SELECTED ☐ FILM CRITICISM 1921-1930 ☐

edited by
Anthony Slide

THE SCARECROW PRESS, INC.
METUCHEN, N.J., & LONDON
1982

In the same series:

Library of Congress Cataloging in Publication Data (Revised)
Main entry under title:

Selected film criticism.

   Includes index.
   Contents: 1. 1912-1920. 2. 1921-1930.
   1. Moving-pictures--Reviews. I. Slide,
Anthony.
PN1995.S426   791.43'75   81-23344
ISBN 0-8108-1525-7 (v. 1)   AACR2
ISBN 0-8108-1551-6 (v. 2)

This volume is dedicated to
the memory of Bert Langdon, a
British film collector of 35mm
nitrate films, at whose regular
Saturday evening screenings I
learned to appreciate the glory
that was the silent cinema.

☐ CONTENTS

vi

viii

□ PREFACE

Selected Film Criticism: 1921-1930 is the second published in
this series of reprints of contemporary film reviews. The present volume offers reviews on more than 200 features, foreign and domestic,
released in the United States between 1921 and 1930. These reviews
have been selected from thirteen periodicals--Cinema, Exceptional
Photoplays, The Film Mercury, The Film Spectator, Life, Motion
Picture Classic, Motion Picture News, The Moving Picture World,
The Nation, The New Yorker, Photoplay, Shadowland, and Variety--
as well as one book, Robert E. Sherwood's The Best Moving Pictures of 1922-1923.

The reviews differ considerably in tone and style, from the
intellectual in The Nation, through the well-written if popular approach in Life and The New Yorker, to the blatantly film trade attitude of Variety (whose Sime Silverman has a language and a gram-
mar all his own). The reviews from Photoplay, as in the teens,
are reliable and intelligently written, matched in film publications
only by the somewhat longer reviews in Exceptional Photoplays. A
number of major critics are represented here, including Richard
Watts, Jr. , Burns Mantle, Alexander Bakshy, Ted Shane, James
Shelley Hamilton, and Robert E. Sherwood.

One critic included in this anthology who is perhaps not as
widely known as he should be is Welford Beaton, editor and founder
of The Film Spectator (later Hollywood Spectator). Beaton's reviews
provide a refreshingly unbiased Hollywood insider's view of the movies, often embellished with personal asides and insights. A Canad-
ian by birth, Welford Beaton had earlier served as film critic of a
Seattle weekly, The Town Crier, and was also the author of a slim
volume on the theory and practice of motion picture production,

Know Your Movies (published by Howard Hill in 1932). He died, at the age of eighty, on December 10, 1952.

Thanks again to the Margaret Herrick Library of the Academy of Motion Picture Arts and Sciences and the Los Angeles Public Library system for their cooperation. Special thanks also to Elias Savada for checking copyright registrations and renewals. The reviews from Variety are reprinted by permission of Syd Silverman and Variety; those from Exceptional Photoplays through the courtesy of the National Board of Review of Motion Pictures, Inc. The reviews on pages 6, 34, 83, 166, 242, 278, and 305 by Will Hays, Jr., Ted Shane, and Oliver Claxton are reprinted by permission; © 1925, 1953, 1981 or © 1926, 1954 or © 1927, 1955 The New Yorker Magazine, Inc.

Anthony Slide

SELECTED FILM CRITICISM:
1921-1930

☐ ABRAHAM LINCOLN (Rockett-Lincoln Film Company/Associated First National, 1924)

A ringing answer to the call for better pictures. One of the finest ever made, and one that should be seen and encouraged by taking the whole family. The rarest kind of entertainment combined with history. If schools could teach as delightfully as this there wouldn't be an uneducated person in America.

No book we have ever read has so brought out the lovable nature of Abraham Lincoln. It is impossible to tell the story in this brief space, but his whole life is shown; his youth, his struggles for an education, his political career, his romance with Ann Rutledge, her death, his subsequent marriage, the cruel ordeal of the Civil War, and his death.

The episode of the love of Lincoln for Ann Rutledge is one of the most beautiful romances of American history. The role of Lincoln's first sweetheart is splendidly done by Ruth Clifford.

We could hardly ask better direction or more sympathetic handling of this epic theme. There is no attempt at great suspense by the usual motion picture tricks. Although there was a great opportunity for a thrilling ride of the Reserve Cavalry, at the time the capital of the nation was threatened by Confederate guns, that would have equalled the ride of the clansmen in the Birth of a Nation.

We have never seen a more delicately handled situation or sequence than the decline and death of the girl that Lincoln loved, or the scene in which Lincoln's firstborn died in his arms while soothing the little chap with a child's story.

Lincoln is wonderfully portrayed by George Billings, a man who had no previous stage or screen experience.
                                        --Photoplay, Vol. 25, No. 4
                                        (March 1924), page 60.

☐ ABRAHAM LINCOLN (United Artists, 1930)

More than an outstanding classic of sound pictures, Abraham

Lincoln eclipses the most conservative illusion of a modernized
Birth of a Nation. It is a startlingly superlative accomplishment;
one rejuvenating a greatest Griffith. In characterization and detail
perfection it is such as to be almost unbelievable. In continuity and
scenes it projects as one smooth roll of literally throbbing pulsation,
pathos, laughter, with never a moment's interlude for audience let-
down. Commercially, for all theatres, it should be Griffith's biggest contribution to the exhibitor.

Next to the direction, with only a tiny margin separating, is
Walter Huston's Abraham Lincoln. Young, aging and aged; playful,
fighting, grief-stricken; commanding, pleading--Huston feels the life
of Lincoln until, many times, it seems as though Hollywood has finally effected the miracle of resurrection.

The broken Robert E. Lee on the eve of his surrender is
likewise summoned for a few moments before the camera in Hobart
Bosworth. The fighting Sherman and his mad plunge in victorious
retaliation is similarly returned for a short time in the commanding
zest of Frank Campeau. The entire cast down to the shortest-lived
extra could be similarly extolled for imparting the sincerity of realism which this picture breathes through at least 90% of its running
time.

What, perhaps, is the most remarkable of all qualities possessed by this classic is the way in which so stupendous a theme
has been shaped for the screen. The reactions before, during and
after the war blend in a finale that teaches only steadfast nobleness
of purpose for the good of the nation.

Robbed of none of its vigor or gunshot, this Griffith masterpiece yet contains not a physical gesture, not a line of dialog, that
would offend race, color, creed or belief. It has achieved that
happy medium whereby both sides are always winning--and both win.

The Yanks' parade past the brownstone fronts is edited as
quickly into the Dixie boys' flag waving, as conferences of the President and his cabinet are turned to the thrills of galloping cavalry,
or the tirades of the lovable Mary Todd Lincoln with the White House
servants.

A vivid prolog, reviewing the times, with camera sweeping
through dark-lit forests, hazy fields and clouded cities, brings the
opening to the little log cabin and the birth of Abe. Romance of
Lincoln and Ann Rutledge is slightly unconvincing in parts. Una
Merkel, at times, seems too light to attract a man of the woodcut-
ter's depth. She as quickly makes up for a childishness of voice
at the death scene, which is one of the impressive scenes. Lincoln
then gives vent to full emotion for the first and last time, falling
upon her grave in a blinding storm.

From the first fight in the country store and the passing of
Ann, Huston then begins to make the personality of Lincoln heighten

in degrees of realism. The maximum of fineness in the actor's performance is unquestionably during the brooding and sorrowing moods
of his characterization.

The scenes at Springfield where he meets the haughty Mary
Todd have considerable comedy. Lincoln's abrupt method of being
introduced, the dance, and later his failure to appear at his own
marriage ceremony--all have a genuine comic side which is aug-
mented by its very human interest.

The association of Lincoln is classically melodramatic. A
study in theatre shadows is capitalized by Griffith, as the murderer
steals to the President's box. The director has availed himself of
innumerable similar opportunities throughout the picture. One particularly good study is the descent of the long Lincoln, his height increased by the stovepipe hat, against a narrow flight of stairs.
Again, as Lincoln enters his first cabinet meeting, the silhouette
camera is used to much advantage.

Exploitation and opportunities for tie-ups with educational
centers are unusual and universal. The picture on the screen,
however, more than substantiates the claims of statisticians.
                         --"Weby" in Variety, Vol. 100,
                           No. 7 (August 27, 1930), page
                           21.

☐ THE AFFAIRS OF ANATOL (Famous Players-Lasky/Paramount,
   1921)

Nothing left of Schnitzler but the title. The subtle craftsmanship, the sentimental melancholy and the humorous cynicism
have given place to crudity and even clumsy vulgarity. We look
upon The Affairs of Anatol as the worst massacre since Custer's
forces were wiped out by the redskins. The silken DeMille is certainly running riot.
                         --Frederick James Smith in Mo-
                           tion Picture Classic, Vol. 13,
                           No. 1 (September 1921), page 89.

☐ ALIAS JIMMY VALENTINE (M-G-M, 1928)

William Haines gives straight drama a fling. He's just as
convincing as in comedy, and wonderfully sincere as Jimmy Valentine, the role Bert Lytell made famous. The modern version of this
popular stage and screen drama is a well-directed, well-rounded
production. Don't fail to see it. Lionel Barrymore, Leila Hyams,

Tully Marshall and Karl Dane head the cast.
                              --Photoplay, Vol. 34, No. 5
                              (October 1928), page 54.

☐ ALIAS THE DEACON (Universal, 1928)

Alias the Deacon, now at the Roxy, is good enough to take
up some of your spare time--if you have any.   It follows the play
with the least possible amount of deviation, and is performed gently
but firmly, and without too much emotion.   Jean Hersholt in the
title role is over-unctuous, and his sweet smiles are a shade too
sweet.   The other characters who wander through the workings of
the plot are satisfactorily portrayed.

You probably know the story, and a gentle reminder of its
theme will suffice.   The Deacon is a card sharp who gets into the
life of a small town, and by deft fingers and big heart is able to
confound wrongdoers, and reward virtue.   Prizefights, races with
trains, and other movie staples assist the picture.
                              --Oliver Claxton in The New
                                Yorker, Vol. 3, No. 19 (June
                                25, 1927), page 51.

☐ ALL QUIET ON THE WESTERN FRONT (Universal, 1930)

When the greatest nations on earth had their representatives
in London trying to reach some agreement that would result in each
having less to fight with when another war takes place, Universal
was putting the finishing touches on the most stupendous piece of
peace propaganda that ever has been presented to the world.   All
Quiet on the Western Front is a great motion picture, but it is still
greater as a document.   It does not preach; it does not plead the
case of either war or peace.   It is content to let us see war as it
is, and to let us make up our minds about it.

But the picture will make more converts to the cause of
peace than any other single argument--except war itself--that has
been advanced.   And it still is a motion picture, a stunning, moving, human film with a mixture of laughter and tears, with rapid,
virile action that will stir those who are looking only for entertainment.   And it will be a feast for those who look for food for thought
in their motion pictures.   It is the first film that plants the audience firmly in the first line trenches and allows it to see and feel
war as it really is; to understand vividly the stupidity of it, its
murderous worthlessness, and the criminal, predatory and ruthless
instinct that inspires it.

It takes the youth of Germany, representing the youth of the world, and shows us what war does to them before it mercifully murders them.   It lifts us from our seats in a theatre and takes us over the top, into the hell of a fierce attack, with shells screaming their way to us before they explode at our feet; it drops corpses in our path for us to step over as we advance to meet the death that is approaching.   It does to us what it did to our brothers and sons when the world went mad and spewed its insanity over Europe. It is the most terrific drama in all the history of the stage, screen or literature.

And without striving for them it has its light moments. There are no comedians in it, but there is considerable comedy. The comedy is not spotted mechanically to follow automatically the scenes that are strong in human tragedy.   It comes in naturally where it belongs and carries its share of the story.   Universal has taken no liberties with the book that is familiar to millions of readers.   There is nothing in the picture that was not in the original work of the author.

When I reviewed the first picture that Lewis Milestone directed in Hollywood I wrote that he was destined to become one of our greatest directors.   With each picture he has revealed more assurance and a firmer touch, and in his direction of All Quiet on the Western Front he displays a comprehensive grasp of the fundamentals of his art that will fix firmly his place as one of our few really great directors.   He makes his actual war sequences something terrific in the way of overwhelming drama, and in his intimate scenes, both grave and gay, he reveals an understanding of human emotions, an appreciation of sentimental values and a sense of humor that makes the entire production a swiftly moving and tremendously compelling glimpse of life in the raw.   In the purely technical aspects of his direction Milestone proves himself a master.   He makes no effort to please our eyes with prettily conceived pictorial treats; but apparently he was conscious always of the dramatic value of effective grouping.

There is one sequence in All Quiet that I would like to recommend to the attention of those directors who distort scenes in order to keep the faces of the characters toward the camera. Eight or ten of the soldiers in whom we are interested have fed themselves into a state of stuffed ecstacy and Milestone brings them into a group for a discussion of the reason for war.   The speech about the hill and the field getting mad at one another is part of this dialogue.   To achieve its greatest effect the grouping should keep all the faces towards the camera.   Milestone gains this advantage naturally by placing his men in a reclining position among the exposed roots of a tree, so constructed that all the characters must face in the same direction.

In keeping with the great theme and the great direction, all the performances in All Quiet are great.   The chief character, the boy who goes all the way through the picture and is the last to be

killed, is played intelligently and impressively by Lewis Ayres, who
gives me the impression that he is going to do something important
in pictures. Louis Wolheim and Slim Summerville are superb in
character roles. Ben Alexander, a lad who was my favorite boy
actor a few years ago, comes to the front with a performance that
is outstanding even in such company. The other boys, Harold
Goodwin, Russell Gleason, Scott Kolk, Owen Davis, Jr., Walter
Browne Rogers and William Bakewell, are entirely satisfactory in
their several parts. John Wray, as the objectionable sergeant, and
Arnold Lucy, as the schoolmaster, also deserve praise. Del An-
drews, who adapted the book to the screen, is responsible for a
notable bit of motion picture writing.

        All Quiet on the Western Front comes at a time when we
are willing to view the world war as it really was. During the
decade following the Armistice we wished to forget the war and all
that pertained to it, but we have passed through that mental stage,
and are willing to face the thing as it was. For this reason I am
satisfied that the picture will be a tremendous box-office success.
Certainly it gives Universal a new dignity as a producing organization, and reflects the greatest credit on Carl Laemmle Jr., that
extraordinary boy who is doing such wonders on his father's lot.

        By way of postscript--Since writing the above comments I
have viewed it again, with the result that my opinion is that All
Quiet on the Western Front is the greatest motion picture ever
made.

                          --Welford Beaton in The Film
                            Spectator, Vol. 9, No. 11 (May
                            10, 1930), pages 6-7.

                      *   *   *

        In the West something new--the hoped-for but hardly ex-
pected production of two non-romantic war pictures not only sincere
and honest in intention but superlatively good in execution, both arriving in the theatre the same month. Close on the heels of the
magnificent Journey's End comes the magnificent All Quiet. Both
are immense credits to Hollywood, the latter perhaps even more
than the former because it is more distinctly a product of Hollywood brains and genius, and a harder job to do.

        It is difficult not to compare the two pictures, not only be-
cause they come along so close together, but even more because
they are both picturizations of remarkable contemporaneous works
about the war. Their essential structural differences come from
one's having been taken from a play and the other from a special
kind of novel. Each, though it is cinematic enough in treatment,
sticks faithfully to its original material. A person who likes the
stage form of drama, building steadily and concentratedly to a
climax, will perhaps prefer Journey's End. All Quiet, broader in
scope, has a looser sort of development, moving forward in episodes that are more narrative in form, without so theatrical an

atmosphere.   For a picturization of a novel it is hard to imagine it
being essentially any better than Universal has made it.

It is the story of some German school-boys moved by an
outburst of patriotism to enlist in the war, and how one after
another they were killed.   No more terrific picture of war has
been made, not even in Russia where they make no effort to soften
horrors.   Worse even than the filth and futility of the wholesale
death-dealing is what it shows happening to the minds and souls of
these boys--the complete ruin of life for them even if they manage
to survive till the war's end.   They have seen something that their
people back home can never even imagine, and never can they fit
into the blind grooves of behind-the-lines again.   Yet there is humor in it--for they do not go insane and must therefore laugh
sometimes--and a stirring kind of comradeship, not at all sentimental, that has profound beauty in it.

Sometimes one wishes there were not quite so much talk.
What could appear in the book as a man's thoughts loses something,
often, when it is heard as uttered words.   Like the prayer over
the first dying boy--being made into a prayer it loses the defiant
force, because its mood and intention is changed, that the same
passage had in the book.   Sometimes, too, the adapters have
seemed afraid that their point would not get over and they have
used too many words--in the beautifully managed scene in the
French girl's room, for instance.

But to say this is to find fault with one minute brush stroke
in a huge and superb canvas.

Back of everything, of course, is the honesty and faithfulness with which the producer attacked the immense task of making
this picture.   Nowhere at all is there the smallest sign of cheap
compromise or poor taste.   And after that, the summit of the
achievement, is Lewis Milestone's directing.   Sound and dialogue
have not made him forget for an instant that he was making a motion picture--that he was telling a story first of all with a camera.
With sound fundamental principles, and abundant skill in exercising
them, he has merely added for whatever they were worth the new
effects that the microphone has brought to the cinema.   Few directors have arrived at Mr. Milestone's mastery of the new medium
of pictures with sound, and none has so splendidly demonstrated
such a mastery.

The cast is remarkably good.   Some of the boys seem to be
more boys than actors--their inexperience shows up now and then.
William Bakewell is the most at home in his part, and the most effective, though Lewis Ayres, with a tremendously difficult role for
a young actor, depends less and less on personality and more and
more on acting as the picture progresses.   There is a particularly
rich performance by Louis Wolheim, beautifully earthy and human,
and a good characterization by "Slim" Summerville.   Raymond
Griffith, too, does excellently something not associated with his
career as a comedian.

What people will find chiefly unforgettable, however, is the total impression of the profoundly pitiable squad of soldiers, the tremendous shattering battle scenes, and the last ghostly glimpse of the boys looking back over their shoulders as they move on into the wide-spread forest of white crosses.

                                        --James Shelley Hamilton in Cine-
                                            ma, Vol. 1, No. 5 (June 1930),
                                            pages 37-38.

☐ ALOMA OF THE SOUTH SEAS (Famous Players-Lasky/Paramount, 1926)

Here is a film of startling beauty, beauty as compelling and as perfect as any the screen has ever shown. It creates the South Seas as we all like to imagine them, palms tall and beautiful against skies piled with sullen clouds, far-flung white beaches lapped by scented seas and native girls as radiant as hibiscus blossoms.

Aloma reveals all this plus Gilda Gray. Almost all of Gilda is revealed, and what a personality she proves to be! Product of Middle Western poverty, product of Broadway's most hectic cabarets, winner of wealth and fame, something has saved Gilda Gray's great simplicity. She is as childlike and primitive as a man's first dream of love. She moves across the screen, undisturbed by it. Watching her, it is almost impossible to believe that it is her first important film rôle. She photographs perfectly and so completely is she Aloma, one's only wonder is whether she can possibly play any other character.

Compared with these factors, the story fades into insignificance, which is just as well, since it is an insignificant story. It's the old one about the soldier who left his sweetheart behind; who was reported killed, but really wasn't, who returns to find the sweetheart married and then goes to the South Seas to drown himself behind a heavy growth of whiskers and a row of whiskey bottles.

Maurice Tourneur's direction is excellent. The playing of the cast, Warner Baxter, as a native; Percy Marmont as the suffering gentleman; William Powell, as the marrying rascal, is all that is necessary. But it is Gilda Gray and beauty that make Aloma a glorious experience. Take the children. It will be good for them.

                                        --Photoplay, Vol. 30, No. 2 (July
                                            1926), page 54.

☐ AMERICA (Griffith/United Artists, 1924)

Mr. Griffith has done it again. Has almost made another
Birth of a Nation--but not quite. Nevertheless, America is an epic
film and one of the greatest thrill pictures ever made. If you miss
this picture, you miss something worth while--something that will
not only give you a greater appreciation of motion pictures, but
something that will make you pause and gaze with added reverence
the next time you see an American flag.

No period in our history is so rich in romance as the struggle for independence and this is the period chosen by Mr. Griffith,
with a story by Robert W. Chambers.

He has caught the spirit of our forefathers as we conceived
it, and transferred it to the screen in such a way that you glory in
being an American.

The first part of the picture treats of the causes of the
Revolution and the events leading up to the battles of Lexington,
Concord and Bunker Hill. Nothing has ever been thrown on the
screen that surpasses the ride of Paul Revere to arouse the Middle-
sex villagers and farmers.

In the second part of the picture, Mr. Griffith, realizing that
it was impossible to tell the story of the Revolution in any one or
any dozen pictures, has selected phases of it that vividly depict the
sacrifices of the patriots in the struggle.

Notable figures of the American Revolution are presented,
including Washington, Patrick Henry, John Hancock, Samuel Evans
and King George III, and into it all he has interwoven a charming
love story of the daughter of a Virginian Tory (Carol Dempster) and
a young patriotic leader (Neil Hamilton).

Mr. Hamilton is pushed into stardom and Miss Dempster does
the best work of her screen career.
                                        --Photoplay, Vol. 25, No. 6 (May
                                          1924), page 55.

                        *   *   *

Patriotism has gone out of style since the last Liberty Loan
drive. The 100% American fervor which was very much in vogue
during the brave days of 1917-18 is now regarded as distinctly bad
taste. The post-war reaction accounts for some of this change, and
the lease of Teapot Dome for the rest.

In spite of this condition, it is extremely difficult to see D.
W. Griffith's new picture, America, without experiencing an exalted
thrill of patriotism. When you watch a shabby band of embattled
farmers fall into line on the main street of Lexington, and march

off to the strains of "Yankee Doodle," you will forget all about
Harry Daugherty, Frank A. Vanderlip and the Ku Klux Klan--and
you will not feel the necessity of apologizing when you say, "I am
an American."

Mr. Griffith shows us the ride of Paul Revere, the early
battles around Boston and the fearful sufferings at Valley Forge,
and he presents them with extraordinary vividness. The courage,
the ruggedness and the indomitable simplicity of these men who
made the United States are magnified mightily by contrast with the
present age of bluster and ballyhoo and bunk.

The effectiveness of these scenes is heightened materially by
the work of Neil Hamilton, Erville Alderson, and Frank McGlynn,
Jr. There is a fine sincerity in all the players.

Unfortunately, Mr. Griffith decided that the patriotic thrill
which he inspires at the start should be developed logically into
bitter enmity towards England. So he fills the latter portions of
his picture with atrocities and general dirty work by the British
soldiers, and thus gets entirely away from his main point.

The spirit of America becomes lost in a general muddle of
petty trickery, sticky love interest and heavy propaganda. From
Valley Forge to the final surrender at Yorktown, the picture is involved and dull, and the first wave of excitement recedes.

Mr. Griffith's mistake is not an uncommon one. He was
misled by the ancient tradition that a man can't really love his own
country without hating every other nation on earth.
                              --Robert E. Sherwood in Life,
                                 Vol. 83, No. 2158 (March 13,
                                 1924), page 26.

☐ ANIMAL CRACKERS (Paramount, 1930)

A hit on the screen before it opened and in the money plenty.
Anyone having seen the stage musical, Animal Crackers, could have
predicted that much with ease. This should get more money than
did the Marx Brothers' Cocoanuts, because Cocoanuts made the
Marx Brothers on the screen. Animal Crackers holds as many
laughs from the same trio of comics.

Perhaps a little trade stuff here might serve better than a
waste of words to tell about a dough film that's already in. The
Marx Brothers suggest a lot in the relation of the screen, stage
and radio to each other, direct or on the reverse.

First[, give] Paramount extreme credit for reproducing Animal Crackers intact from the stage, with not the least of that re-

production the excellent sound and entire synchronization and without too much of the songs and musical numbers. That is of such benefit it asks why Animal Crackers on the stage at $5.50, when even the ruralites know they will see it later on the screen at 50 or 75 cents? It parallels the prevailing threat against the film road show, paying $2 for a picture shortly showing at pop prices.

This is not a matter of the legit now. And not only musicals, but the drama. Which seems to say that until the legit can compete with the talking theatre's scale, it cannot seriously consider itself in line for a comeback. Excepting the metropolitan centers, particularly Broadway. On Broadway the weekly average in season is 55 legit houses and maybe 12 box-office draws. The public hears about the hits and doesn't care about the flops.

After Cocoanuts played on the screen, the Marx boys went out once again, trouping with Animal Crackers on the stage. Immediately it was noted that the upstairs draw had increased, and that continued. It was their screen popularity from Cocoanuts.

Loew's tried eight names during last season as possible draws for as many weeks in its vaudfilm houses. The only name of the eight to show any real box-office strength was Belle Baker. Of the eight on name value previously she had ranked about fourth. Miss Baker had been on the air. That was the reason.

Floyd Gibbons was at the Palace, New York, last week at $3,500. His first vaude appearance, and not an actor. It was the air.

Frank Fay is at the Palace this week at $4,000. The last time Fay played the Palace his salary was $1,750. That's the screen.

Al Jolson can have a $15,000 salary from the Palace for a single week, with that only big time vaude theatre left knowing it can not make much money at such a salary. Gross record for the Palace to date is $36,000. Jolson can go in any mammoth picture house for a week and earn $25,000 on a percentage basis. Jolson is a freak show attraction. His name has not been helped by pictures. He was made for all time before The Jazz King and he has not had a real screech hit since Singing Fool. But he's worth $15,000 to the Palace, New York, twice as much as it has ever paid any headliner.

But the screen has helped the Marx boys. And in so helping, it now tells the world at large it is no longer necessary to pay $5.50 to see them in person on the stage, for in this Paramount picture they are just the same.

If the screen must wait for the stage to perfect a musical comedy such as Animal Crackers before its principals will return, then valuable picture material of the highly commercial kind is being withheld from the films for too long intervals. Cocoanuts came out in May last year. The Marx Brothers should have done three since then, instead of one.

A theory with comedians like Cantor, Jolson and the Marxes is that if in a stage-play, they can season the material. Then removing it with most of the original cast for the camera, it's air tight for pictures. Which is right as far as that goes, but pictures can not afford the long lapses. Reproduced comedies like Crackers and Whoopee can't flop, unless their producers in pictures cause it. Rain or Shine is another example.

Drawing stars, valuable screen properties and comedy above all will sooner or later have to go directly to the screen from the writers. A George Kaufman can, if he will, write as well for the screen as for the stage, if the screen, as the stage does, leaves him alone while he is writing. When the studios tell writers they don't have to punch a clock in Hollywood, the writers may give to the studios the best they write, instead of holding it out later for the stage, in fear that some butcher around the studio will chop it to bits in ignorance, as so many have done.

In Animal Crackers among the Marx boys there is no preference. Groucho (Julius) shines; Harpo (Arthur) remains a pantomime clown who ranks with the highest, while Chico (Leo) adds an unusual comedy sense to his dialog as well as business and piano playing, and Zeppo, if in on a spit, is lucky.

Lillian Roth may have been cast here to work out a contract, that being a favorite practice on the coast, it seems. She can't hurt because the Marxes are there, but if Miss Roth is in for any other reason it doesn't appear. She sings one song in the ingenue role. That song is useless. Opposite is Hal Thompson, a juv who doesn't prove it here.

Others look as though from the original stage troupe, which explains their respective good performance.

Whether the picture is cut or not is immaterial. For good showmanship it should be cut. There is too much fidelity to story causing drags, especially toward the finish. It runs over 95 minutes. At the Rialto the turnover is the picture and a news reel, all within 105 minutes, or one and three-quarter hours.

--Sime Silverman in Variety, Vol. 100, No. 8 (September 3, 1930), page 19.

☐ ANNA CHRISTIE (Ince/First National, 1923)

The notable feature of this faithful and effective transfer to the screen of Eugene O'Neill's play is the remarkable acting of

Blanche Sweet in the title rôle. Those who wanted Pauline Lord,
the stage star, to play the rôle, may be consoled. Miss Sweet
does the finest work of her career and leaves nothing to be desired.
It isn't a pleasant story, but it holds the attention, and the direction of John Griffith Wray is notable for its directness and simplicity. There is no lost motion. Everything counts. Second only to
the acting of Miss Sweet as the unfortunate Anna, is that of George
Marion as her father, Chris, all of whose troubles are due to "that
davil sea." Mr. Marion repeats the masterly performance he gave
on the stage. While it may not be a picture for the children, no
adult should miss it.

--Photoplay, Vol. 25, No. 2
(January 1924), page 68.

*   *   *

The picture version of Eugene O'Neill's Anna Christie marks
an important advance in the artistic integrity of the screen. It is
an honest attempt to give the play and its spirit for what they are
worth and let the eloquence of the camera and of fine acting
achieve their legitimate results.

Too often, in the past, plays, like novels, have been ac-
quired for the advance publicity which they carry or for some sensational feature. They have then been subjected to a process of
distortion in order to make them a standardized movie product.
This has usually resulted in killing the very flavor and individuality
which made the play a success. Incidentally it also gave another
explanation of why the intelligent public was alienated from the
movies, besides causing conscientious dramatists to hesitate to turn
their plays over to the motion picture industry.

Mr. Thomas H. Ince and his director, Mr. John Griffith
Wray, are to be congratulated upon having departed from this short-
sighted policy in picturizing the first play of our greatest living
dramatist that has reached the screen. As far as is humanly possible they have been faithful to the spirit of the play in story, setting and acting. Mr. O'Neill, well known as he is for his artistic
sensitiveness and his very proper insistence upon a correct rendition
of his plays, has every reason to be satisfied.

The difficulty of the task accomplished here becomes evident
the moment we consider the theme of Anna Christie. For the heroine of Mr. O'Neill's play is a girl who has become a woman of the
streets at the age of twenty. She comes to New York from the
Middle West to find her father living a degraded life along the water
front of the city. She has formed a vague longing to see her father
from whom she has been parted since she was a child, and wants
to rest up after a disastrous experience of imprisonment and sick-
ness.

There is a first awakening of tenderness between the two,
with the father's remorseful affection for his neglected child making

him utterly blind to her way of living.   A trip on a coal barge
along the coast to Boston removes Anna far from her former life,
both physically and spiritually, and makes her come to honest terms
with herself.   But now she meets and falls in love with a stoker,
and when the question of marriage arises she feels compelled to
tell both men the truth.

At first they react conventionally and turn upon the girl.
But the father realizes at last how far his neglect of his daughter
has contributed to her downfall and seeks to make amends.   The
girl's lover, more primitive in his rage, nevertheless cannot put
her out of his heart even though he only feels bitterness and hate.
But when Anna, without excusing herself, turns the double standard
against him, and makes him see that her love for him has lifted
her out of herself, he follows the lead of his heart without further
reserve.

Here certainly is a play which at first blush seems far re-
moved from the smugness of the movies and their tricky moralising.
Mr. O'Neill's honesty, the realism of his dialogue, the incisiveness
of his character drawing, and above all his method of establishing
the fundamental morality of his theme without sentimental concessions, were so many more obstacles to deter the conventional
scenario writer and director.   Anna is not a girl who is made good
or who turns out to be a misunderstood model of virtue.   She is
simply that rarest thing in the movies or, for that matter, in the
theatre too--a convincing human being.

Now the notable success of the picture lies in the fact that
it has done precisely what Mr. O'Neill did, in terms of motion
pictures.   There is no padding, no change of characterization, no
tampering with the author's intention.   Every scene that enlarges
the horizon of the play by virtue of the greater mobility of picture-
making is a legitimate expansion of what is suggested by the text.
Thus we see Anna as a girl of five in Sweden, while her father is
roaming the Seven Seas and acquiring the habits that make sailors
notoriously unfit for the duties of parenthood.   We see her again as
a drudge on a Minnesota farm, subject to the abuse of farm hands
and defenceless.   Matt Burke, the man who loves her, is shown in
the stoke-hole of the doomed steamer in accurate picturization of
the boastful words in which he describes the event in the play.

But these episodes do not interrupt the flow of the picture.
The story strikes its pace in the water front saloon where Chris
spends his time when he is not working on the coal barge, and
proceeds in a series of simple but powerful sequences with almost
as few changes of scene as we find in the play.   Chris, in a fever
of excitement over the coming of his daughter, is at pains to present an air of sober respectability to the good and beautiful daughter
whom he expects to see.   Anna, tired and ill, stumbles into the
back room of the saloon, recognized immediately for what she is
by an older sister.   Soon the whole saloon knows about her except
her father.   The first big mood of the play, the groping growth of

affection between a wastrel father and his unmothered daughter, is established unerringly by the same economy of means and power of suggestion which makes Chaplin's A Woman of Paris, a technical masterpiece.

From this point the story moves naturally by its own momentum through Anna's voyage on the barge with her father to her meeting with Matt Burke, the shipwrecked stoker. We see her in tarpaulin, feeling the freedom of the sea and the symbolic cleansing which mankind has always associated with it.

In the cabin of the barge Anna faces her great crisis, the telling of her story to Matt, even though it may destroy his love for her. This is the most powerful scene in the picture, altogether modern in its appeal, with the woman, claiming no absolute sainthood for herself, yet challenging the complacent morality of two men, one of whom contributed to her degradation while the other, in his hurt vanity, would keep her in it.

This simple and honest treatment of the play is seconded by acting of a rare quality. The picture marks the triumphant return of Blanche Sweet, formerly D. W. Griffith's leading lady, after many regrettable years of absence from the screen. Her success is as great as Pauline Lord's in the play and will help to re-establish a reputation that should never have been dimmed. Her interpretation of Anna is realistic but restrained, a consistent impersonation which gathers strength and conviction as it progresses through the picture. The climax of her work coincides with that of the play; when she finally confesses her past she remains absolutely still with only her lips moving, but she has made us hear what she says by what has gone before.

The rest of the cast also lives up to the picture. William Russell as Matt Burke suggests Mr. O'Neill's blundering, passionate Irishman with great freshness and charm, and Mr. Marion, who played the original Chris in the play, is equally convincing when transferred to the screen.

Anna Christie stands out as one of the most striking achievements of the year in motion pictures. It courageously lifts the screen to the level of the best on the contemporary stage and will stand as a landmark in the photodrama's coming of age.

                                   --Exceptional Photoplays, Vol. 4,
                                   Nos. 1 and 2 (October-Novem-
                                   ber 1923), pages 1 and 2.

☐ ANNA CHRISTIE (M-G-M, 1930)

When I wrote in the last Spectator that Greta Garbo's going talkie was a calamity, I was aware that probably before the article

appeared I would have an opportunity of judging of her ability as a
talking artist. I have seen the first picture in which she uses her
voice, Anna Christie, directed for Metro by Clarence Brown. It is
a superb picture, masterly, poignant, gripping and dramatic, and
is certain to rank among the most artistic things done by the
screen this year. Miss Garbo is magnificent. She is a really
great artist. When she makes George Marion, her father, and
Charles Bickford, her lover, sit down in the dingy cabin aboard
the coal skow and listen to her while she relates to them the blows
that fate dealt her until finally she became a prostitute, she is
simply superb. She has a rich, well rounded and impressive
speaking voice, with just a trace of an accent which in Anna Christie is an advantage, as her part is that of a Scandinavian girl.
This great scene, wonderfully directed by Brown, is in its essentials a stage scene, and is not one of the sort upon which Miss
Garbo's fame is founded. I see nothing in Anna Christie to make
me change my mind about the folly of making a talking artist out
of this talented girl. I enjoyed every reel of Anna Christie. It
absorbed me, and at times I was spellbound, but still I regretted
that this superb artist had not continued to be the sole remaining
and great exponent of the fine art of the silent screen. However,
I must review the picture as I saw it and not as I wished it might
have been. I just have come from it, and still while under its
spell I feel that it is the finest thing that yet has been presented on
the talking screen. Certainly Clarence Brown never did a better
job, and never did Greta Garbo give a finer performance. It is a
drab story, set in sordid surroundings with very little change of
locale, yet Brown keeps it moving and intensely dramatic. The
director and star, however, do not supply all the merit there is in
the production. Marie Dressler contributes one of the grandest
performances I ever saw on the screen. She plays a drunken, old
hag who is the plaything of any seagoing man depraved enough to
want her. She dominates every scene she is in, even those which
Miss Garbo shares with her. Every flutter of her eyelids, the
twist of her lips, her faintest gesture, everything she does, is an
exquisite example of screen acting. George F. Marion duplicates
in this version the great success he achieved in the stage and silent
versions of the same story, and Charles Bickford handles his robust
part with skill. Brown tells his story in an unrelenting manner.
It is an unbeautiful story of unimportant people, and he tries to put
no beauty into its telling. He is another director who rapidly is
augmenting in the new medium the reputation he established for
himself in the old. He shows again that he has a fine eye for
pictorial value, and he was fortunate in having for his chief cameraman William Daniels, who has contributed so much superb photography to other pictures directed by Brown. It will give satisfaction
to those who enjoy screen art in its highest form, but I am not
quite sure that it is screen art that the public wants to buy. Our
most popular stars are not our best actors, which would indicate
that acting has not as much market value as personality. However,
if I were an exhibitor I would jump at a chance to show Anna Christie.

                                        --Welford Beaton in The Film
                                        Spectator, Vol. 9, No. 3 (Janu-
                                        ary 18, 1930), page 6.

*   *   *

The case of Greta Garbo is one that is so rare that there is
no great exaggeration in calling it unique.   Here is a young actress, a foreigner, with only a brief fame in Europe which had not
yet reached this country, coming almost by accident--certainly not
by the solicitation of any producer--to America and here immediately achieving a phenomenally rapid and wide-spread success.   She
is not only enormously popular with the millions who give box-offices authority, but people to whom box-offices mean nothing at all
are fascinated by her and admire her.   She is that rarest of things
in the motion picture world, a fan idol and an acknowledged artist.

Apparently she could have gone on with undiminished success
in silent pictures, but there is probably no one who admires her
who hasn't been curious to hear her voice.   For her vocal début
they have chosen a play in which any accent she may have is a
natural part of her rôle, a play which is moreover a good play,
with a central character worthy of any actress.

Transferred to the sound screen Anna Christie turns out to
be of very little importance except as a vehicle for some extremely
good acting.   Much more pains would have been taken--and were
taken, a few years ago--in translating it into a silent movie.
Scene painters and carpenters and prop men and electricians have
done their best to make it look like a motion picture, but it has
only the appearance: there is simply no cinematic movement in it.
Each fade out and time-lapse title has the effect of a curtain falling
and an entr'act, and each episode is as distinctly a set and separate
scene as if it were being done on a stage.   Any intelligent script
clerk could have turned out as good a scenario as the one Mr.
Brown was given to direct, and no director in the world could have
made more a motion picture of it than Mr. Brown has.   It does not
grow--it is merely a series of scenes hitched together.

But the picture is worth--well worth--any mature person's
visit, if only for the sake of four remarkable characterizations.
Greta Garbo is an Anna Christie that only a poet could write of
adequately--and I am no poet.   It is one of Eugene O'Neill's best
creations, and no actress is likely to embody it more effectively.
What we have come to expect of her is there--a profound understanding of the woman she is portraying, and complete technical
skill in expressing that understanding.   Her voice--a dark voice but
not a sombre one--adds more than one would have thought possible
to her acting, which seemed so complete when she was silent.
More and more it seems sure that this girl's success is not an
accident of personality and striking opportunities--it is the result
of a real artistic power whose limitations, if there are any, have
not yet been disclosed.

Charles Bickford is the Irish sailor, much more the real
thing and much less like an imitation of Synge than the part seemed
when acted on the stage.   He fills the rôle up to the brim with
moving, authentic life.

Marie Dressler is not much given to subtlety and over-re-
finement in her methods, but every stroke of characterization, even
when it is exaggerated, is so sure and to the point that her picture
of the sodden old barge-woman is a complete delight. I wonder
what George Marion will do now that he has played old Chris in the
talkies. He has done it on the stage and in the silent movies--
there remains only a possible operatic version for him to do it in.
It is the same Chris it has always been. If it stands out a little
less prominently this time it is not because it isn't as good as ever,
but because the other parts are so much more glamorous than they
have been before.

--James Shelley Hamilton in
Cinema, Vol. 1, No. 3 (April
1930), page 37.

☐ ANNIE LAURIE (M-G-M, 1927)

A new and picturesque locale for a story--the Scottish Low-
lands. Annie's home is neutral ground in the fight between the
clans of Campbell and MacDonald. And how they fight! The story
has swirl and dash, sometimes spoiled by over-cutting. Moreover,
the studio carried the Scotch idea too far by using painted scenery
instead of the real thing.

Norman Kerry as the mountain clansman who "has a wae
wi' him" steals the picture from Miss Gish. He is a magnificent
figure. John Robertson's direction is excellent--both spirited and
charming. And Lillian Gish displays a vivacity heretofore unsus-
pected. But Kerry's performance is the thing that sets the girls
to humming "Annie Laurie" with a far off look in their eyes.

--Photoplay, Vol. 32, No. 2 (July
1927), page 55.

☐ APPLAUSE (Paramount, 1929)

Mr. Rouben Mamoulian, the pride of the Theatre Guild, having a grand time with his newest toy, the camera, and being a bit
self-conscious about it. The story is nothing to cheer for and even
those of us who are almost as enamoured as is Mr. Mamoulian of
mobile, subjective pictorial effects are likely to find the work too
much of an exercise in mannered technique for comfort, but, with
all its faults, it does suggest that its director, now that he has
finished his roadwork, is destined to do great things for the photoplay. The best thing about Applause is the simple, honest and sincerely moving performance of Miss Joan Peers, in the ingenue role.

--Richard Watts, Jr. in The Film
Mercury, Vol. 10, No. 11 (November 1, 1929), page 6.

*   *   *

It is silly to complain of how many back-stage tales we have had
on the screen, or how many mother-love stories, when something
so good as Applause comes along.

It is the odyssey of a burlesque queen--an easy-going perox-
ide who probably wouldn't know a moral if she saw one. A dumb,
generous, flabby creature, sentimental and cheap and most likeable
and pitiable. She drifts improvidently through life, doing a lot of
foolish things and never anything really bad or mean, toward the inevitable bedraggled end of such a one. She is already facing the
pathetically tragic moment when a popular favorite has to step aside
for younger faces and fresher talents--her affection for her daughter
suddenly prompts her to sacrifice herself for her daughter's happiness, and instead of long and dreary years of growing older and
older, she makes a quick, clean finish.

It sounds a bit sordid, and in spots a bit theatrical. It's
not, really, in spite of the dingy theatres and dingy rooms where
Kitty Darling spent her days and nights, and in spite of the sacrifice motif at the end. Because it rings true.

A fortunate combination of talents has given the life of this
shallow, amiable, good deal vulgar woman the dignity of tragedy.
Not the superficial tragedy of a "sad" ending, but the deeper and
much more significant tragedy of a simple soul asking for only affection and fun from life and becoming the victim of her own simplicity. The story, the characters, supply flesh and blood material
for such a tragedy. Well conducted research and excellent technical assistance has made a vivid atmospheric background for such a
story.

Several people new to the screen lay down solid foundations
for their screen careers in this picture. Rouben Mamoulian, associated with some of the best recent Theatre Guild productions, as
a director--Helen Morgan, Joan Peers, Henry Wadsworth as actors.

Mr. Mamoulian brings a fresh eye and a surprisingly pro-
ficient hand to his first movie. His camera seems to be groping
sometimes as if he were not quite sure what he was after, but that
is easy to overlook in a man who generally seems so sure of what
he wants, and how to get it. Many a situation that might have been
made trite comes out with the sunny newness of something just discovered for the first time. This is particularly so in the boy-and-
girl scenes, which are bright and innocent without ever getting
mushy. Their courtship, for instance, away from the grime of the
theatre and the cheap hotel, on windswept Brooklyn Bridge or the
top of a down-town skyscraper. This way of putting fresh air into
old and dusty situations is far more effective than shifting to the
apple-blossoms and singing birds of country lanes. Only in the
convent scenes does real beauty give way to mere prettiness.
There is something of the over-sweetness of Easter chromos in the
setting where Kitty's little girl spent her innocent childhood.

The sordidness of the burlesque life is somehow mellowed
with a kind of humorous pathos--it has the faded yellowed glamour
of old theatre programs, evoking memories wistful and kindly.   A
gay accompaniment of old songs--a series happily selected, from
"Alexander's Rag Time Band" down to today--dates the different
episodes better than any calendar.

Helen Morgan is either a fine actress or she has found in
Applause the part that fits her like her own skin.   With nothing
but musical comedy appearances to compare this performance with,
it is hard to say.   It doesn't matter, though.   She is Kitty Darling,
the blond burlesque beauty, through and through.   Her lazy, tawdry
life, her clinging affections like the purring affection of a kitten,
her cheap and flamboyant good times--even her end, inspired by
just the theatrical ideal of sacrifice such a woman would have--all
these things Miss Morgan has made wonderfully and pleasantly real.
The "wages of sin" touch is altogether absent.   You never blame
Kitty, or reflect that she got just about what she deserved.   You
wish, instead, that she had got a better break.

Joan Peers, who plays the convent-bred daughter of the burlesque lady, has a much harder part, and she plays it just as
brilliantly.   To capture sympathy for herself without taking it away
from her mother, to be "good" without being goody-goody, to be
the exponent of common-sense and virtue without ever being tire-
some--all that isn't easy, but Miss Peers does it with all the apparent ease in the world.   One scene--where she has to break with
her young sailor-man and has to make him think she doesn't care
for him any longer--she does better than I have ever seen such a
scene done, on the stage or on the screen.

The two men, too, are excellent--Fuller Mellish, Jr. , hitting a note of rather obvious villainy sometimes but on the whole
pretty life-like--and Henry Wadsworth, who is a wholly fitting mate
for Joan Peers.

                              --James Shelley Hamilton in
                                Cinema, Vol. 1, No. 1 (Janu-
                                ary 1930), pages 36-37.

☐ THE ARAB (Metro, 1924)

This latest--and possibly final--directorial effort of Rex Ingram has a fascinating background, the very Sahara itself, but the
story limps.   The action revolves around a missionary and his
daughter, with a young native on the sentimental horizon.   In this
it is suggestive of Where the Pavement Ends.   But there the comparison ends.

This mission is a pawn in the hands of the wily Moslems.
They plan to send away the government troops, let the desert

tribesmen wipe out the Christians and politely disclaim all responsibility. But the dashing dragoman, Jamil, son of a desert chieftain, prevents the tragedy. There is an indefinite ending, with the
girl returning to America but promising to come back. All this
may sound like a story of considerable action. The Arab, however, is turgid. There are few romantic scenes and the sentiment
is meager. The Moslem attack is worked up without creating any
real suspense. But there is more than a measure of picturesque-
ness in the rôle of the dragoman, Jamil, who has politely lied his
way in and out of Christianity four times. And there is a distinct
pictorial appeal to Mr. Ingram's production.

Mr. Ingram seems to have fallen down most in his plot development but he has performed something of a miracle with his
native players. They seem excellent actors, indeed. There are
some finely atmospheric scenes of the East, notably in the Algerian
dance halls and in the streets of the Oulad Niles.

Ramon Novarro is the Jamil and the rôle seems to us to be
better played than anything this young actor has yet done. Alice
Terry is the missionary's daughter and Alexandresco, a vivid Russian actress, makes her film debut in the colorful rôle of an Oulad
Nile.

--Photoplay, Vol. 26, No. 4
(September 1924), page 43.

☐ ARE PARENTS PEOPLE? (Famous Players-Lasky/Paramount,
1925)

Everybody has been anxiously awaiting the release of this
picture for two reasons: first, to see if Betty Bronson would
measure up to her performance in Peter Pan; second, because this
is the first production that the youthful director, Mal St. Clair,
has done for Paramount. We could write pages and pages about
Betty but it can be summed up in this: she is a marvellous actress, natural and human at all times. The story shows a young
girl whose parents suffer from incompatibility. She decides to give
them a mutual worry to bring them together. Every member of the
cast is perfect--Adolphe Menjou, Florence Vidor, Lawrence Gray
and Andre De Beranger. BUT what is foremost is the direction.
The picture moves along smoothly with a finesse of touches that
are subtle and amusing. See this!

--M. B. in Photoplay, Vol. 28,
No. 3 (August 1925), page 50.

☐ BARBARA FRIETCHIE (Regal Pictures/P. D. C. , 1924)

        The poetic "shoot if you will this old gray head but spare
your country's flag" has little to do with the heroine of this adaptation of Clyde Fitch's play.   Once again there is a lovely Southern
gal in desperate love with a handsome Northern officer.   The flag
episode is dragged in.   Conventional and slow moving Civil War
stuff.   The direction makes Florence Vidor's Barbara super-sweet.
                                --Photoplay, Vol. 27, No. 1
                                (December 1924), page 53.

☐ BARDELEYS THE MAGNIFICENT (M-G-M, 1926)

        So long as King Vidor and John Gilbert take Raphael Saba-
tini's story seriously, this picture remains just another costume
production, smoothly told, artfully acted, but not guaranteed to give
any ticket-seller a nervous breakdown.   But when star and director
say;

        "Come, come, enough of this seventeenth century intrigue.
Let's make a comic movie, " then it snaps into great entertainment.

        It's a story of another one of those mediaeval male Peggy
Joyces, who sets out to win a hard-to-get-Gertie of the provinces,
in spite of the fact that Louis XIII simply can't bear to have his
favorite wisecracker leave Paris.   Once the boy vamp sets eyes on
the champion "No girl" of France, he gets a bad case of honorable
intentions and risks his life in her service.   Vidor tells the conventional story smoothly and sincerely, even if his atmosphere of
those careless days is a little too spick-and-span.   When he kicks
over the traces at the climax, he hits a really gorgeous combination of farce and romance.

        And there's a love scene, in a boat drifting among the wil-
lows, that has genuine poetic feeling.   It's enough to make any picture.

        Mr. Gilbert's performance is bold, fiery and immensely
clever.   Eleanor Boardman acts with her brains; in spite of the
beauty of her romantic scenes, there is a refreshing sharpness
about her performance.   As the villain, Roy D'Arcy makes some
mean faces and John T. Murray, as the King's "yes man, " does
great work.   Of course, your season won't be complete unless you
see this picture.   It's safe enough for the children.
                                --Photoplay, Vol. 30, No. 6
                                (November 1926), page 53.

☐ THE BAT (Feature Productions/United Artists, 1926)

Eeeeee! The Bat! It's thrilling. It's chilling. It's a
scream of laughter and spookiness. Your spine quivers and your
hair stiffens every moment.

Perfectly written, originally by Mary Roberts Rinehart and
Avery Hopwood and scenarized by Julien Josephson, this Roland
West production is simply superb. Each detail dovetails properly
into every other. Lights flash, guns are fired, secret panels
swing, and the laughter and the creeps alternate till you chew your
fingers in excitement and delight.

The involved plot is centered around a criminal with the bat
as his trademark and his operations in a Long Island household.
Beyond that we refuse to tell. But when The Bat flies in your
neighborhood, don't fail to see it and take the youngsters, if it's
not too late at night.
                                        --Photoplay, Vol. 24, No. 6 (May
                                        1926), page 48.

☐ THE BAT WHISPERS (United Artists, 1930)

Of the clutching hand school that the stage smash, The Bat,
was probably the real parent of, The Bat Whispers, in its talking
version, must rise somehow above all of the others since the original, silent and sound, to get into the money.

One point in this talker's favor is the production, another
the direction, still another the photography, while at the Rivoli the
wide film and screen* lend aid, with the legit begotten comedy here
rather than the blatant sort, not to be overlooked. These may all
be exploitation angles, and the picture needs them, for it's a follow
up of all the others. With Chester Morris's name for its b. o.
value, whatever that may be.

The wide film, United Artists' first, permits the scenic end
of the film, which includes directorial and photographic touches, to
become somewhat grandiloquent. Bits of direction, with the camera
aiding, particularly early, are very endearing. They send forth an
impression of big and good production, with the wide screen probably the forceful factor, although the same effects will come in a
lesser way on the standard size.

Most of the comedy that is so legitimately secured is by
Maude Eburne, as the lady's maid. Miss Eburne is an English

*The Bat Whispers was initially released utilizing a widescreen
system, Grandeur.

stage comedienne. Some more is quietly injected by Spencer Char-
tres. It's not the noisy kind of ghostly slapstick so long associated
with haunted house stories.

Mr. Morris has but little to do. It's some time before his
appearance and shortly after that he's knocked out for another lapse.
At the finale the audience is halted by a cry from the screen not
to leave, and as a sort of epilog or something, Morris reappears
to request the audience not to divulge the identity of the Bat in the
picture. Other cast players take care of their portions without distinction either way. Una Merkel is the girl, with William Bakewell
opposite.

The Bat Whispers is a mystery haunted house and detective
tale. It has its creeps, thrills and some suspense. Its denouement is quite unanticipated and marks an excellent finish.

It can be paraded as a good picture in the class division, for
shivers and smiles. There is always an audience for either. Those
items and the advance work should do the rest.
                                   --Sime Silverman in Variety, Vol.
                                        101, No. 6 (January 21, 1921),
                                        page 17.

☐ THE BATTLE OF THE SEXES (United Artists, 1928)

A light-heavyweight drama, not as belligerent as the title
implies, but human, sophisticated and worth while. Jean Hersholt
as a business mogul greatly distresses a happy family by becoming
entangled with a gold-digging blonde, Phyllis Haver. Don Alvarado
is good as the power behind the blonde, and Belle Bennett adds
suspense as the distraught wife. Worth your while.
                                   --Photoplay, Vol. 34, No. 4
                                        (September 1928), page 56.

                         *   *   *

D. W. has given us what I think is the best picture he ever
made. The Battle of the Sexes lacks the epic sweep of The Birth
of a Nation, and is without the romantic atmosphere that assisted
in the success of some of his other pictures. It is an ordinary
story about ordinary people, but so superbly has Griffith directed
it that it is a notable example of screen art. Its appeal will be
general. Women, particularly, will find it engrossing. It is made
a great picture by the quality of its performances, yet there is not
a broadly sketched character in it. Griffith's facility for handling
numerous people and for grouping a few in intimate shots is much
in evidence. He introduces no arresting light effects, contenting
himself solely with telling his story directly and briskly, and without any frills. D. W. has shed all but one of the old fashioned ideas

that he has clung to throughout the years. In The Battle of the
Sexes there are no stilted titles that tell what is going to happen,
and in only one instance did I see a close shot that did not match
its medium shot, a weakness that has been a feature of all Griffith
pictures. The one habit that remains is that of defying convention
by fading out in the middle of a sequence instead of cutting. It is
odd to see a return to a scene that has faded out, but I hope that
D.W. sticks to it. He will, if he has a sense of humor, and he
must do something eccentric to show that he is no ordinary director. He has some exquisite touches in this picture. It deals with
a family, Belle Bennett being the mother, Jean Hersholt the father,
Sally O'Neil the daughter, and Billy Bakewell the son. I think
D.W. will agree with me that with such talented artists in one
group almost any director should give us some fine scenes, but I
think there are few who could make them as compelling as Griffith
manages to. In the opening sequence Hersholt gives Miss Bennett
a jeweled bracelet as a birthday present, and it is done with such
tenderness and feeling that it brought a tear to my eye, for I am
an emotional old ass. Another beautiful touch is in a scene showing Belle reading a letter from Jean in which he tells her that he
is leaving her. The strength of the scene lies in the fact that
while she is reading the letter she is standing directly below a
photograph of her and Jean in their wedding clothes. When she
finishes reading she looks up at the photograph, and anyone who
would not be moved by the scene has no place in a picture audience. Miss Bennett gives a superb performance, and Hersholt's
is one of the best of his career. For the first time we see the
real Jean on the screen. He plays the part straight, and it was a
brilliant bit of casting to put such a talented character actor in
such a role. Sally O'Neil is an actress. I said that once before,
and I am even surer of it now. She does magnificent work throughout. Billy Bakewell is the same ingenuous boy as usual, a capital
trouper with a rare screen personality that should be on the screen
much oftener. Phyllis Haver is in the picture. In a field with
less talented competitors she would be the picture. As the unscrupulous gold-digger she is simply great, again demonstrating
that she is one of the most capable girls on the screen. Don Alvarado has a mean sort of part which does not allow him much
latitude, but the acting excellence of the production suffers no re-
lapse when it is his turn to sustain it. In a few places Griffith
uses closeups where I think medium shots embracing all the characters in the main scene would have been more effective, but the
fault is not aggravated sufficiently to prompt me to become catty
about it. The picture is a splendid one, human and entertaining,
and that is all that matters. Of interest to Hollywood, but of none
to audiences, is the fact that Griffith shot it nine days under schedule and for quite a few thousand dollars under budget. The United
Artists production department, under that wise youth, John W. Con-
sidine Jr., is working efficiently and is turning out some of the
best pictures that we are getting.

--Welford Beaton in The Film
Spectator, Vol. 5, No. 13
(August 18, 1928), page 6.

☐ BE YOURSELF! (Joseph M. Schenck/United Artists, 1930)

     All Fanny Brice needs is what they call a vehicle, though
vehicles are not the easiest thing in the world to come upon.   No
less an expert carpenter than David Belasco once tried to fashion
one for her, and the result was appalling.   The trouble seems to
be that when a story is stretched out to what is considered the
right "dramatic" length it is deemed indispensable to include a
serious heart interest in it, with some sort of emotional climax.
As if comedies were not successful every time they are funny!

     Miss Brice is--need one say it?--a comedian.   Even a
comedienne, if you prefer.   She has had her greatest success in
revues and in vaudeville, where her different acts could be spotted
or strung together without bothering at all about plot or heart interest.   "Situations" should be the last thing in the world she
ought to be hampered with, and the man who can write a story
without situations hasn't happened along yet.   But it ought not to
be so hard to sew a few situations about other people together,
and let Fanny barge in and out of them in her own grand way.
She doesn't need a part if she has even half a chance to be herself.

     Be Yourself is a really good attempt to let her be herself.
To be sure, she is allowed to fall in love, and have a bit of heart-
ache, but there is not enough of it to be depressing.   The fact that
she falls in love with a prize-fighter whom she has to contrive a
defeat for before she can settle down comfortably with him prevents it from being too serious.

     For the rest she has a pretty free hand in doing her stunts.
They include one lugubrious song--ever since "Mon Homme" she
seems fated to be lugubrious at least once during a performance--
but they also include her classic dance and her operatic aria.   The
songs provided for her are not among the best she has had.   To
be frank, they are very feeble.
                                   --James Shelley Hamilton in
                                     Cinema, Vol. 1, No. 4 (May
                                     1930), pages 37-38.

☐ BEAU BRUMMEL (Warner Bros., 1924)

     An absorbingly interesting picture, from the famous play by
Clyde Fitch in which Richard Mansfield made such a success.   The
title rôle is in the hands of John Barrymore and permits him to
give one of the finest performances of his screen career.   Brummel, disappointed in love, determines to advance himself by sheer
insolence, and does so until he loses the friendship of his patron,
the Prince of Wales.   He is exiled from England and dies in a

French hospital. Mr. Barrymore's performance is masterful always. His expressions, his mannerisms, depict all shades from
impertinence to the most studied insolence. The direction is excellent, and some of the photography is wonderful. Second only
to the star are the performances given by Willard Louis as the
Prince of Wales, and Mary Astor as Lady Margery.

--Photoplay, Vol. 25, No. 6
(May 1924), page 54.

☐ BEAU GESTE (Famous Players-Lasky/Paramount, 1926)

They're advertising this special as a man's picture, but,
girls, don't let that keep you away. Glance over the cast: Ronald
Colman, Ralph Forbes and Neil Hamilton play the heroic Geste
brothers. Noah Beery is that remorseless scoundrel of the Foreign Legion, Sergeant Lejuane, and William Powell is a sly and
sinister Legionnaire. That's a cast!

Beau Geste is a mystery story, first and last. The screen
has too few good mystery tales. The love element is pretty slen-
der, but the swing of adventure makes up for it. Perhaps you
read Percival Wren's best seller. In filming it, Director Herbert
Brenon has followed the original with a lot of fidelity. We aren't
going to tell you about the mystery here, save that there is a
stolen sapphire, "the Blue Water," of great value. All three
Gestes shoulder the blame of the theft and run away to join the
Foreign Legion, that little army of lost men trying to forget and
be forgotten in the African sands.

If you read Wren's novel, you will recall the fascinating
and startling opening of the story. A detachment of the Legion is
moving to the relief of Fort Zinderneuf. Approaching through the
shifting sands, the advance guard hails the fort. At each battle-
ment soldiers can be observed standing, gun in hand. But there
is no answer to the rescuers' calls. Each man is dead, standing
at his post.

The brave Gestes are splendidly played by Messrs. Colman,
Ralph Forbes (here's a good bet), and Hamilton. But the real acting honors go to Mr. Beery for his Lejuane and Mr. Powell for
his cringing Boldini. Watch those two boys cop the picture.

--Photoplay, Vol. 30, No. 6
(November 1926), page 52.

☐ BEGGAR ON HORSEBACK (Famous Players-Lasky/Paramount,
1925)

James Cruze hits the high spot of his career in his screen
translation of the play by George Kaufman and Marc Connelly. We

might call it Art, but we won't, because too many dull and pre-
tentious films have been shoved on the public in the name of Art.
This film is gorgeous entertainment and as much fun as anything
we have ever seen.

The story is that of a young composer who is tempted to
marry for money. He falls asleep and dreams a fantastic nightmare of his life as the husband of a rich woman. The dream sequence is a brilliant satire of American life. It is a picture of
the revolt of an artistic imagination against a standardized and
mechanical world. The whole unreal atmosphere of a dream has
been strikingly created, thanks to some of the finest settings and
most remarkable photography ever conceived in an American
studio. It's downright funny, too, in the cock-eyed burlesque
manner of the comic supplements. The satire is swift, dazzling
and amazingly amusing.

It is something considerably more than trick photography and
grotesque settings that makes the dream sequence an extraordinary
achievement. In its curious mixture of sense and nonsense, of
fantasy and satire, of the ridiculous and the true, it has a quality
of greatness that reminds you of Alice in Wonderland.

The picture is a triumph for Cruze, but Edward Everett
Horton comes off with honors and so does Gertrude Short. Esther
Ralston and Cyril Chadwick also deserve mention. As for the
producers, they have every reason to be proud of a picture that
sets a new standard for intelligence and imagination. If you miss
it, you'll be passing up one of the best shows of the year.
                                  --A. S. in Photoplay, Vol. 28,
                                     No. 2 (July 1925), page 50.

*   *   *

James Cruze is known primarily as the man who directed
The Covered Wagon, but it has seemed to me that the most representative and finest examples of Cruze's work were to be found in
One Glorious Day and Hollywood. Both of these were fantasies,
and both were flops.

In Beggar on Horseback, the undaunted Cruze goes back to
the realms of insanity, and he proves again that he is a real master in this highly unprofitable form of expression. He and Walter
Woods, his faithful collaborator, have caught the spirit of George
Kaufman and Marc Connelly's play, and have sustained it beautifully. In setting forth the weird ramifications of Neil McRae's
nightmare, they have gone far beyond the restrictions that were
necessarily imposed when Beggar on Horseback appeared as a play.

They have made one bad mistake: in the earlier scenes,
before the dream starts and while the horrors of great wealth are
first being impressed on Neil's imagination, they have been just a
bit too fanciful. Thus the contrast between the dream and its basis
of reality is not sufficiently marked.

There are several excellent performances in Beggar on
Horseback, by Esther Ralston, Erwin Connelly, Ethel Wales and
Gertrude Short.   As the harassed genius, Neil McRae, Edward
Everett Horton is somewhat uncertain; his work is generally good,
but there are sour moments.

Although not addicted to music criticism, I must voice the
opinion that the score which accompanies Beggar on Horseback
ranks, in effectiveness, above any that I have ever heard.   It was
arranged by Dr. Hugo Riesenfeld.

--Robert E. Sherwood in Life,
Vol. 85, No. 2225 (June 25,
1925), page 24.

☐ BEGGARS OF LIFE

Beggars of Life interested me hugely, not because of possessing qualities that I think will interest the average audience,
but because it is an interesting cinematic study.   It has a consistent story from beginning to end; it was directed by William A.
Wellman with the force and conviction that he is putting into his
productions on an increasing scale; it contains excellent performances by Wallace Beery and Richard Arlen, and the story is told
in scenes and settings that preserve its atmosphere and enhance
its drama.   Can you think of anything else that a picture needs to
make it successful?   There is just one thing, and Beggars of Life
lacks it: it must be about something in which we can take a personal interest.   Nearly nine reels of nothing but tramps will not
find favor anywhere, even when dished up with the trimmings I
have mentioned and which are all that are necessary to make a different kind of picture successful.   Jim Tully's books, I understand,
achieved a certain success.   I suppose Beggars of Life had a respectable number of readers, but if one hundred people view the
picture for every one who has read the book, the picture still
would be a lamentable financial failure, the point I am making being that just because a certain story was a success as a book, it
does not follow necessarily that it will be a success as a motion
picture.   I do not understand why anyone wants to read Jim Tully's
uncouth utterances about tramps, and still less do I understand
why Paramount believes that anyone will care to follow the utterances for nearly two hours while they are being interpreted on the
screen.   But on behalf of Paramount, I would like to add that the
only way it can determine as a fact what the public wants, is to
provide it with every kind of entertainment and allow it to demonstrate its preference.   I criticize Paramount neither for making
Beggars of Life, nor for making it in the manner in which it was
made.   All I can say is that it is a really fine picture which did
not interest me at all, for I am interested in hoboes only when
they do things that I would not expect hoboes to do; and the picture,
with meticulous care, shows us hoboes doing only what we would

expect from them, and I can't derive any entertainment from that.
Wellman handled the romance between Louise Brooks and Dick Arlen with sympathy and good taste, but I could take no great sentimental interest in it, but whether the fault is mine or the picture's
I don't know. Perhaps it was because Miss Brooks was not equal
to the demands of the romantic scenes, which made Arlen's splendid work greatly overshadow hers. This young fellow has a marked
ability for submerging himself in a role. In Beggars of Life he is
not a movie actor; he is a good-for-nothing young tramp who is
not quite past the possibility of rehabilitation. The more I see of
Arlen on the screen the more I am convinced that he has the making of a great actor. He is wasted in conventional leading roles,
but when he gets a characterization into which he can get his teeth
he gives us something worth while now and which promises us
something really brilliant in the future. The old Wally Beery
comes back to us in this picture, Wally the actor who can act,
not the buffoon of those terrible comedies. He is just a tramp,
like everyone else in the picture, but he makes his characterization stand out as a fine piece of work. I don't know how Paramount is going to figure it out with both Bancroft and Beery on its
hands, but I hope it hands some of the plums to the latter. The
romance is the big part of Beggars of Life, but I am afraid it is
not going to carry the picture into popularity for the reason that
we see too many romances in settings much more pleasing. As a
five-reel production it would be better.

--Welford Beaton in The Film
Spectator, Vol. 6, No. 6 (October 27, 1928), pages 6-7.

☐ BELLA DONNA (Famous Players-Lasky/Paramount, 1923)

        Pola Negri's first American production seems troubled by
too much conscience. They were trying to observe all the rules
of censorship. They were trying to make Pola a sympathetic sin-
ner. And they were trying to make Bella Donna--the story of a
bad woman if there ever was one! As a result the story and the
characters seem straining under effort. They know they are in a
bad business but they are trying to think right!

        Even Pola is strained. She seems determined to be a good
woman, even if she dies of ennui. They have taken this passion
flower and made a poinsettia. A more beautiful flower, perhaps,
but without the seductive power.

        Pola Negri is a great actress. Even in the most artificial
absurdities of this film she registers subtleties of thought and
emotion that are impressive. But she hasn't the spontaneity, the
camera-free abandon of Carmen and Du Barry. She is timed down
until every little movement seems an effort all its own.

Conway Tearle plays Baroudi, the Arab of sinister animal attraction. He wears a turban and pantaloons and a henna complexion, but nothing can spoil that fine Irish face. He squints his eyes at Pola but otherwise does nothing that wouldn't be considered gentlemanly by the ladies and gentlemen of the Pennsylvania state board. The part required a Valentino.

Both Conrad Nagel and Lois Wilson are automatons. In fact, no one interests you. They are all papier-mâché.

We are too patriotic to compare this picture with Pola's foreign ones except to say that it's technically far superior. Indeed it is a triumph of technique over realism.

--Frederick James Smith in
Photoplay, Vol. 24, No. 1
(June 1923), page 64.

☐ THE BELOVED ROGUE

If the famous François Villon could see himself as he is burlesqued on the screen, he would probably writhe in agony in his grave. All the charm and romance in the life of the roguish Villon has been turned into regular slapstick comedy. Though lavishly mounted, this has little to offer. John Barrymore is in this picture.

--Photoplay, Vol. 32, No. 1
(June 1927), page 139.

☐ BEN-HUR (M-G-M, 1926)

Four million dollars and several years' time and infinite patience went into making Ben-Hur. The finished version justifies all of it. Elsewhere in this issue is related the story of its accomplishment.

Ben-Hur is not a flat picture upon a screen. It is a thing of beauty and a joy for ten years at least.

Reverence and emotion serve as background for the undying drama of Christ interwoven with the story of Ben-Hur, the young Jew who aimed to serve Him.

The screen has yet to reveal anything more exquisitely moving than the scenes at Bethlehem, the blazing of the star in the heavens, the shepherds and the Wise Men watching. The gentle, radiant Madonna of Betty Bronson's is a masterpiece.

Novarro is a perfect Ben-Hur. He gives an inspired performance. The story carries him from early boyhood, through the

Roman occupation of his city, through his years as a galley slave, through shipwreck and temptation until the final great moment in the Circus Maximus when he drives his chariot to victory over Messala and wins the love of the gentle Esther. Francis X. Bushman, as Messala, is very fine, indeed, and screens magnificently.

The gore and glory of the galleys, the thrill and beauty of the racing horses, the mobs at the Joppa gate, the desolation of the lepers among whom are the mother and sister of Hur, the furious excitement of the Circus, all these pass before the tense stillness that precedes the death of Christ. The Last Supper, the judgment of Pontius Pilate, the shadow of Calvary--all are touched with imagination and reverence.

This is a truly great picture. No one, no matter what his age or religion, should miss it. And take the children.
                              --Photoplay, Vol. 24, No. 4
                                (March 1926), page 54.

                          *   *   *

It would seem that, having attained his first $505,000,000, Mynheer Marcus Loew was hard put to know what to do with the odd $5,000,000. Whereupon some bright literary office boy stepped forward and proffered the suggestion that since Ben Hur, the mighty creation of our Gen. Lew Wallace, had not been done more than eight times during the past twenty years, and was resting peacefully and forgotten in its grave, why not do it again? Presto, chango and e voilà! Again we have Ben Hur, edition No. 1359m44, revived for $5,000,000 cold cash. It opened at the George M. Cohan one night last week, before a rubbernecking movie audience, which showed taste enough, at one time, to applaud the Madonna. We recommend it to you at your own risk.

To this strictly partial observer, edition No. 1359m44, represents the expenditure of $4,999,999.95 on massive effects and the remaining $.05 on drama. It resembles a tiny boy with a huge head resting on his puny shoulders. For as a hippodromic spectacle it has hardly ever been equaled, containing all the elements going to make Amazing, Gargantuan, Stupendous, and Mighty Biblical Pageantry. Which grandeur includes: (a) a Terrifically Impressionistic Galley manned by a thousand slaves; (b) a Thundersome sea battle between the Romans and ancient pirates; (c) a horribly effective Valley of the Lepers; (d) wondrous pictorial touches taken from the life of Christ; and of course, (e) ye good old chariot race, staged in a woolworthian, mammoth stadium with every Los Angeles man, woman, and child lying about as a super. Why, in scale, the thing almost resembles Opera.

As for the $.05 worth of drama, the fault would seem to be our General Lew Wallace's. His piece of bric-à-brac romance is nothing more than a super Rover Boys story touched up with a biblical background.

Ramon Novarro plays his best as <u>Ben Hur</u> and gives the
part plenty of adolescence, if nothing else. Francis X. Bushman
seemed well cast as Messala, his nose at least giving him that
Roman Look which a program note asserted was sought after in
casting for types. Summarily, after watching this Roman Jewish
Holiday, should the estimable M. Loew ever again have $5, 000, 000
to chuck away, why not call a conference and be a bit more careful as to just where to chuck it?

>   --Ted Shane in <u>The New Yorker</u>,
>   Vol. 1, No. 47 (January 9,
>   1926), page 30.

                              *   *   *

way.
Ramon Novarro as a Jewish boy who made good in a big

>   --Robert E. Sherwood in <u>Life</u>,
>   Vol. 87, No. 2266 (April 8,
>   1926), page 32.

☐ BEYOND THE ROCKS (Famous Players-Lasky/Paramount, 1922)

Written, supervised and dominated by the personality of Elinor Glyn. A little unreal and hectic as though the continuous presence of the stars was the desired object. But those who like Valentino and Swanson will not be disappointed. A glynish tale of true
love, baronial halls and the treacherous Alps, with Gloria's makeup
whiter than the snows.

>   --<u>Photoplay</u>, Vol. 22, No. 2 (July
>   1922), page 54.

☐ THE BIG HOUSE (M-G-M, 1930)

Not a $2 talker, but virile, realistic melodrama, a cinch
for every weekstand and hold-overable generally. A he-man picture, but oke for the wife and kiddies, gripping with its stark
drama, yet not without an element of underlying preachment and
utterly devoid of comedy.

As Butch, Morgan and Kent, Wallace Beery, Chester Morris
and Robert Montgomery are a great trio in "the big house, " where
each is serving a stretch for homicide, forgery and manslaughter,
respectively. Latter (Montgomery) is in for 10 years for killing a
man while driving stewed in his car; a criminal only by fate, unlike
the other two hardened law-breakers.

Butch (Beery) is the bullying guerilla of the Big House, only
recognizing in the sleeker forger (Morris) a mental superior.

Prison life on the half-shell is plainly exposed and with it a few of the problems which undoubtedly face every warden of every crowded prison institution, who must know how to temper justice with humaneness and yet be subject to an internal degree of corruption through the bullying "screws," stool pigeons (who are promised jail commutation for double-crossing plots for prison breaks), and the like.

The big wallop, timely enough in view of the recent Auburn and other jail breaks, is the prison revolt, resulting in several deaths and an exposé of how the officials deal with foolhardy prisoners. The hand grenades, barrages, stench bombs, tractor attacks and other means to conquer rebellious prisoners, with variations in the dungeon, etc., are all graphically dovetailed into the tense story.

Outside of the leading male trio, Leila Hyams contributes little as the femme interest, although Eddie Foyer in a Ben Turpin-esque stuttering role scored in the little he did with his comedy relief.

The Big House will go generally. Also susceptible to timely exploitation.

                                        --Abel Green in Variety, Vol. 99,
                                          No. 12 (July 2, 1930), page 25.

☐ THE BIG PARADE (M-G-M, 1926)

War, not from the cushioned seat of a government job but the mud-splashed perspective of a cootie-bitten private, has been brought to the screen by King Vidor's masterly direction of The Big Parade.

Bitter, grueling, muddy strife in all its tragedy and ironic humor has been superbly interwoven with rollicking comedy, captivating love episodes and tender romance. It is not make-believe. It is war as war actually is, with soldiers and women playing their parts bravely as plain human beings.

The story is simple--but the telling is great. A French maiden, an American doughboy and his two modern musketeers. But Vidor's vast sympathy with the subject, his utter lack of mock heroics and flag-waving and the genius he displays in sweeping his audience with him, even to the shell-pocked battleground, is unsurpassed in any war picture ever filmed.

John Gilbert, as the wealthy private, gives a splendid interpretation of the character's evolution from pampered youth to soul-shocked veteran. Renée Adoree, as the charming Melisande, wins the hero and the audience by her great performance of the French

peasant girl. The laughs and many of the tears go to Karl Dane
as the gangling member of the wartime trio, and Tom O'Brien
garners his share of glory as the third musketeer. Claire McDow-
ell's mother rôle is illuminated by the beauty of her sincerity, and
Hobart Bosworth, Claire Adams, Robert Ober and Rosa Marstini
are excellent.

This is a truly great picture, for it blends the color and
feeling of a war canvas with the homely intimacies of a doughboy's
kodak record.

--Photoplay, Vol. 24, No. 2
(January 1926), page 46.

*   *   *

I could not detect a single flaw in The Big Parade, not one
error of taste or of authenticity--and it isn't as if I didn't watch
for these defects, for I have seen too many movies which pictured
the war in terms of Liberty Loan propaganda.

The Big Parade is eminently right.   There are no heroic
Red Cross nurses in No Man's Land, no scenes wherein the doughboys dash over the top carrying the American flag.

This is due primarily to the fact that Laurence Stallings
wrote the story, and was allowed to select the director and the
most important members of the cast.   Mr. Stallings kept his story
down to the simplest possible terms, avoiding anything that might
remotely resemble a complication of plot, and he displayed remarkable judgment in choosing King Vidor as director, and John Gilbert
and Renée Adorée as stars.

For these reasons The Big Parade is a marvelous picture, a
picture that can be ranked among the few genuinely great achievements of the screen.   The initial credit must go to Mr. Stallings,
but the final honors belong to King Vidor, who thus substantially
justifies all the loud salutes that, I am happy to say, have been
fired in his behalf in this department.   He proves here what he
indicated in Wild Oranges: that he is a director of intelligence and
imagination.

He has made war scenes that possess infinitely more than
the usual spectacular thrill; he has made war scenes that actually
resemble war.   When he advances a raw company of infantry
through a forest which is raked by machine gun fire, he makes his
soldiers look scared, sick at their stomachs, with no heart for the
ghastly business that is ahead.   What is infinitely more important,
he causes the sleek civilian in the audience to wonder, "Why, in
God's name, did they have to do that?"

He has shown an American soldier, suddenly wild with the
desire to kill, trying to jab his bayonet into the neck of a dying
German sniper.   He has shown the look on that sniper's face, and
the horrible revulsion that overcomes the American boy.   I doubt

that there is a single irregular soldier, volunteer or conscripted, who did not experience that same awful feeling during his career in France--who did not recognize the impulse to withdraw the bayonet and offer the dying Heinie a cigarette.

Although the war scenes are naturally predominant in The Big Parade, the picture itself is essentially a love story--and a supremely stirring one at that.   Renêe Adoree, who appears for a very short time in the early part of the story, and again at the finish, manages to impress herself so vitally on the audience that her presence, in the dim background, is never for an instant forgotten.   Both she and John Gilbert are brilliantly effective.

There is great work by Tom O'Brien and Karl Dane, as two rough and blasphemous but typical crusaders of the A. E. F.; indeed, the entire army that moves forward with The Big Parade is recognizable and real.

It is recorded that when Laurence Stallings went to Hollywood to write The Big Parade, he failed to endear himself to the denizens of that strange community.   In fact, he intimated in print that the great majority of them were dim-wits.

This caused all the local mental giants to pray feverishly that Stallings' maiden effort as a photodramatist would prove to be a flop.   It seems that these embittered yearnings are not to be gratified.

The movies need some more men who can insult them and, at the same time, produce pictures like The Big Parade.
                    --Robert E. Sherwood in Life,
                      Vol. 86, No. 2249 (December
                      10, 1925), pages 24-25.

☐ THE BIG TRAIL (Fox, 1930)

The Big Trail will do a certain business because of its magnitude, but it is not a holdover picture and it cost around $2,000,000 to produce.   Failing to own a kick or a punch, other than scenically, and with no outstanding cast names, Trail, as big as it is and 125 minutes long, remains still a "western" of the American pioneering sort, so thoroughly made familiar by those silent epics preceding it.   In this talker day, Fox in The Big Trail has turned out only a noisy Covered Wagon.   Still it has expansive possibilities in tie-ups with educational chances.   At the Roxy it should stay the second week, owing to its New York exploiting campaign that must have cost over $30,000.

The big puzzle to The Big Trail is why it was not given drawing names, and more young people.   According to this film,

only elderly people started to hike from the Mississippi to Oregon,
other than the juvenile leads, John Wayne and Marguerite Churchill.
Wayne is entirely unknown and Miss Churchill has yet to make herself famous on the screen.   Among all the others not a half-dozen
youngsters, and no young men--nearly all heavy gaited males with
whiskers, and their wives who had to ply axes.   You see them always, like the cattle, going forward toward Oregon, over cliffs
and across streams, in the desert, etc. , for 125 minutes.   By and
by you commence to recognize them, even the cattle.

A big screen effort and an elegantly directed job by Raoul
Walsh, the only person connected with this picture who is starred.
A few of the actors are featured.   The recurrence of the same
things, interrupted now and then by a "big scene, " such as the
river or cliff crossing, or El Brendel's dragged-in comedy with his
mother-in-law, or the simple romance and the silly melodrama,
commences to weary, for it's the same thing over and over again,
including the Indian attack on the wagon train made corral.   Brendel by himself does get a gagged laugh here and there, but they are
too far apart.

This leaves the historical portion, the Oregon trail, as the
single interesting part.   And that perhaps only interesting to those
who relish looking back upon the hardships of developing America,
but perhaps not so entrancing to those who would prefer Charlie
Farrell and Janet Gaynor in any Fox picture.

The narrative has a romance and John Wayne, a studio property man, was chosen by Mr. Walsh to play the role of Breck
Coleman, a trapper, who undertakes to officiate as scout for the
wagon train.   Mr. Wayne acquits himself with no little distinction.
His performance is pleasingly natural and even if he is somewhat
fortunate in settling matters in a closing scene with the ignominious
Red Flack and his cohort, Lopez, one feels that he is entitled to
this stroke of luck.

In the early scenes the wagons and their occupants are seen
preparing for the long journey.   Marguerite Churchill plays Ruth
Cameron, who arrives on a river boat, aboard which she encounters
Wellmore, a stereotyped villain who intrigues the gullible passengers
with the more or less fascinating shell game.   For some time Ruth
is ungracious to Breck, but, as one surmises, she eventually learns
that he is a man among men and the story winds up satisfactorily
for this young couple.

Red Flack has a voice that reminds one of Captain Hook in
Peter Pan.   He talks in English to Lopez, who replies in Spanish.
Then there is Gussie, who is always in trouble either with his mule
or his mother-in-law.   Gussie is acted by El Brendel, whose comedy is often obtrusive, but yesterday afternoon it sometimes aroused
laughter from the audience, notably when Mr. Brendel has his sad-
dening experiences with his mount.

40   Selected Film Criticism

Tully Marshall, who was one of the pillars in The Covered
Wagon, does well in the film as Zeke, a good-natured and understanding old trapper.   Tyrone Power plays the raucous-voiced Flack.
Louise Carver gives an energetic performance as Gussie's ubiquitous
mother-in-law.

The vocalization is for the most part well done, the tonal
quality being modulated and life-like, but now and again yesterday
afternoon the voices did not seem to come from the mouths of the
players.   As this was an early performance it is presumed that
this infrequent failing was subsequently corrected.

No one will find anything to say against the Walsh direction.
If there is any objection, it would have to be made by the animals,
who had to struggle so fiercely so often.   Especially in the fording
river scenes.   The manner in which Walsh handled them and the
big scenes, in fact the entire picture, is okay as far as that goes
for a modern talker.

Young Wayne, wholly inexperienced, shows it, but also suggests he can be built up.   He certainly has been given a great start
as the lead role in a $2,000,000 production.   Wayne does a walk
through as far as he is able.   His greatest anxiety must have been
to appear natural as the wagon train's scout.   At least he looks it
and his athletic build did much for him to get over as well as he
has done.

Miss Churchill is set much in the same key, with not a
great deal to do.   Hers is mostly a silent role through being continually in a scrap with her sweetheart Wayne, and not speaking to
him.

Of the other actors, Ian Keith, as one of the heavies, perhaps leads, because he was not disguised with a beard.   Tully
Marshall and the rest are pretty well covered up with hair on their
face as the Oregon trailers or mule drivers.   In fact the players
mean nothing, nor does the story.   It's just the moving caravan,
going ahead at 10 miles a day as the captain mentions, with Oregon
2,000 miles away and the film getting there in 125 minutes.

At the Roxy the picture is in Grandeur on film and screen.
That isn't so material to the trade, as The Big Trail will be shown
upon only two Grandeur screens, in Hollywood and New York.   Otherwise it will exhibit in standard size.

In Grandeur is where the magnitude of the picture is made
evident.   The wide screen is employed throughout at the Roxy.   But
the Grandeur screen seems to dim the photography; leaves ensemble
scenes indistinct, except for figure or form, in person or with animals.   Grandeur is sharp enough in photography when in closeups,
but even in closeups other than with the ensembles or mobs, the
standard 35mm size might be preferred.

This Grandeur leaves the same impression its first demonstration did at the Gaiety by Fox some months ago; that it is required only for mass scenes or sport events; that the exhibitor can
go along with the standard size and that the wide screen is not big
enough in itself to become an additional stimulant at present to the
picture house trade.

> --Sime Silverman in Variety, Vol.
> 100, No. 16 (October 29, 1930),
> pages 17 and 27.

                              *   *   *

Here is a picture that can truly be classed as epic.   The
Big Trail is done on such a massive scale that it completely over-
shadows its actors.   And that is a tribute to the direction of Raoul
Walsh as well as to the human, simple characterizations of the
players.   It is another Covered Wagon.   Greater, because of Grandeur Film, and now you hear the people speak, the blood-curdling
shrieks of Indians and the creaking of prairie schooners.

This is the romantic story of the old Oregon Trail, a nation
in exodus to the promised land of the West.   The plot itself is
sparse, but the picture moves with such a breathless sweep, with
such smashing climaxes, that the story is relatively unimportant.
The highlights include a buffalo hunt, crossing a swollen river, and
an Indian attack.

Photography is excellent.   One long shot, the circling attack
of the corralled wagons by the Indians, has the beauty of Reming-
ton's pictures of the old West.   John Wayne, a screen newcomer,
in the leading rôle of the young scout, plays with a winning mixture
of boyish diffidence and self-assurance.   Fine characterizations by
Marguerite Churchill, Ian Keith, El Brendel, and by Tully Marshall
as an old scout.   Walsh has surpassed his past achievements and
produced a thrilling record of an important American epoch.

> --Photoplay, Vol. 38, No. 6
> (November 1930), page 52.

☐ BLACK BEAUTY (Vitagraph, 1921)

The simplicity and naturalness of Anna Sewell's original
"autobiography of a horse" has been preserved, and Black Beauty
on the screen becomes not only a possible picture, but an interesting one.   The story the horse tells is lifted practically in its entirety from the pages of the book and relates those adventures in
which Black Beauty figures.   The story Mr. and Mrs. George
Randolph Chester have added, to connect these scenes, tells the
story as Black Beauty could not have heard it, the story that was
told in the house about the persons who took part in the adventures.
There is, therefore, the "inside" story of the humans and the "out-

side" story of the horses, and they dovetail so well there is no
break in the interest and no resentment at the frequent changes
from one to the other.   The story of the humans tells of pretty
Jessie Gordon, who was being forced to marry wicked Jack Beckett
in order, as she thought, to save her brother's good name.   The
story that Black Beauty sandwiches in concerns his opinion of the
kind masters he loves and the cruel masters he hates; his account
of the carrying of the squire to town and his refusal to take the
bridge he knew was unsafe, even though he was whipped for it; his
race for the doctor; his terrifying adventure when the stables burned
and finally the long race he ran which saved the heroine and brought
the picture to a somewhat prolonged but exciting close.   Jean Paige
is a fine little heroine, justifying pictorially the romance that during
the making of the picture, sent her producer, Albert E. Smith,
scurrying out her way with a marriage license.   She also gives a
good account of herself as an actress.   Jimmy Morrison is her
leading man.

--Burns Mantle in Photoplay, Vol.
19, No. 5 (April 1921), page 53.

☐   THE BLACK OXEN (Frank Lloyd/Associated First National, 1924)

Somehow, as Corinne Griffith plays her, the rejuvenated
Countess Zatianny is a real flesh and blood woman who lives and
loves and suffers.   She might, in less capable hands, have been
the puppet of a novelist's imagination.

The story, of course, is not an everyday affair.   It tells of
a woman who, after sixty years of swiftly moving life, becomes
young again.   This is done through--business of quoting--"A modern
miracle of science."   With the face and figure of youth, with the
experience and subtlety of age--she re-enters the society that knew
her as a girl.   And many men fall victim to her charms.   The one
whom she loves, in return, is Lee Clavering--a dramatic critic and
playwright; the part is well acted by Conway Tearle.

Well cast and well directed by Frank Lloyd.   For adults.
--Photoplay, Vol. 25, No. 4
(March 1924), page 61.

☐   THE BLACK PIRATE (Elton/United Artists, 1926)

A roistering tale of the Spanish Main is The Black Pirate,
and I pity the man whom it does not waft back to the days of his
boyhood, when he dreamed of himself climbing aboard the pirate
craft and cleaning the seas of the bloodthirsty buccaneers, "Yo, ho,
ho--fifteen men on a dead man's chest."   Into it the ever-youthful

Doug has injected the very spirit of boyhood romance and adventure,
and it would be a hard-hearted parent, indeed, who would not will-
ingly advance the price of the tickets for every youngster in the
family. Incidentally, they should include themselves in the entertainment and adventure.

The entire picture is done in colors, not the usual colored
photography, but soft tints that delight the eye and emphasize rather
than detract from the story value. Nothing has ever been done in
colors on the screen that approaches it in beauty and uniformity.
The year of experimentation and study that has been put into this
phase of the production has been well repaid. In it, Mr. Fairbanks, for the first time in motion pictures, has secured the beautiful effect of mural paintings.

The plot? What do you care about that? It's all about pirates, with Doug, single-handed, capturing a huge galleon to prove
he's a good pirate himself. Imagine that!

Billie Dove is the beauty in distress, captured by the tough-
est pirate that ever slit a throat or scuttled a ship. Donald Crisp
runs away with the acting honors, and it is a delight to watch the
way in which Doug gives way to him on the screen and lets the
audience enjoy Crisp's characterization of an old Scotch pirate:
Go see The Black Pirate.
                              --Photoplay, Vol. 24, No. 6 (May
                              1926), page 48.

                              *   *   *

There is a quality of courage evident in every one of Douglas
Fairbanks's pictures--and I don't refer to the mock courage displayed by the characters he portrays in their acrobatic antics, their
duals and their desperate, eleventh-reel rescues. It is a form of
courage associated with those eleventh who are pioneers in some field of
endeavor, who are not afraid to blaze fresh trails or to experiment
with new and untried tools.

Doug Fairbanks is, and always has been, a progressive force
in the movies. Each of his productions has represented a definite
departure from the old forms; he has never been content to sit back
and say, smugly, "Now I have discovered the formula of success;
I'll stick to it," as so many of his brethren in Hollywood have done.

In The Black Pirate, Mr. Fairbanks has employed the Technicolor process of photography, an extremely daring experiment, in
view of past results. With characteristic taste, he has toned down
his tints to such an extent that the spectator is almost unconscious
of them; he has made no attempt to duplicate the realism of a mir-
ror, but has made his scenes in the form of impressionistic paintings. Thus, The Black Pirate stands at the top of all the movies
I have seen in point of rich, glamourous beauty.

In collaboration with Mr. Fairbanks was his director, Albert Parker, whose imagination and knowledge of the power of a camera have enhanced the value of The Black Pirate immeasurably. The arrangement and composition of the scenes is simply extraordinary; furthermore, it is never obvious. It is the work of artists who know how to reach the brain through the eye.

At this point, I might easily embark on a discussion, "Resolved: That the public's brain is non-existent," but that would take up too much valuable space. Suffice it to say that the audiences at The Black Pirate gasp with wondering approval as each new visual thrill is revealed.

The dramatic values in The Black Pirate are subservient to the pictures themselves. Messrs. Fairbanks and Parker seem to have realized this, and they have kept their story down to the essentials; the picture is much shorter than most of Mr. Fairbank's previous efforts.

The plot, such as it is, tells of a young Spanish nobleman whose father is killed by pirates. He then enlists under the Jolly Roger, aids the buccaneers in their nefarious activities and ultimately delivers them into the hands of the law. That is all; but it is enough.

Supporting the muscular but still slim Douglas are Billie Dove, beautiful but unimportant, and the villains of Robin Hood and Don Q--Sam De Grasse and Donald Crisp. The pirate crew is composed of all the unemployed boxers and wrestlers in the United States, and a terrible-looking outfit they are, with battered faces, and muscles bulging under the habiliments of desperadoes.

The sub-titles, be it said, are absolutely flawless in style, and are further distinguished by their commendable scarcity.

I hope that every one will seize the opportunity to see The Black Pirate before its marvelous beauties have been blurred by constant association with projection machines.

--Robert Sherwood in Life, Vol.
87, No. 2264 (March 25, 1926),
page 26.

☐ BLACKMAIL (British International Pictures/Sono Art-World Wide, 1929)

At one bound the British picture makers jump among the leaders in the talkie race. British International deserves much credit for this splendid phonoplay. Love and murder combine in the story, with a shopgirl, a dastardly blackmailer and a lad from Scotland Yard as the key characters. Some excellent acting by Donald

Calthrop as the miscreant. A few such will deliver British producers from their inferiority complex.

--Photoplay, Vol. 37, No. 1
(December 1929), page 54.

☐ BLOOD AND SAND (Famous Players-Lasky/Paramount, 1922)

We foresee a highly popular career for this screen version of Vicente Blasco Ibáñez's novel, Blood and Sand. There are several obvious reasons. One is the presence of Rudolph Valentino in his most decorative role since his Julio in The Four Horsemen. Another is the color and swiftly unswerving movement of the story.

Ibáñez wrote Blood and Sand as a lasting indictment of the bull fight and its cruelty. As far as the film is concerned, however, we fear that the Spaniard's message has gone to the Dead Letter Office. The bull fight, as the silversheet catches it, is highly attractive. The film follows the original tale fairly closely, tracing the harum-scarum peasant lad who grows up to be the matador idol of Spain, and who comes to know fame and temperamental vanity. His haunting love for his wife becomes hopelessly tangled in a mad, consuming passion for a philandering young woman of birth and wealth and he comes to know the fickleness of the public before he dies, mangled and broken, a hero toppled from his pedestal. As the toreador breathes his last, from the bullring drift the cries of the populace, cheering a new hero.

All this is told admirably. Mr. Niblo's direction is sane and now and then stirring. There are flashes of a glowing Zuloaga background. Valentino's matador is rife with sex and passion, with a breathless touch of brutality here and there. Indeed, it is this note of savagery recurring through Blood and Sand that lifts it, stark and palpitating, above the sugary, milk and water tales of our screen.

Valentino's toreador lacks subtlety but it is as real in many ways as Joseph Schildkraut's Liliom of the footlights. We place it well in advance of his Julio. And Nita Naldi's Dona Sol is quite unforgettable.

--Photoplay, Vol. 22, No. 5
(October 1922), page 58.

* * *

It is a Herculean job to picturize, according to the standards of the American picture industry, a novel like this one of Blasco Ibáñez's, and leave anything of the quality of the original. Most of the redness has to be taken out of the blood, and the sand must be arranged so prettily that no aridity is apparent. June Mathis was given this job to do, and considering the limitations put upon

her by the exhibitor point of view she has done it remarkably well.
She has had to inject probably the most tiresome old moralizer
known to motion pictures--a man who intrudes upon the story at
regular intervals to point out to the eight-year-olds that certain
things are wicked.   She has had to throw overboard--naturally--
most of the fascinating detail of a bullfighter's life, as well as the
keen tragedy of an idolized athlete who eventually falls off his pedestal because his physical prowess wanes, and concentrate chiefly
on what is called the love-interest.   But with what she has left she
has made something vivid and colorful and interesting--rather more
a tourist's picture of Spain than a glimpse into the heart of Spain--
through which moves a real, flesh-and-blood man.   This story
Fred Niblo has translated into exceedingly good moving pictures.
Then, Valentino plays his part with the imagination and authority
of a real actor.   His matador is a real person, a son of the people,
who becomes an idol of the people, spoiled, vain, but generous and
always a boy at heart.   It is a more unsophisticated and puritanical
character than the novelist created--his adventure in passion has
been so managed that he seems to be tricked into it against his
will instead of striding into it with bold, Latin abandon.   But Valentino does it for all that has been left in it, extremely well.

                           --Exceptional Photoplays, Vol. 3,
                             No. 1 (November 1922), page 4.

☐   THE BLOT (Lois Weber/F. B. Warren, 1921)

          Or Do Schoolteachers Eat?   Apparently not, according to
Lois Weber, who here pictures a starving professor, his wife and
daughter, Claire Windsor, in a series of pathetic episodes.   Luckily the rich young college lad, Louis Calhern, appears just in time
with roast chicken and a wedding ring.   Typical Weber exaggeration, and rather tiresome.   Censor proof.

                           --Photoplay, Vol. 20, No. 6
                             (November 1921), page 113.

                           *   *   *

          In The Blot Lois Weber champions the cause of the under-
paid college professor and the struggling minister whose salary is
insufficient for his needs.   The story she has written has a strong
human theme but she has smothered it under a mass of plausible
but unnecessary detail.   In a four-hundred page novel where time
is no object and the book may be picked up and read in sections,
such a method of constructing a story is permissible.   By using a
dozen or so minor characters and introducing frequent bits of local
color that do not advance the story, the author-director has weakened the vital points in the picture and deprived the theme of half
its punch.   Building a scenario is a question of elimination, as well
as of selection.   It may be quite within reason that a pretty girl
should inspire love in the hearts of a wealthy college boy and a poor

minister, and also in the breast of the young fellow next door, but
when the action halts while the brothers and sisters and chums of
the last named suitor drive the head of the house out of his own
parlor and start a jazz party, the piece of business becomes a dis-
traction and not an asset. Miss Weber's character drawing is seldom at fault, but she uses so many characters that they frequently
get into one another's light.

A piece of business that is in rather poor taste is the close
proximity of scenes showing the Olsen family at dinner and the
Griggs cat foraging in the Olsen garbage-can. Heroic cutting would
leave a well-balanced and entertaining picture.

The cast, headed by Louis Calhern and Claire Windsor, is
excellent. The details of production relative to location, lighting
and settings are all high grade.

> --Edward Weitzel in The Moving
> Picture World, Vol. 51, No. 10
> (August 27, 1921), page 930.

☐ THE BLUE ANGEL (Ufa/Paramount, 1930)

Emil Jannings' performance in The Blue Angel is so brilliant
that, as a sort of cinema paradox, it ends by inflicting an injury on
the picture. It is actually so good that it hurts. As the stern, upright German school teacher, who falls into sentimental, middle-
aged love with a reasonably promiscuous cabaret singer, and thereupon loses position, dignity and life, he is--to employ a word that
has lost most of its force in cinema criticism--magnificent. He
does, it is true, drift from time to time into that familiar German
acting vice of ponderous detail; of playing a scene at too great a
length, until he has squeezed from it every drop of emotion, powerfully but far too slowly. It is this insistence of his on lingering
over an episode that gives rise to the careless charge that he is
guilty of over-acting. He isn't, by any means, but he is guilty of
that serious venial sin of lethargy.

It is not, however, in this excess of detail that Jannings in-
jures The Blue Angel. The trouble is that he is so infernally moving in his portrayal, so tremendously vivid and real in his portrait
of collapse, mental, moral and physical. He builds his picture of
the dignified pedant so thoroughly and so earnestly that, as you
watch his gradual degradation, you are seeing a man you know and
believe in collapse before your eyes and you are suffused with a
feeling of shame, knowing that you have no right to be there. You
have burst in on a private tragedy and you feel that the only thing
for you to do is to mumble an apology and withdraw amid embarrassment. You are an intruder, not a playgoer.

There can, of course, be slight question that when a performance creates in a casual spectator so personal a reaction, then

it is brilliant acting. There is, it appears, such a thing as an actor being too good. Certainly, though, no one could want the Jannings portrayal to be less striking. It does have the effect of making the resulting photoplay seem, not great tragedy, with the purg-
ing effect that great tragedy is supposed to possess, but something
more personal and less exalting. The fate of the unhappy professor
becomes a painful, embarrassing, almost a shameful thing to watch;
a thing that is not stirring or poignant so much as it is terrible and
infinitely depressing. Some of the spectators, I am told, find the
public garrotting of the two Chinese hostages in the Theater Guild's
version of the Russian play, Roar China, difficult to witness. When
you consider how theatrical is such a scene in comparison with the
realistic horror of The Blue Angel, you are inclined to wonder how
these same spectators would react under the spell of the Jannings
portrayal.

It is only fair to warn you that if you are nearly as impres-
sionable in the theater as you should be, you will find the later
scenes of the photoplay painfully real, even though you are theoreti-
cally an admirer of stark tragedy. At the same time, it is equally
reasonable to remind you that if any such qualms keep you from
visiting the picture you will be missing two of the finest performances that the talking films have yet provided. The other one, of
course, is Miss Marlene Dietrich's.

Before passing to that young lady's contribution, however,
something should be said about Mr. Jannings' possible return to
America. His brief Hollywood sojourn was terminated rather hast-
ily just about the time that the talking pictures arrived, but that
was, to a certain extent, a coincidence. It is true that the excuse
was that he was unable to speak English, but added to that there was
the fairly important reason that his pictures were, outside of in
their New York showing, not bringing in the proper economic returns. One of the few pleasant things that can be said for the
talking screen is that it has built up audiences for more adult pictures and more adult performers. (That adjective, "adult," has
always seemed to me one of the most annoying conceivable, but it
is the only word possible here, so please forgive it.) It happens,
also, that the Jannings English is entirely satisfactory for cinema
purposes. Perhaps, therefore, the local film producers will be
wise enough to attempt to lure this First Actor back to Hollywood.
Whether he would be wise to surrender to any such blandishments
is a matter he can talk over with Miss Dietrich, who is spending
her holidays in the Fatherland.

Knowing practically nothing about showmanship, I cannot say
whether the all-seeing Paramount organization was wise in billing
Miss Dietrich as the New Garbo or whether it merely failed to
realize the German girl's qualities as a personage. Of course, it
is true that the newcomer does look a bit like the Incomparable
One, but the resemblance is hardly as striking as publicity has
made it. The chief reason why she was at first regarded as an
imitation is that her first scene in Morocco was so arranged that,

in character appearance and manner, she was made to seem merely an impersonation, attractively done, of Greta Garbo in Anna Christie. After that episode she seemed less and less an imitation and more and more an original person. Now, in The Blue Angel, made before Morocco but shown here after it, it is proven conclusively that she is neither a synthetic nor a publicity-made star.

In both pictures, though, she is an excellent actress. Taken in one way or another, she is quite sensational in Morocco, but regarded merely as an actress, she is undeniably more real in The Blue Angel. Anyway, now that we have seen her in two pictures, it is possible to say with considerable dogmatism that she is a brilliant performer, who possesses all the necessary qualities from beauty and poetic appeal to histrionic skill and a gift for merciless realism, to make her another Garbo in influence, if not in style or ability to create a legend.

Possibly it is now time to mention the picture, itself. It is a heavy, ponderous German sentimental fable, that gloats with beefy tearfulness over the details of amorous tragedy, and it has a lot of trouble passing a given point. Granted those weaknesses, though, it is a moving drama, brilliantly directed by von Sternberg, admirably acted in the supporting roles--particularly by Kurt Gerron, as Jannings' chief tormentor, the magician--and providing a great actor with the vehicle for what is probably his finest performance.
--Richard Watts, Jr. in The Film
Mercury, Vol. 12, No. 1 (December 22, 1930), page 7.

☐ THE BRIGHT SHAWL (Inspiration/Associated First National, 1923)

This production of Joseph Hergesheimer's highly colored tapestry of revolutionary days in Cuba a generation ago marks an interesting milestone in the career of Richard Barthelmess. It is his first stellar venture into the field of the costume drama. The result, under the careful guidance of John Robertson, is a pretty play of distinct atmospheric charm. The Bright Shawl, as Hergesheimer wrote it, was a tale of Havana intrigue, with Cuban strugglers for liberty on one side and soldiers of Spanish oppression on the other. Into this maelstrom was dropped Charles Abbott, a young American who attaches himself to the Cuban cause. He is largely the pawn of circumstances (which make him a negative screen character) but he moves among a maze of interesting folk, including one of Hergesheimer's most picturesque creations, La Clavel, a dancer of old Andalusia. Another is Pilar de Lima, a pretty but sinister half caste Peruvian-Chinese spy.

Barthelmess does surprisingly well with his character of Charles Abbott. Into it he puts all his technique and intelligence--

and no young actor has more of either.   But he never can quite
overcome the negative quality of the role.   Dorothy Gish is La
Clavel, but not the dancer as Hergesheimer painted her.   Still, it
is a surprising departure for the "little disturber" and, no doubt,
will interest motion picture followers.   We should have preferred
Hergesheimer's La Clavel but Miss Gish's version will be more
appealing to screen audiences, we suspect.   Jetta Goudal, the Pilar,
may or may not be a film find.   Seemingly she had a distinct film
personality.   One of the real hits is William Powell's dashing Spanish officer.

> --Frederic James Smith in Photo-
> play, Vol. 24, No. 2 (July
> 1923), page 68.

☐ BROADWAY (Universal, 1929)

      The original of all the night club and underworld dramas--
and still the most effective.   You may quarrel with the too lavish
settings given the Dunning-Abbott play, but you'll have no complaint
against Director Paul Fejos' direct and sharp handling of the story.

      Here you will find no hodgepodge talkie, trying to get by on
the strength of its novelty, but an expert drama, with concise dialogue, tense melodrama and, for the most part, good acting.

      Glenn Tryon plays the rôle of the innocent hoofer embroiled
in a bootlegging murder.

      Tryon is surprisingly good in a difficult part.   But he has
keen competition in Thomas E. Jackson, a member of the stage
cast, and Evelyn Brent, as the vengeful chorus girl, who steal the
show.   Mr. Jackson is decidedly a talkie find.   What a voice!
Paul Porcasi, as the proprietor of the night club, also duplicates
the hit he made on the stage.   Merna Kennedy is not so good and
is swamped by superior performances.

      Broadway is tricked out with theme songs, with special danc-
ing acts and with a mammoth cabaret scene, three times as large
as any New York night club.

      But these bits of over-elaboration are immediately forgotten
in the rush of the melodrama back-stage in the night club.

      And so you will not be disappointed in Universal's version of
one of the most entertaining plays presented in several seasons.
All Talkie.

> --Photoplay, Vol. 36, No. 3
> (August 1929), page 54.

                        *   *   *

The first and greatest of the nightclub melodramas has lost most of its effectiveness in its screen adaptation. It is buried under a mass of extravagant production and its casting of the role of Roy Lane, the hoofer, has not helped it. The best things about the work are the performances of Thomas E. Jackson and Paul Porcasi, of the original stage production, in their familiar parts of the noble detective and the troubled cabaret owner.

--Richard Watts, Jr. in The Film Mercury, Vol. 10, No. 3 (July 12, 1929), page 4.

☐ THE BROADWAY MELODY (M-G-M, 1929)

There is a widespread belief, I am told, that those arrogant fellows, the New York cinema critics, find an evil joy in reversing the verdicts issued by their colleagues in alien centers. Particularly do they delight, the theory has it, in objecting to the opinions advanced by their fellow archons in distant Hollywood. Let a West Coast observer hail a picture with enthusiasm and the New Yorkers will denounce it as trifling and unworthy. Should the Californian find serious faults with a production, then the Broadway critic will likely hail it as a masterpiece.... As in the case of most theories held about critics, this belief has the important defect of being entirely false.

For example, there is the instance of The Broadway Melody, which, I gather, was enthusiastically approved of in Hollywood. Did the Manhattan reviewers, determined to put their Western brethren in their place, gaze upon the picture, therefore, with scorn and superiority? If you think so, then you haven't had the good fortune to read the notices that appeared in the local newspapers. The only signs of a fight in evidence arose from the determination of the boys and girls of the New York press to eject the Californians from their positions in the front of the cheering section.

I certainly wouldn't go so far as to say that my colleagues were influenced by a desire to outcheer their rivals, much less that they were unconsciously swayed by the extraordinarily vigorous and skillful advertising campaign waged by the photoplay's sponsors. Anyway, there couldn't have been much more critical enthusiasm manifested had we been reviewing Hamlet with the original cast. The reviewers were rendered everything but speechless by a masterpiece that, I gathered, must be greater than the combined works of Ibsen, Shakespeare, Sophocles, O'Neill, Shaw and Samuel Shipman.

Miss Irene Thirer, of The Daily News grew so excited that even her best superlatives sounded too quiet and she had to fall back on the eloquent and expressive, "Zowie!" to relieve her feelings. Miss Katherine Zimmerman, of The Telegram compared the photo-

play to "a Jed Harris production, with entr'acts by Prof. Flo Ziegfeld," which, for your information, I might say is intended as a
compliment. The other observers, if less picturesque in their applause, were about equally enthusiastic.

Having noted down the newspaper and, apparently, the public
reaction to The Broadway Melody, I wonder if you would permit me
to add, in my calm way, that the ecstacy aroused by the work
seemed to me just a trifle excessive. That the picture offers the
best show the talking and singing films have yet devised is, I think,
true. The acting, likewise, seemed to me exceptionally good and
Mr. Beaumont's direction was shrewd and always effective. Then,
there was the work of Mr. James Gleason.

It is true that Mr. Gleason is set down as but one of three
authors of the piece, sharing program credit with Edmund Goulding
and Norman Houston. Possibly many of the things I liked best were
not the work of Mr. Gleason, and he may even have been responsible for a moment or two that I found trying. Nevertheless there
was manifest with pleasant frequency throughout the picture a quality
of dialogue and characterization that many of us have come to expect of the man who put something into The Shannons of Broadway
that caused us to have an affection for that slightly ramshackle piece
infinitely greater than we felt for offerings of considerably more
aesthetic merit. "Heart-warming" is the way the quality is expressed, I believe.

It was the frequent presence of the hard-boiled, sentimental
humors that I insist on ascribing to Gleason that gave The Broadway
Melody its chief merit, but the virtues of the film were immeasurably assisted by the grand acting of Charles King, Anita Page and
Bessie Love. Mr. King's romantic song and dance man seemed to
me not far inferior to Lee Tracy's classic portrait of a somewhat
similar hoofer in the original company of Broadway. Miss Love's
impersonation of the sacrificial sister was moving, understanding
and credible, providing a come-back for an unfortunately neglected
screen actress. In many ways, though, it was Miss Anita Page's
characterization of the beautiful member of the sister team that
seemed the outstanding histrionic feat of the photoplay. In a part
that might easily have been of secondary importance in the face of
the more sympathetic role of the older girl, the increasingly astounding Miss Page was so believable, so true to type and so emotionally right as to make her work stand out in a trio of fine performances. Any one who can play such different roles as the evil
virgin of Our Dancing Daughters, the show girl of The Broadway
Melody and the conventional ingenue of The Flying Fleet and do them
all so well is a real actress.

These, then, are the most inconsiderable virtues I discerned
in The Broadway Melody and I will not deny that they make the picture worthy of the economic success it is bound to achieve. There
are, however, a number of things about the work that are not quite
so praiseworthy. For example, the situations and even, upon occa-

sion, the dialogue are too directly reminiscent of Broadway, The
Shannons, The Butter and Egg Man, Burlesque and Is Zat So to
make it quite first rate as an original creative effort.

There is, also, at least one situation that is insufficiently
clarified. It is never made quite clear whether the younger sister
is listening to the advances of the villain through infatuation or because she is doing a little sacrificing of her own and doesn't want
to break up her sister's romance. The speech of the villain offering Miss Page an apartment, jewels, a car, etc., was, come to
think of it, pretty terrible. Warming to my subject I might even
express regret that the three song numbers were not a bit more of
musical comedy hit caliber.

One more objection and I am through. I wonder why it is
that the talking films have decided that a stuttering man is the most
hilarious figure imaginable. The part in The Broadway Melody is
well played by Jed Prouty and some of his lines are really amusing,
but it doesn't seem to me that the close-up of a mouth in the act
of stuttering is excruciatingly comic.

It is perhaps true that all of my objections, save possibly the
one on the score of imitation, are somewhat trifling, but then they
were intended to be. I think The Broadway Melody is a good picture. But it certainly isn't the overwhelming masterpiece that will
provide the final death blow to a silent screen capable of turning
out Potemkin, The End of St. Petersburg, Variety, The Patriot and
The Big Parade.

--Richard Watts, Jr. in The Film
Mercury, Vol. 9, No. 13 (February 22, 1929), page 6.

☐ BULLDOG DRUMMOND (Goldwyn/United Artists, 1929)

This is a corking melodrama--and Ronald Colman gives the
best talkie performance to date. He's suave and easy before the
terrorizing "mikes." Voice gives him a new charm. Bulldog
Drummond puts Ronald Colman right at the top after some recent
wavering, if lavish, films.

The English writer of shockers, Sapper, dashed off Bulldog
Drummond as a stage melodrama. With the advent of the talkies,
every producer was after it. But Sam Goldwyn reached first.

Goldwyn took a lot of pains with the film. It is intelligently
and tastefully done. The sounding is highly expert. Here a rain-
drop can be made to act in the sound pictures as excitingly as a
Rolls-Royce. The cutting (one of the drawbacks of the talkies up to
now) is finely done. In a phrase, Bulldog Drummond is great stuff.

Bulldog is a demobilized officer who wearies of his dull club life. He puts an advertisement in the "agony column" of the London Times, asking for adventure. Out of the avalanche of letters, he selects one signed Phyllis. It requests him to be at the Green Bays Inn at midnight, if he is sincere in his quest for adventure.

It develops that Phyllis' uncle, a millionaire American, is being held prisoner in a fake hospital by three master crooks, aided and abetted by a host of bloodthirsty Malays.

Colman gives a superb performance and he gets fine aid from an excellent cast. The best work is done by Claude Allister, as a new sort of silly ass Englishman, and by Lilyan Tashman, as the tough baby who leads the crooks. All Talkie.

--Photoplay, Vol. 36, No. 2 (July 1929), page 54.

☐ THE CABINET OF DR. CALIGARI (Ufa/Goldwyn, 1921)

Change, say the psychologists, is rest. From which basis it might easily be argued that The Cabinet of Dr. Caligari is as good as a week in the mountains for any movie fan tired of the conventional picture. Certainly it is a complete change. However relaxing it may be depends greatly upon the susceptibility of the spectator. Being a reasonably calm, ordinary sort of individual we left the theater believing strongly that the author of the picture was a little mad, the director a little madder, the actors engaged quite mad indeed. The American distributors bought the picture from its German owners. Yet we were conscious of having seen a perfect sample of that cubistic art of which we have read so much since the first nude descended the staircase looking like a patchwork quilt in eruption. Caligari, then, is the weird story of a German scientist who carts a somnambulistic youth about the country in a coffin-like cabinet, sets him up at county fairs as an exhibit and releases him at night that he may commit a murder or two between bedtime and breakfast. It is a story told, and seen, by a disordered mind, with all the scenery jumbled in fantastic shapes and the features of the players weirdly angular and wildly staring. But it is momentarily returned to normal at its conclusion and the effect is one of having seen an Edgar Allan Poe thriller cleverly transferred to the screen. We would not, however, take the children. They will be just as well off and a lot happier if they do not meet Dr. Caligari. The German actors are excellent, Werner Krause giving a good performance as the weird doctor and Conrad Veidt an uncanny subject.

--Burns Mantle in Photoplay, Vol. 20, No. 2 (July 1921), pages 58-59.

*   *   *

The Cabinet of Dr. Caligari is a revelation and a challenge.
It is a revelation of what the motion picture is capable of as a
form of artistic expression.   It challenges the public to appreciate
it and challenges the producer to learn from it.   The revelation is
there for all to see.   If the appreciation fails, the motion picture
itself, and all that it has promised, is in danger of failing.

In The Cabinet of Dr. Caligari the motion picture for the
first time stands forth in its integrity as a work of art.   It is one
of the paradoxes of art that it is at the same time an abstraction
and something tangible in terms of our bodily senses.   It is form
and idea.

The story of Doctor Caligari is a phantasy of terror told
with the virtuosity of a Poe, in terms of the screen.   Its emotions
appeal directly to a universal audience.   Even if stripped to its
barest outline it would still compel our attention, for it deals with
the fascinating problem of one person's supernatural control over
another person.   But it acquires the irresistible quality of all true
art because it is told with such complete mastery of medium that
its terror becomes an aesthetic delight.   We find that we have
shared the experiences of a madman without suspecting that he is
mad; we have been transported into that sphere where man creates
his own imaginative realities as an escape from the realities of life
which constantly overwhelm without ever completely satisfying him.

Specifically, there is an evidence in this picture, for the
first time in America, at least, of something of the point of view
of the "Dadaist" to whom everything in the world is equally impor-
tant--a sort of reflection in the world of plastic representation of
the conceptions of relativity which are agitating mathematicians and
astronomers.   Thus, the picture stands in the current of living
thought.   It becomes a motion picture with an underlying significance
that is worthy of serious discussion.   The picture itself questions,
makes sanity relative as insanity is relative--and constitutes a valuable offset to the American tendency to oversureness of intellectual
values.   Moreover, it is related through its use of form and decoration to the modern art movements of the Continent.

The plot is a simple one.   It concerns itself with the strange
happenings in a fantastic town of problematic reality, where a Fair
is being held.   To this Fair comes a Dr. Caligari with his cabinet
in which he keeps a wonderful sleeping puppet named Cesare, whom
Caligari alone can awaken to somnambulistic speech and action.
Soon after Dr. Caligari sets up his attraction at the Fair and Cesare has been made to perform, strange murders begin to occur in
the town.   Suspicion points to Caligari.   And now is perpetrated the
crowning outrage--the abduction of a beautiful girl on the very night
her lover, who has already numbered a student friend among those
murdered, is keeping watch over Dr. Caligari.   The authorities are
called and arrive at the Fair only to find Caligari sitting beside the
cabinet in which is seen the form of the sleeping Cesare.   But in-
vestigating further they find that the real Cesare, who, acting som-

nambulistically at the hypnotic direction of his master, has been the
direct cause of the crimes, has been replaced by a dummy. Dr.
Caligari, seeing that his ruse has been discovered, makes good his
escape and is pursued up a bleak and tortuous hill and over an eery
bridge, beyond which he enters through the gates of an insane asylum. Within this asylum a denouement takes place as uncanny as
any that ever unravelled a tale of nightmare mystery.

The impact of this picture upon the spectator is overpower-
ing. The expressionistic treatment of the background loses its
bizarre quality almost at once; it is justified by its appropriateness.
The story unfolds swiftly, with an astonishing economy of description. It does not wait for you; it compels you to follow. It baffles
you without leaving you at a loss; you try in vain to outguess it.
The titles do not usurp the cinematographic function; when they occur they appear merely as footnotes. The actors appear anony-
mously; their excellence is sufficient introduction. Everything is
sacrificed to the potency of imaged action.

The picture is not a story told; it is a story moved. Everything is moving and fluid. The background enters into the action.
Its bizarre, cubistic design suggests grotesqueness and distortion.
These reflect both the character of the story and the mental state
of the people in it. The leaning, top-heavy houses and the crooked,
winding, cul-de-sac streets seem to crush and overwhelm; they suggest lurking danger and reflect the growing dread of the characters.
The effect is sustained throughout. The design on the floor of the
insane asylum suggests mental confusion. The girl's bedroom, with
its fleecy draperies and lofty Gothic lines, suggests the very spirit
of sleep.

The whole picture is expressive of the eloquence of pure action. The murders are swift, relentless stabs of motion. When
the somnambulist breaks into the girl's room he does not merely
break the window. He utterly destroys it with a single movement
of his hand. He becomes the spirit of destruction. When he carries the girl out of the room he takes the whole room with him.
He gathers up an interior and turns it inside out. He projects us
out of the room with him. When he staggers under the burden of
the girl, his weariness comes over us like sudden torture. The
picture is a continual rush of movement. We feel emotion rising
from motion as an immediate experience. That is the quintessence
of cinematographic art.

The Cabinet of Dr. Caligari owes its preeminence to the perfect fusion of its elements. It has a plot which would remain effective under almost any treatment because it is one which stands on
its own merit as a folk narrative, besides possessing essentially
cinematographic qualities. It is told to us on the screen against a
novel background which is a contribution to the art of the moving
picture in itself. The photography is a masterly piece of experimentation, and the direction is of a quality whose virtuosity shines
through its apparent unobtrusiveness. All this is crowned by superb

acting. We know of nothing in this country that can approach either the impersonation of Dr. Caligari, which is a triumph of the art of pantomime, or that of Cesare, the somnambulist. The latter is a puppet for the imagination of an artist to play with. A figure that alternately rouses our pity and inspires us with dread. The actor who plays it seems superhumanly tall, with thin, shrunken legs that suggest the emaciation of the somnambulist's life-in-death, and eyes grotesquely enlarged whose "lead lids" take an eternity to open. His movements in the scene where he approaches the house of the girl are a lesson in the art of stalking. He literally winds his way through the tortuous passages and appears at the window with a sharp and sudden surprise of a genie rising mysteriously out of the earth.

The girl Jane is acted with admirable restraint. She is pictorially beautiful. She suggests the woman with a few short strokes of action, and carries the complete story of her love in a few flashes of her face. The scene where she learns of the death of her lover is one of the finest bits in the picture. The sharp movement of shrinking from the teller is full of sudden horror and alarm. The eloquence of grief flashes over her face like a swift transformation. The thing is done without titles in less than a dozen feet of film, showing again that where a part is conceived in terms of motion, captions become artistic impertinences.

In The Cabinet of Dr. Caligari the motion picture has proved its kinship with the other arts. Its popularity ought to be assured. It comes to us at a critical period of our motion picture industry when the public is jaded by many inferior domestic pictures and our producers themselves are still at a loss as to how to get out of their rut. It should give the public a new standard and imbue the producers with the courage to live up to it. Its release has all the aura of a great advent. Is it too much to assume that the American public can appreciate the best when it is given a chance to see it?

--Exceptional Photoplays, No. 4
(March 1921), pages 3-4.

*   *   *

The Cabinet of Doctor Caligari is the only serious picture, exhibited in America so far, that in anything like the same degree has the authentic thrills and shocks of art. This tale of a madman unfolded thru mad scenery by mad characters has greater intrinsic reality than any of our flat photographic pictures. It ceases to be merely a succession of photographs, and becomes alive--a creation, spiritually real and vital in a way peculiar to the screen, as unthinkable in any other form as are the poems of Heine.

This expressive explosiveness--this dynamic reality--has been achieved in pictures only by Chaplin and the creators of Caligari. But that they have achieved it is an indubitable fact of overwhelming importance. For the motion picture is, impertinently, the perpetual butt of the pseudo-intellectual and the pundit. They

58   Selected Film Criticism

can be silenced with a gesture.   For Charlie Chaplin and The Cabinet of Doctor Caligari, in divergent and equally convincing ways,
have established beyond cavil the integrity of the motion picture as
an art.   There is no longer any need for doubt or discouragement.
                                          --Albert Lewin in Shadowland,
                                             Vol. 9, No. 2 (October 1923),
                                                pages 46 and 75.

☐ CAMEO KIRBY (Fox, 1923)

        A romance of the river boats that once plied up and down
the Mississippi, of a man who had forgotten his name and his social standing to become a professional gambler, and of a girl who
gives his ideals back to him.   A period seldom pictured, packed
though it is with possibilities for both stage and screen.

        Cameo Kirby joins in a dishonest card game for the sake of
saving the fortunes of an old man who is being fleeced.   He wins
everything--with the intention of giving it back--but the old man,
not realizing his opponent's altruism, commits suicide.   And then
it turns out that the orphaned daughter is the woman of Cameo Kirby's heart.   Of course, in the end, she is made to understand Kirby's real nobility of purpose and generosity.
                                          --Photoplay, Vol. 25, No. 1 (De-
                                             cember 1923), page 73.

☐ THE CAMERAMAN (M-G-M, 1928)

        Buster Keaton clicks again, and we don't mean perhaps.
He's a reformed tintype photographer this time, trying to break into
the newsreel service all because his heart aches for the office
stenographer.   He takes his famous poker face through fire, water
and jail for the type-writing lady, and gets all tied up in hard knots
trying to scoop a Tong War.   Great story, original gags--and
Buster's irresistible.   See this and bust!
                                          --Photoplay, Vol. 34, No. 5 (Oc-
                                             tober 1928), page 54.

☐ CAMILLE (Metro, 1921)

        The dominant role in Nazimova's Camille is that of artificial-
ity.   The characters are unreal, the scenes are absurd fabrications
of pasteboard, and even the famous Camille cough is unconvincing.
Never once does the picture touch actual humanity, largely because

Madame Alla persistently poses rather than acts.   The Armand of
Rudolph Valentino is as good as it is permitted to be.
                              --Photoplay, Vol. 21, No. 1 (De-
                                cember 1921), page 62.

☐   CAMILLE (Norma Talmadge/First National, 1927)

        This was a boxoffice picture before a single scene was shot.
The famous tragedy of Alexandre Dumas, fils--the poignant story
of the Parisian courtesan who finally found real love only to lose
it--is sure fire stuff.   Norma Talmadge shifted the background to
the present day.   This change seems to have affected the story itself but slightly.

        Camille has one fault.   It is too long.   Too much footage is
given to planting reasons for the mode of life followed by the Lady
of the Camellias.   She is beaten and pursued for over two reels.
We suspect that Miss Talmadge will be a popular Camille.   She has
some excellent moments toward the end of the film.   Gilbert Roland is
the Armand.   Rather actory but with IT.   Supersexy stuff, this.
                              --Photoplay, Vol. 32, No. 1
                                (June 1927), page 54.

☐   CAPTAIN BLOOD (Vitagraph, 1924)

        This Rafael Sabatini romance naturally bears a resemblance
to his The Sea Hawk.   It is of the old roystering days of the seven-
teenth century and revolves around a series of sea fights.   However, its action lies in and about the Barbadoes and its story revolves around a young Irish physician sold into slavery for a political offense.   At Bridgetown, Barbadoes, a romance develops between the handsome slave and the niece of the military governor.
Captain Blood gets his Arabella after he saves Port Royal from the
French fleet in a sea battle in which miniatures are sunk with awe-
inspiring abandon.   Still, this version, although it is obviously
handicapped by a lack of money in production, has considerable
color and vitality.   It is splendid entertainment.
                              --Photoplay, Vol. 26, No. 6
                                (November 1924), page 60.

☐   THE CAT AND THE CANARY (Universal, 1927)

        Here is a corking melodrama.   Mysterious fingers reach out
of mouldy draperies to steal jewels and trick bookcases swallow up
unsuspecting victims.

It all happens in an old, shabby mansion once occupied by
the eccentric recluse, Cyrus West. It is exactly twenty years from
the date of his death to the second and his will is being read to his
anxious relatives while a storm beats upon the broken windows.

It develops that Annabelle West, his pretty niece, is the
heiress, provided she sleeps that night in his dusty, cobwebby bedroom and is able to prove her sanity next morning. Annabelle's
sanity gets a stiff test, we'll tell the world, between disappearances
and murders. To help things along an asylum keeper happens in,
searching for a runaway maniac.

Of course, there is a guilty person who hopes to inherit the
estate. This person is the instigator of the dire doings.

The Cat and the Canary is adroitly directed by Paul Leni, the
German who made The Three Wax Works. He uses trick angles
galore, but they all help the atmosphere of mystery and murder.
Leni is a director to be reckoned with.

The Cat and the Canary, which, by the way, is based on
John Willard's Broadway mystery shocker, has an excellent cast.
Laura La Plante is the blonde heroine, Annabelle. Creighton Hale
overdoes the nervous comedy hero, Paul Jones. Indeed, the comedy is the one weak element in The Cat and the Canary. Well done
bits are contributed by Lucien Littlefield and Martha Mattox.

--Photoplay, Vol. 32, No. 2 (July
1927), page 55.

☐ CHANG (Paramount, 1927)

Major Merian Cooper and Ernest Schoedsack, those two
young chaps who filmed Grass, have returned from the Siamese
jungles with this new study in elemental life. It compares favor-
ably with Robert Flaherty's Nanook and Moana and provides a big
dramatic kick of its own.

Chang shows the eternal battle between man and nature. The
protagonists are a native, his wife and their three children, not to
mention a pet white gibbon. Their daily combat with tigers, ele-
phants and other jungle inhabitants equals the tribulations of even a
Chicagoan with machine-gun inhibitions. Reviewers are requested
not to reveal the meaning of the title, Chang. So we pass it by.

--Photoplay, Vol. 32, No. 1 (June
1927), page 55.

☐ THE CIRCUS (Chaplin/United Artists, 1928)

Being his first since The Gold Rush, Charlie Chaplin's The
Circus will suffer by comparison with its predecessor. The Gold
Rush was a great picture on account of the deep human vein that
stretched between the comedy high spots, and there was a sweep to
the production that raised it almost to the level of an epic. We
had a right to assume that it signified Charlie's farewell to slapstick
and that thereafter the human note would be stressed in all pictures
and that their settings would be on a broad and comprehensive scale.
To the extent that we held such expectation we will be disappointed
with The Circus, for its greatest sweep is within the borders of a
circus lot and its human note is more implied than stressed. The
Circus is a good picture, one of the best Charlie has made, and his
reputation as an actor, producer, author, and director will not suffer by it, but to enjoy it to the utmost you must forget The Gold
Rush and close your mind to the exquisite tenderness of The Kid.
These two pictures taught us what Chaplin can do, but in his last
offering he reverts to what we knew he could do before he made the
others. There is much rich comedy in The Circus, but it lacks
such a screamingly funny sequence as that of the rocking house in
The Gold Rush. There are many directorial and acting gems in it,
and from a motion picture standpoint these features are above criticism. In one scene showing Charlie in a cage with a lion his acting is brilliant. Every moment he is on the screen is a treat to
the audience. His extraordinary pantomimic powers show increased
development with each succeeding picture. All the comedy hits in
the picture have their place in the unwinding of the story. In that
respect The Circus might well serve as a model for such comedies.
Also it might serve as a valuable lesson in direction. Charlie
commits none of the standard faults that we find in nearly all other
pictures. He knows the value of medium and long shots as opposed
to close-ups, and resorts to the latter but seldom. He knows also
that the way to create sympathy for a character is to show him as
a small creature in a big setting, and he does not resort to mugging to gain sympathy for himself. In one scene, in which he urges
Harry Crocker to marry the girl that he (Charlie) loves, he does
not face the camera. During most of the scene we see the back of
his head, and in the rest of it we see only the side of his face.
But his failure to make the most of the opportunities to build up
sympathy for himself is the greatest weakness of the picture. His
appearance is not as pathetic as usual, and the fact that he loves
the girl is not stressed sufficiently. There are none of the charming one-sided love scenes that made The Gold Rush notable. In
fact, I am not sure that I would have gathered from the picture itself that Charlie loved the bare-back rider. Before I saw it Charlie
outlined the story to me, consequently I was aware of the love element, and knowing it was there, I recognized it. I doubt if audiences will grasp it sufficiently to give point to Charlie's sacrifice
in the end when he recognizes that the girl is not for him and brings
to her the man she loves. Charlie is the tramp again. He comes
from nowhere, is forced by circumstances to enter circus life, has

a glorious romance, the circus moves on and leaves him sitting in
the deserted ring, watching the wagons disappearing in the distance.
It is a beautiful ending to a picture that will rate high, even though
it will be felt that such a great artist could have done something
greater. Merna Kennedy, the girl of the picture, will prove to be
another of Charlie's gifts to the screen. She is beautiful, natural
and talented. Harry Crocker, Henry Bergman and Allen Garcia
contribute good performances. Charlie's titles are models of what
titles should be. They are brief and simple, and confine themselves to telling the story.

> --Welford Beaton in The Film
> Spectator, Vol. 4, No. 8 (De-
> cember 10, 1927), pages 7-8.

*   *   *

Looking at our great and incomparable Charlie Chaplin I feel
like patting myself on the back. Did I not argue as long as fifteen
years ago that the ordinary "legitimate" actors should be barred
from the motion picture? It was of these actors that I said in
1913: "Are they aware that the cinematograph play is the most ab-
stract form of the pantomime? Do they realize that if there is any
stage on which the laws of movement should reign supreme, it is
the cinematograph stage? If they did they would not have monopo-
lized the cinematograph play, but would have left it to the dancers,
clowns, and acrobats who do know something about the laws of
movement. " A few years later came Charlie, the perfect clown and
acrobat, and by way of confirming my dictum at once leapt to such
heights of artistic distinction that ever since there have been only
two kinds of motion picture actors: Charlie Chaplin and the rest.
The classification is based not only on the singularity of Chaplin's
genius, but equally so on the singularity of his methods as an actor. This fact, however, is often ignored. Chaplin's mannerisms,
the peculiar traits of the screen character he has created, have
been imitated and plagiarized times without number. On the other
hand, his consistent pantomime acting (I cannot recall a single picture in which Chaplin moves his lips as if actually speaking), his
emphasis on expressive movement (his gait, for instance), and his
puppetlike, essentially nonrealistic treatment of his role--these are
the characteristics of Chaplin's acting which have found but few
imitators, and certainly none to show anything like Chaplin's appreciation of their meaning and importance.

In The Circus, his latest picture, Chaplin is again at his
very best. His inexhaustible comic imagination has provided the
picture with a more than ample supply of side-splitting "stunts" of
characteristic Chaplinesque quality, the most striking of these being
the scenes at Noah's Ark and the lion's cage. The "big scene" of
the picture, in which Charlie performs some amazing feats in tight-
rope walking (with the help of an attached wire), is funny too, but
suffers somewhat from the attempt to join the wistful buffoonery of
Charlie's little trick to the cruder and different fun of his helpless-
ness in disengaging himself from the attacking monkeys. And

through all these mirth-provoking scenes there flits the unforgettable image which has so endeared itself to the world--the image of a childishly simple and quixotically noble Pierrot who occasionally borrows the impishness of Harlequin.

In The Circus Chaplin's is a solo performance. The rest of the actors are not more than competent, and the direction of the picture as a whole lacks distinction. This last feature is disappointing. Chaplin showed his mettle as director in A Woman of Paris, and though there is no place for realism of this kind in his own grotesqueries, there is place in them for something which he is pre-eminently fitted to accomplish. His style of acting and all his dramatic upbringing proclaim Chaplin for what he actually is: a superb vaudeville comedian. We have motion pictures that are equivalent to comedy and drama. But we still have no motion picture vaudeville, i. e., entertainment shunning illusionist effects and making its appeal direct to the audience simply and solely as entertainment. I cannot help hoping that perhaps one day Chaplin will turn his mind to this richly promising field of experimental effort. There is waiting for him a full-size job worthy of his genius.

--Alexander Bakshy in The Nation, Vol. 126 (February 29, 1928), pages 247-248.

☐ THE COCOANUTS (Paramount, 1929)

The Cocoanuts also is another kind of picture that will belong wholly to the sound device. It sets out to achieve one purpose, that of making the audience laugh, and as I laughed during almost its entire showing I must credit it with having scored a success insofar as my personal taste goes. The New York critics did not like it. They disapproved of it unanimously, acridly and with much enthusiasm. I had read the New York reviews and was prepared for something rather terrible. But instead of something terrible, I found something highly amusing and diverting, adequately mounted and containing quite a lot of clever photography. Thus far in the history of the talking screen, the experience has been that those pictures that Broadway liked well are not doing well on the Main Streets. Broadway did not like The Cocoanuts, but I will be surprised if Main Street does not like it. I never have seen the Four Marx Brothers in the flesh, consequently the fact pointed out by so many of the New York reviewers that the picture was merely a series of photographs of the things that they had done on the stage, in no way lessened my enjoyment of the picture. They came to me as a refreshing novelty, as something exceedingly funny, original and clever. The only distressing spots in the production were those in which the story took itself seriously, and tried to become melodramatic. There were many silent stretches which were among the most enjoyable. The picture had two directors, Joseph Santley and Robert Florey. I imagine it is Florey whom we have to thank

for the occasional bits of silent screen technic that mark the production.   The whole thing--in case you have not seen it or the
Marx brothers--is a hodge-podge of frivolity, delightfully silly and
brilliantly unreasonable.   For the most part sound is handled intelligently.   We hear doors slam only when the slamming means
something, but to offset the wisdom of this is the folly of having
two thieves plot a theft in a hotel room in voices loud enough to be
heard from one end of the corridor to the other.   From the business standpoint this form of entertainment has one weakness.   It is
not a repeater.   The Marx brothers have been doing certain things
on the stage so long that they have them perfected, and apparently
they have put all of them into one picture.   What will they do for
an encore?   Of course, as Paramount can find another combination
to provide the encore, it need not worry about the business aspect
of the situation, but how long can it go on finding such combina-
tions?   Such pictures now are successful in building bank accounts,
but are unsuccessful in building a permanent asset.

--Welford Beaton in The Film
Spectator, Vol. 8, No. 4 (July
27, 1929), page 4.

□ COLLEGE (Joseph M. Schenck/United Artists, 1927)

        Another variation of the grind who sets out to become the
varsity athletic star.   Buster tackles the baseball nine, the track
team and the crew but, of course, he wins the heroine.   He cops
the boat race by strapping the lost rudder to his back and sitting
in the water behind the shell.   The dead pan star isn't as funny as
he was a year or so ago and College is just a fair farce.

--Photoplay, Vol. 32, No. 6
(November 1927), page 55.

□ A CONNECTICUT YANKEE AT KING ARTHUR'S COURT (Fox,
1921)

        You are safe in placing A Connecticut Yankee at King Arth-
ur's Court on your list of pictures not to be missed.   It is the
second best screen comedy of the year, counting Chaplin's The Kid
as the first, and, curiously, it is as dependent upon its titles as
the Chaplin picture was notable for its absence of titles.   The
printed witticisms are responsible, I should say, for at least a
third of the laughs.   And though they are frankly "jazzed," as they
say in the studio, the jazzing has been cleverly and intelligently
done in a spirit of high burlesque.

        In the screen version of Mark Twain's story the dream form
is widely used.   The hero, a great lover of the Yankee's written

adventures, sits late reading the book.   On retiring, he encounters a housebreaker.   There is a fight, the hero is knocked down and out, and loses consciousness just as the burglar grabs a pikestaff from a stand of armor and stands above him menacingly.   When he awakes in his dream he is being poked in the ribs with the pikestaff of Sir Sagramore ("Saggy" of the round table) and is made captive.   Taken to the castle, he is condemned to death by King Arthur and about to be burned at the stake, when, by nicely timing the sun's eclipse, he convinces the king that he is a much better magician than the wicked Merlin and is allowed to live.   His adventures thereafter are many and fantastic.   He introduces modern methods in the conduct of the kingdom, and soon has the knights punching a time clock and spending the noon hour "shooting craps." In the jousting tournament the Yankee sees himself as a Bill Hart who ropes the startled "Saggy" and pulls him from his horse, armor and all, and then repeats the performance "for the benefit of those who came in late."   He rescues the Princess Alisande (he calls her "Sandy" for short) from the dungeon of the wicked Queen Morgan le Fay with the aid of his "enchanted Gat," with which he shoots holes through several surprised gentlemen, and from the armor discarded by the knights after the incident of the joust he builds a flivver.   When he and the king are captured by the "four horsemen of the eucalyptus" in the employ of the queen, they are rescued by Sir Launcelot and "Sandy."   "As Sir Boss has often said, 'Give her the gas, Kid,'" advises Launcelot in hurrying the rescue, and as the flivver scurries toward the castle it is followed by a couple of hundred knights mounted on motor cycles.   It is all good fun, and has pictorial value as well.   Emmett J. Flynn has made a name for himself as a director who is not dependent upon the slapstick and the swift kick in creating low comedy on the screen, and Bernard McConville has done well with the scenario.   Ralph Spence, I am told, had much to do with the titling.   Mark Twain himself, could he have had a hand in the rewriting of his story, would probably have objected to some of the liberties Mr. Fox's young men have taken, but I venture that if the earth above his grave should be discovered to have been recently disturbed it was caused by the laughter and not the writhings of the well-loved humorist.   Harry C. Myers is consistently amusing as the Yankee, Pauline Starke is the "Sandy," Rosemary Theby the vamping queen, William Mong the Merlin, Charles Clary the King Arthur and George Siegmann the "Saggy."

--Burns Mantle in Photoplay, Vol.
20, No. 1 (June 1921), page 51.

*   *   *

A spectacular comedy which is a long way from Mark Twain's novel--but a long way in the right direction.
--Robert E. Sherwood in Life,
Vol. 77, No. 2009 (May 5, 1921),
page 652.

▢ THE CONQUERING POWER (Metro, 1921)

The result of the Rex Ingram method of producing a film story is to give life on the screen to the men and women conceived in the brain of an author. The characters in Balzac's Eugenie Grandet, which forms the base of The Conquering Power, live and move through the picture with the convincing reality of life itself-- an achievement that is always aimed at, and often missed, in screen drama. The combination of correct casting, adequate directing, proper lighting and skilled individual effort on the part of the actors necessary to the complete illusion sought after is found in this worthy successor to The Four Horsemen of the Apocalypse, the picture that marks the most ambitious production under the Metro banner. A simple story compared to the sweep and extent of the Ibáñez novel, The Conquering Power has been made important and lifted into a place among first rank screen dramas by the uniform excellence in every department of production. In this respect it is superior to the screen version of the Spanish novelist's work. Mr. Ingram has applied his knowledge of sculpture to the faces of the cast with even greater success, and improved upon the best of his previous light and shade effects.

Another mark of merit is the direct and dramatic way the story is told. The local color is never absent, but it never has the scene to itself. The dramatic action is unbroken; the human interest always holds the center of the stage.

Among the most famous of the French novelist's tales, Eugenie Grandet is a powerful and absorbing "slice of life." Students of Balzac may resent the bringing of the story down to the present time and the use of automobiles and fountain pens, but the claim put forth in one of the subtitles--that the story belongs to this day and age as well as to the first half of the last century--is proved before the end of the scenario written by June Mathis is reached.

Alice Terry is an ideal Eugenie in appearance, and acts with corresponding truth and understanding. Rudolph Valentino as Charles Grandet is again eminently fitted for the part he plays. Ralph Lewis as Pere Grandet gives a supremely able impersonation of a man whose miserly instinct grows until it destroys him, without resorting to the facial contortions and bodily indications of decrepitude which generally accompany the acting of such a part. Edward Connelly contributes one of his masterly character studies as Cruchot, and the parts of lesser importance afford the cast the proper balance. The Conquering Power has no sensational sets or vast armies of extra people, but it is a distinct triumph for the screen by reason of the fine intellectual quality of the story and its production, and its high entertainment value.

--Edward Weitzel in The Moving
Picture World, Vol. 51, No. 3
(July 16, 1921), page 339.

*   *   *

Now let us consider Rex Ingram's production, The Conquering Power, an adaptation of Balzac's Eugenie Grandet. Just why
Director Ingram and June Mathis, the scenarist, have bothered men-
tioning Balzac is beyond us. They have shifted the time from the
last days of the eighteenth century to more or less the present day,
have played battlecock with the characters, and twisted the story
from a grim tragedy of romance crushed by gold into a typical
flapper love idyl. Balzac's Eugenie Grandet was the plain daughter
of an old miser, a woman who waits for years with slipping hope
after an affair with a lover who never really cared. Her romance
ends in a marriage of convenience with another. Mr. Ingram and
Miss Mathis have seen to it that Eugenie is both beautiful and innocent, that the lover is a dashing young man from Paris, who
really cares, and that their romance is but temporarily blocked by
a brutal and miserly father.

From a directorial standpoint, The Conquering Power is away
above the average. There are moments of singular camera beauty--
photographically and artistically in points of balance and light and
shade. The whole story moves amid a finely sustained atmosphere
of provincial France. As in Mr. Ingram's The Four Horsemen,
there is nothing of the human note. One cares little for the fate of
the various characters. But there is beauty. One can't have everything. Mr. Ingram has stepped up among the first six of our directors with his Ibáñez and Balzac adaptations.

Mr. Ingram has made Eugenie a charmingly pretty picture
in the person of Alice Terry, while Rudolph Valentino, the tango
hero of The Four Horsemen, makes a gracefully sophisticated and
pleasantly romantic hero. Mr. Valentino, indeed, does an excellent
piece of work. We take exception to one thing, his polished patent-
leather hair. There is an admirable characterization of a scoundrelly old notary by Edward Connelly.

                                        --Frederick James Smith in Mo-
                                          tion Picture Classic, Vol. 13,
                                          No. 2 (October 1921), pages 65
                                          and 86.

☐ THE COVERED WAGON (Famous Players-Lasky/Paramount,
   1923)

Here is the biggest picture of the screen year--two hours of
celluloid with a fine epic sweep. Emerson Hough wrote The Covered Wagon of the pioneers who packed their small belongings into
a prairie schooner--and crossed the horizon into an uncharted world
of strange menaces. These men and women were the makers of
America.

68   Selected Film Criticism

The Covered Wagon has a simple love story but mainly it
concerns itself with the panorama of a wagon train making its way
from that outpost of civilization, Westport Landing, later destined
to be Kansas City, to far off Oregon, across the plains and the
Sierras. It is a tortuous passage, between hostile Indians, prairie
fires, dangerous river fordings, lurking starvation and the internal
dissension which always comes to humans surrounded by danger.
Indeed, news of the gold strike in California turns most of the
wagon train aside, to pick its way over the Rockies to California.

All this has been screened with a fine sense of the bigness
of the theme. Cruze has been remarkably successful in catching
the reality of his backgrounds. His wagon train is real and living,
his pioneers of '49 are flesh and blood.

Photoplay wants to recommend The Covered Wagon without
reservation. It is a big thing--in many ways the biggest thing since
D. W. Griffith did The Birth of a Nation. The acting is excellent.
Lois Wilson is a real and charming heroine, J. Warren Kerrigan
something more than a conventional hero. But the guide of Ernest
Torrence, superb bad man of Tol'able David, is a joy forever. And
only a little behind is Tully Marshall's uncannily fine playing of an
old trader of the plains.

                              --Photoplay, Vol. 23, No. 6 (May
                                1923), page 64.

                          *   *   *

When a schoolboy, struggling manfully with exams at the end
of a term, is asked for an outline of American history, he generally
lists these major events:

Discovery by Columbus (1492), Settlement of Jamestown
(1607), Arrival of Mayflower (1620), French and Indian War (1756),
Revolution (1775-1781), Constitution Ratified (1788), War of 1812,
Monroe Doctrine (1823), War with Mexico (1846-1848), Civil War
(1861-1865), Steve Brodie's leap from Brooklyn Bridge (1886), and
War with Germany (1917).

There is one glorious period of American history which is
usually omitted from such lists. Indeed, it has received but little
recognition, except in the works of Francis Parkman, and in those
humble, paper-covered dime novels that used to be frowned upon by
the same type of person who now sneers at the movies. This is
the period of expansion which commenced about 1846, and which resulted in the settlement of the Pacific Coast. It was then that the
pioneers--men, women and children--struggled across the prairies
and over the mountains in their trains of covered wagons, passing
through incredible hardships and cordons of belligerent Indians that
they might ultimately drive their ploughs into the soil of Oregon and
California.

They were adventurers, these pioneers, but adventurers of a
peculiarly sturdy and heroic type. For them, there was none of the

romance that inspired Pizarro, Raleigh or Drake; they were not
bold, reckless swashbucklers embarking on perilously fascinating
voyages in quest of gold and glory.   It is one thing for a man to
start off on an expedition in company with a band of fellow adventurers as fearless as he--and another thing for a plain farmer to
stride out into the unknown in company with his wife and his children, with no object in view other than the discovery of virgin soil.
For this reason, I have a deeper respect for the heroism of the
pioneers of the Oregon Trail, and of the Pilgrims of the Mayflower,
than for the more sensational exploits of the daring heroes whose
blades have flashed in the pages of romance.

Emerson Hough, who had an opportunity to study the old
West from the point of view of an eye-witness, wrote a novel called
The Covered Wagon, which was published in the Saturday Evening
Post.   There it caught the eye of the movie people, who saw in it
material for another good, rousing cow-boy picture.   They bought
it--and it was not until they had actually started the work of pro-   ·
duction that they realized the true significance of Hough's story.   It
turned out to be the one great American epic that the screen has
produced; and when I say "epic," I use that much-abused word in
its legitimate, or pre-press agent, sense.

With the presentation of The Covered Wagon, I venture to
say that the pioneers of the Oregon Trail will receive honorable
mention on every school-boy's list, even if he flunks out on all other important dates.

The Covered Wagon was a great picture, not so much because it was based upon a magnificent theme as because it was produced with genuine skill.   Jesse L. Lasky, Vice-President of the
Paramount Company, was one of the first to recognize its potentialities, and he backed it to the limit.   He assigned it to James
Cruze, a director who had been advancing rapidly in popular esteem,
and he entrusted the adaptation of the story to Jack Cunningham.
Both men stuck closely to the point.   They refrained from trim-
ming Hough's story with any movie hokum, having sense enough to
appreciate the essential simplicity of the drama.

Cruze saw to it that the dust raised by the covered wagons
was real dust, that the Indians who battled to save their lands from
the white invaders were real Indians, and that the beards on the
protruding chins of the pioneers were real beards.   As Cruze himself has explained, "there wasn't a false whisker in the picture."

Of the actual acquisition of the story, James Cruze has this
to say:

The Covered Wagon had a curious history before it fell into
my hands.   The original Emerson Hough novel had been turned down
by a number of stars when Mary Miles Minter saw it--and was attracted to it.   As I understand it, she had a clause in her contract
giving her a certain choice of story.   So the Famous Players-

Lasky Corporation bought The Covered Wagon for her. Then the
first difficulties presented themselves, with the result that three
directors declined the script and Miss Minter finally did another
picture instead. In brief, it was not possible to spend a large
amount of money on any production where the star received a salary
of the Minter magnitude--and still release the photoplay at a profit. "

This may be considered a miracle of good luck, for if The
Covered Wagon had fallen to the lot of Mary Miles Minter, it would
undoubtedly have been lost forever. Of all the stellar collapses
that the silent drama has known (and it has known plenty of them),
Miss Minter's was undoubtedly the most dismal. Moreover, The
Covered Wagon was not a star picture--any more than was Nanook
of the North--and it would have been seriously damaged if it had
been converted into a vehicle for the advancement of personal vanity.

When James Cruze was finally empowered to go ahead with
The Covered Wagon, he cast about for a suitable location in which
to stage its scenes. The action of Hough's story started in the
settlement called Westport Landing (now Kansas City), and continued
with the wagon train across the prairies to Fort Bridger, where
the first whispers were heard of the discovery of gold in California.
Beyond Fort Bridger the train divided--one unit, composed of the
more adventurous youths, going to the gold fields, and the other
proceeding as originally planned to Oregon.

Cruze finally found a place, in the Snake Valley of Nevada,
which would serve for all the scenes, from Westport Landing to the
Rocky Mountains. Thither he went, with a company of one hundred
and twenty-seven people and a large staff of carpenters and technical
men. He recruited a thousand extras from the inhabitants of that
sparsely settled district (some of them came as far as three hundred miles for their ten dollars a day). He also enlisted the services of seven hundred and fifty Indians, who did a thriving business
on the side selling souvenirs to the members of the movie company.

As the location in the Snake Valley was eighty-five miles
from the nearest railroad, Cruze had to employ a fleet of motor
trucks to carry supplies for his large army of workers. He pitched
a camp of some five hundred tents, where his entire company re-
mained for eight weeks. Living under these adverse conditions, the
players in The Covered Wagon forgot that they were actors, and
there was, in their work, an understanding for the hardships of the
original pioneers that never could have been simulated in the luxuri-
ous atmosphere of Hollywood.

Of the four hundred covered wagons used in the picture, some
were actual relics of the plains, furnished by the farmers whose
fathers had used them in the brave old days. The rest were built
on the spot.

After the eight weary weeks in the Snake Valley, Cruze
moved his company to Antelope Island, in Great Salt Lake, where

he made some scenes of a buffalo hunt. He then returned to the
Hollywood base, with many memorable reels of film and a thoroughly worn-out troupe of movie actors.

"At that time," Cruze explains, "The Covered Wagon ended
on the plains. There was nothing of the present California and
Oregon sequences. We had thought that the continuous scenes of
the pioneer caravan wending its way across the country would grow
monotonous. So we ended the tale out there near Fort Bridger.

"But, when we returned to California and put the print together, we revised our estimate. The wagon train curiously became the star, with a personality all its own. Then we decided to
show the actual consummation of the long migration across the
plains and the Sierras.

"So, three months later, we went to Sonora, California, for
the snow scenes and there rebuilt the wagon train, for the old
wagons had been discarded, broken up or sold back in Nevada.
This added a big expense, but it gave The Covered Wagon its logical culmination. Don't forget that Mr. Lasky deserves his praise
for adding this huge item to the final cost--and adding it purely
with the thought of bettering a picture which could have been sold
as it was. "

The outstanding quality in The Covered Wagon as it appeared
in its final form, was its absolute honesty. There was nothing false
in it, nothing that was insincere, or trumped up, or phony. James
Cruze obtained his effects by legitimate methods, without recourse
to the mechanical tricks which have spoiled so many potentially good
pictures in the past. In Jack Cunningham's adaptation of the story,
the same spirit of straightforwardness prevailed. He had the wisdom to realize that he must set forth the details as simply and directly as possible; he shunned spurious hokum in his drama, his
sentiment and his humor, and relied instead on the intense vigor of
reality.

The most stalwart and picturesque figure in the cast was
Ernest Torrence, a lean Scotchman who quitted musical comedy
three years ago to play the villain in Tol'able David. Since then,
he has become an actor of undisputed prominence in the movies.
There have been few characterizations on the screen so vital, so
elementally human as his impersonation of a rugged old frontiers-
man in The Covered Wagon. Tully Marshall was splendid in a similar role--and had the distinction of raising the best beard in a production which was literally rich with honest whiskers. Lois Wilson
was a calm, charming heroine, and Charles Ogle made a sturdy
pioneer.

The hero of the piece was J. Warren Kerrigan, a star who
dates back to the earliest days of Western melodramas in the
movies. He was a screen celebrity long before Harold Lloyd,
Douglas Fairbanks or Rex Ingram came into prominence--before

Jackie Coogan was born. In The Covered Wagon, he displayed his
great horsemanship to good advantage, but his performance was not
in harmony with the picture as a whole. In fact, he was the one
figure in the entire picture who suggested that, after all, it was
only a movie--and not an actual record of the real conquest of the
West.

Such were the elements which went into the preparation of
The Covered Wagon. That they were strong elements, and well
blended, is proven by the picture's astounding success. Although,
at the time of writing, it has not gained anywhere near its full cir-
culation, it has already established itself as the greatest money
maker that the motion picture industry has ever known. It cost,
according to the most reliable estimates, $782,000, with a great
deal more added for advertising and exploitation. It is believed
that this figure will be covered by the returns from only two theatres, the Criterion in New York and Grauman's in Hollywood, in
each of which the picture has been playing to capacity for six
months.

As there are over fifteen thousand movie theatres in the
United States alone, it will be seen that The Covered Wagon is
destined to turn in an extraordinarily neat profit. Nor can anyone
conscientiously begrudge the Paramount Company a nickel of this
tremendous gain. It was a far-sighted, intelligent piece of work on
their part, and whatever they make will be well deserved.

Of Emerson Hough, the author of The Covered Wagon, much
could be written--for he was a character as picturesque as any that
he created. In his early life he travelled all over the West--from
the Rio Grande to the Columbia River--and saw it before it had
been surrendered to the oil stock promoters, the real estate men,
E. H. Harriman, James J. Hill, and the film producers. After he
had knocked about aimlessly for many years, he started to set down
his impressions in stories and novels.

The Covered Wagon was his greatest success, and after its
production as a movie, he received some of the recognition that was
his due. Almost all of his earlier books were bought by the picture
people, who are always ready to trade on an established reputation.

In May, 1923, Hough died. He had the ultimate satisfaction
of knowing that he had honestly reflected a period in American History of which every American has a right to be proud.

--Robert E. Sherwood in The Best
Moving Pictures of 1922-1923
(Small, Maynard and Company,
1923), pages 71-77.

☐ THE CROWD (M-G-M, 1928)

Even if The Crowd were not as good as it is, Metro would
deserve a lot of credit for having made it.   It is a peculiar organization.   In rapid succession it turns out pictures that give little
evidence of the expenditure of any thought on them, and then it
comes along with something like The Crowd that is so full of thought
that it will not be a box-office success, in spite of the fact that it
is one of the finest and most worthy motion pictures ever made.
King Vidor's conception was an extraordinary one and he has put it
on paper with a degree of faithfulness and conviction that could be
attained only by a master craftsman.   When he reached into the
crowd his hand fell on the shoulder of one of its standard parts,
and out of that part he made a motion picture.   His hero is one of
the men upon whom nature relies to keep intact the integrity of its
crowds, a man without either virtue or vices, and lacking the mental equipment to lift himself by his thoughts above the level of the
others whose elbows always were touching his.   With this thought,
and with his average man, Vidor proceeds to write an essay and
spread it on the screen.   In so doing he presents us with two performances of extraordinary merit, those of Eleanor Boardman and
James Murray.   The acting of these two young people is enough in
itself to make a picture notable purely as a picture, but a dozen
such performances in such a picture could not make it notable as
screen entertainment.   It has the fundamental weakness of attempting
to interest us in something inherently uninteresting.   We are not interested in average things, whether animate or inanimate.   We are
interested in anything in the degree that it is above or below the
average.   We are interested in Lindbergh because he is a fine,
brave boy who soars above the average; we are interested in Hick-
man because he is a beast so far below the average that he attracts
our attention.   We are not interested in young Johnny Sims, one of
several hundred clerks in an insurance company's office.   He is one
of hundreds in the same office and of untold millions throughout the
world, and there is nothing about him to attract our attention.
Vidor presumed that we would become interested in Johnny when he
was pointed out to us, but pointing at him does not make him more
interesting.   I am aware that great plays and great books have been
written about average people, but in them the average people did
things or thought thoughts that we would not expect from average
people, proving, after all, that they were not true to the average.
The Crowd gets all of its merit from the fact that it deals with
people who do not rise above or fall below the mean average.   In
short, it tries to interest us in the most uninteresting thing on
earth: an average product.   The most successful picture always
will be the one which deals with the most interesting subject in the
most interesting way.   It can not be a picture that possesses only
one of these superlatives.   There are some things so uninteresting
that they can not be made interesting by any kind of treatment.
The average man is one of them.

But The Crowd was a fine thing for Metro to do.   I am
afraid, however, that the poor box-office record that it is going to

make will have a blighting effect on the organization's output. In
the future when a director wishes to get Mayer's permission to
make a picture with a thought in it, The Crowd will be trotted out
as proof that the public does not wish to think. The Vidor picture
would not have been made if the Metro executives understood the
business that they are in. If they knew anything about screen fundamentals they would have seen that the picture could not be successful. While we go to the film houses primarily for entertainment, we go to them also for inspiration. The reason the public
enjoys a picture whose logical ending is happy, more than it does
one which, to be logical, must have an unhappy ending, is the inspiration it derives from the former. Johnny Sims and his friends
are paying over ninety percent of what the world pays to see motion pictures. The screen has become practically their only source
of inspiration. The discouraged stenographer is inspired by the
fact that the stenographer in the picture marries the boss, and the
traveling salesman is given fresh hope when he sees Dick Dix or
Bill Haines, playing a salesman, cop the millionaire's daughter in
the final reel. Johnny Sims sees that there is a future for him
when the picture shows the clerk becoming vice-president and marrying the president's daughter. But what does anyone get from The
Crowd? The comfortable citizen who drove to the theatre in a car
of his own and who can sleep at night without worrying about the
grocery bill, sees paraded before him on the screen every heart-
ache he and his wife endured during the years of their upward
struggle. Out of locked closets come spectres of the past that the
screen breathes life into and makes real again. And what do the
friends of Johnny Sims get out of it--the young people who constitute the crowd? The only thing that keeps their heads up and eyes
front is the thought that some day they will rise above the multitude, as the heroes in motion pictures always do. But this picture
has no such inspiration. With extraordinary vigor and conviction it
plants the utter futility of endeavoring to battle one's way to success. It shows that the crowd is too powerful to be combatted, and
it breathes hopelessness and despair. All these drawbacks are accentuated by the excellence of the production from a motion picture
angle. I do not think a finer example of intelligent direction ever
reached the screen. As an example of cinematic art The Crowd is
a success, but as a medium of screen entertainment it will be a
failure. It is too depressing, and carries realism just a little
farther than the public will prove willing to follow. But it should
not discourage further adventures into realism, which should be applied to themes that strike a more optimistic note. Metro is to be
commended for discarding the superlatively happy ending that was
tacked onto The Crowd at one stage of its evolution. It ends now
just as it should.

        At the time of one of its previews The Crowd had a wildly
ridiculous ending tacked on to it, as I pointed out at the time. I
suppose it cost some thousands of dollars to shoot. It destroyed in
half a reel what King Vidor so powerfully built up in seven. The
impossibility of it was so obvious that finally even the Metro executives saw it. They recalled the prints that had gone out, and re-

placed them with the version that was shown in Los Angeles. It is not an unusual thing for a studio to make two or more endings of a picture, and to give each one a chance to make good at a preview. It is a sensible practice that should be adopted by other arts. Take architecture. At present when an architect is planning a twelve-story building he builds from the basement up, and designs a roof that is in keeping with the rest of the structure. That is, he thinks it will look well. Anyway, the contractors go ahead and finish off the building with the roof that the architect deemed the most logical for it. Picture people would have used more intelligence in finishing the building. How could the architect know that Iowa tourists would like the roof he designed? Logical? My dear boy, you and I know that the architect has the right idea, the artistic idea, but we are not erecting buildings for you and me. We must think of our public, dear fellow. And to please the public several roofs would be built, one after the other, and each given a turn on the top of the building until the final choice was made. My illustration is not an extravagant one. Despite the fact that alternative endings have been shot for some of our best pictures, I maintain that such a practice is an artistic idiocy and an economic folly. There is but one ending that any story can have: that dictated by logic. There may be discussion during the story-building stages of what ending logic would dictate. Opinions would differ, but before shooting begins such differences should be composed and the picture given the ending that the majority mind decided was the logical one. To shoot two or more endings is a childish practice, a sad confession by the production staff that it does not understand the story it is putting on the screen. The practice is an off-shoot of executive indifference to waste. Dollars are the cheapest things to be found on any of the big lots. On the payrolls are men who could recognize the proper ending for a given story, but in the executive offices are men who are afraid of themselves and who squander scores of thousands of dollars each year while trying to make up their minds, with which they are furnished quite scantily. When exhibitors fail to be impressed by the cost of a picture a move may be made to reduce the cost. Metro will sell The Crowd to exhibitors on the strength of the large sum it took to make it, which puts a premium on extravagance. Exhibitors reason that if it took that much money it must be good, and buy it on that theory. They should remember that the cost figure presented to them by the salesman consists of three parts: the amount that what reaches the screen really cost; the amount wasted, and the amount that the liar who sells the picture throws in for good measure.

--Welford Beaton in The Film
Spectator, Vol. 5, No. 4 (April
14, 1928), pages 6-7.

*   *   *

Here you have Life. Life as it is lived by millions in New York and other big cities where the crowd walks, pushes, tramples each individual member.

A tremendous production; a powerful story of a man who was born to be "something big" but has a furious fight for mere existence.

Cocky, self-confident, blind to his own failures, James Murray, as John Sims, holds the love and the sympathy of his audience from beginning to end just as he holds the sympathy and love of his frail, self-sacrificing wife, Eleanor Boardman.

You have lived the same experiences as this simple, devoted couple.

You have suffered and struggled, laughed and rejoiced, worried and fretted in the same manner.

No picture is perfect, but this comes as near to reproducing reality as anything you have ever witnessed. Yet it loses none of the suspense and thrills of a great picture because it is a real-life story.

The photography is splendid, the titles are as heart-yearning as the picture.

James Murray makes his initial bow to the public in a manner that will not be forgotten, while Eleanor Boardman is nearly perfect.

Take several handkerchiefs, because you will cry with laughter and weep with sympathy while viewing this unusual King Vidor production.

Don't miss it.

--Photoplay, Vol. 33, No. 1
(December 1927), page 52.

☐ DANCING MOTHERS (Famous Players-Lasky/Paramount, 1926)

Herbert Brenon scores again. The renowned creator of film fantasy has here turned out a realistic, fast moving drama of smart night life.

It concerns a gentle wife who would a-flappering go. Her sub-deb daughter and her distinguished husband leave her home, night after night, while they seek the white lights. Finally, mother puts on her smartest evening gown and rebels. The complication is that she falls in love with the same handsome bachelor who is loved by her daughter and her husband's sweetie.

Clara Bow's performance as the peppy little daughter is beautifully handled. Norman Trevor does very well by the father.

But Alice Joyce and Conway Tearle as the mother and the lover are
rather disappointing.

> --Photoplay, Vol. 24, No. 5
> (April 1926), page 54.

*   *   *

For those who would like to see a picture called Dancing
Mothers.

> --Robert E. Sherwood in Life,
> Vol. 87, No. 2266 (April 8,
> 1926), page 32.

☐ DISRAELI (Distinctive Productions/United Artists, 1921)

This is a thoughtful interpretation of the Louis N. Parker
play which George Arliss made famous on the stage several years
ago.   Its screen success is surprising in view of the fact that it
seemed to be reliant upon the spoken word for its value.   It seemed
too subtle, too epigrammatic, for the screen.   George Arliss, however, is one of the most skillful pantomimists since Deburau, and
he makes Disraeli, the wily British statesman, the most perfect
reproduction of a historical character that has ever been made.
The direction, by Henry Kolker, is intelligent, if uninspired.   In
fact, one might say that the only fault to be found with Disraeli is
that it is only a fine picture, when it might have been made a very
great picture.   The sets are amazingly real; but some of the people
who walk through them are most un-English.   There is Reginald
Denny, very much mis-cast; and E. J. Ratcliffe, as the Governor
of the Bank of England, who doesn't look it.   Mr. Arliss has a
wholly delightful co-star in Mrs. George Arliss, who plays the patient Mrs. Disraeli.   She is a charming woman and an accomplished
actress.   There should be a law against Mr. Arliss ever appearing
on the stage or screen without his wife.   Louise Huff is a quaint
sweet Clarissa; she is perhaps the most modest of all our ingenues;
we are glad that she has returned to the films.   The Honorable
Benjamin Disraeli held the screen for two weeks at the same Broadway theater, which proves that he is considerably more popular
now than he was in Victorian England.

> --Photoplay, Vol. 20, No. 6
> (November 1921), page 61.

☐ DISRAELI (Warner Bros. , 1929)

A fine camera record of a great stage performance.   Not a
motion picture at all in the strict sense of dependence on the use
of movement and pictorial effects, it merely sets down, in semi-

close-up form, the brilliant portrait that George Arliss has drawn of England's Semitic prime minister, and it does it beautifully and tastefully.   The highest tribute to the film is that it can take the matter of whether Victorian England or Czarist Russia wins control of the Suez canal and get an American screen audience excited about it.

--Richard Watts, Jr. in The Film
Mercury, Vol. 10, No. 11 (November 1, 1929), page 6.

*   *   *

There isn't much to say about Disraeli after all these years except that in the talkies it is better than ever.   It isn't much different from what it was when first seen on the stage.   The scenarist and director have chosen to transfer it to the screen as directly as possible, without elaboration and without cinematic experimenting.   They were undoubtedly wise in so choosing.

Disraeli always has been, and still is, nothing more than a vehicle for the peculiar talents of George Arliss.   It is only mild drama--if it can be called drama at all--it is inaccurate history, and it is the most superficial kind of biography.   It probably would never have been written--it certainly would never have survived so long--if Mr. Arliss had not been able, with so very little trouble, to make himself look like the portraits of Queen Victoria's favorite prime minister.

One doesn't expect a popular play to have the brilliance and penetration of a Lytton Strachey historical study.   It serves well enough if some of the surface aspects are caught.   The English-Jew who was Gladstone's greatest rival--who made Victoria Empress of India, and in his private correspondence used to call her the Faery--was a man of such mixed and fascinating characteristics that no intelligent portrait of him could help being interesting.   His strange combination of realistic insight and grandiose romanticism, his practical craftiness and piercing wit, his world-wide breadth in state policies and his singular depth of sensitiveness in personal relations--these and dozens of other extraordinary traits made him a figure well worth putting on the screen.

The Louis Parker play puts him in the center of some not very thrilling intrigue about the Suez Canal.   Spies in the pay of Russia eavesdrop hoveringly, in a stagey fashion, and it hardly needed a Master Mind to circumvent them.   But Mr. Arliss has a way with him that gives an extremely vivid theatrical effect of a Master Mind performing tremendous feats--he could ask for lemon in his tea and imply that questions of vast international fatefulness hung upon his request.

Mr. Arliss is one of the actors for whom talking pictures might well have been specially created.   His manner of speech, peculiarly dry and unemotional, sounds, even on the stage, as if it

were mechanically produced, and his characterizations, whether sinister or quaint, always have an individual quality of aloofness, likeable without ever being warm, so that more than most actors he
gets himself over in screen shadows as completely as in the flesh.
Nearly everything is done by suggestion--he has the gift, even on
the screen, of having the audience so completely in his confidence
that the merest hint is enough to tell them volumes. People come
away with a feeling of having seen a good deal more than their eyes
have actually beheld.

Mrs. Arliss is Mrs. Disraeli--Lady Beaconsfield--and it was
well worth the dramatist's while to twist the facts a bit and keep
her alive for the Queen's first reception as Empress of India.
Those two figures--aging wife and aging husband, moving hand in
hand toward the throne room--represent what was after all one of
the most significant things in Disraeli's life. And they give a
romantic touch to the picture even more moving than the delightful
young lovers so nicely done by Anthony Bushell--completely English
--and Joan Bennett--completely un-English.

--James Shelley Hamilton in Cinema, Vol. 1, No. 1 (January
1930), page 42.

☐ THE DOCKS OF NEW YORK (Paramount, 1928)

The most distinctive motion picture I have seen since The
Patriot is Josef von Sternberg's The Docks of New York. Certainly
it is not in any way as fine and stirring and heroic a piece of work
as the Lubitsch-Jannings masterpiece. As a matter of fact, it is
slow-moving, less than brilliant in story and, with all deference to
my favorite cinema critic, Miss Anabel Lane,* its ending is unsatisfactory. Yet as completely as any photoplay of recent seasons
it bears the imprint of a definite personality, a definite style and a
completely characteristic approach. These, you may have suspected
before this, are the marks of a first rate contribution to this possibly dying art of the silent drama.

If you follow the films with any care, you are bound to have
noted how emphatically an outstanding director gives his own personal quality to a picture he makes. You can tell a work of Stroheim, Lubitsch, Griffith and even DeMille as completely as you can
identify the literary style of a James Branch Cabell, a Percy Ham-
mond or a Joseph Conrad. It is a sign of Josef von Sternberg's
importance that he, too, is now revealed as a definite cinema sty-
list. The Docks of New York is the perfect example of his photoplay manner.

*Anabel Lane was the wife of The Film Mercury's editor and pub-
lisher, Tamar Lane.

Possibly it is von Sternberg's attitude towards plots that offers the chief clue to his methods.   There is a suggestion of his feeling in The Last Command and Underworld, but it comes out far more noticeably in his latest work.   In all of these films, the director has been concerned with highly colored, melodramatic events, but, in each one, he has given the impression that he regarded them as of secondary importance.   I think you will find this point of view rather cautiously advanced in the two earlier pictures and frankly admitted in the latest.

In The Docks of New York, von Sternberg has a story that is essentially melodrama in story, background and characterization. His hero is one of those hard-boiled he-men, given to smashing up waterfront dives at the slightest opportunity.   His heroine is one of those sad-eyed sentimental prostitutes so often encountered in the works of Mr. Eugene O'Neill and his lesser colleagues.   The other characters include a somewhat more hard-boiled prostitute with the usual heart of gold, a lecherous chief engineer, a comic stoker, the proprietor of a dive and a waterfront clergyman.   You probably heard of all of them in previous motion pictures.

The outline of the story hardly comes under the head of novelty, either.   The he-man stoker, with a night's shore-leave, rescues the O'Neill lady of the docks from an attempted suicide; marries her, half in jest, half in earnest, during a saloon celebration, and casually deserts her the next morning to return to the sea.   In the end, he changes his mind, returns to her and takes a jail sentence that was destined for his wife.   There are, also, a shooting and a number of pleasant bar-room brawls.

To all of this potentially sensational material, Mr. von Sternberg adopts the most casual attitude imaginable.   His plot always seems a distinctly side issue with him.   He starts just as if he were all set to build up to a vigorous climax and then he calmly refuses to get excited, while his narrative, all set for something smashing, slides off into semi-placidity.   In many a director, you would say that this neglect of the climactic was the result of an inability to accomplish it.   But in The Docks of New York it is so obvious that this truncated manner of melodramatic narration is intentional, that you realize it comes from the intent of a man who knows just what he is doing.

The reason is that von Sternberg has other and more important concerns.   He is interested in characterization, in background, in pictorial and atmospheric values, in cinematic style, not in the more commonplace items of plot.   This preoccupation with matters usually regarded as secondary is bound to make the director stand out as a distinctive figure, but it is skill with which he gives way to his concern that really gives him his importance.   Pictorially and atmospherically, The Docks of New York is nothing short of superb.   Each scene is a superior example of the cameraman's art and the whole is a passing canvas worthy of the art critic.

The excellence of its characterization is undoubtedly abetted
by the fact that each figure in the drama, in the process of being
moving and credible, also knocks over most of the important con-
ventions belonging to the part.   George Bancroft is the hard-boiled,
he-man hero-villain; Betty Compson, the sentimental prostitute;
Baclanova, the vengeful wife; Mitchell Lewis, the heavy, and Clyde
Cook, the comic relief.   You have encountered every role in the
cinema before, yet here they are different.   They are no longer
stock figures; they manage to be here utterly believable.

During his comparatively brief thespian career, Bancroft has
revealed himself, not only as one of the most expert of character
actors, but also as that rarest of cinema players, the man who
could portray a hard-boiled, roistering, two-fisted gentleman of the
aforementioned he-man school, with the propensity for socking people, and still make him entirely sensible.   In The Docks of New
York, Mr. Bancroft is both honest in his impersonation and thoroughly moving.   I imagine it is his ablest portrayal.   Miss Compson does marvels with her comparatively sympathetic role for a
change, is fine in it, even if she has less than her usual opportunity.

And now to disagree with Miss Lane.   I agree with her entirely that a happy ending is not essentially a sin against the honesty
of the drama and when she suggests that the critics may not realize
this, I am unable to oppose her views.   But I do think that The
Docks of New York, not from the point of honesty, but from the
standing of pure theatrical effect would have been more impressive
had it closed with the departure of the errant husband, rather than
with the current conclusion.

Incidentally Miss Lane is a bit unfair to O'Neill when she
says that he has been contemptuous towards the films.   In the first
place he was enthusiastic about the screen version of Anna Christie
and, in the second, he is so interested in the medium that he has
entirely rewritten The Hairy Ape and Desire Under the Elms in
photoplay form, concerning himself with their pictorial and cinematic
qualities to the extent of changing his stories to conform with them.
He is one of the few creators of literature, who not only does not
scorn the films, but is actively and intelligently interested in their
problems.

> --Richard Watts, Jr. in The Film
> Mercury, Vol. 8, No. 19 (Oc-
> tober 26, 1928), page 6.

☐ DON JUAN (Warner Bros. , 1926)

Hey, Mr. Fairbanks, come home quick!   John Barrymore is
stealing your stuff.   He climbs balconies, he rides horses, he fights

duels and he makes hot, hot love.   Here is a young feller who is
determined to live down his dark past as a Shakespearean actor.
And here is an actor who is more than just a star; for you cannot
tell this reviewer that Barrymore didn't have an active hand in
producing this film.

        Don Juan is a lively burlesque of The Great Lover of legend.
This boy is so mean with women that the girls won't let him alone.
As soon as he sights a good girl, however, he reforms.   You can't
blame him; good girls were a novelty in Renaissance Italy.   In the
course of enacting the adventures of the wicked Spaniard, Barrymore
gives us Jekyll-and-Hyde, Don Q, Zorro, Hamlet and Beau Brummel.   His is such a boundless talent that he can afford to be pro-
fligate.

        He acts with an abandon that will arouse the disapproval of
the School of Eyebrow Lifters.

        The whole production has a lavish beauty.   Surely never were
so many beautiful girls assembled in one cast.   Estelle Taylor gives
one of the great performances of the year as Lucrezia Borgia.

        Montagu Love and Warner Oland are a couple of sinister
heroes, while Mary Astor is the girl whose glance has the purifying
effect.

        Here is a picture that has great acting, thrilling melodrama
and real beauty.   Anyone taking a child to Don Juan is nothing but a
silly.

        With the Vitaphone, a real film event.
                                        --Photoplay, Vol. 30, No. 5
                                        (October 1926), page 52.

                          *   *   *

        At Warner's Theatre John Barrymore in Don Juan and also
the Vitaphone have arrived.   The latter is a device to further the
cause of talking pictures by synchronizing sound and action in a
moving picture.   What happens is that when a figure appears on
the screen, whatever sound it makes comes through a loudspeaker.
In this endeavor the device is most successful and probably very
extraordinary, but beyond this synchronization there is nothing much
to shout about.

        A photograph of Mr. Will Hays made a speech that in the
hot and far reaches of the balcony was largely a blur of sound.
Pictures of various noted fiddlers and songsters performed as be-
fitted them, but the result seemed to lack the snap, or edge, of
direct acoustics.   The Philharmonic Orchestra, via the loudspeaker,
accompanied first a picture of itself, and later Mr. Barrymore's
love-making, and left the impression of an orchestra not so good,
that in the theatre, would be more pleasing than its secondhand efforts.

After the heat and the Vitaphone, which lasted about an hour, had reduced me to the point of exhaustion John Barrymore was brought to view in what the subtitle announced as a story based on the Don Juan legend. The basis turned out to be slight. By very indifferent acting Mr. Barrymore depicted a farceur, an acrobat, a poser, and a super swordsman. In a word, a combination of every ham hero the screen has held.

A prologue is attached to justify any ensuing evilness and preserve the moral sense of the far reaches of the nation. The action is in Rome at the time of the Borgias and the initial action lays down the impression of Juan being a most efficient lover. Lucrezia Borgia makes a play for his affections but is balked by the Don sighting a good girl and getting lofty in his outlook on such affairs. He pursues the sweet young thing, Lucrezia pursues him, and after a lengthy series of intrigues and climaxes he gallops with his true love into the sunset toward Spain and "happiness."

Mary Astor strikes the proper note of insipidity as Don Juan's true love, and Estelle Taylor fails utterly to live up to a conception of Lucrezia Borgia. The rest of the cast does better.

--Oliver Claxton in The New Yorker, Vol. 2, No. 26 (August 14, 1926), pages 33-34.

* * *

Some press matter issued in connection with the showing of Don Juan assures us that, in the course of this lengthy film, John Barrymore receives or delivers exactly one hundred and ninety-one kisses.

This figure is probably correct, but it seems extremely conservative to me. Certainly, Mr. Barrymore has established a new record for running broad osculation over the twelve-reel route. As the most celebrated lover in history, he literally leaps from lip to lip, with optional stopovers at each point of interest.

Among the actresses who are favored by his lingering caresses are Estelle Taylor, Mary Astor, Jane Winton, Phyllis Haver, June Marlowe, Helene D'Algy, Hedda Hopper and various unidentified but luscious extra girls.

More darned fun. ...

Don Juan has been as liberally panned by the United Brotherhood of Movie Critics as has any picture within my memory. Strain my ears as I might after its New York opening, I could hear no kind word for it from any one.

For all that, I confess that I enjoyed it. The backgrounds are awful, and the costumes grotesque in their inaccuracy; Mr. Barrymore himself is almost as bad, at times, as he was in The

Sea Beast; the story is dragged out and frequently confused. But the
fact remains that Don Juan engaged my humble interest and provided
me with considerable entertainment.

Much of this merit is traceable to good direction by Alan
Crosland, and to the efforts of a generally good cast. There is
one splendid performance by Nigel de Brulier, and some effective
work by Willard Louis, Warner Oland, Phillipe de Lacy and Myrna
Loy.

As the father of Don Juan, Mr. Barrymore is his old self.
When he steps down a generation into the title rôle, he becomes
the movie Barrymore, with a few flashes of brilliance and a great
many glints of supreme silliness.

You may take or leave Don Juan, as you yourself may
choose. I hesitate to recommend either course.

In connection with the "world première" (as it is fatuously
called) of Don Juan, there was a demonstration of the Vitaphone, a
new devise for the synchronization of shadow and sound.

There can be no doubt that the Vitaphone is a real triumph.
It is as far ahead of De Forest's Phonofilm as the Phonofilm was
ahead of Edison's ill-fated Kinetophone (I think it was called that).

The Vitaphone has reproduced speeches, songs and instru-
mental numbers by Marion Talley, Will H. Hays, Mischa Elman
and others. On the female voices, the choruses and the violin
solos it is a trifle unsure of itself, but in a solo by Giovanni Mar-
tinelli and a ukulele number by Roy Smeck it proved to be extraordinarily impressive.

Don Juan was accompanied by the New York Philharmonic
Orchestra via the Vitaphone, indicating that it will be possible in
the future to dispense with orchestras and organists in movie theatres.

Well, I for one will shed no tears. I'm tired of hearing
"Hearts and Flowers" during the views of the United States Cavalry
riding to the rescue, and "Horses--Horses--Horses" during the
tender love scenes.

--Robert E. Sherwood in Life,
Vol. 88, No. 2286 (August 26,
1926), page 26.

☐ DON Q, SON OF ZORRO (Elton/United Artists, 1925)

"If the little boys in the front row promise not to scream,
Douglas Fairbanks will blindfold his eyes and, with one flick of the
whip, put out a candle...."

That's the sort of picture Don Q is; it is guaranteed to drive little boys into frenzies of stunts until they break an arm or a new fad comes along.   It is romance all snapped up with vaudeville tricks, adventure told in terms of athletics.

In case you haven't heard, Don Q is the son of our old friend, Zorro.   There are, of all things, a few scenes from the first adventures of Zorro and the old man, played by Mr. Fairbanks himself, in a white wig, appears in the story so you have a double-barrelled climax with two sword fights.   The young Don Q, however, is most of the show.   And the joy of all the stunts--the new ones and the old ones--is the feeling you have that Mr. Fairbanks really knows his stuff.   It's all real and no fooling.

The story is lively but clumsy; it is full of over-seeing and over-hearing and dark doings.   But as it is laid in the beautiful and mythical Spain of romance, it has the advantage of taking place in a rich and gorgeous background.   And Mr. Fairbanks, in Spanish clothes doing a Spanish dance, is a sight to behold.   In fact, in all his pantomime, he's really more of a dancer than an actor.

Next in interest to Mr. Fairbanks is Warner Oland, who gives a splendid performance of a gay Archduke.   When the Archduke dies, the story never quite recovers from the blow.   Mary Astor is so beautiful as the heroine that she doesn't seem quite human.   She is the ideal lady for romance.   Donald Crisp, the director, makes a swell sneaking villain.

And now, Mr. Fairbanks, won't you tell us the adventures of old man Zorro's grandson?
                              --A. S. in Photoplay, Vol. 28, No.
                              3 (August 1925), page 51.

☐ DOROTHY VERNON OF HADDON HALL (Pickford/United Artists, 1924)

This new effort of Mary Pickford, one of the late Charles Major's historical romances, is exceedingly beautiful pictorially. If it does nothing else, it will establish a new high water mark in animated photography.

Dorothy Vernon of Haddon Hall moves along conventional historical lines.   Dorothy is being pushed by her father into a marriage with her worthless kin, Sir Malcolm Vernon, when she loves the son of the neighboring Earl of Rutland.   Actual folk of history move across the background, now and then becoming pawns in the story.   Dorothy, petulant, headstrong, violent tempered and lovable, wins her choice.

Miss Pickford is Dorothy and the rôle will please her army of followers.   Although lovely optically, it offers little new.   Work-

manlike of technique, her acting strikes no big spark. It is careful
and considered all the way. This mood of care seems to run all
through the production. It moves slowly. It lacks pace and, in a
measure, spontaneity. There are two performances of vitality in
the production. Claire Eames' Queen Elizabeth is admirable. Her
Virgin Queen will linger among your celluloid memories. Estelle
Taylor's few moments as the tragic Queen of Scots have poignancy.
Miss Taylor has been steadily advancing. Actually, "Dorothy Vernon" comes pretty near being old home week for the Pickford family. You will find Lottie Pickford as a serving maid to Dorothy,
and Allan Forrest, her husband, as the heroic John Manners.
Even the redoubtable Doug is there to be caught by those with keen
eyes. Marshall Neilan is the director and his hand is apparent in
the frequent little comedy sequences. Charles Rosher, cinematog-
rapher extraordinary, deserves a medal of honor for the photography.

--Photoplay, Vol. 26, No. 3
(July 1924), page 44.

☐ DOUBLING FOR ROMEO (Goldwyn, 1921)

    Will Rogers, collaborating with Will Shakespeare, has written
a good comedy about a small town Romeo who doesn't know how to
make love, and who goes to Hollywood to learn. Both of the talented authors deserve credit. In the cast is young Jimmie Rogers,
who is counted upon to sustain the family bankroll when his decrepit
old dad retires from the screen--eighty years hence.

--Photoplay, Vol. 20, No. 4
(September 1921), page 57.

*   *   *

    Doubling for Romeo has what is perhaps the rarest quality in
a motion picture story--genuine wit. Many motion pictures have
real humor, and not only of the slap-stick variety, but those that
are distinguished for their wit can still be counted on a one-armed
man's fingers. The reason for this is not far to seek. For genuine wit is a purely intellectual exercise, very hard to get down upon
the screen and very hard to hold there. It is a question of give
and take between producer and actor on the one hand, and the audience on the other. The actors must be able to see themselves as
others screen them and the spectators must be able to relish having
their favorite pictures turned inside out for them and their favorite
emotions burlesqued.

    The whole picture is a delicious burlesque of the conventional
film. Will Rogers is a clumsy cowboy who goes to a picture studio
in order to learn how to make love in proper movie style to please
his girl. He is shown every variety of movie love-making by the
obliging director and tries his hand at each variety, emerging with

a strong preference for the strong-arm method.   Presently he falls
asleep while reading Romeo and Juliet and dreams that he is Romeo,
with the girl he loves, but canot make love to, as his Juliet.   Here
the fun is at its best with Rogers playing Romeo a la Douglas Fairbanks, plus his own witticisms.   On awakening he decides that
strong-arm methods are, after all, the best for a man of his cast
of features and proceeds to use them on his girl with eminent success.

   Doubling for Romeo invites comparison with Sennett's A
Small Town Idol, which has already preceded it on the screen as a
brilliant example of motion picture burlesque.   There is undoubtedly
more virtuosity and more Gargantuan humor in the Sennett picture.
Its vein of satire cuts deeper and goes into more malicious detail
in its caricature of the methods of different directors and of various types of pictures.   But it suffered from inadequate titling, so
that the spectators were not always sure of their ground, and the
picture was at times done too much from the inside, so that its
extraordinary merits may not have fully reached its larger audiences.   The Rogers picture makes a safer bid for popularity on
this score.   It is easily the best picture Mr. Rogers has ever done.
                         --Exceptional Photoplays, No. 10
                           (November 1921), pages 9 and
                           10.

□ DOWN TO THE SEA IN SHIPS (Whaling Film Corporation/Hod-
kinson, 1922)

        Here is a story with an idea.   John Pell wrote Down to the
Sea in Ships to depict the whaling industry, the adventurous record
of which is the history of our New England sea coast.   Pell placed
his action in the golden days of 1850, when the hardy whalers swept
the seven seas.   This isn't all the idea.   The rest concerns itself
with the way the picture was produced, for it was financed by descendants of these very seamen themselves.   The result is an oddity
and an interesting one.   There is a superb freshness to the whaling
scenes--and brand new thrills to the hand to hand combats.   And
the land episodes among the Quakers of the day have quaintness.
Unfortunately the story as it is developed now isn't just right.   Cutting and editing are needed.
                         --Photoplay, Vol. 23, No. 3
                           (February 1923), page 64.

                    *   *   *

        Almost every movie costume drama is described, by its
press agents, as an "epic."   Occasionally there are films that justify this overworked description.   The Covered Wagon is one; Down
to the Sea in Ships is another.

Down to the Sea in Ships is unique as a motion picture in that it represents the result of a severe attack of community spirit among the citizens of a small city. The good people of New Bedford, Massachusetts, were inspired by Elmer Clifton with the idea that they could get together and make a movie of their own--one which would tell the story of New Bedford's heroism, and spread the glory of New Bedford to the four corners of the earth. Mr. Clifton, having read Moby Dick and other books about the noble old whaling days, realized that there was great dramatic material here; and he set out to convince New Bedford that he was right.

Oddly enough, he succeeded. New Englanders are notoriously hard-shelled folk; they can never be "sold" on anything. They do all their buying by themselves. So it is greatly to Mr. Clifton's credit that he persuaded the New Bedford citizenry not only to co-operate in the production of his picture, but to pay for it as well.

Elmer Clifton, like Charles Brabin, had done nothing much in the course of his career to indicate that he was qualified to produce a picture of the magnitude of Down to the Sea in Ships. He started out in the movies, as so many others have started, under the tutelage of David Wark Griffith--first playing in The Birth of a Nation and Intolerance, and later directing a number of feeble comedies in which Dorothy Gish was starred. His greatest success was made in the Babylonian episode of Intolerance, wherein he played a number of memorable scenes with the then obscure Constance Talmadge.

It was this picture, and these scenes, that propelled Miss Talmadge to the lofty estate of star. Mr. Clifton, however, waited seven years and more before Down to the Sea in Ships gave him his opportunity to establish himself.

The production of this picture was a great story in itself. Having persuaded New Bedford of the feasibility of his project, Mr. Clifton had to assemble his cast--largely from local talent--and then go down to the sea himself to do his actual shooting. As he had but meagre capital to work with, and no studio at hand, he was compelled to fall back upon realism--an element which is steadfastly ignored by movie producers. His ships were real ships, his sea was a real sea--not a Hollywood tank churned by an aeroplane propeller--and his whales were real whales. There was no trumpery about it. Moreover, the interior scenes were nearly all real; Mr. Clifton set up his lights and his cameras in New Bedford homes and meeting houses, and reproduced them exactly as they are.

The costumes of the period--one hundred years ago--were designed from old prints, and from models still in existence in New Bedford attics. Every detail of make-up was perfect, down to the last whisker.

The good ship Charles W. Morgan, which provided the scene for most of the action, is the oldest whaling vessel afloat. Her aged skipper, James A. Tilton, was taken along with Mr. Clifton's company on their long cruise. He had hunted whales for forty years and it is safe to assume that, under his supervision, there were few mistakes made in the technique of this manly art.

Of the start of his adventurous expedition, Mr. Clifton writes: "The Rev. Thurber of the Seaman's Bethel, who for over thirty years, with his choir, has wheeled his little organ down to the wharf in a barrow to chant his blessing for those sturdy men who go 'down to the sea in ships,' repeated this benevolent process for our benefit. From the time that prayer was given, I never doubted for a moment the ultimate success of the picture. There was too great a sincerity in the minds of the people to permit failure."

This sincerity was markedly evident in the picture itself. There was a sense of genuineness about the whole thing that stamped it as an honest effort.

Mr. A. G. Penrod, who was Mr. Clifton's head cameraman, furnishes the following account of the whale-hunt:

"We left New Bedford, Massachusetts, on our whaling voyage the twenty-second of February on an old square rigger, the veteran of many greasy voyages, amid songs, prayers and booming of cannon, the customary prelude to such a hazardous undertaking. Our officers were the most expert whalemen obtainable. The crew was composed of adventurous young men going out to perpetuate the thrills and hardships of their whaleman ancestors. Captain Tilton, a whaleman of forty years' experience, commanded the bark.

"After a two-weeks' voyage, in which time we passed through such experiences as being seasick, getting accustomed to a whaleman's grub and his mode of life, and learning to sleep in a bunk just wide and long enough to squeeze into, we finally arrived at San Bay down in the Caribbean Sea, just south of Haiti in the West Indies.

"This small body of water is considered the mecca of sperm whaling. It very soon turned out to be, for the very next morning after arriving, just as we were ready to eat our breakfast of salt horse, we heard that glorious sound, which quickens the pulse and causes every muscle in the body to become tense with excitement, wailed out from the mast-head: 'B-l-o-ows--B-l-o-ows--B-l-o-ows.' Every man instantly sprang to his post and did what he had been so thoroughly drilled to do. Breakfast and everything were forgotten in the thought that we were about to enter into deadly combat with one of the greatest monsters that have ever lived on land or sea. Cameras were quickly loaded into the small, frail whaleboats that hung along the sides of the mother ship, and at the signal to lower, we were fairly deafened by the squeaking of pulleys, the shouting of orders and the banging of boats

against the side. It took only a few minutes to be off,
and then everything was as quiet as death. After the
pursuit starts the least noise will frighten the whale and
cause it to sound, and then it may not be seen for many
minutes and perhaps will be lost altogether.

"Our sails were quickly set, and every man strained
at an oar. Suddenly we found ourselves in a sea of
plunging monsters blowing large volumes of vapor out of
their lungs every time they breathed. The boats separated, as there were whales in every direction. The mate
of each small boat was captain of his crew and upon him
depended the success of his unit. Every man pulled on
his oar with every ounce of his strength, and under the
stifling heat of the tropical sun it was a real test of his
courage and mettle. The whales evidently sighted us, as
they sounded, and it was several minutes before we again
caught sight of them. Everything became quiet and motionless. We dared not move lest they hear us and not
come up again. During this breathing spell we noticed
that the calm, peaceful blue waters had become infested
with large gray sharks from fifteen to thirty feet long,
with large mouths lined with triangular teeth which had
saw-toothed edges. These sharks always follow the
whales, for they are scavengers of the sea and prey upon
the whales themselves as well as their victims. A shud-
der ran through us. We looked at each other with the
realization that if any of us should be spilled into the
water in the forthcoming struggle it meant practically certain death. We were in the camera boat and consequently
were not equipped for catching, or defending ourselves
against whales or sharks.

"Suddenly there appeared on the surface of the water
only a few feet away the backs of four huge whales, each
emitting a spray of vapor, with loud snorts such as a
herd of wild steers might make magnified a hundred times.
We were so taken by surprise that hardly a man moved,
not a word was spoken. There was nothing to do except
keep perfectly still; this was our only means of defence.
They were too close for us to make an attempt to escape.

"On they came, puffing and blowing, spraying us with
their white vapor breath until we could almost touch their
noses with our hands. Then, very slowly, they submerged and passed under only a few inches below the keel
of our boat. We were practically sitting on three hundred
tons of unsuspecting wrath and energy. We had been too
close for them to see us. They did not know we were
there. It is difficult for them to see objects close to
their noses, as their eyes are located about one-third of
the way back on the sides of their bodies. The thing that
had frightened us most had saved us. This was our first
thrill. But was by no means the last. Fortunately, I got
some very fine close-ups.

"Although the ocean seemed to be alive with these mon-

sters, it took some time for one of our boats to get
'fast.' To harpoon a whale it is necessary to have the
boat right up against his back. The whalemen call it
'Wood to Black Skin.' We noticed our boat getting rather
close to a group of whales, so we manoeuvred for a
position from which to photograph the harpooning. These
were tense moments; for when the whale feels the pain
of the harpoon sinking in his side he is sure to start a
wonderful disturbance. One flip of his flukes or tail and
all is over. Smashing a boat and hurling its occupants
into the air is no more to him than crushing an egg in
the hand is to us. The code of the whalemen, however,
permits of no compromise. Their slogan is 'A Dead
Whale or a Stove Boat.' A whale is considered of more
value than a human life.

"Gradually we were closer and closer, until the mate
in the other boat was thoroughly alarmed at the dangerous
position we had attained and violently waved his arms for
us to be careful. The motion picture cameramen also
have a code of ethics which is as stern as the whalemen's,
and that is--GET THE PICTURE. We had only one thought
and that was to get real photographs of real action at any
cost.

"Suddenly we saw our leading man, who was standing
in the prow of his boat with the harpoon in his hands high
above his head, stiffen himself and with all his might hurl
the harpoon into the back of his victim. It was a huge
bull whale, the largest of the school. He was at one end
of the rope, with the small boat and its occupants at the
other. Instantly making a great splash he lunged forward,
throwing thousands of gallons of water high into the air.
The race was on. He plowed through the water at tremendous speed, leaving a violent wake behind him, and at
times the tiny boat seemed only to touch the tops of the
waves he created. We were able to keep alongside of this
action by the motor which had been installed in our camera
boat for just such emergencies. The chase continued at
intervals for several hours, the whale first plowing through
the water at great speed, then sounding or going down under the water, then again coming to the surface for breath,
when, seeing us, he would repeat the operation. The
other boats, realizing the enormous size of the whale we
were fast to and not wanting him to escape, came up and
made fast also.

"We noticed he kept coming up closer and closer to
our boats. We thought he was becoming more accustomed
to us. This was soon disproved, for suddenly he ran up
alongside one of the boats and started thrashing at it with
his huge twenty-foot flukes, knocking the oars into the air
and jostling the boat around in such manner that the men
went headlong into the water. Then with a final effort he
sent the boat high in the air, smashing the sides and
leaving the crew to the mercies of the sharks. They were

quickly picked up, were given another boat from the mother ship and renewed the chase.

"His efforts kept getting weaker and weaker until we were able to get quite close, and then came the final flurry or death struggle. They had begun throwing long sharp lances into his very vitals. This aroused in him all the hate and fury it was possible for his huge body to contain, and an unbelievable amount of strength.

"Being very anxious to get some wonderful close-ups we drew nearer. Then almost before we could realize it he had changed his course and was bearing down upon us with all his speed. We were barely able to get out of his way by a few feet as he shot past us, his large mouth wide open and his wonderful strong white teeth plainly visible. This final effort seemed to discourage him; soon he turned over on his side and was dead. 'Fins out! Fins out!' was yelled from every throat. We had won our fight and obtained some of the most wonderful motion pictures that have ever been made of such a combat. "

Whether Mr. Penrod's enthusiasm has run away with him in the foregoing description, I am unable to say; but I do know that the whale hunt is one of the most realistically thrilling episodes that I have ever seen on the screen. It is a glorious instance of swift, stark action.

In recording the indisputable excellence of Down to the Sea in Ships, one is apt to pass over the story hurriedly. This element of the picture was unimportant--which is fortunate, for it was decidedly foolish. Indeed, a great many people can see Down to the Sea in Ships without realizing that it has a story at all.

The plot, such as it was, centered in the person of a stalwart young Harvard man of the class of 1823, who falls in love with Patience Morgan, a fair Quakeress. Asking her father for her hand, he is met with the inexorable decision that no man shall marry the girl until he has first killed a whale. So the young hero goes out boldly and brings home the blubber--coming in time to prevent a marriage ceremony between the heroine and one Samuel Siggs, a horrible, leering villain.

Raymond McKee, as the hero, performed in a manly, straightforward manner, and a little girl named Clara Bow scored an emphatic hit in a minor part.

Down to the Sea in Ships stands as a fine achievement for Elmer Clifton and for the people of New Bedford. The fact that they undertook the job is commendable in itself; the fact that they made a success of it is little short of miraculous.

                              --Robert E. Sherwood in The Best
                                Moving Pictures of 1922-1923
                                (Small, Maynard and Company,
                                1923), pages 63-70.

☐ DREAM STREET (Griffith/United Artists, 1921)

Father Griffith seems to feel that he should apologize for
Dream Street. "We do not make any great promises one way or
the other," he writes in the program; "we have done the best we
could." There really is no call for an apology. And if apology
must be made, a better basis for it would be the length rather than
the quality of the picture. It is not a super-feature picture. Which
is to say it is not a $2 picture. But it is an interesting and beauti-
fully screened "regular" picture. If it were sharpened by being cut
from twelve to seven reels it would retain all its stronger points
and lose nothing but its padding and repetition, and a dozen or so
close-ups expressing grief, or fear, or terror, or surprise. With
his Dickensian flair for over-emphasizing character D. W. slips into
the habit of holding his close-ups so long the character itself fades
and you hear nothing but the stentorian tones of the director himself shouting: "Hold it, Carol!" "For God's sake, weep a little,
Charlie!" "Get the terror into it, Ralph!" Or, if you know nothing
of the methods of picture-taking, you wonder just why you must be
shown again and again how the heroine looks when she is in trouble
and mightily upset about it.
                              --Burns Mantle in Photoplay, Vol.
                              20, No. 2 (July 1921), page 58.

                    *   *   *

Somehow, David Wark Griffith reminds us of an old-time
magician. You never could tell whether the prestidigitator was going to take a beautiful dove or a lowly cabbage from the silk hat.
Griffith leaves one in the same state of expectancy. However, he
surely pulled forth a cabbage in his latest production, Dream Street.

Mr. Griffith has combined two of Thomas Burke's Limehouse
Night stories, chloroformed the characters into tame insensibility
and then practically devised a new tale. If you have read Burke,
you will realize the state of the dilution. Suffice it to say that the
heroine, Gypsy Fair, is one of those guileless little flappers who
plays at a Limehouse music hall without the slightest damage to her
unsullied ideals. There are two brothers, one a brute bully and
the other a poetic weakling, who love her in their varied ways. In
the end, the brute becomes a hulking angel, winning Gypsy Fair's
love.

Dream Street delves into symbolism, but with little success.
There is a corner preacher who stands for a very orthodox sanctity
and a weird street musician who wears a mask and represents an
equally orthodox hell. The thing is crude.

Mr. Griffith has not once touched life anywhere. Nor does
he anywhere touch the art of Broken Blossoms, laid in the same
colorful surroundings. There is one manifest reason: in the earlier production Griffith was well-nigh uncompromising in his disre-

gard of what our public is supposed to want in the last he is playing Pollyanna for the exhibitors.   Moreover, he is playing it with
an exceedingly weak cast of interpreters.   None of them in any
way stands out, save in the matter of overplaying.

--Frederick James Smith in Motion Picture Classic, Vol. 12,
No. 6 (August 1921), pages 50-51.

*   *   *

A lengthy foreword in the program of D. W. Griffith's new
picture, Dream Street, announces that the play is a conflict between
the forces of darkness and light.   It might better be described as a
conflict between banality and bunk, in which the audience figures as
the heaviest loser.

From which our readers will gather that Dream Street is not
a colossal achievement of cinematographic art; and they will gather
correctly.   It is a thoroughly bum picture, and the fact that D. W.
Griffith sponsored it makes it just so much more easily a target
for criticism.   For one is entitled to demand something better from
the man who produced The Birth of a Nation and Broken Blossoms.

Thomas Burke receives credit for the idea back of the story
(the word "credit" is used in a purely rhetorical sense), but there
is really little of "Limehouse Nights" in Dream Street.   Some of
the characters bear faint resemblance to Burke's people, but the
resemblance is purely external.   The atmosphere of the play--usu-
ally Mr. Griffith's strongest feature--is woefully bad.   The scenes
and some of the costumes give a suggestion of the West India Dock
Road, but the language and manners smack of 14th Street and Second
Avenue.   There are references to "stool pigeons," "sweeties," a
request to "quit your kiddin'," and a Scotland Yard detective remarks that somebody "croaked this guy."

Many people (who claim to be "in the know") have told us
that the actors in Mr. Griffith's productions are mere puppets, who
do everything just as he tells them to, without knowing why they are
doing it.   If this is so, Mr. Griffith evidently had a series of off
days during the production of Dream Street, for he has failed to inspire any of the cast with the emotional intensity of Lillian Gish, or
the eloquent restraint of Richard Barthelmess.   Carol Dempster,
Ralph Graves and Charles Mack perform acceptably, but they are
so utterly lacking in variety that they pall dreadfully after the first
few reels.   Miss Dempster has three tricks, Mr. Graves two and
Mr. Mack one--and they use these over and over again.

There is somewhat more than the usual quota of Griffith al-
legory and symbolism, and, this time, it doesn't ring true.   In fact
Mr. Griffith, who used to be known as "The Master" at this sort of
thing, might now be designated more appropriately as "Symbol Simon."

--Robert E. Sherwood in Life, Vol.
77, No. 2010 (May 12, 1921),
page 692.

☐ DYNAMITE (M-G-M, 1929)

This picture has some fine touches that Cecil DeMille should be proud of, but it is too long. While there is delightful comedy relief, in the sophisticated handling of some of the domestic relations, the story is stark drama, with several exceptionally tense scenes.

Cynthia Crothers, to save her fortune, bargains with a murderer to marry her a few hours before his execution. She plans to marry another man whom she has bought from his present wife. The big surprise is Charles Bickford who wins all the female hearts by his first screen rôle--a he-man. Kay Johnson, also new, delights with her work. A harrowing mine explosion, a weepy court room scene, love scenes à la Glyn, beautiful sports events, a whoopee party de luxe, and last, but not least, a new DeMille bath tub. All Talkie.

                                        --Photoplay, Vol. 36, No. 5
                                        (October 1929), page 53.

☐ THE EAGLE (Art Finance Corporation/United Artists, 1925)

Rudolph Valentino changes his personality three times in his new picture, and each one is dashing and fascinating and very Valentino.   First, he is a young lieutenant of the Czarina's regiment, brave and handsome and desired of Catherine.   When he deserts because he objects to "boudoir service," young Dubrovsky becomes a bandit, the Black Eagle, seeking to avenge a wrong done his father.

Next we see Rudy impersonating a French tutor in the house of his enemy, teaching the enemy's beautiful daughter.   Dubrovsky falls in love.   Shall he break his oath of vengeance?

The story really begins when Dubrovsky becomes the Black Eagle.   The finish is weak and the characters not well drawn. Vilma Banky is Sam Goldwyn's gift to the screen.   You will like Rudy and Vilma and the picture, in spite of its faults.
                                        --Photoplay, Vol. 24, No. 2
                                        (January 1926), page 46.

☐ ELLA CINDERS (John McCormick Productions/First National, 1926)

Probably you know Ella Cinders of the comic strips.   Ella is a great-great-great-granddaughter of Cinderella.   Note that her name is Cinderella in reverse.   The 1926 heroine goes to Hollywood

instead of Prince Charming's grand ball. Does the plain little Ella
make good. Does she? Well. Colleen Moore is Ella. This isn't
one of Miss Moore's best comedies, by any means. It is slow in
spots. But it has another inside glimpse of Hollywood.
                              --Photoplay, Vol. 30, No. 3
                                (August 1926), page 56.

☐ EXIT SMILING (M-G-M, 1926)

       A picture which had such possibilities and of which so much
was expected that the result is disappointing. In the effort to make
this a rip-roaring comedy, the human interest and pathos have been
overlooked, and had these been stressed the picture would have been
excellent. Beatrice Lillie, the English comedienne, is not particularly impressive. In fact she has a lot to learn in camera technique. Photographically--she is not a camera study.
                              --Photoplay, Vol. 31, No. 2
                                (January 1927), page 54.

☐ FAUST (Ufa/M-G-M, 1926)

       This German-made visualization of the Faust legend is an
extraordinary motion picture, one of the really fine things of the
screen.

       Goethe's panoramic poem has been used as its basis and the
adaptation has followed, in the main, as closely as the screen permits.

       The medieval legend of the philosopher, who sold his soul to
Satan that he might regain his youth, has been told many times and
in many forms. This celluloid version testifies to the directorial
abilities of F. W. Murnau and proves that his The Last Laugh was
no mere chance success.

       Murnau has caught the medieval atmosphere with surprising
success. Under his adroit direction, the interest never lags. Mur-
nau was aided by three fine performances: of Emil Jannings as
Lucifer, of Camilla Horn as Marguerite and of Gosta Ekman as
Faust. Indeed, for once, a picture is stolen from the redoubtable
Jannings.

       This Berlin newcomer, Fraulein Horn, is a remarkable ac-
tress. Playing the rôle that was offered to Lillian Gish, she gives
what is, in our opinion, a better performance than Miss Gish could
have offered. It is a superbly tender and unaffected bit of work.

This, of course, isn't taking credit away from Jannings, who contributes a roystering and amazing Satan.

Murnau has developed any number of scenes extraordinary in directorial technique and photography. The opening curiously parallels the start of the Griffith film, Sorrows of Satan, with Lucifer at the gates of Heaven. The Murnau handling is vastly superior, however.

--Photoplay, Vol. 31, No. 2
(January 1927), page 52.

☐ FLESH AND THE DEVIL (M-G-M, 1926)

Here is the picture filmed when the romance of Jack Gilbert and Greta Garbo was at its height. Naturally, the love scenes (and there are several thousand feet of them) are smolderingly fervent.

Based upon Sudermann's The Undying Past, the tale revolves around the devastating Felicitas, wife of an elderly count. Felicitas is one of those sirens who move through life with the destructiveness of a Missouri cyclone. She is faithless to her husband and she well-nigh breaks up the life-long friendship of Leo and Ulrich. Indeed, she dies, just as the boyhood pals face each other in a duel. Miss Garbo gives a flashing performance of Felicitas, Gilbert is a dashing Leo, although he does overshade some of his scenes, and Lars Hanson is excellent as Ulrich.

--Photoplay, Vol. 31, No. 3
(February 1927), page 52.

*   *   *

While this film has its entertaining moments and is marked by three or four clever touches, it is nevertheless a most unsatisfactory offering judged in its entirety. It will be all the more disappointing to those who looked forward with keen anticipation to the playing of John Gilbert and Greta Garbo in the same film.

While there are one or two good flashes of these two players, neither Miss Garbo nor Mr. Gilbert at any time equal the characterization or dramatic heights that they have accomplished in other releases.

While the story offered splendid opportunity for impassioned playing between these two artists, there are but a few brief moments wherein the love scenes attain the effectiveness or ardor that might be expected.

Apparently, director Brown is somewhat out of his element with a picture of this sort. He had failed to get anything approaching the results which both the film colony and the general public had anticipated.

Brown has treated certain of the scenes with originality, as far as camera angles, etc., are concerned, but he has notably missed at other times in getting the most drama out of the situations.

The story sags badly in the middle and will take considerable editing to bolster up.

The character in which Miss Garbo is presented is badly drawn. According to the continuity she is a vacillating personality and there is no logical explanation for many of her actions.

When previewed at a local theatre, the audience roared with laughter at several of the dramatic and emotional high spots in the picture. There were certain good psychological reasons for this that are easy to explain--but I will let the M-G-M production geniuses figure it out for themselves.

This laughter, however, takes some of the edge off the drama of the picture and results in much tittering throughout the remainder of the serious moments of the production.

The ending, too, is neither convincing nor satisfying.

Greta Garbo is photographically appealing but does not equal her previous work in this country. Let it also be said in passing that two more pictures of this nature and a reaction will set in against Miss Garbo among American theatre-goers that will result in much less popularity.

John Gilbert gives the weakest and most colorless portrayal he has presented to the screen in an age. On the other hand Einar Hanson gives a superb performance as the husband, actually taking many scenes away from the heretofore invincible John.

If he would protect his fair name as M-G-M's foremost thespian, Gilbert had in future best refrain from playing in films in which Hanson has a prominent role.

With Greta Garbo and John Gilbert as the two featured players, The Flesh and the Devil should be one of the big box office draws of the season. The film, however, will draw because of these two players and not because of its own merit. To those who had not looked forward to the production with keen relish, it may prove a good night's entertainment; but to those who expected something sensational The Flesh and the Devil will be frankly disappointing.

--Tamar Lane in The Film Mercury, Vol. 5, No. 4 (December 24, 1926), page 19.

☐ FOOLISH WIVES (Universal, 1922)

The long-evolving "million dollar movie" written and directed by Erich von Stroheim, Foolish Wives, has reached Broadway at last. Its reception was an interesting commentary upon our modes and manners, for von Stroheim, of the Junker physiognomy, was accused of everything from arch treason to studied insolence before all things American. That is, he was accused of all save one thing: demonstrating a superb directorial technique. We feel sure that von Stroheim will forgive us for adding this accusation to the others.

Foolish Wives has moments--indeed, whole stretches--of greatness. It is not for the provincial or the prude. Von Stroheim has taken the one real theme of life--sex--and played upon it with Continental discernment and, let us say, abandon. Where the Pollyanna American viewpoint dresses up sex in tinsel and spangles, von Stroheim looks upon it with the worldly and half cynical, half humorous Viennese viewpoint of a Schnitzler. Briefly, where we love to dress our sex illusions in Santa Claus whiskers, von Stroheim sees only the stocking at the fireplace.

We have said that Foolish Wives is not for the prude. For instance, we can imagine with what chuckles of unalloyed satisfaction the New York state board of censors dived into it with eyes and shears agleam.

Von Stroheim built his story around a renegade Russian count, Sergius Karamzin, who can most happily be described as living by his wits. Together with two pretty adventuresses, he occupies a cozy palace overlooking Monte Carlo and the Mediterranean. With a quiet little gambling rival to the famous Casino in full swing, Karamzin finds time to devote himself to the chase-- with women as the hunted. Karamzin is not the connoisseur, for he takes all comers, from serving maids to half-witted peasant girls.

The wife of an American envoy falls within his wiles, and the Russian almost sweeps her from her feet when fate circumvents in the hands of the aforementioned maddened servant maid. The woman sets fire to the castle, with the count and the "foolish wife" locked in a lonely tower-room. Here von Stroheim works to a thrilling climax as the flames lick their way up the winding tower steps and force the prisoners to a tiny balcony high above the ground.

The firemen stretch a net and the count--master egotist first and last--adjusts his monocle and leaps to safety. A second later the foolish wife half falls, half jumps to the rescuing net. Here von Stroheim might have ended his theme, but he went onward to show the ultimate fate of the dissolute Russian.

The end comes when, on the eve of a duel with the American envoy and with an empty evening on his hands, he climbs into the bedroom of a half-witted peasant girl. Awakened by the girl's cries, the father kills Karamzin and--here is a grim touch--drops his body thru a street sewer man-hole. A dead black cat, reposing hard by, is tossed into the darkness after the degenerate. Thus ends the tale.

Von Stroheim both wrote and directed the opus. Badly constructed at best, it is apparent that he lost all grip and perspective as the production progressed. The result is a story which collapses in its last hour, as shown in its original fourteen-reel form at the New York première. The theme completely spluttered and fizzled out.

Yet there are--as we have intimated, even in the face of being declared un-American--many marvelous moments. No one in this country has directed scenes to compare with his expansive shots of throbbing Continental life on the Monte Carlo boulevards and terraces. The vitality of actuality is captured, for the handling of the ensembles is touched with genius. And--in the intimate scenes--von Stroheim imbues his action and characters with subtlety and suggestion as keen as a Damascus blade. The flash of intrigue, the flame of passion and the criss-cross shading of thought are all there.

Von Stroheim has apparently never been popular with the "100 per cent Americans" of our photoplay. These folk went to Foolish Wives seeking something--and they professed to find it in the way von Stroheim presents Karamzin as shrewdly winning the foolish wife away from her American husband and also (here is the deadly count against the director), in the way he paints the envoy as a sort of good-natured boob. Knowing the calibre of some of our American representatives abroad, we find nothing but realism in this. But the parlor patriots, who recently were weeping over the subtle propaganda of the Pola Negri photoplays, call it "studied insolence. "

All of which we dismiss as absurd stuff to frighten naughty children. We know some of the limitations under which von Stroheim worked and we congratulate him upon proving--in an unqualified way--that he is one of the rare cinema elect. At the same time, let us declare ourselves as against the waste of money on huge extra reel spectacles. Also, that we fully realize that von Stroheim lost his story and, in a large measure, failed with Foolish Wives. Which is but another proof that one cannot do all things well. Von Stroheim should let some one else write his stories. Imagine, for instance, what he could do with the The Affairs of Anatol. The Cecil DeMille drivel would fade into nothingness. But von Stroheim needs a strong leash. Right here we predict that this man will do more things of fine worth. If he does not, then the photoplay is the loser.

We have stepped from the narrow path of criticism.   To return to Foolish Wives.   Von Stroheim himself gives an almost uncanny performance of Karamzin--dissolute, dapper, monocled, a
reckless player with passion, drinker of perfume, base student of
feminine psychology, unscrupulous thief, scoundrel guilty of all the
sins on the calendar; yet fascinating withal.   We guarantee you won't
forget his Count Karamzin.

The foolish wife is played by Miss DuPont, and the envoy-
husband mostly by Rudolph Christians, altho there are some shots
with Robert Edeson doubling for Mr. Christians, who died during
the making of Foolish Wives.   The adventuresses are adroitly done
by Maude George and Mae Busch and Dale Fuller, a former Key-
stone comedienne, contributes a striking bit as the maid who so
effectively brings out the Monte Carlo fire department.
                         --Frederick James Smith in Mo-
                           tion Picture Classic, Vol. 14,
                           No. 2 (April 1922), pages 48,
                           49 and 87.

                    *   *   *

So much publicity has been given this picture, which was
released too late to be included among the Shadow Stage reviews,
that we feel our readers would like to know what it is all about.

This--the much-heralded million-dollar production--has been
shown at last, in fourteen reels.   It is the most eccentric film ever
put together.   At times startlingly beautiful, at other times repul-
sively ugly, it is an amazing hodge-podge.

The American public cannot be expected to pay the million
dollars that Universal, and Erich von Stroheim, have wasted, not
spent.

An unworthy theme, the ugly amours of a pseudo-count from
Russia, it has been produced with consummate care and unceasing
imagination.

There is no doubt that Mr. von Stroheim probably spent almost the press-agented million on his sets and other effects; if he
had spent as much time on his story--if he had had a tale worth
telling--he would have earned the applause of that Broadway first-
night audience and every other audience in the world.

As it is, he has made a photoplay that is unfit for the family
to see; that is an insult to American ideals and womanhood.

To point a doubtful moral, von Stroheim has adorned a gruesome, morbid, unhealthy tale.   That he could give to it his admitted
genius for detail and artistic talents is nothing short of incredible.

Portraits such as Griffith himself never dreamed of.   Beautiful bits of acting.   Monte Carlo, as real as itself.   Photography and

decoration of unsurpassed appeal. And an insight into continental morals and manners such as only, so far, we have been able to get from certain books and paintings.

All wasted, on a story you could never permit children or even adolescents to see. A story that sickens before you have seen it half told. Your verdict is ready before the end.

Absurdities and atrocious melodrama; astounding subtleties and keen beauty--a beautiful waste.

Von Stroheim wrote the story. It is, as we have said, morbid; more, it is unreal. He has lifted one of his most effective episodes right out of Frank Norris' masterpiece, McTeague. At other times, he is almost original. He never knows when to let a scene alone; he whips it into insensibility before he lets it go. Consequently, every sequence is twice too long.

This picture, which has been advertised, actually, as "a one hundred per cent American" enterprise, is an insult to every American in the audience. Consider: an American, of sufficient prestige and importance to be selected by the President of the United States as a special envoy in charge of a vitally important mission to the Prince of Monaco, is depicted as a man who does not know how to enter a room or wear formal dress!

His wife is represented as the type of woman who strikes up a terrace flirtation with a Russian count who accepts money from a serving maid! To say nothing of the continual innuendoes to American ideals; the little sly thrusts at our traditions and our sentiments.

The actors are all good. Rudolph Christians is excellent; Miss Du Pont pretty and perfumed and exceedingly commonplace as the Foolish Wife--there is only one of them. Mae Busch is sparkling and would have been more if she had had an opportunity; Maude George makes the most of her role; she has it--the talent and the temperament; Dale Fuller is exceedingly good. Von Stroheim, who is a competent actor at all times, projects himself into too many scenes.

He has abused his directorial privileges.

This film may make money. That is a question. It is not a picture that will do you any good. It is not good, wholesome entertainment.

It is not artistically great.

It is really nothing.

--Photoplay, Vol. 21, No. 4
(March 1922), page 70.

☐ FOR HEAVEN'S SAKE (Harold Lloyd/Paramount, 1926)

For your own sake, go see this Harold Lloyd production. It's as merry as a summer day and as clean as April and what laughs it holds!

For Heaven's Sake proves that Harold is just as funny as ever.

The plot, which doesn't matter in the least, concerns a man with a mansion--that's Harold--and a girl with a mission, Jobyna Ralston. Harold's so rich nothing disturbs him. He wrecks and buys ten thousand dollar limousines with equal indifference. Jobyna and her minister father are so poor every doughnut counts--for they feed doughnuts to the poor.

Harold, slumming about, burns up the coffee stand accidentally. He gives the minister a check for $1,000 for it, only to find they've built a whole mission with that much money and put his name over the door. He goes down to stop it and sees Jobyna.

Then it's all over but the fun.

Wait till you see Harold trying to eat a powder puff, thinking it's a cookie Jobyna has baked; wait till you see him recruiting a congregation for the mission, stopping at nothing short of murder to get a crowd. You'll laugh until the tears stinging your eyes and the pain in your ribs force you to stop.

And if you've ever driven a car, go see what they do to a traffic cop.

The gags are all wows. The direction by Sam Taylor is intelligent, but then we've only praise for the whole thing.

Take the entire family to see it and then you won't need to spend money on spring tonics.
                              --Photoplay, Vol. 30, No. 1
                              (June 1926), page 53.

☐ FOUR DEVILS (Fox, 1928)

Here is the long-awaited F. W. Murnau film--the successor to Sunrise. For this picture Murnau took his cameras to the top of a circus arena, since the Four Devils are aerialists extraordinary.

Murnau goes back to the childhood of the Four Devils. A quartet of forlorn orphans, they are trained and beaten by a brutal circus proprietor.

This episode is so beautifully and tenderly filmed that it is worth seeing the picture for. And the work of little Dawn O'Day deserves special tribute.

A kindly clown helps the children to escape and they grow up to be a famous troupe of acrobats.

The two young women love their Charles and their Adolf and all goes well until a wealthy divorcée tosses a rose to Charles in the arena.

The boy loses his head over the adventuress and the broken-hearted Marion finally lets herself fall from a trapeze. That plunge brings the Four Devils back together--and the final shot implies a happy ending.

Janet Gaynor gives a sympathetic, sincere and touching performance. She has remarkable personality and persuasive charm. Charles Morton and Barry Norton are extraordinarily fine and you'll like Nancy Drexel. The weakness of the film is Mary Duncan's old-fashioned vampire. In dress and direction, the rôle is exaggerated, a flashback to the days of Theda Bara. Perhaps all the fault is not Miss Duncan's.

The film will probably be cut to eliminate the overdrawn scenes before it is generally released.
                                   --Photoplay, Vol. 35, No. 1
                                   (December 1928), page 52.

☐ THE FOUR HORSEMEN OF THE APOCALYPSE (Metro, 1921)

A film version of Ibáñez's widely known novel held out the interesting possibility of giving us something better than the original or something inferior. Mr. Rex Ingram, the director, has preferred simply to transcribe the original in terms of the screen. For that very reason the picture does not stand by itself, and any serious review of it must take into account the defects of the Ibáñez novel. With this reservation, the picture achieves distinction, through its sheer bulk and its linking up of widely separated places and events.

The first three reels are devoted to the spacious, open air life of the Madariaga family in the pampas of the Argentine where Madariaga's two sons-in-law are presented to us as contrasted prototypes of the opposing forces in the great European war. As in the novel, they are transported with their families to France and Germany respectively just on the eve of the conflict. This early part of the picture is distinguished by a careful detail study of a South American tango resort where the tango is danced as it was intended to be performed. This is one of the bright spots of the

picture from an artistic point of view though perhaps too strong in
its Latin flavor for our less sophisticated standards.

The war is soon under way and each wing of the family takes
part in it according to the temperament and blood of each; the offspring of Hartrott, Madariaga's German son-in-law, with the blind,
automatic devotion supposedly characteristic of all Germans, while
Julio Desnoyers, the libertine, Madariaga's half-French grandson,
holds aloof against the hopes and wishes of the elder Desnoyers.
We see the war in its panoramic aspects, the first great assault
of the Germans, the destruction of whole towns and the plundering
of estates, and a few titbits of atrocities thrown in, until the turning point of the Marne is reached.   Julio renounces his libertinism
at the last moment and is killed in action, while Madame Laurier,
with whom he had been having an intrigue, turns nurse and devotes
herself to her heroic, blind husband.   The echoes of the war gradually fade away and a mood of resignation succeeds the turmoil of
conflict.

The pleasure which such a film affords to the spectator is
largely the pleasure of recognition.   First the pleasure of recognizing what we have already read and secondly the pleasure of
recognizing, or rather re-creating, the mood which dominated us
two years ago.   The picture undoubtedly helps us to see ourselves
as we were in those stirring times.   Its war images are vivid.
But the argument remains one-sided throughout and, if it is to be
taken at all seriously as a presentation of historical truth, is really
dishonest because all the horror and atrocity of war are credited to
one side and all the idealism and sacrifice to the other.

Skillful as the producer has been in evoking the old war
mood in us, the picture as a whole shares most of the defects of
Ibáñez's novel.   In its unfolding it is entirely too prolix and could
easily have been done in fewer reels.   Also it lacks an absorbing
human story to pull it together.   After the outbreak of the war we
have only the thin thread of Julio's unedifying intrigue with Madame
Laurier to carry us along until Julio is killed.   There is very little
characterization.   The Hartrotts are plain caricatures and the figure
of the elder Desnoyers is robbed of all true pathos by a theatrical
interpretation.   None of the figures compel our interest by any
tragic greatness.   This is the more to be regretted because Mr.
Ingram has collected an astonishingly good cast with a fine feeling
for type.

From a purely cinematographic point of view the picture
reaches its finest moment in the sixth reel.   Here the vision of
the Four Horsemen is handled with real imagination.   These symbolic figures of War, Plague, Famine and Death are finely conceived and boldly executed.   They dominate the scene like the Furies
of old, as they gallop through the clouds high over a battle-torn
world.   This is the real core of the story and a picture written
around these figures and more continuously focussed upon them

would have had astonishing screen results.
                                    --Exceptional Photoplays, No. 4
                                      (March 1921), pages 5 and 7.

                              *   *   *

      We may talk all we like about the perfect picture, the tech-
nically fine and the disappointingly slipshod, the possible and the
impossible, the ideal and the commonplace picture, but, so far as
I have been able to discover the real and practically the only test
the public that supports pictures applies to the screen is the test
of entertainment. It is either a good picture or a poor picture as
it amuses or thrills, interests or bores; as it is convincingly told
or stupidly exaggerated, as it is artificial or real. There is a
public that likes "war stuff" and a public that doesn't. But roll
them together and you will find they represent one public when the
picture is entertaining. The Four Horsemen of the Apocalypse is
interesting, and sufficiently away from the conventional story of the
screen to give it a distinctive value of its own. It is a war picture, and the war scenes are its big scenes. Yet it has a character and story value that in effect, put the war in the background.
The horrors of the great conflict, the still remembered ruthlessness
of the German invasion, the fine thrill we get from the stand of the
French at the first Marne, are as graphically reproduced as it is
possible for the camera to reproduce them with a dummy village
and a trick army to shoot at. But I am inclined to believe the
scenes that will be longest remembered are those of the prologue,
the South American cattle country, the tango district in Buenos
Aires, which is particularly well done, and the gradual wakening of
the young Argentinian to his duty to his father's country. Rex Ingram is to be credited with a good job of directing. The cast is
well chosen, with an attractive boy, Rudolph Valentino, playing
Julio, and Joseph Swickard giving an intense characterization as
the father. Smaller parts are well played by Alice Terry, John
Sainpolis, Edward Connelly, Wallace Beery and "Bull" Montana.
                                    --Burns Mantle in Photoplay, Vol.
                                      19, No. 6 (May 1921), page 52.

                              *   *   *

      In a hundred years there will be no one left in the world
who can give a first-hand account of the great war--no one who
can say, "I was there; I saw it as it was"--and people will have
to get their knowledge of it from the books and plays that it inspired. The vast maelstrom of words which has flowed since the
machine guns and the typewriters first started clicking in 1914 will
remain, in greater or lesser degree, throughout all time, and by
them will we and our actions be measured.

      It is quite important, therefore, that we get the record
straight, and make sure that nothing goes down to posterity which
will mislead future generations into believing that this age of ours
was anything to brag about. Imagine the history which some H. G.

Wells of the Thirtieth Century would write concerning the world
war, basing his conclusions on such books as From Baseball to
Boches, such plays as Mother's Liberty Bond, or such songs as
"Hello, General Pershing, Is My Daddie Safe To-night?" It might
be entertaining reading, but hardly instructive.

Rather let us hope that this future Wells will depend upon
the books of Philip Gibbs and Henri Barbusse, and the poems of
Rupert Brooke, Alan Seeger and John MacRae.   And if, after reading these, he is still doubtful of the fact that war is essentially a
false, hideous mistake, then let him go to see the production of
The Four Horsemen of the Apocalypse and be convinced. It took
us a long time to get around to that statement, but the picture is
well worth the trip.

Blasco Ibáñez wrote the novel, and achieved widespread
fame thereby.   There are many, including the present reviewer,
who believe that this fame was not altogether deserved.   In fact,
we must confess that we belong to that society (recently organized
by F. P. A.) of "Those-who-started-but-did-not-finish The Four
Horsemen of the Apocalypse."

The motion picture adaptation, however, succeeded in holding our undivided attention more consistently than any dramatic
production since the day when, at the age of seven, we broke down
at a performance of Uncle Tom's Cabin and were carried out in a
sinking condition.

The great strength and vigorous appeal with which The Four
Horsemen of the Apocalypse has been endowed is largely due to the
superb direction of Rex Ingram, who produced it.   His was a truly
Herculean task, and he has done it so well that his name must now
be placed at the top of his profession.

June Mathis did the work of adapting the story, and her
scenario is coherent, and strongly constructed on logical lines, with
a fine sense for dramatic values.   At no time does the action drop
or the suspense weaken, except for a few moments near the end
when a crowd of frolicsome doughboys and Salvation Army lassies
are dragged in just to give the orchestra a chance to blare out
"Over There."

The cast is uniformly good, and selected with such great
care that every part--Spanish, Indian, French and German--is
played by a character who is actually true to type.   In the leading
role is a newcomer to the screen, Rudolph Valentino, who has a
decided edge--both in ability and appearance--over all the stock
movie heroes, from Richard Barthelmess down.   He tangoes, makes
love and fights with equal grace.   Both he and Alice Terry, who
plays opposite him, will be stars in their own right before long.

It is impossible to detail the work of the others in the large
cast, but more than passing mention should be made of Joseph

Swickard, Pomeroy Cannon, Nigel de Brulier, John Sainpolis, Stuart Holmes, Wallace Beery and Beatrice Dominguez.

The pictures themselves are at all times striking, and occasionally beautiful--for Ingram has evidently studied closely the art of composition, and almost any one scene, taken at random from the nine reels, would be worthy of praise for its pictorial qualities alone.

The four horsemen--Conquest, War, Pestilence and Death-- are convincingly frightful figures, and the fleeting pictures of them galloping through the clouds in a stormy sky are decidedly impressive.   Usually, when movie directors attempt to introduce an allegorical note, the result is little more than laughable.

Comparisons are necessarily odious, but we cannot help looking back over the brief history of the cinema, and trying to find something that can be compared with The Four Horsemen of the Apocalypse.   The films which first come to mind are The Birth of a Nation, Intolerance, Hearts of the World, and Joan the Woman; but the grandiose posturings of David Wark Griffith and Cecil B. DeMille appear pale and artificial in the light of this new production, made by a company which has never been rated very high. Nor does the legitimate stage itself come out entirely unscathed in the test of comparison, for this mere movie easily surpasses the noisy claptrap which passes off as art in the box office of the Belasco Theatre.

It is our belief that the film will not be an unqualified success in the United States, where the entire war now resolves itself into terms of Liberty Loan Drives and George Creel.   But in France, The Four Horsemen of the Apocalypse will be hailed as a great dramatic achievement; one which deserves--more than any other picture play that the war inspired--to be handed down to generations yet unborn, that they may see the horror and the futility of the whole bloody mess.   Ingram has recorded the martyrdom of France as no writer could have done.

Praise is difficult to compose, for it is always easier to be harsh than it is to be ecstatic.   The reviewer's task would be much simpler if every movie was of the calibre of Man-Woman-Marriage, for instance.   Nevertheless, we have told our story, and we shall stick to it.

The Four Horsemen of the Apocalypse is a living, breathing answer to those who still refuse to take motion pictures seriously. Its production lifts the silent drama to an artistic plane that it has never touched before.

--Robert E. Sherwood in Life,
Vol. 77, No. 2003 (March 24,
1921), page 433.

☐ THE FRESHMAN (Harold Lloyd/Pathe, 1925)

It's the finest picture that Harold Lloyd has made because,
like Grandma's Boy, it is more than just a series of gags. The
gags are there, of course, and some of them are the funniest that
Lloyd has ever presented; but there is a spirit back of the picture
that makes it something greater than just an extraordinarily funny
comedy.

As you know, it is the story of a boy who goes to college.
He's the greenest freshman of them all and got all his ideas of
college life from the movies. He wants to be the most popular man
in college and so he gets so collegiate that he is the joke of the
place.   The institution is just one of those "big stadiums with a
college attached," so he goes in for football. In the scenes of the
football practice and in the game itself, Lloyd surpasses himself.
The climax of the picture--the big game of the year--is an achievement in picture making. Not only is it overwhelmingly funny, but
it has all the excitement of a real game.

The scene in which Harold is thrown out of the line and
lands just at the moment to catch a twenty-yard forward pass will
always remain one of the Big Moments of this reviewer's life.

The comedy gains a lot by having its quiet moments; some
of them border on pathos. All of them are human.   Nevertheless,
Lloyd has never done better farce comedy than the incident of the
dress suit that has been only hurriedly basted together in time for
the party. Countless other comedians have lost their clothes, but
none of them has been so subtly and insidiously shorn of his cover-
ing.   Lloyd can do this sort of thing in such a way as to make
even a censor laugh.   And what greater praise can there be than
that?

                              --A. S. in Photoplay, Vol. 28,
                                No. 4 (September 1925), page
                                51.

                        *   *   *

There is a football game at the conclusion of this Harold
Lloyd comedy which atones for many dreary moments at the start.
                              --Robert E. Sherwood in Life,
                                Vol. 86, No. 2248 (December
                                3, 1925), page 56.

☐ THE GARDEN OF ALLAH (Metro-Goldwyn, 1927)

This is the best picture Rex Ingram has made since he tore
up his return ticket and decided to remain in France.   An excellent

telling of Robert Hichens' famous novel--of the monk who ran away
from his vows but couldn't get away from his conscience.   Ivan
Petrovich is admirable as the run-away Trappist, and Alice Terry
is satisfying as the woman the man of religion marries.   Beautiful
desert backgrounds.

--Photoplay, Vol. 32, No. 6
(November 1927), page 54.

☐ THE GENERAL (Buster Keaton/United Artists, 1927)

They're kidding everything now and any day you may expect
to see U. S. Grant and Robert E. Lee break into a Charleston.
Not that they do it in The General, but Buster Keaton does spoof
the Civil War most uncivilly in his new comedy.   Buster is a loco-
motive engineer who saves a whole Confederate army single-handed.
There is an undercurrent of heroic satire in the way Buster is always saving the moron heroine in crinolines.   Annabelle Lee is a
gorgeous laugh at all the helpless young ladies of historic fiction,
if you read between the pictures.

They spent a lot of money on The General.   A whole train
is wrecked in a deep ravine, if that means anything to you.   We
mustn't neglect to add that the basic incidents of The General actually happened.

--Photoplay, Vol. 31, No. 4
(March 1927), page 52.

☐ GENTLEMEN PREFER BLONDES (Paramount, 1928)

Those who read Gentlemen Prefer Blondes, the book, will be
disappointed in the picture made from it; those who have not read
the book will find the picture uninteresting.   It is a faithful recital
of the exploits of the little gold-digger as set forth in the book, but
it does not sparkle as the book does, and it builds no sympathy for
anyone in it.   When I read the book I was beguiled so much by the
sheer artistry of Lorelei's methods that I wanted to see her turn
up gold every time she dug.   When I watched her on the screen
her methods seemed so crude that it was a matter of indifference
to me whether she succeeded or not.   The book interested me because it is a superb example of humorous writing and an extremely
clever, searching analysis of the character of a fascinating girl with
but one idea in her head.   The action of the written story contributed nothing to its entertainment as reading, its attraction being
the manner in which it was set forth.   In the picture we have the
action stripped of its garb of scintillating humor, and there is
nothing in the action, even when we visualize it, to hold our interest for seven reels.   In the book Lorelei puts over her deal for

the diamond tiara with fascinating subtlety; in the picture she merely asks the Englishman for the money, and the scene in which she
does it does not develop sufficiently to make it reasonable for the
Englishman to give it to her.   He is not established as being the
easy mark he proves to be.   But Paramount is to be commended
for the effort it made.   It is what might be called an honest picture.   It has put the book on the screen as faithfully as possible,
and Anita Loos, the original author, wrote for it some clever titles.
And it cast Ruth Taylor as Lorelei.   When Ruth talks salary with
Paramount she will be reminded that she was given her chance to
demonstrate her value, which will be advanced as a reason why she
should accept but a fraction of it as salary.   Instead of demanding
gratitude, Paramount should offer it to the superb little creature it
was lucky enough to secure.   Whatever success Gentlemen Prefer
Blondes meets with, and it will be considerable, will be due to Ruth
Taylor, not to the story, the direction, or the supporting cast.
She is a find.   I will be surprised if she ever develops the range
of expression of Dolores Del Rio and Janet Gaynor, the other finds
of the year, but as a delineator of ingenuous precocity she will
reign supreme.   When I've said she makes a perfect Lorelei I've
said it all.   She has great beauty and personality, a combination
that spells success.   I would judge from the care that was exercised
to avoid photographing her profile that such shots of her would not
be as attractive as those to which we are treated in the picture,
but they could be a lot less attractive and still be treats to the eye.
Some of her close-ups are breath-taking in their beauty.   The very
first one will hit you right between the eyes and make you her slave.
But do not get the impression that she is of the beautiful-but-dumb
type.   She has brains, and plays her part with as much ease as if
she had a score of years of experience behind her.   This picture,
of course, will make her, but she will reciprocate handsomely by
making the picture, which relieves her of the necessity of feeling so
grateful to Paramount that she will allow it to retain the greater
portion of what should go to her in the way of salary.   Another fine
bit of casting is that of Alice White as Dorothy.   She and Ruth make
a pair that might have stepped from the book.   Miss Loos must have
had the two of them in mind.   Alice is a clever girl.   In this picture she is the wise-cracking gold-digger to the life, but she reveals a talent that would indicate that she is not in any way limited
to that kind of characterization.   She is astonishingly like Clara
Bow in appearance, and I would not be at all surprised if she ultimately will not go farther than Clara.

There are other excellent performances in Gentlemen Prefer
Blondes.   As I said in the previous paragraph, it is an honestly
made picture.   Paramount exercised the greatest care in casting and
filled each part perfectly.   Whether the public, with its preconcep-
tions derived from the book, will accept all the characterizations is
another matter.   Certainly I can not understand what Paramount was
thinking of when it decided upon the characterizations of Sir Francis
and Lady Beekman.   In this country Mack Swain and Emily Fitzroy
will be immensely popular in the parts, and will be responsible for
many laughs, but wait until the picture reaches England!   There is

one shot so obviously a caricature of Queen Mary and the hats she
wears that it will raise such a storm of protest that I predict the
picture will be withdrawn, even if it be shown at all.   Imagine if
a picture made in England and containing a scene reflecting on the
good taste of Mrs. Coolidge, were shown in this country.   We
would resent it.   Well, multiply the resentment by one hundred and
you have an idea of how England will receive Emily Fitzroy's characterization.   America is having a struggle to retain the European
market, and it is the height of folly to send over pictures that will
aggravate the existing prejudice against our productions.   Swain's
characterization will not be popular in England either.   There was
no reason why it should have been drawn so broadly.   It is an excellent performance, though.   Ford Sterling is an admirable Eis-
man.   It is another character that might have stepped from the
book.   Holmes Herbert, as the millionaire whom Lorelei finally
lands as a husband, is entirely adequate.   Trixie Friganza's characterization as a poor, demented old woman is clever, but it adds
a melancholy note to the picture.   There is nothing notable about
the direction of Mal St. Clair.   Farther along in this Spectator you
will read my praise of St. Clair's direction of Breakfast at Sunrise.
Whatever merit that picture has is due to the direction.   Whatever
merit Gentlemen Prefer Blondes has is in spite of the direction.   I
would have assumed that the Loos story was one made to order for
St. Clair, but he directs it as almost any of our established directors, not so skilled in his particular line, might have directed it.
It is just ordinary direction, with no inspiration back of it.   One
variety of fault that gradually is getting on my nerves is committed
frequently.   It is the common one of lining up characters facing the
camera.   It is crude direction.   I have said it many times and I
repeat it: two people conversing with one another do not stand
shoulder to shoulder.   They face one another.   When three people
stand and converse they form a triangle.   No scene showing them
standing in any other formation is convincing.   The greatest crime
that St. Clair commits is in a scene showing Ruth, Alice and Sterling lunching in a cafe.   They are at a round table, and are fairly
glued together--and leaving about three-quarters of the space at the
table unoccupied.   St. Clair groups them that way to make all of
them face the camera, which is inexcusable direction.   No scene
that betrays a consciousness of the position of the camera is a good
scene.   The three people at the small round table should have been
seated in a triangle, not in one straight line and so close together
that they do not have elbow room.   Another fault of the picture is
the over-indulgence in close-ups.   There is one scene that is ruined
by them.   It shows Herbert confronting Sterling in Ruth's room.   It
is one of the high spots of the picture, and gains its strength solely
from the reaction of the players to one another, consequently all
the players should be in it all the time.   But it is cut into fast
flickering close-ups, each one of which shows but one-third of the
scene.   Swain, depicting a titled Englishman, enters the room of
Lorelei and Dorothy and does not remove his hat.   More inexcusable
direction.   Swain is presented as a silly ass, but even silly asses
who have achieved sufficiently to be knighted learn somewhere along
the line that it is customary to remove your hat when you enter a

drawing room and address women.

                              --Welford Beaton in The Film
                              Spectator, Vol. 4, No. 8 (De-
                              cember 10, 1927), pages 8-9.

☐ A GIRL IN EVERY PORT (Fox, 1928)

Victor McLaglen is featured in this picture because of the
popularity he won in What Price Glory. McLaglen, as Spike Mad-
den, a deep sea sailor on a tramp schooner, finds that another
seafaring youth is stepping in his love affairs in the various ports
of call. McLaglen and Robert Armstrong are excellent as the roving rivals. Their adventures will intrigue and amuse you.

                              --Photoplay, Vol. 33, No. 4
                              (March 1928), page 55.

☐ THE GLORIOUS ADVENTURE (J. Stuart Blackton/Allied, 1922)

It was only a question of time before some director would
conceive the idea of using the Prizma effects or some other natural
color scheme for a feature picture. J. Stuart Blackton's unique
innovation is certain to arouse a deal of comment. Taking a swashbuckling story based around the court intrigue of Charles II, he has
realized that such effects could be more expressive in such a period
when milady and the gentleman in waiting, and brigands bold stamped
their personalities in song and story. It is such a marked departure
--this natural color scheme--that people will flock out of curiosity
to see it. From this argument it is worth a booking.

Certainly high class houses who cater to a discriminate clientele will add prestige to their showmanship by capitalizing its
conspicuous high-light. Experimentation must be made before all
pictures are made with a natural color process. But it is a feather
in Blackton's cap that he, at least, has shown the way. While the
figures are in movement their faces are almost indistinguishable.
It is as if the colors merged too readily, leaving the spectator in a
maze guessing their identities. Particularly is this noticeable in the
long shots. The close-ups compensate for making the effort as the
players in repose bring out the desired effect. We are speaking of
actual movement. The costumes are always in harmony--colorful
and picturesque. And the colors are held. Not so much success
seems to have been made in bringing forth cerises, pinks, blues,
oranges and yellows. Red and green are dominant and the former
color, if one may be excused for using a vulgarism, splashes the
other effects too readily. For instance it often shows a man's
arm or a woman's neck a deep carmine.

The Glorious Adventure is a tapestry--a mural decoration.
Its story is of less consequence because the natural color design
is really the motif. However, through it all runs a fantastic tale
of the days when knights were bold. And despite the tendency to
pay attention to the colors and losing the story interest as a result,
one becomes transported. Mr. Blackton has directed long enough
to know something of situation and climax incident and emphasis.
He tells us of a band of rogues who seek to compromise the fair
heroine, cheating her at the gaming table and carrying on an intrigue in the best Cromwellian manner. Quaint humor accompanies
the dramatic scene when she pledges herself to marry a murderer
awaiting execution following a custom when a wife's gambling debts
fell upon the head of a condemned husband. So he reaches a thrilling climax and the color scheme is vividly presented when London
burns. The criminal is a medieval "Hairy Ape"--a veritable cave-
man. He tosses the royal lover into a caldron of flames and is
shocked to discover his victim much alive the next moment. So
he actually rescues him and the fair lady from the cathedral, the
roof of which is pouring molten lead about them. The continuity is
not of the best and the plot is not easy to follow owing to the confusion of introducing a vast number of characters, who are ever
appearing up to the final reel.

     The picture is interpreted by a British cast of players some
of whom look like living Rembrandts or Gainsboroughs. Lady Diana
Manners appeared too much in repose. Perhaps she seemed so to
us on account of Lois Sturt's animated Nell Gwynn. All in all The
Glorious Adventure carries an opulence and richness of background
that makes it a distinctive achievement. The vivid silks and satins,
frills and furbelows--and the fire certainly offer a feast for the eye.
                              --Laurence Reid in Motion Picture
                                News, Vol. 25, No. 20 (May 6,
                                1922), page 2592.

                         *   *   *

     It's one of those "in the days of old when knights were bold"
things. For people who have a weakness for kings and sword-play
and old inns and faire ladies.

     This first photoplay in color is a novelty but hardly a knock-
out. Lady Diana Manners is the perfect English beauty. She can't
act, but then you can't have a perfect English beauty, a title and
talent.
                              --Photoplay, Vol. 22, No. 2
                                (July 1922), page 54.

☐ GO WEST (Buster Keaton/Metro-Goldwyn, 1925)

     It's rather a sad state of affairs when our old friend Buster
Keaton can't put over the laughs. He prances around with that

frozen look on his face trying to be funny and with the aid of a big
cow does his best with an improbable story.   The gags are not
what they should be and they don't come fast enough.   But all
tastes are different--you will get a few laughs out of it, anyhow.
--Photoplay, Vol. 24, No. 2
(January 1926), page 49.

☐ THE GOLD RUSH (Chaplin/United Artists, 1925)

The long-awaited Charlie Chaplin picture, The Gold Rush, is
at last released, and it is an amazingly pleasant thing to see Chaplin once more in person upon the screen.

This new picture of his, which is the first ten-reel comedy
ever to be sent out, is one of the best things Chaplin has ever done.
The story is a simple and logical one, and some of the "gags" and
situations are enormously funny.   But the picture is, by no means,
Chaplin's best.

Chaplin's individual performance as the lone prospector is,
of course, a joy.   His gay, pathetic little figure against the great
backgrounds of ice and snow moves with all the Chaplin genius for
touches of rare comedy and real pathos.

The scene in which Chaplin waits for the dance hall girls to
come to dinner is delicately played and it is moving, but it is built
upon too thin a premise and upon too unsympathetic an incident, to
afford the real heart-twist of The Kid or Shoulder Arms.

The final scenes on the boat are among the best in the picture, showing Chaplin as the Alaskan millionaire who still clings to
his habit of "shooting snipes."

No doubt everyone will enjoy this new Chaplin offering.   It
is Charlie Chaplin, lots of him, and it is filled with merriment.
But that it is a great development in the comedy field, or that it
brings a new comedy era to the screen, certainly is not true.   It
is simply ten reels of very good Chaplin comedy, which ought to be
enough for anybody, but it is no more.

Viewed as a picture, it meets a high standard.   As Chaplin's
masterpiece, as the result of two years' work touted as a supreme
effort, it falls short.   But it is infinitely better than The Pilgrim
or The Idle Class.
--Ivan St. Johns in Photoplay,
Vol. 28, No. 4 (September
1925), page 50.

☐ THE GOLEM (Ufa/Hugo Riesenfeld, 1921)

This new German picture is a masterpiece. It is perhaps
the most worthy of all the celluloid importations. The legend of a
Rabbi of medieval Bohemia who creates and brings to life a gigantic
figure of clay, it is presented with a sweep and a sincerity of purpose that thrills and amazes. It is, racially, Jewish; artistically
it is international. A picture that is a credit to the screen.
                                        --Photoplay, Vol. 20, No. 4
                                        (September 1921), page 57.

☐ THE GOOSE WOMAN (Universal, 1925)

An impressive and original mystery story--one of the best
things of its kind ever filmed. Rex Beach drew on America's most
famous murder for some of his incidents.

One great character study dominates the picture. The Goose
Woman is a drunken old witch who had once been a prima donna.
The birth of her son robbed her of her voice. She has taken to
drink and nourishes a deep hatred for the boy. When a murder is
committed nearby and reporters flock to the scene, she gets a whiff
of printer's ink and all the old Mary Garden rises to the surface.
In seizing her last chance for publicity, she nearly sends her boy to
the gallows. This weird study in the prima donna temperament is
superbly acted by Louise Dresser and wonderfully directed by Clarence Brown.
                                --A. S. in Photoplay, Vol. 28, No.
                                4 (September 1925), page 50.

☐ GOSTA BERLING'S SAGA (Svensk Filmindustri, 1924)

This was the only European film appearance of Greta Garbo
before she was sold down the river to Hollywood. * Moreover, it
was directed by Mauritz Stiller, who discovered her. It need only
be said that Hollywood has made the Glamorous One. In the picture
she photographs execrably, and acts like an anemic clam. Stiller's
work is in evidence, and there is a good performance by Lars Hanson. You won't die in vain even if you miss this one.
                                        --Photoplay, Vol. 35, No. 2
                                        (January 1929), page 92.

*Incorrect, of course!

☐ THE GRAND DUCHESS AND THE WAITER (Famous Players-
Lasky/Paramount, 1926)

A dramatic bonbon that will not improve your mind nor help
you hold your husband nor solve how to pay the mortgage. But how
it will delight you if you belong to that class which finds an unlifted
eyebrow more stimulating than a heaving chest.

It is love in high society with a charm as gentle and exhilar-
ating as spring about it. Like all well made bonbons, it is pure
and sweet and ultra-sophisticated.

Malcolm St. Clair has directed it flawlessly. Another picture
of this calibre from this young man and his will be a name well
worth following to any box office.

The title tells the whole story. In fact, the story matters
not at all in this picture. It is the talents of Adolphe Menjou and
Florence Vidor shining forth from it like bubbles in champagne that
make it the delicious thing it is.

Florence, appearing more beautiful and smartly gowned than
ever before, plays an impoverished and very grand Duchess. Menjou is a French sportsman, who pretends to be a waiter simply to
know and serve her. Suspecting his lowly love, the Grand Duchess,
not suspecting his wealth, determines to humiliate him into leaving.
She makes him wash the dogs. She makes him take them, four
wolfhounds and two poms, for a walk in the park. She makes him
sleep on her doorstep and retrieve her book from her bathtub.
Menjou executes all her commands, suave and smitten to the end.
And then when love begins to dawn on the Grand Duchess--well, go
see it for yourself.

Sophistication and sex at their merriest are here. Yet so
beautifully is it all handled it is safe for everyone from grandma
down to the baby.
                                        --Photoplay, Vol. 24, No. 5
                                        (April 1926), page 54.

☐ GRANDMA'S BOY (Roach/Pathe, 1922)

This picture is to Harold Lloyd what The Kid was to Chaplin
--his first five reeler, his first real approach to a seriously dramatic subject and also the high water mark of his career.

In Grandma's Boy, Lloyd appears as a mild young man, who
is actually afraid of his own shadow. So pronounced does his cowardice become, that his little old grandmother decides to adopt
drastic means to inject a little pep into his system. She tells him

how his grandfather (also played by the energetic Harold, with side
whiskers and square spectacles) outwitted the entire Union army
during the Civil War.   She even gives the boy the charm which had
inspired his grandfather to do the trick.   Armed with this, he goes
out and tears up the community, capturing a dangerous criminal and
beating out his formidable rival for the love of a sweet young
blonde.   (Yes, it is Mildred Davis.)

    Words are inadequate to describe the various virtues of
Grandma's Boy.   It is genuinely marvellous.

--Photoplay, Vol. 22, No. 2
(July 1922), page 52.

*   *   *

    Nine-tenths of the native product for which may be claimed
some measure of freshness and creative ingenuity, falls into the
general category of comedy.   And of this nine-tenths the greater
part is strongly tinctured with slapstick.   In the past year, however, there has developed a definite tendency to inject a social
satire into the films, using for the machinery of doing this a combination of straight comedy and certain elements of the so-called
garden variety.   To these elements, as in the notable examples of
One Glorious Day and The Kid, a certain quantity of the grotesque
has sometimes been added, and the result has been an indication
of something new to come, peculiar at once to the genius of American humor and to the terms of the cinema medium.

    Harold Lloyd's latest vehicle, "Grandma's Boy," is an in-
vention somewhat along these lines.   It carries on what The Kid
began as a form of picture, developing its comedy around a trivial
but definite plot, utilizing a concept of character, and putting across
through a series of buffooneries its cartoon of human nature.

    In the case of Grandma's Boy the satire is not incisive;
there is neither the originality and daring of The Kid nor the whimsy and subtle implications of One Glorious Day; but it is all done
with a grin and a chuckle and a fine sense of the incongruous, with
a sure technique of building the preposterous on the ridiculous until
a clear and well proportioned idea is presented.

    Mr. Lloyd, in his steady rise to prominence as an actor
and picture-maker, has in a way been marked by a cleverness, an
ingenious ability to construct carefully planned, swift-moving,
smooth-running farce situation.   Only in his most recent pictures
has his intellectual interest become apparent.   Grandma's Boy
evinces a keenness, a dry witticism, that at once lays claim to
recognition for being more serious entertainment than the majority
of the audience who will have the joy of seeing it, will in all like-
lihood detect.   For the first time Mr. Lloyd becomes somewhat
more than a droll figure projecting his nimble frame through a
series of twirling hoops.   In the inhibited and trampled upon Harold, peering hopelessly at life through berimmed goggles, one is

aware of one of life's failures, more pathetic than mirth-provoking.
It is a tribute to Mr. Lloyd's acting that one can always find the
heart to laugh at him.   It is as if he had said, "I will give you a
comedy, if that you must have, but it will all be a very serious
matter for my character Harold!"

Space is too brief to go into the detail of this story of a
country boy, victimized by the bully who is his rival, laughed at
by the neighbors, understood only by the wizened old lady who perceives the latent valor in her grandson's narrow breast and by a
pure gem of imagination eggs him on to a finding of himself.   Lest
one think this smacks of heroics, it shall be disclosed that Harold's
metamorphosis is accompanied by pitching down wells, sitting upon
pitchforks, slipping from pigs' backs, and the loss of seat of at
least one pair of breeches.   There is also about the most ludicrous
and at the same time convincing fight that has ever been placed
upon the screen for the delectation of the blood-thirsty, as well as
a whiff of love aroma far too delicate to be a stench in the nostrils.
Everything, indeed, is there for those who are weary of life and of
business and just want to laugh--and something more besides.
That something is another signpost on the way that American producers must travel if they wish to keep the interest of the public,
as it is whispered they do, providing they could only find out how.
And that something is also a little flag, not of truce, but of defi-
ance, to those godly souls crying in the wilderness for clean pictures whilst they whittle the brambles to sharper points in order to
impale the motion picture with the thorns, so to speak, of censorship.

--Exceptional Photoplays, Vol. 2,
No. 2 (March-May 1922), pages
6 and 7.

☐ GRASS (Famous Players-Lasky/Paramount, 1925)

Here is an engrossing motion picture.   It makes one stop to
ponder if a lot more time isn't being wasted than critics say by producing in studios so much popular fiction and such, frequently with
unnotable results, when, by going into the great natural amphitheatre
of real life and people, the cinema camera can be made to furnish
dramatic and entertaining film of such unusual, refreshing order.

There is only one other picture so far exhibited that can be
compared to Grass, that is Nanook of the North.   The latter picture, which can never be mentioned too often, was a photographic
record, like Grass, of real people in actual combat with Nature.
Like Grass, it was drama of the most thrilling order; instead of
plot and characters, we had Man and the elements that represented
the circumstances that sought to overcome him, the force against
which he struggled and over which he prevailed.   Both Grass and
Nanook prove conclusively that no medium approaches that of the

motion picture in its power to portray such a conflict; both pictures
also go a long way to suggest the kind of thing that the motion picture can do best and should do more often.   It is not being over-
sanguine to say that in time, as such pictures take hold on audiences, they will preempt the attention now commanded by so-called
dramatic films.   For such pictures are the real photoplay and their
range of action is the world.

Grass is the picture of an exodus into a promised land. It
affords a vicarious experience through the sun and wind of the desert, across a deep and swirling Asiatic river, up a deep and for-
bidding mountain side in bleak snow, and through a craggy pass into
a valley of rest and plenty where the tents are unfolded and the
portion of the flocks that has survived is turned loose in the
dreamed-of grass.   It is a theme of conquest, of the defeat of heat
and icy water and snow and mountain blast to the ultimate winning
of the pleasant meadows.   The driving impulse of its actors is the
need for sustenance.   The gaining of that sustenance is the measure
of Man's courage and his beasts' endurance.   The picture might
well be called The Will To Live.   We of this modern civilization
have forgotten what this will entailed upon our primitive forefathers
and still entails upon the primitive peoples of the earth.   Grass
teaches us, for in its scenes we see the living problem of this
tribe of the Bakhtiari who ever so often must move their habitation,
carrying with them all their earthly possessions, in order to provide the food for their herds and flocks, and so for themselves,
that Nature in her malevolent moods of drought has taken away.
Thus the lives of these people are lived in the expectation of mi-
gration--in a moving onward in the past, present and future, in the
lives of their fathers, themselves, their children and their children's
children, when the hand of Nature closes on their food supply.
Such migration is in the consciousness of their race and in their
dreams; the hope of grass is their racial aspiration.

The art of this picture lies in the perception of the motion
picture camera and in the imaginative selection of the things it is
asked by its operator to record.   The picture opens with a fine
suggestion of the distance across the desert by horse and camel
voyage to the land of the tribe whose travail it will portray.   Need-
less to say, it is not a movie desert that is traversed.   It is a
desert of wind-burning days and cold nights in crumbling old court-
yards--broken stone oases filled with tired camels and strange
faces, where simple supper is prepared with utensils used before
the pyramids were raised.   At last we come upon the tribe which
at the moment is expectant of the drought.   There is a fine old
stoic chief, who is the counterpart of Nanook.   We make his acquaintance about the moment his tribesmen come in from an inspec-
tion of the flocks to confirm his own estimate of the situation.
Without any ado, he gives the order, the belongings are packed,
the tents struck, all the little things of everyday life collected, the
livestock rounded up, and the nomad community set on the move.
As it progresses, other communities, other herds and flocks, join
it.   Soon we have the picture of a whole people journeying, hardly

pausing to sleep or eat.   The tribes come to a swirling river which
must be crossed in order to climb the mountains beyond and reach
fertile land.   We have been aware of impending drama.   The situation in which the characters must untangle themselves from the
circumstance that holds them reveals itself startlingly with the first
view of that wide yet sinuous rapid water curving like a sword laid
between waste and plenty.   Here is the great act.   The tribes set
briskly, as if they were on a business venture or an excursion,
about the task of crossing the river.   They blow up goat-skins, tie
them together and make rafts.   They truss up the goats (which it
appears cannot swim) and lay them on their backs on the rafts.
The women-folk, with tents and a great conglomeration of para-
phernalia, climb aboard the rafts with them.   The rafts are
launched, each with two men paddling furiously at the bow.   Then
the flocks and herds are dragged or driven into the water until the
current seizes them and they are swept off to swim or be sucked
under.   With the animals go men wildly whirling on the surface
each on his inflated goat-skin, strangely like children on water-
wings swimming in the undertow.   Soon the scene is one continuous
processional of rafts, goat-skins with their single passenger, and
thousands of dots representing the heads of struggling drowning animals.   A subtitle tells us that one out of every ten of these is
sucked down in the passage.   Then we see this happening.   Heads
in the wake of the raft bearing the camera point up a moment from
the furrows of the current then vanish as if their bodies were
seized by the legs and pulled under.   Here and there a man on a
goatskin reaches out and holds up a calf or a lamb until the further
bank is reached.   It is like the river in Kubla Khan, rushing down
toward measureless caverns to fall into a sunless sea, but with a
multitude foolishly trying to cross it.   We have the feeling of fan-
tasmagoria.   It is a greater spectacle than any of the Barnums of
the movies have invented.   It is the sight of Man's will against
Nature's.   Doré's imagination might have conjured it.

        Then comes the scenes of the surviving flocks and herds
swirled against the further shore, struggling out of their immersion,
being dragged to safety by the ever-busy tribesmen, who launch
themselves on their bloated-skin boats time and again, swirling off
toward the rapids, to get as many of their possessions as possible
safely to shore.   Everlastingly, it seems, the tribesmen keep
crossing.   As soon as they have landed they unload, repack, and
start the climb to the highlands, sometimes hoisting the animals
straight up cliffs.   We have the feeling of weariness, of endless
effort.   Through the last sequences of the picture, we too begin to
look hopefully for the grass.   Yet through it all, the hardy nomads
are astonishing in their stoical optimism, their endless resource of
strength and cunning, their assumption of hardship as if they were
doing a casual thing.

        The picture closes in a mood of quiet, of danger overcome,
in the good sight of tents going up and the beginning of rest and of
the tired flocks and herds in this new and hard-won land putting

their muzzles in the spreading grass.

--Exceptional Photoplays, Vol. 5,
Nos. 5 and 6 (February-March
1925), pages 1-2.

* * *

A genuinely great picture--with no actors, no scenario and
no bunk.

--Robert E. Sherwood in Life,
Vol. 85, No. 2222 (June 4,
1925), page 35.

☐ THE GREAT GABBO (James Cruze/Sono Art-World Wide, 1929)

If you are interested in such a theoretical matter as Hollywood irony, you may possibly be entertained by the sight of Erich
von Stroheim acting away for comparatively dear life in the title
role of a picture called The Great Gabbo. It is not that there is
anything inherently comic in this juxtaposition of names, or a detail
lacking in the distinguished Austrian's performance. The point is
that it seems a bit curious to come upon von Stroheim, divorced
from every trace of managerial authority, his characterization
guided by a director of less than his quality, playing in a picture
perfectly suited to his strange perverse directorial genius.

You will remember, provided you read cinema criticism with
reasonable care, that The Great Gabbo was the drama that combined the absurdities of one of those irritating screen comedies with
a shrewd psychological idea that was amazingly distinctive for either
photoplay or stage.

This curious amalgamation of the two most contradictory elements possible in the current theatre resulted in a shambling and
thoroughly ineffective mass that wasted one of the grandest dramas
recently offered. When the screen tries an enormously ingenious
amalgamation of Strange Interlude, Strindberg and The Picture of
Dorian Gray, which must certainly be the most extreme thing that
this essentially conservative medium has yet dared, it really deserves a chance to make something of it. It seems to me, therefore, that when a major handicap is offered the idea in the form of
one of those routine musical comedies that insist on cluttering up
the cinema, an entirely unforgivable sin is committed against a
dramatic form that is striving desperately to get somewhere.

The story, it is only fair to remind you, is one of the most
ingenious of recent fables, a narrative that is likely to provide more
respect for the skill of the erratic Mr. Ben Hecht than his other
achievements have recently aroused. Its hero is an arrogant, ego-
tistical ventriloquist, who, though at heart sentimental, is afraid to

express his romanticism in person and must use his dummy as the
vehicle of his poetry.   It is, therefore, fairly logical that the girl
he loves, but is afraid to provide with tenderness, cries out for
the mechanical figure's sympathy.

Slowly she comes to hate the arrogant, strutting, imbecile
who had been cruel to her and to love the lifeless dummy, who had
expressed all the vagrant kindness that the savage, but inherently
sentimental, egoist had silently felt for her.   Under that feminine
influence, the man lapses into a cold, mechanical inhumanity that
is soulless and savage, while the wooden figure slowly takes on an
aspect of humanity which makes the ventriloquist hate it and the
girl worship its gentleness.   It is the climax of the narrative that,
at the end, the Nietzschean ventriloquist becomes so jealous of the
mechanical figure that he is driven to murder a wooden image that
is more human than he and that the image has become so alive that
it cries out in despair when it is being throttled.   Then, having
smashed the doll which was, after all, merely a prop in his act,
the Great Gabbo feels that he has become a murderer and falls
wildly into an assassin's insanity.

That, at least, is the idea of the motion picture which features this somewhat neurotic plot.   In the films, though, it is so
carelessly handled, so obviously unconcerned with the import of its
story and so completely wasted in the morass of its cheap and
clumsy musical comedy scenes that it is difficult to recognize its
potential value.   It rambles clumsily and it wastes every dramatic
opportunity that should be so obvious to the most immature of the
cinema directors.   Since Mr. Cruze, who made The Great Gabbo,
is by no means anything like that, the failure of the picture can
only be ascribed to a sinister carelessness of manufacture.   A
magnificent idea is wasted and you can regard that as one of the
greatest sins yet committed against the oncoming talking photoplay.

The point of this jest about von Stroheim is that, after failing to do justice to one of his ideas, the film manufacturers beg
him to save them.   The Great Gabbo was an ideal directorial vehicle to the man who, next to Chaplin, is probably the one authentic
genius that the cinema has yet offered us.   Instead of allowing him
to produce the work, however, the Hollywood magnates, who still
insist on building up the fiction that he is the most extravagant,
impractical and generally destructive of the film makers, merely
hired him for the all-important title role and, without giving him
any chance to handle the treatment of the work, depended on his
acting to write in every quality of the narrative and its idea that
they were unable to achieve.

It seemed to me that von Stroheim overacted a bit too much
for comfort, that he was too pompous, too strutting and generally
too emphatic for credibility, even as the self-centered ventriloquist
of the fable.   His portrayal, however, was so brilliantly devised,
so shrewd and, in its gruff way, so sensitive, and, above all, it
wrote in those qualities, by the sheer force of a brilliant perform-

ance, that the director and the authors were unable to devise, that
one can hardly deny that his is a great characterization and an
added proof of the departmental belief that he is one of the few
really significant figures in the motion picture. If the cinema would
just realize that and, as a conclusion, recognize that it should have
some consideration for the eccentricities and weaknesses of such a
valiant personage, it might be a more important force in our cultural life.

--Richard Watts, Jr. in The Film
Mercury, Vol. 10, No. 9 (Octo-
ber 4, 1929), page 4.

☐ GREED (Metro-Goldwyn, 1925)

Greed, the much talked of picturization of Frank Norris'
McTeague, is a picture of undeniable power. Erich von Stroheim
has let himself go and has produced a picture which by virtue of
choice of subject, treatment, and emphasis represents a logical
development in the work of the creator of Blind Husbands, The
Devil's Pass Key and Foolish Wives. Mr. von Stroheim is one of
the great stylists of the screen whose touch is recognizable in
everything he does. He has always been the realist as Rex Ingram
is the romanticist and Griffith the sentimentalist of the screen, and
in Greed he has given us an example of realism at its starkest.

Like the novel from which the plot was taken Greed is a terrible and wonderful thing. McTeague is one of the most savage,
uncompromising, ugliest novels ever written. It achieved fame and
continues to be read as an example of the horrible. It must be
considered in any survey of the development of the American novel.

In judging the picture which Mr. Stroheim has made from it
we must use the widest possible perspective. For motion picture
art has by this time attained its majority. It is entitled to experiment in any form from the ultra-sentimental to the latest fad in
symbolism. The days of censorship in that sense, the feeling that
motion pictures must always be pretty pictures, are over. The
time has come when we can invite the spirit of Matthew Arnold to
the screen to see what he saw in literature, namely a criticism of
life.

Most emphatically there is and should be a place for a picture like Greed. It is undoubtedly one of the most uncompromising
films ever shown on the screen. There have already been many
criticisms of its brutality, its stark realism, its sordidness. But
the point is that it was never intended to be a pleasant picture. It
is a picture that is grown up with a vengeance, a theme for just
those adults who have been complaining most about the sickening
sentimentality of the average film. Nobody can complain of being
deceived when he goes to see it; Zola did not compete with Gautier

and Frank Norris would never have sent any story of his to True
Romance.

Lest it be considered that so far this review has been propaganda rather than criticism, we hasten to add that Greed is not our
idea of a perfect picture.   It is sometimes easier to make a perfect picture than a real one.   Scaramouche, which has just won the
Adolph Zukor $10, 000 prize, is one of those perfect pictures.   It
is slick and polished, deftly acted, correct in setting and costume.
But it is not really very much alive.   Its perfections satiate rather
than stir.   Stroheim could do that sort of thing; in fact he has done
it.   But it is entirely to his credit that he has preferred to do
some pioneer work.   His picture, it is true, has generated the
heat of controversy but the very picture people who today are saying that he has gone beyond what is permissible on the screen tomorrow will be copying him.

The picture follows the novel with considerable accuracy.
It gives the essentials of McTeague in so far as that could be done
upon the screen.   Just how far Stroheim succeeded in this respect
will, however, never be known.   For the original picture was made
in no less than forty reels which were first cut down to twenty-four,
then to twelve or less.   Inevitably much must have been sacrificed
in this process of reduction and one certainly misses some of the
motivation.

But these omissions hardly impair the primitive impact of
the story and the Death Valley sequence would stand out in any picture as a sort of travelogue through Hell.   Some of the details of
the picture, the sheer animalism of the characters as reflected in
their every manner, have been the subject of much criticism.   But
Stroheim set out to show that greed is an ugly cankerous thing and
in his conception everybody and everything in the picture becomes
smudged with this quality.   Sometimes the sense of ugliness becomes overwhelming so that it disturbs our aesthetic reaction.   The
best form of realism in any art does not do this and to that extent
Stroheim has failed to do what he set out to accomplish.   But that
is one of the penalties of experimentation and should not become an
unconditional criticism of the picture.

The acting honors of this remarkable production are so evenly divided that it is hard to say whether the characterization of Mc-
Teague by Gibson Gowland or of his wife by ZaSu Pitts is the more
memorable.   Both create the illusion that they are not acting at all.
They build up the characters slowly and carefully and carry the
spectator with them at every point.   Jean Hersholt's impersonation
of Marcus Schouler, McTeague's false friend, is hardly less skillful though it, together with the other characters, shows some of the
exaggerations of low comedy into which the actors were undoubtedly
pushed by Stroheim's over-direction.   There are times when Stroheim squeezes the lemon a little too hard.

--Exceptional Photoplays, Vol. 5,
Nos. 3 and 4 (December-January 1925), pages 2 and 3.

*   *   *

The New York newspaper critics acclaimed it as a masterpiece. Greed is sordid.   Greed is depressing.   Greed is brutal. Greed is shocking.   It reeks with good acting and wonderful direction.   Translated to the screen from Frank Norris's McTeague, Director von Stroheim has emphasized the detail of a sordid story until it becomes almost repulsive.   It is the realism of vulgarity to the nth degree, and if that is art, von Stroheim has produced a masterpiece.   This is not one of Photoplay's six best, and it is given a place on this page only because of its news value.

--James R. Quirk in Photoplay,
Vol. 27, No. 3 (February 1925),
page 55.

*   *   *

Ferocity, brutality, muscle, vulgarity, crudity, naked realism and sheer genius are to be found--great hunks of them--in von Stroheim's production, Greed.   It is a terribly powerful picture--and an important one.

When von Stroheim essayed to convert Frank Norris's McTeague into a movie, he assumed what is technically known as a man-sized job.   There was absolutely nothing in this novel of entertainment value, heart interest or box-office appeal--none of the qualities that are calculated to attract the shrewd eye of the movie mogul.

Nevertheless, there were the elements of fierce drama in McTeague, and these have been taken by von Stroheim and turned loose on the screen.   He has followed copy with such extraordinary fidelity that there is no scene in the picture, hardly a detail, that is not recognizable to those who have read the book.

The acting in Greed is uneven: Gibson Gowland is practically perfect as McTeague, as are ZaSu Pitts and Jean Hersholt as Trina and Marcus Schouler; but von Stroheim has been guilty of gross exaggeration in his treatment of the subordinate characters.   They are an artificial lot, derived from the comic strips rather than from reality.

Atmospherically, Greed is marvelous.   The costumes, the settings and the properties are just as Norris described them. McTeague wears a plaid cap which may be rated as the most appropriate article of attire ever displayed on the screen.

There are two defects in Greed--one of which is almost fatal.

In the first place, von Stroheim has chosen to be symbolic at intervals, and has inserted some very bad hand-coloring to emphasize the goldenness of gold.   This detracts greatly from the realism of the picture.

In the second place, von Stroheim has been, as usual, so
extravagant with his footage that Greed in its final form is merely
a series of remnants.   It has been cut to pieces--so that entire
sequences and important characters have been left out.   Thus the
story has a choppy quality; many of its developments are abrupt.
We see Trina in one instant the tremulous young bride, and in the
next the hard, haggard, scheming shrew of several years later.
The intervening stages in her spiritual decay are not shown, although von Stroheim undoubtedly included them originally.

This is von Stroheim's own fault.   He must learn to acquire
some regard for the limitations of space.   Greed, I understand,
was produced in forty reels, which would take eight hours to un-
wind; and the eight-hour day for movie fans has not yet dawned--
thank God!

Von Stroheim is a genius--Greed establishes that beyond all
doubt--but he is badly in need of a stopwatch.

--Robert E. Sherwood in Life,
Vol. 85, No. 2200 (January 1,
1925), page 24.

☐ HALLELUJAH (M-G-M, 1929)

Hallelujah is a magnificent motion picture, a magnificent
tribute to the genius of King Vidor, and a magnificent achievement
that reflects the greatest credit on Metro-Goldwyn-Mayer as a producing organization that is striving for the best there is in screen
art.   Not even superlatives can do it credit.   It is a gorgeous poem
of the South, both dramatically and pictorially.   Its all-Negro cast
gives us some superb performances, and Gordon Avil with his camera gives us a succession of views of surpassing beauty.   The
story is a gripping one, emotional, dramatic and human, and even
though the production is strong in atmosphere and many of the
scenes are notable for their composition, lighting, and photography,
Vidor tells the story briskly and without circumlocution.   Eastern
writers who have seen the picture disagree about the faithfulness
with which Vidor has caught the spirit of the Negro and presented
it on the screen.   Not being qualified as an authority on the subject, I cannot take sides in the controversy, but I am content with
what he gives us.   If he has caught the spirit accurately he is to
be congratulated upon the efficiency with which he screened it; and
if he failed to catch it accurately, he is to be congratulated even
more upon the extraordinary attractiveness with which he gives us
his conception of the South.   There is no doubt about the honesty
of the camera, which caught scenes that make the picture an entrancing journey through an idealized South.   In addition to dealing
with the joys and sorrows of the colored people the production follows the progress of cotton from the field to the factory, to that
extent giving the film an educational value.   As is the case with

most of the productions that have come to us from the cradle of
the sound device, this one in places is more noisy than it need be,
and the sharp cutting that apparently was necessary to bring the
picture down to length causes too many abrupt terminations to entertaining musical numbers.   At first I thought a weakness of the
story would be its difficulty in enlisting our sympathies for characters who have no personal appeal to us, but soon I found myself
being swept along with the current of the story, and admiring
greatly the superb performances of Daniel L. Haynes and Nina
Mae McKinney, who have the leading parts.   I even went so far
as to sympathize with the villain, William Fountaine, and I loved
the dear old mammy of the picture, Fannie Belle DeKnight.   Harry
Gray, Everett McGarrity, and Victoria Spivey also are to be credited with splendid performances.   But Vidor is the man to whom
the major praise must be given.   As a creation it is entirely his,
as he wrote as well as directed the story.   He has a place of his
own among American directors.   He is as fearless as are those
foreign directors who give us beautiful works of screen art that
enrich the screen even if they do not enrich their producers.   I
can not imagine that Hallelujah will fail to earn a large profit, but
even if it should fail to do so, it is of tremendous value as a contribution to the art of the screen.   There is one sequence in it
which I think is the finest thing ever done by an American director.   Toward the end of the picture the villain lures the girl away,
and the hero, after the girl dies, goes out in pursuit of the man
who wrecked his home.   The villain flees in terror through a
swamp that Avil has photographed with extraordinary effect.   Behind him comes the relentless pursuer.   The villain runs, stumbles,
and sometimes falls, but the pace of the hero always is the same,
a deliberate, deadly, menacing advance straight toward his quarry.
The sequence is directed and cut in a manner that makes it an
outstanding example of the steady building of dramatic intensity.
Directed less skillfully and acted with less understanding, it would
not justify the footage devoted to it, but as handled by Vidor,
Haynes, and Fountaine, it is extraordinarily effective.   In sharp
contrast to this sequence is the note struck in the one which follows it, and with which the picture ends.   The homecoming of
Haynes, after serving a term in prison for the murder of Fountaine, is another fine bit of intelligent and human direction.   It
gives us again a shot which we saw earlier in the picture, a
camera etching of superlative beauty in which Avil seems to have
caught the whole spirit of the picture.   Hallelujah should go into
every motion picture theater in the world.

                              --Welford Beaton in The Film
                                Spectator, Vol. 8, No. 11
                                (November 2, 1929), pages 4-5.

☐ HANDS UP (Famous Players-Lasky/Paramount, 1926)

        A mild and harmless comedy not up to the standard of the
usual Raymond Griffith comedies.   All about the adventures of a

Confederate spy who tries to prevent the North from receiving
gold.   He almost completes his mission when peace is declared.
Raymond Griffith's goings on and dainty Marion Nixon and Virginia
Lee Corbin in the cast give the picture its chief claim to your attention.
                                   --Photoplay, Vol. 24, No. 4
                                     (March 1926), page 56.

◻ HE WHO GETS SLAPPED (M-G-M, 1924)

     When Victor Seastrom presented his version of Hall Caine's
Name the Man we were disappointed.   He failed to rise much above
the level of a fourth rate novel.   But this adaptation of Leonid Andreyev's He Who Gets Slapped is a superb thing--and it lifts Seastrom to the very front rank of directors.

     This fatalistic Russian drama is a bizarre thing; of a sci-
entist who, wrecked by a faithless wife, seeks to forget as a clown
in a small traveling circus.   He becomes the famous and mysterious "he who gets slapped."   In the same circus is a pretty little
rider, daughter of a derelict count.   He comes to love the girl,
Consuelo, but he masks his longing behind his grotesquely painted
face.   Consuelo loves a young rider.   The count tries to sell his
daughter to another but He saves her for her lover, and gives his
life that she may live on and be happy.

     All this is unfolded in a series of beautiful camera pictures,
technically faultless.   It is told clearly and directly in pantomime,
as is the right function of the photoplay.   True, there are subtitles, but in the main they are philosophic (and well written) com-
ments upon the action.   Andreyev's play was elusive behind the
footlights.   Enmeshed in celluloid by Seastrom, it gains immeasurably in clarity.   The director has taken liberties with the original
story, but they seem to us logical and in the spirit of the Russian
dramatist's original theme.

     The acting is remarkably fine.   Lon Chaney does the best
work of his career.   Here his performance has breadth, force and
imagination.   Tully Marshall, as usual, gives an outstanding performance, and Norma Shearer and Jack Gilbert, as the lovers, are
delightful.
                                   --Photoplay, Vol. 27, No. 2
                                     (January 1925), page 61.

◻ THE HEADLESS HORSEMAN (Sleepy Hollow Production/Hodkin-
     son, 1922)

     No matter what the difference of opinion may be as to the
Will Rogers screen production of The Legend of Sleepy Hollow

(The Headless Horseman) as a whole--whether one is inclined to be
satisfied or disappointed--there will probably be general agreement
as to Mr. Rogers having given us a unique and whimsically original
character in his figure of the gaunt and comical Yankee schoolmaster of the Irving tale. The crane-like quality, the scare-crow
grotesqueness, of the original is missing. On the other hand, the
original misses somewhat of the drawing of Mr. Rogers--notably,
in the element, of human pathos and clown-like likeability, on the
part of the poor alien who, striving to knock some learning into
the thick pates of their children, finds himself the butt of the
burghers' sturdy Dutch humor. Thus, it is an original, but none
the less honest, reading of the role; it stamps Mr. Rogers as an
actor of versatility--as an artist more concerned with doing truth
to human nature than doing human nature at the expense of truth.
Not that Mr. Rogers needed to furnish proof of this virtue, or to
give further assurance that as long as he continues in pictures
credit will be reflected on the American screen.

--Exceptional Photoplays, Vol. 3,
No. 1 (November 1922), page 4.

☐ HELL'S ANGELS (Caddo/United Artists, 1930)

        Hell's Angels, which took three years and several lives to
make, is sorely handicapped. Only in spots is it great, notably in
the immensity and daring of its flying stuff. Ben Lyon and James
Hall, as the brothers, are splendid. Jean Harlow, newcomer,
tries hard with an unsympathetic rôle. The rest of the cast is
fine. Now, don't mistake. Hell's Angels is worth seeing. But
$4,000,000 worth?

--Photoplay, Vol. 38, No. 3
(August 1930), page 55.

☐ HIS PEOPLE (Universal, 1925)

        A marvelous picture dealing with the simple happenings from
the everyday life of the Ghetto folks. The story is filled with the
human interest stuff that is appreciated by so many fans. The
Comisky family is no different than a goodly number of families
now living on the East Side today. Many have the same high ideals
as the father, a Russian immigrant. Realism is the keynote
throughout the picture and never does it become stagey.

        The production ranks high in quality, which speaks for the
masterly direction of Edward Sloman.

        The cast, consisting of Rudolph Schildkraut, Gordon Lewis,
Blanche Mehaffey and Kate Price, is excellent. Schildkraut, as

the father, gives one of the most impressive performances seen on
the screen this year.

--Photoplay, Vol. 24, No. 1
(December 1925), page 46.

☐ HOLLYWOOD (Famous Players-Lasky/Paramount, 1923)

Moving pictures, like plays and novels, travel in cycles; one
thing leads to another, and a successful film will inevitably inspire
a legion of imitators.   Thus, The Birth of a Nation started a deluge
of patriotic spectacles; Is Any Girl Safe? promoted a number of
"daring" exposés of the white slave traffic, and incidentally provoked the first agitation for motion picture censorship; The Miracle
Man was followed by a dreary array of "moral" pictures, in which
the religious note was heavily stressed; The Spoilers pointed the
way for innumerable red-blooded, two-fisted, he-men melodramas
of the Great Northwest; Intolerance discovered the possibilities in
ancient Babylon; Passion was responsible for the recent abundance
of costume dramas; Over the Hill established the box-office value
of mother love.

The current cycle of Hollywood pictures dates from the publication of Harry Leon Wilson's novel, Merton of the Movies, and
from the poisonous wave of scandal which swept through the yellow
journals of our fair nation after the Arbuckle and Taylor cases.
Hollywood became the most notorious community on the face of the
earth, being associated in the public mind with such historic bor-
oughs as Nineveh, Tyre, Babylon, Sodom and Gomorrah.   It was
the subject of many an ardent sermon, and consequently it became
a Mecca for tourists.   Solid citizens from all over the country
journeyed out to the citadel of the silent drama in quest of a thrill.

The movie producers, ever ready to cash in on a burst of
publicity, started in to make pictures which would draw aside the
veil of secrecy surrounding themselves.   In doing so, most of them
succeeded only in increasing the thickness and opaqueness of that
veil.   They gave us several movies about Hollywood that were very
bad indeed.

There was one standard plot for all these films: a small-
town girl goes out to Hollywood in search of work, finds it and becomes in no time at all a world-famous star.   There was practically
no variation to this theme.

Frank Condon, a flippant member of Hollywood's younger literary set, decided to write a burlesque of the many stories then
current--telling of a girl who went to California and found neither
fame nor fortune.   He sold his yarn to Photoplay Magazine and it
occasioned considerable talk among the readers of that publication;
by violating all the accepted tenets of movie fiction, it shook their

faith in the theory that determination, willpower and adherence to all the moral laws will inevitably win out in the end.

Of the history of this sacrilegious story, Mr. Condon writes:

> "Hollywood was originally a short story, called in California a 'reading' story, to distinguish it from other forms of narrative. When it was quite a young thing, I did not expect ever to see it grow up, put on long pants and become a motion picture, although such a future was discussed. It was the opinion of several experts in motion pictures that nothing could be done, pictorially speaking, with the plot of Hollywood, because of its obvious frailty. It was too thin. There was not enough plot to it, and furthermore, it had no villain at all, which of course, settled it.
>
> "It was laid upon the shelf, with all the other little half-dead stories, and remained there for many weeks, until one day Mr. J. L. Lasky heard about it and remarked casually that he didn't see why it wouldn't make a picture. After that, its health improved noticeably.
>
> "In writing the story, I aimed at no great moral reform, nor did I strive to satirize, or reveal secrets of the movie folk, who, as a general rule, have no more secrets than other people. All I planned to do was to write a yarn wherein the beautiful and innocent young heroine did not get a job. I realized that this would be difficult, when I started, and likewise unprecedented. Worthy maidens have been descending upon Hollywood for several years, in fiction, and I have noticed that about seven paragraphs from the end, the ambitious lady invariably signs a contract with the largest film corporation in California and becomes a star. There has never been any departure from this formula. When I spoke to my friends about it, they shook their heads and advised me not to monkey with a time-honored tradition, and that if I did, no good would come of it.
>
> "This general feeling about heroines only annoyed me. I decided that I would have a heroine who not only did not get a job in the movies, but who did not get a job anywhere. She could starve, for all I cared, but she certainly would not go to work, as long as I had anything to do with her. I even refused to find employment for her in a restaurant, or a drug store.
>
> "When it came to making the motion picture, numerous persons put the heroine to work, and I fired her. This continued for weeks and it was contended by the experts that you could not make a motion picture unless the heroine finished in a blaze of glory, seated before the desk of a famous producer, with the contract ready for her signature."

Several unsuccessful attempts were made to write an adequate continuity for Mr. Condon's story, but the job was finally done, and

with considerable skill, by Tom Geraghty. The directorial duties were
assigned to James Cruze, who had just completed The Covered Wagon.

At Condon's suggestion, it was decided to fill in the background
of the picture with prominent stars, whose countenances would be
familiar to the public and who could consequently appear in their own
identities without undue explanation. Of course, everyone in the
Paramount corral was used, with an imposing list of outsiders dragged
in. Tom Geraghty prevailed upon Douglas Fairbanks, Mary Pickford
and Charlie Chaplin to appear fleetingly on the scene, and their pres-
ences added materially to Hollywood's popular appeal.

However, this assemblage of stars, impersonating themselves,
proved a source of embarrassment in one respect: to avoid any overlapping between the real characters and the fictional ones, it was
necessary to recruit the actual cast of the piece from the most obscure
sources. Thus, the principal parts in Hollywood were played by actors
and actresses who had never been heard of before.

Hope Drown, who appeared as the hapless heroine, came
from a stock company in San Diego--this being her first appearance
on the screen.   Luke Cosgrave, another of the principals, was discovered by Cruze in a Salt Lake City stock company during the
period when The Covered Wagon company was out on location.   G.
K. Arthur had only just arrived in California from his native England when he was called upon to play the small-town hero of Hollywood.

Frank Condon's story started in the hamlet of Centerville,
where lived the Whitaker family, composed of Grandpa and Grandma
Whitaker, Aunt Margaret Whitaker and Angela Whitaker--the last an
average girl of average beauty and more than average ambition.
She and the other women of the family were devoted to the onerous
task of caring for Grandpop, a feeble, crotchety and utterly worthless old loafer.

Angela was a movie fan who attended regularly at the local
picture palace and dreamed of the day when she herself could go to
Hollywood and occupy a room and bath in the Celluloid Hall of
Fame.   Finally, she went--taking Grandpa along with her, in the
hope that the widely-advertised climate of California might either
kill him or cure him--it didn't much matter which.

On her first day in Hollywood, Angela started out on the
round of the studios in quest of employment, leaving Grandpa parked
on the hotel veranda and complaining bitterly.   Angela had been fed
with the stories of girls like herself who had gone to this strange
place and achieved instantaneous success; consequently she believed
that she need only present herself at any casting director's window
and wait for the celebration to start.

She trudged about from one studio to another, walking along
miles of boulevards while the sad pepper trees of Hollywood nodded

their sympathy; but none of the movie producers evinced the slightest interest in her, and she didn't see a single contract all day.

So, weary and worn, she returned to the hotel--to find that Grandpa had been picked up by William de Mille as a valuable "type," and had been working in pictures all day. From then on Angela met with one discouragement after another, while the rejuvenated Mr. Joel Whitaker stepped from triumph to triumph. The rest of the family travelled out from Centerville, and all of them found work in the silent drama.

Angela followed the dismal career mapped out for her by Frank Condon, and never succeeded in getting a job. However, there was some consolation. She married the young pants presser from Centerville, who had been her first beau and who had subsequently developed into a film star of the first magnitude, and the twin children which resulted from this union were engaged to act in the movies even before they had been graduated from the cradle.

James Cruze treated Hollywood as a fantasy rather than as a grimly realistic drama. Together with Tom Geraghty, he kidded his subject from start to finish, introducing elements of the wildest absurdity. In this way he avoided the semblance of propaganda; he never attempted to defend Hollywood, or the art of the motion picture; he never preached or moralized or drew conclusions.

In one episode he visualized a dream in which the Centerville pants presser imagined himself a knight errant who had journeyed to the Twentieth Century Babylon to rescue his girl from the clutches of that dread dragon, the Cinema. It was utter insanity. The various stars, garbed as sheiks, licentious club-men, aristocratic roués, bathing girls, apaches, and the like, moved about in weird confusion through a distorted nightmare. There was slow motion photography, reverse action and double exposure; no sense was made at any given point.

In another scene, Angela was shown making a futile application for work at the Christie Comedies studio. When she joined the line before the casting director's window, a corpulent gentleman stepped aside and politely gave her his place. When she had been firmly refused, the fat man walked up to make his plea but the window was slammed in his face and the word "CLOSED" displayed before his eyes. The camera was moved into a close-up, and Fatty Arbuckle was shown gazing at that one final word.

It was a superbly forcible touch, inserted in the picture without comment. Whether one feels sympathy or contempt for Arbuckle, one cannot deny that his was a vitally dramatic moment in Hollywood.

James Cruze worked over Hollywood for a long time--about eight months, in fact--for it wasn't easy to catalogue all the stars in that eventful community and at the same time maintain the con-

tinuity of his story. It was a weary, painful job, but he and Geraghty kept at it until they were sure they had done it right.

While Hollywood was in course of production, Rupert Hughes
was working at the Goldwyn studio in Culver City on a movie version
of his own novel, Souls for Sale, which purported to be another
revelation of life in the film capital. Souls for Sale was a highly
melodramatic story, designed to show the frightful risks that movie
stars must make for the sake of their art. It was all deadly serious, and it reeked with propaganda.

In its earlier form, Souls for Sale did not shape up as a
particularly stalwart success; but Rupert Hughes decided to follow
the example which Cruze was setting, and to insert a number of
well-known stars as "atmosphere" for his picture. So he dragged
them in by the ears, introducing them in batches of a dozen and
accounting for their presence in the picture in no logical way.

Because of the deliberate pace of Cruze's production, Souls
for Sale beat Hollywood to the screen by several months, and
achieved a tremendous financial success. But for all that, it was
an imitation--and a very bad one.

For one thing, Hughes had several well-known stars appearing in his purely imaginary rôles, and other stars appearing as
themselves--which caused a great deal of confusion. One never
knew, in Souls for Sale, where the plot ended and the propaganda
began.

The cast in Hollywood, composed of actors and actresses
who might just as well have been anonymous, gave a better account
of itself than did the stellar assemblage in Souls for Sale. G. K.
Arthur, who impersonated the Centerville tailor, contributed a performance of great sincerity, and the Whitaker family was capably
represented by Luke Cosgrave, Ruby Lafayette, Eleanor Lawson and
Hope Drown.

Miss Drown, as Angela, was wistful, appealing and supremely pathetic. Her wide eyes seemed to increase in depth and in
softness with each fresh disappointment. Indeed, there was something terribly sad about Hope Drown, entirely aside from the nature
of her part in Hollywood. Even her name carried a connotation of
inevitable doom.

She made a tremendous success in this, her first picture,
and everyone who watched her work was anxious to know whether
she would go on with the screen career that had started so aus-
piciously, or sink back into the obscurity from which she had come.

After the release of Hollywood, no announcements were made
as to Miss Drown's future plans, and she was permitted to drop out
of sight until a play called Peter Weston arrived in New York. On
the program of this piece, in the cast of characters, was the line:

"A Maid .... Hope Drown."

So the little Cinderella returned to the ashes, after all--
proving that Frank Condon's cynical story had a regrettably firm
basis of truth.

--Robert E. Sherwood in The Best
Moving Pictures of 1922-1923
(Small, Maynard and Company,
1923), pages 78-85.

*   *   *

Seeing yourself as others see you is said to be good medicine.   Showing yourself as others might see you if they had a six-
cylinder sense of humor certainly is good fun.   James Cruze has
tried the latter experiment in Hollywood, made from a story by
Frank Condon originally published in Photoplay, and the result is
one of the most successful of Paramount pictures.   Angela Whitaker
felt the urge to twinkle in Hollywood.   So she took her ill and aged
grandfather, and made the trip.   Angela didn't get a job.   Grandpa
did.   Angela's beau and her family felt something must be wrong,
so they followed after, and got jobs, too.

All the motion picture people you ever heard of are in this
picture.   By laughing at himself and his crowd Mr. Cruze has
turned out a rattling good film.

--Photoplay, Vol. 24, No. 5
(October 1923), page 72.

☐ HOLLYWOOD REVUE OF 1929 (M-G-M, 1929)

This is a great show for the money.   And there's something
in it for everybody.

Like Shakespeare?   Well, you'll find Jack Gilbert and Norma
Shearer as Romeo and Juliet.   Like low-brow slapstick?   Well,
there are Laurel and Hardy in a comedy act as low as they come.
Like big musical numbers with glorified gals singing and dancing?
All right, there's the hit, "Singing in the Rain," and many breath-
taking girl numbers.

Besides all this there are your favorite screen stars who do
their bits expertly.   Marion Davies is remarkably good in "Tommy
Atkins on Parade."   And can that girl tap dance?   Watch her!
Marie Dressler, Polly Moran, Bessie Love, Ukulele Ike, Charlie
King and Gus Edwards are howlingly funny in a Gay Nineties number.   Gus, by the way, does more than his share by appearing in
the show, writing most of the numbers and directing some of the
dancing acts, although Sammy Lee, of Ziegfeld Follies, directed
many of them.

Conrad Nagel and Jack Benny deserve especial praise for their work as masters of ceremonies. Besides those mentioned there are Joan Crawford (photographed rather badly), William Haines, Anita Page, Nils Asther, Buster Keaton, Karl Dane, George K. Arthur, Gwen Lee, the Brox Sisters, Natacha Natova and June Purcell.

Whether picture revues will ever be as good as the real thing is still conjecture. This is strictly a revue with no semblance of a story, for which Producer Harry Rapf deserves credit. There are bad spots, but it is, to date, the best of its kind and great entertainment. All Talkie.

--Photoplay, Vol. 36, No. 4
(September 1929), page 55.

*   *   *

A lively and entertaining screen musical show, with the high spots furnished by an admirable number called "Singing in the Rain," the slapstick antics of the Messrs. Laurel and Hardy and a sketch based on Romeo and Juliet, in which Miss Norma Shearer and Mr. John Gilbert perform attractively. The low point, it can hardly be disputed, is supplied by an incredibly mawkish ballad called "Your Mother and Mine," which must certainly be one of the most embarrassing songs ever written.

--Richard Watts, Jr. in The Film
Mercury, Vol. 10, No. 11 (November 1, 1929), page 6.

☐ HOTEL IMPERIAL (Famous Players-Lasky/Paramount, 1927)

Here is a new Pola Negri in a film story at once absorbing and splendidly directed. The credit on this last item may be divided safely between Mauritz Stiller, the director, and Erich Pommer, the production chief, late of Ufa and now of Hollywood.

Actually Hotel Imperial is another variation of the heroine at the mercy of the invading army and beloved by the dashing spy. This has been adroitly retold here, until it assumes surprising qualities of interest and suspense. The scenes of Hotel Imperial take place in a deserted hostelry in Galicia, between the Austrian and Russian lines. In the dark, shadowy halls of the half-medieval hotel, the action develops swiftly and surely around a hotel slavey, a spy masquerading as a waiter, and the heads of the Russian divisional army, at the moment in triumphant advance.

Miss Negri at last has a rôle that is ideal. Moreover, she gives a corking performance of the Galician slavey. It is her best characterization since she came to Hollywood. James Hall, as the Austrian, and George Siegmann, as the Russian general, give ad-

138   Selected Film Criticism

mirable performances, and the bit of a Russian spy is finely done
by Michael Vavitch.

Hotel Imperial places Mauritz Stiller at the forefront of our
imported directors.   It will give high interest to his forthcoming
work with Emil Jannings.   Credit for directorial supervision goes
to Erich Pommer, under whose guidance The Last Laugh, Variety
and most of Metropolis were filmed on the Berlin Ufa lot.

Don't miss Hotel Imperial.   It has Pola Negri in her best
rôle since Passion.
                                        --Photoplay, Vol. 31, No. 2
                                          (January 1927), page 53.

☐ HUMAN WRECKAGE (Ince/F. B. O. , 1923)

        Not a cheery story for the whole family and yet a picture
that will probably do the old world a lot of good.   The drug evil
has never known so stiff a celluloid uppercut.   Human Wreckage
starts out to show the inevitable breaking down of the physical and
moral fiber of a narcotic victim--and does it very completely.
The story deals with a young lawyer who falls a victim to dope and
who comes face to face with complete failure--and death.   How he
fights back, aided by a faithful wife, is the theme.   Human Wreckage is well played and very well acted, particularly by Bessie
Love and George Hackathorne.   Special merit attaches to the excellent performance given by Mrs. Wallace Reid, and it was largely
through her instrumentality that the production was made.   She
gives a portrayal that is most effective.
                                --Frederick James Smith in Photo-
                                  play, Vol. 24, No. 4 (Septem-
                                  ber 1923), page 65.

☐ THE HUNCHBACK OF NOTRE DAME (Universal, 1923)

        It may be said at the beginning that this photoplay reproduces
the spirit of Victor Hugo's book.   Not that it does not depart at
times from the narrative of his story, but, whatever its twists
away from the original for better or worse for picture purposes, in
its vigor, its swift and comprehensive pictures of Paris of the time,
in its culminating power, its manner of creating a final thrill, it
leaves the impression of strong dramatic events, compact of suffering, of brutality, of intrigue, of love, arising out of dungeons and
sewers and palaces and most of all out of the grey, pervading atmosphere of the great Cathedral.   In a dramaturgic sense--when
Quasimodo pours the boiling lead on the populace near the end of
the picture--it is almost made to mean the vegeance of the Cathedral
on a cruel and barbarous world of dark and torturing passions.

The Hunchback of Notre Dame   139

The Hunchback is curiously uneven in its technical qualities
and the histrionic display of the actors, but, slow and divergent
and sometimes stilted as are its means of getting under way, it
suddenly looms big and thrashes out and delivers the punch. Unlike most pictures, its power is at the end, where its power should
be--it does not fail at the critical moment.

And, quite properly, the chief character is not allowed to
grow bigger than the picture--and that brings up another curious
thing about it: in spite, ofttimes, of inferior acting in the leading
roles, in spite of close up handling that is often far less finished
than the handling of the background, the picture itself stands strong
in its power to interest, so that you say, "That fellow doesn't act
entirely like a Frenchman--he's a bit Hollywood; but that place
where he is, is surely old Paris and those things are surely happening there." This is largely due to the physical features of the
production. The perfection of the picture from the standpoint of its
scene architecture, the ability of that architecture to create the
atmosphere needed, the response of its shapes and tones to the
flicker of the camera, has not been outrivalled by any motion picture dealing with the medieval period and depending on paint and
beaverboards for materials of scenery.

You see the old plaza, upraised, with the heavy railing
around it, that spread out under Notre Dame in those days before
the whole square was made the same level; and "The Court of
Miracles" gray and scabby as the bodies of the beggars who con-
gregated there; and many a massive-pillared street and cobbly alley
full of the shadows that surely lay in them when thieves and plotters,
women pursued and horsemen in mail, went their devious ways
through the darkness of a city still arising from barbarism. These
are given by a photography that often has the sinister quality of
etching. You say then, "That is the picture that Hugo had in mind;
that is where his imagination led his characters." The public, and
the intelligent public as well as any other part of it, will like The
Hunchback for many reasons, and doubtless most of them good ones,
but it is to the things just mentioned that the critical mind goes
back, that make The Hunchback faithful to the spirit of Hugo's dark
and powerful romance, that make the picture true as a shadow from
the screen, and that give it life out of the past such as few period
pictures have possessed.

As for the actors, few of them, except at moments, make
persons of the characters portrayed. The Clopin of Ernest Torrence, the Louis XI of Tully Marshall, and the Sister Gudule of
Gladys Brockwell are all acceptable, but it is the histrionic contribution of Mr. Lon Chaney as The Hunchback that fastens the eye to
the exclusion of the others; certainly Quasimodo raises his hump
commandingly over the rest of the cast. You may say that Mr.
Chaney has pasted upon himself too much hair (when he is stripped
to the waist in the flogging scene he looks like a piece of moth-eaten
upholstery with the stuffing bursting through); and you may say he
has so masked his face with putty that its features can make no

movement and force through no expression; but somehow this Quasimodo, like the picture he is in, bulges into a definite impression,
gathers power and meaning, becomes at once a symbol and a force
--so that you think that Hugo, for all the oakum pickings and hard
mould that Mr. Chaney has burdened himself with, would quite
probably, could he have seen him, not disowned this strange being
but would have said, "Somehow this Quasimodo is like the creature
I saw and gave to the world." Surely he would have said something
like that could he have seen him in that fine moment of Mr. Chaney's
imagination when Quasimodo in a monstrous glee at having brought
Esmeralda into the sanctuary of the Cathedral, stands swaying in
rhythm with the great bell and then leaps exultingly upon it as it
swings.

It is unfortunate, and unnecessarily so, that the characters
and the story have been altered and distorted. But in one regard
in particular, The Hunchback is marked with great good taste--there
has been no endeavor anywhere to inject into it a false element of
"comedy relief;" it has been allowed to go untainted in its body of
grimness, monstrosity and terror to show forth in the end its
sinews of human fidelity and love; there has been the recognization
from the first that The Hunchback of Notre Dame had to be melodrama of weighty sort, through which it would be perilous to let
any light humor run.

--Exceptional Photoplays, Vol. 4,
Nos. 1 and 2 (October-November 1923), page 4.

*   *   *

In spite of the liberties taken with the Victor Hugo novel,
this picture is a superb and remarkably impressive spectacle. The
Hugo story is pure melodrama, and the picture is just that, with
the addition of some of the most stupendous and interesting settings
ever shown. The reproductions of the Cathedral of Notre Dame
and of the squares and streets of old Paris are extremely well
done, as are the scenes in the bell tower.

The only fault that can be found is that the story suffers for
the benefit of the spectacular features of the picture, the continuity
being somewhat jerky. Setting aside even the marvelous spectacular
features, the picture is very much worth while because of the acting
of Lon Chaney in the title rôle. His performance transcends anything he has ever done, both in his make-up and in his spiritual
realization of the character. He is weird, almost repellent at
times, but always fascinating. He falls short, perhaps, in creating
the sympathy which is the due of the Hunchback, but he more than
atones for this by the wonderful acting. The scenes in which he
hurls logs and boiling pitch on the mob attacking Notre Dame, and
his wild glee at the effect of his bombardment must be seen to be
appreciated. Director Wallace Worsley has handled the crowds
with much skill. The scenes in which the mob flows up the steps
of Notre Dame and batters in the doors of the old cathedral are

extremely striking. Ernest Torrence contributes a masterful performance as Clopin, king of the beggars. And Patsy Ruth Miller
is always appealing as Esmeralda. This picture should be placed
on your list and not missed by any means.
                              --Photoplay, Vol. 24, No. 6
                                (November 1923), page 74.

                              *   *   *

     A gorgeous and vigorously acted medieval spectacle--but try
to find Victor Hugo.
                              --Robert E. Sherwood in Life,
                                Vol. 83, No. 2151 (January 24,
                                1924), page 31.

☐ IN OLD ARIZONA (Fox, 1929)

     This picture probably goes further to show the possibilities
of sound and dialogue on the screen than any other film to date.
The limitations and confinements which have marked other talkie
offerings to date have been brushed aside by the producers of In
Old Arizona and the result is refreshing, at least, to those who
have become "fed up" already by the new and noisy cinema.

     The plot and situations are by no means new, they have been
done over and over again in the silent past, but there is a certain
novelty and effectiveness to them in dialogue form, particularly in
view of the fact that it is the first time film audiences have had an
opportunity of viewing and hearing a sound film wherein much of
the action is laid out of doors and in its natural settings. This
allows of more sweep and movement in the telling of the story and
undoubtedly enhances the entertainment value of the film.

     In this respect the directors of In Old Arizona are to be
highly commended for the naturalness and simplicity with which they
have staged the action and handled the sound elements of the drama,
making them synchronize with sincerity and a forceful yet restrained
impressiveness that lifts the picture out of the ordinary run of
raucous sound "entertainment."

     Both R. A. Walsh and Irving Cummings are credited with the
direction of In Old Arizona, and it is therefore rather difficult for
the reviewer to know upon which brow to pin the major laurel
wreath. In Hollywood film circles it is generally reported that
Cummings was responsible for the greater part of the production as
it now stands, and this is somewhat borne out by the fact that Cummings is known to have directed all those portions of the film in
which Warner Baxter appears--and which are among the best in the
picture.

In Old Arizona is rather sketchy and episodic in spots. It
is marred somewhat by a weak ending, after building up to a climax
which gave much promise of some kind of a powerful dramatic punch
to come.

Warner Baxter gives one of the most polished and compelling
performances that the talkies have had up to the present time. His
voice seems ideally suited to microphone work.

Edmund Lowe delivers an interesting portrayal of the tough
army sergeant but is completely excelled by Baxter. Dorothy Bur-
gess is pleasing as far as her vocal efforts are concerned, but
seems to lack a magnetic screen personality. She may improve
with more work before the camera.

In Old Arizona is entirely different from any sound production
released so far. This may help it at the box office. Film offers
good exploitation possibilities and it will be interesting to note how
the production draws when released throughout the country.

> --Tamar Lane in The Film Mer-
> cury, Vol. 9, No. 6 (January
> 4, 1929), page 14.

☐ INNOCENTS OF PARIS (Paramount, 1929)

This picture is Maurice Chevalier's (pronounced She-val-yay)
first screen appearance and, because of his great popularity in
Paris, his screen debut has been awaited with unusual expectancy.

Dispel your doubts, he can stay as long as he likes. He
sings with joy. He plays with abandon and his personality gets you.
He renders half his songs in French and half in English, but it is
not just his pleasing voice, nor even his perfect pantomime, that
makes him a success.

The plot is inconsequential and much of the dialogue is stilted
and unnatural, but the sparkling, lovable personality of Chevalier
lifts the story out of the commonplace--and makes it delightful entertainment. Fans will love Chevalier. All Talkie.

> --Photoplay, Vol. 36, No. 2 (July
> 1929), page 54.

☐ IRENE (First National, 1926)

This picture is entertaining hokum in a beautiful setting.
Colleen Moore is a poor little Irish tad who gets befriended by a
young fellow, part owner of a modiste shop. Does he make her
the head mannequin? You guessed it.

The story begins in Philadelphia where Irene is a member of the shanty Irish aristocracy. Mom takes in washing and Pop takes in anything containing one per cent alcohol. Irene is constitutionally unsuited for remunerative work. As a window demonstrator of the resiliency of somebody-or-other's patent bed spring, she takes a terrible flop. Then she tries salamanding with a girl friend, and is obliged to skate home.

Next Irene runs away to New York, meets the nice fella and goes to work in Madame Lucy's gown shop. She is not exactly Madame Lucy's idea of a mannequin, but the boss likes her, so there you are. Mom and Pop and the kids soon follow to live off Irene's swell job.

Comes the fashion show. In color. The four seasons are represented by beautiful girls in beautiful gowns and handsome settings. Of course, there isn't a stitch that you could ask your local dressmaker to copy, but what a feast for the optics! And Colleen looking like a rose petal, leading the show.

Everybody in the picture is funny except that terribly earnest young man, Lloyd Hughes. Colleen's pantomimic talents are hampered here and there by unnecessary subtitles. George K. Arthur's characterization of Madame Lucy is well thought out and decidedly clever. His work is one of the outstanding points of the picture.

The direction leaves something to be desired.
                              --Photoplay, Vol. 29, No. 5
                              (April 1926), page 55.

                    *   *   *

There is some color photography in Colleen Moore's latest masterpiece, Irene--the color being employed, doubtless, to distinguish it from Sally, of which, in all other respects, it is an absolute reprint.

In Irene Miss Moore appears as a mannequin ... and by the way, mannequins are now threatening to surpass rising Young District Attorneys and Royal Northwest Mounted Policemen as the most thoroughly commonplace lay figures of filmdom.

Miss Moore is a good actress, and it is this type of picture that earns for her the greatest amount of popularity and money. But I can't help wishing that she would do something just a shade more legitimate.
                              --Robert E. Sherwood in Life,
                              Vol. 87, No. 2264 (March 25,
                              1926), page 26.

144   Selected Film Criticism

☐   THE IRON MASK (Elton/United Artists, 1929)

        The greatest argument against gabby pictures that has been
advanced since we've had them, is The Iron Mask, the latest Douglas Fairbanks picture. It is a superb example of screen art in its
highest form, the new art that employs the sound device with intelligence, discretion and sympathy. There is no dialogue in the
picture, but there is an ennobling theme, superb acting and glorious
photography; a story that moves swiftly when the spirited action demands it, that hastens along with a chuckle and a joyous ring of
steel when it is happy, and pauses and becomes sober when it is
sad. Through it all, the glitter of it, its royal trappings, its
romance and its tragedies, shines the bright light of an exquisite
sense of humor, an exuberant boyishness that is uplifting to the
spirits and a balm to the mind. Doug makes different kinds of pictures. It is difficult to compare The Gaucho with The Thief of
Bagdad, or Robin Hood with Three Musketeers; and it is equally
difficult to compare The Iron Mask with any of the others from the
box-office angle, but I have no hesitation in giving it as my opinion
that never before has he given us such an exemplification of the
real meaning of screen art. In every scene The Iron Mask reflects
the contact it had with mature picture minds. There are directorial
subtleties in it, little touches of rare genius, that will delight those
who know something about screen art, and which help to make it
screen entertainment that will delight those whose only demand on a
motion picture is that it please them. Doug again proves the honest
merchant. He is giving his customers full measure. The Iron
Mask has a great production, and Henry Sharp has photographed it
with a skill that is amazing. I have seen no shots on the screen
that give a more vivid impression of the third dimension or which
make such individual portraits out of the members of groups. The
perfection reached in all the mechanical and physical arts that enter
into the making of a picture, is matched in the story and the manner of telling it. In every way The Iron Mask gives us a riper
Doug. As usual, he wrote his own story--under the name of Elton
Thomas--and he put into it more feeling and a richer humor than
have characterized any of his previous screen writing. The historical and personal elements have been blended with rare skill in
both the writing of the story and the editing of the picture. With a
nicety that is fascinating, the capacity of the audience to assimilate
history is judged. Just before we come to the point of missing
Doug and his jovial companions, they come bounding into the picture
again with joyous abandon and carry on with the zest that made
The Three Musketeers one of the landmarks of screen history.
And as an actor we have a riper Doug, one who reminds us of the
athlete of the years that reach back and holds out a promise of the
screen artist of the years to come. Never has he given a finer and
more finished performance. And when we pause to think of all he
has done for this picture as author, producer and actor, the only
feeling we can have for him is one of deep and real admiration.
The cast is a long one and a perfect one. You will find it farther
along in this Spectator and you can write "well done" after each

name in it.   It brings back to us a splendid little actress in the
person of Marguerite de la Motte, whose talents have been overlooked through the film industry's unexplainable habit of neglecting
some of those who have served it well.   She gives a notable performance which I hope will lead to her more frequent appearance
on the screen.   William Bakewell proves himself to be a boy with
a man's acting skill.   He has a dual role, a good and a bad personality, and carries both parts admirably, providing a study in
transitions that should please all those who can appreciate what is
good in screen acting.   Nigel de Brulier and Ulrich Haupt are
among the others who make big contributions to the production.
Allan Dwan's direction is flawless.   He brings out the full value of
every scene.   Coming at a time when the industry is talking talkies,
The Iron Mask should serve to restore its sanity and to bring it
back to its regular business of making motion pictures and not artistic hybrids that can not be classified.   Also it is a complete answer to those who feel that screen art has lacked something.   It
proves that it most decidedly does not need dialogue, although it
might do with a few more Dougs.

> --Welford Beaton in The Film
> Spectator, Vol. 7, No. 5
> (February 9, 1929), page 3.

☐ ISN'T LIFE WONDERFUL? (Griffith/United Artists, 1924)

Isn't Life Wonderful? marks a distinct departure from Mr.
Griffith's style, choice of theme, and method of treatment.   The
pioneer of historical spectacle, the master of super-melodrama
has entered the modest field of naturalism.   In Isn't Life Wonderful? he has given us a sad-eyed idyll of the poor, a drink from the
cup of poverty wreathed with a bit of shy romance and the unobtru-
sive heroism of want and privation gladly born for the sake of love.

Mr. Griffith has found his theme in post war Germany, in
an attempt to picture the debâcle after the war when a starved and
humiliated people were trying to find themselves.   But he has re-
sisted the temptation to treat this theme in terms of a national
panorama with mob scenes and obvious contrasts between gilded
palaces and wretched hovels.   We have had a surfeit of these things
and Mr. Griffith himself has at time surfeited us with them.   He
has wisely preferred to concentrate upon the vicissitudes of a single
family and show us in detail how they have come to suffer from the
effects of a war which others had willed.

Yet the sufferings of this one family become typical for millions of Germans and reflect the condition of a whole nation.   The
hero and heroine are known only as Inga and Hans and are really
Polish refugees fleeing from even worse conditions in Poland, but
they stand as symbols of the crushed yet hopeful youth of a country
which is fighting its way out of the darkness.

The story, reduced to its simplest terms, is the effort of
a family to subsist on a diet of white turnips and an occasional
potato. The head of the family is a timid, unworldly professor
whose services nobody wants in these distressful times. He sits
about with a lean moth-eaten look, staring vacantly into space, an
intellectual who has never faced the struggle for existence in the
raw. A gaunt, big boned aunt and a charming wise old grandmother
keep him company. Inga, the girl, with her bright sparkling eyes,
is the one bright ray with her rather naïve Pollyanna philosophy that
life is somehow wonderful despite hunger and privation. Hans is in
love with her and the two would fain get married but the practical
grandmother asks on what, on white turnips, perhaps?

But Hans has not lost his initiative and secretly builds a
little shack for himself and Inga while he cultivates a potato patch
in a small public garden. Meanwhile, an illness of the grandmother,
due to malnutrition, provides an opportunity to show the desperate
food conditions in the Germany of 1918-1919. Inga has saved
enough money to buy a precious pound of beef for the invalid and
takes her place in the long line waiting at the door of the butcher
shop. But it requires three hours of waiting for her to get anywhere near the shop and when she arrives there the price of meat
has risen from 9,000,000 to 15,000,000 worthless paper marks on
account of the fluctuations in exchange. Poor Inga's savings don't
reach that far. This scene, which is more truth than fiction, is
powerful in its simple appeal and will give any well-fed audience a
thrill.

Inga's brother, however, has had some food given him.
Hans contributes his first peck of potatoes and a hen which they
have been boarding lays a wellnigh golden egg for the grandmother.
It is a feast seasoned with tears which the imaginative spectator
may well share.

Of course, love and the courageous will to survive and make
the best of things triumph in the end, despite the dastardly theft of
Hans' entire potato crop by a hunger maddened mob. Inga and
Hans are married and a faint hope of better times comes over the
scene.

Isn't Life Wonderful? is a picture done in simple terms with
a minimum of plot or forced situations. It may even prove not
very exciting to the picture fan who insists upon his thrills, but
only the callous will miss the appeal of Mr. Griffith's treatment
and the sorrowful beauty of Miss Carol Dempster's wan but confident smile.

                                        --Exceptional Photoplays, Vol. 5,
                                          Nos. 3 and 4 (December-January
                                          1925), page 5.

*   *   *

No doubt, this is one of the finest pictures of the typical
Griffith type. We are quite sure that any other director would have

made a flop of it owing to the absence of a plot. Yet, one never loses interest for a moment; in fact, we seemed to share the hardships and sorrows of the half-starved Polish family and we rejoiced in their few happy moments.

The technique of the picture bespeaks perfection--direction, photography, acting. Grace and ease characterize each player's performance. At first we could hardly believe our eyes that Inga was our own Carol Dempster with her beautiful curly hair brushed straight back into a knot at her neck. Neil Hamilton is splendid as the German lad. Special mention must be made of the delightful but simple love scenes between him and Inga. Another fine character is Erville Alderson, a German professor. Lupino Lane and his impromptu acrobatic dancing supplies the comedy relief.

But getting back to the story--an impoverished family of Polish refugees settle in Germany after the war. Wretched and deplorable conditions of the times are vividly depicted. Each and every member of the family do their utmost to raise funds to buy food. Famine threatens and marks are valueless. One night, the younger son, who earns a livelihood as a waiter, brings home the bacon--pardon us--we mean liverwurst; Hans arrives with potatoes and Inga's hen lays an egg--and, oh--"Isn't Life Wonderful?" Taken for profiteers, Hans and Inga have their hard-earned possessions (potatoes) stolen. But as Inga crawls over to Hans and whispers, "I have you and you have me and, oh--Isn't Life Wonderful?" we felt like standing up and shouting, "It is." The same thrill awaits you--don't pass up this sterling Griffith effort.

--Photoplay, Vol. 27, No. 3 (February 1925), page 55.

☐ IT (Famous Players-Lasky/Paramount, 1927)

At last Elinor Glyn has sidestepped her famous royal characters and has given us a story of the everyday working girl. And Clara Bow is the girl--so you know what to expect. Clara is just marvellous as the peppy little saleslady who has IT personified. From all appearances Clara is the only person who will fill the niche in Paramount stardom left vacant by Gloria Swanson. And Paramount feels the same way--just watch Clara from now on. Good stuff.

--Photoplay, Vol. 31, No. 4 (March 1927), page 54.

☐ JANICE MEREDITH

This romantic tale of the American Revolution, written by the late Paul Leicester Ford in the old days of the swashbuckling novel, is likely to be the last big costume picture to reach the public in some time. The pendulum of favor seems to have swung away definitely from wigs and furbelows.

As an example of its kind, Janice Meredith is fair to middlin'. Marion Davies' Janice does not approach her work in Little Old New York. Still, it is far better than her Yolanda. Janice Meredith represents a huge outlay of money. Several fortunes have been tossed into the making of the story, which, incidentally, is neither clear cut nor well motivated.

Basically it represents the love of Janice, daughter of a Tory father but at heart a true American, for Charles Fownes, a bond servant who wins laurels as an aid to Washington. As in every other romantic opus, the characters in Janice Meredith are in intimate touch with all the notables of the day. This is a panorama of famous folk.

The story's chief fault is that it is repetitious. The hero is captured continually, only to be liberated by the heroine. The script is a wandering one and the direction loose. Janice Meredith has its own ride of Paul Revere, which, however, does not compare in electric qualities with that of Mr. Griffith's. Janice Meredith reaches its high point in a presentation of Washington and his forces crossing the ice-bound Delaware.

We are convinced that Miss Davies' metier is comedy. We feel sure she would be at her best in imtimate comedy minus lavishly oppressive trappings. Let's hope she gets such a rôle soon.

--Photoplay, Vol. 26, No. 5
(October 1924), page 53.

☐ THE JAZZ SINGER (Warner Bros. , 1927)

The Jazz Singer definitely establishes the fact that talking pictures are imminent. Everyone in Hollywood can rise up and declare that they are not, and it will not alter the fact. If I were an actor with a squeaky voice I would worry. There is one scene in The Jazz Singer that conclusively sounds the knell of the silent picture: that showing Jolson at the piano, playing idly and talking to his mother. It is one of the most beautiful scenes I ever have seen on a screen. How anyone can view it without seeing the end of our present noiseless screen entertainment is something that I can not understand. What immediately succeeds it is so flat by comparison that it becomes ridiculous, and you can not point to any art that has clung to anything ridiculous. The whole program that we saw at the Criterion makes silent pictures out of date. The curtain-raiser, a short reel in which the story is told entirely by voices, shows what can be done, and to argue that the public will be satisfied with motion only after it has been shown that voices can be added is to argue that the mind of the public has become stagnant. I am in a combatative mood about speaking pictures because I just have left the office of a producer who proved conclusively that such screen entertainment never would be popular, and who urged me not to advance a contrary view, because it would give my readers the idea that I am an impractical dreamer. The silly ass! I suppose that if he had been toddling about when Bell invented the telephone he would have produced proof that the public never would accept it. It is possible to tell stories on the screen better with voices than without them, and to declare that the public never will demand the best is to combat all the history of human achievement. If I were a producer I would give sound devices my major attention and I would develop artists who can talk and directors who know color, for if there be anything certain about the future of pictures it is that in two years or less we will be making talking pictures in color and that no others will be shown in the big houses. The Jazz Singer demonstrates how sound devices will change motion picture technic. They will allow simultaneous action. A scene shows a Jewish congregation singing, and we hear the singing. We see a cut to another scene while we still hear the voices, registering that the service continues in progress while the boy visits his home; then we come back to the congregation and end the sequence when the singing ceases. Off-stage sounds will be reproduced without cuts to show their origin, which will simplify shooting. When we have a scene showing people standing in a window looking down on a band which is marching on the street below, there will be no need for a cut to the band, as we can hear it and do not need to see it. No sound device that I yet have heard is perfect, but all of them are good enough even in their present state of development to be used generally. As speaking pictures become better known the public will demand them, and producers who do not keep up with a public demand will be forced out of business by those who do. It is the same way with color. It will take only a few all-color features to make the public clamour for more of them, and the way to make most money is to give the public what it clamours for. It will be only a short step then to a demand for action, sound, and color in the same picture.

Usual motion picture standards can not be applied to a criticism of The Jazz Singer. What it lacks in story interest is compensated for by the fact that it is a pioneer in a new screen adventure, and every reel of it is interesting on that account. We have had lots of pictures showing people singing songs, but this is the first time we have heard some of the songs. In silent pictures the singing is indicated by cuts to the singer, while in The Jazz Singer the camera is held on the singer until the song is completed, the most obvious variation in screen technic, for which the general use of sound devices will be responsible. I noticed that apparently no effort was made in the long shots to synchronize the lip movement of the singers with the words they recorded, a defect that was minimized by quick cutting. And it was the only defect I noticed in the Vitaphone. The reproduced musical accompaniment was a notable feature of the evening's entertainment. An attachment that

will bring symphony orchestras into moving picture houses will make
the program more attractive. I would like to see the Vitaphone applied to a story with more universal appeal than The Jazz Singer
possesses. It is too Jewish, a fault that I would find in it if there
were too much Catholic, Mason or anything else. Al Cohn made a
worthy adaptation of the story and Alan Crossland directed it well,
although he gives us many more close-ups than were warranted.
Most of them mean nothing. There is one that emphasizes the fact
that no intelligence is exercised in their use, and that those who
cut them into pictures do not know what they are for. Jolson returns to the home he left when a boy. In the early sequences the
home is planted and the boy's place in it shown. When Jolson returns he embraces his mother, and the embrace is shown in a large
close-up which effactually blots out the home and gives us only the
two heads. Such treatment destroys the spirit of the scene, as so
many close-ups do. The scene should have been presented in a
medium shot which preserved as much of the home as its frame
would have permitted. Jolson did not return only to his mother;
he returned to his home as well as to her, and the spirit of the
scene demanded that a portion of the home in which we had seen
him as a boy should have been part of the picture of the reunion.
The facial expressions of the mother and son were matters of no
value to the scene, for we could imagine what they were. The only
value of the scene was the presence of the two once more in the
home in which we had been accustomed to seeing them, and the close-
up robbed it of that value. I was not impressed particularly with
Jolson as a screen actor. He is too jerky, and is entirely devoid
of repression. I like his voice when he does not stress the sobbing quality. May McAvoy is the girl and is as delightful as she
always is. Long before I started The Spectator May became one of
my screen favorites and her every appearance strengthens my liking
for her. The love element in The Jazz Singer is handled admirably.
Warner Oland gives a feeling and convincing performance as Jolson's
father. Despite the handicap of a comprehensive beard he gives a
telling impression of the proud old Jew, his eyes being used effectively to register his emotions. Eugenie Besserer makes an impressive and sympathetic mother, and Otto Lederer contributes
another strong characterization. The Jazz Singer will have a definite
place in screen history and Warner Brothers are to be congratulated
upon blazing a trail along which all other producers soon will be
travelling.

                              --Welford Beaton in The Film
                                Spectator, Vol. 4, No. 12
                                (February 4, 1928), pages 7-8.

☐ JOURNEY'S END (Welsh-Pearson-Elder/Gainsborough/Tiffany,
   1930)

        Here was the most honest and the most effective picture of
the World War that had yet been made in America until All Quiet

came along--for the first time material worthy of the best kind of production, and a production worthy of the material.

The history of <u>Journey's End</u>, that extraordinarily moving play of English officers in a dug-out under fire, doesn't need to be repeated. The play itself has made a tremendous impression not only in England and America but on the Continent. It is not merely sincere--many ineffectual things are sincere enough, in intention-- it was written by a man with the gift for seeing truth and the skill to tell what he saw in dramatic form. It has surface strength enough to hold, and hold powerfully, those who look no further than mere story. It also has deep and subtle currents and conflicts for those to whom the inner things are important: the nerves and emotions, the mysterious entanglement of loves and hates, that when we get hold of them and speculate about them we call soul-knowledge --psychology. It is probably one of the most important plays of this generation.

The adaptation of it to the screen is amazingly good. It will stand, triumphantly, comparison with any war film that has been made anywhere, though one must remember--as a matter of ac- curacy and not with any apologetic feeling--that it deals with Eng- lishmen, not with Americans, Frenchmen, Germans or Russians. The whole technique of production is in true key with the characters and emotions of the play.

The text has been almost literally transposed from the stage to the screen, with additions of action in the trenches and in No Man's Land that prevent the monotony that might come from always watching one single set. But everything that is added helps to con- centrate the emotions upon that dug-out where war is playing its game with a little group of officers, from the first sight of men stumbling through ruins and muddy trenches to their quarters, --to the last heart-breaking glimpse of Lieutenant Osborne waiting for his men to come back to him from the raid on the enemy.

The man who directed the stage productions in England and in this country also directed the picture--James Whale. With al- most the first shot you get the feeling that he knew just what he was doing and just how to do it: you can surrender yourself with- out any fear that fumbling and uncertainty and inadequacy are going to bob up and spoil things. He has not done anything revolutionary or even novel in technique--in fact the production may easily be made a theme for argument among those who like to discuss the relative merits of stage and screen. For myself I find that the screen brings the characters closer to me, in spite of their being shadows instead of flesh.

This is of course intensified by very excellent acting, not in two or three leading actors only but in the whole cast. People who have seen the stage production will make comparisons, finding this or that one more or less to their liking. There is little room

for disappointment whichever direction your preference runs in.
                        --James Shelley Hamilton in
                            Cinema, Vol. 1, No. 5 (June
                            1930), page 38.

☐ THE KID (Chaplin/Associated First National, 1921)

The most outstanding figure in our moving picture world is
an Englishman who seems to have found this country entirely congenial and who has never used his leisure moments to dash off a
book to tell the world what he thinks of America. Instead, he has
put much sweat and labor into giving us a criticism of life. To do
this he has relied upon a trick moustache, a small bamboo cane, a
tilted derby, a pair of enormously large, flat shoes, and a pair
of the most ominously threatening yet never quite descending pair
of trousers in which mortal man has ever dared to walk forth.
These have been, so to speak, his artistic resources, and with
them he can bring tears or laughter to the largest audience in the
world with less apparent effort than any other actor on the screen.

Charles Chaplin's method is what is commonly called "slapstick. " The term is used in disparagement. In many quarters
Chaplin is considered very lowbrow, very vulgar, very unaesthetic.
The endless beatings which he gives and takes, his tumbles and
recoveries, his waddling walk, are not accepted in the upper circles. That is, they are not officially accepted, for it is very curious how surreptitious many people are about what they really enjoy
in a picture. They will often roar their heads off and then turn up
their noses. They say it is nothing but "slapstick, " and that seems
to anger them enormously.

You would think that slapstick had been invented in the movies. It happens, however, that slapstick has been used to entertain
mankind ever since monkeys started to throw cocoanuts at each
other. The classics are full of it. The Don Quixote of Cervantes
contains more slapstick than all the movie comedies thus far made.
The comedies of Aristophanes are so full of the frankest kind of
slapstick that only scholars of the chastest reputation are allowed
to read them in the original. Suppose you were to put Falstaff and
the Merry Wives of Windsor into a movie. Would you cut out the
slapstick? Goethe would laugh at you. Think of the tricks he made
Doctor Faust play. Yet these antics are often cause for disapproval
in the movies.

The plain fact of the matter is that it is quite absurd to
criticise an artistic method if the effect is genuine. Laughter is
achieved by incongruities and distortions. On the screen this must
be done in terms of action. If you can upset the bumptious hero by
making him slip on a banana peel or ruffle a false sublimity by
tickling it with a feather, you are producing valid satire. Pity

often lurks in the ludicrous just as much as in the pathetic.   Watch Chaplin closely and you will find that when he wishes he can be a master of irony.

Something of this revolt against the dishonor of slapstick must have been in his mind when he made The Kid.   He is telling the story of a foundling who is taken in by an itinerant mender of window panes and is reared to young boyhood.   He does not alter his method, though he refines it.   There is still lots of rough-and-tumble.   But there is also more feeling, and more understanding of childhood, than in a hundred Little Lord Fauntleroys.   Slapstick triumphs over sentimentality.

The mother deposits the child in an empty limousine with the hope that the rich owner will adopt it.   But the car is stolen and the thieves throw the child on a heap of refuse where Charlie finds it.

Charlie becomes a parent.   He becomes both parents.   He sits upon the edge of the bed and cuts diapers out of an old bedsheet and folds them with the gravity of the All Mother.   Meanwhile baby hangs suspended from the ceiling by four strings and a bag and drinks his milk contentedly from the spout of an inverted coffee pot which swings in the air nearby.

The child has grown into a boy of five.   Very few children grow into such irresistible boys or such marvelous actors as little Jack Coogan, who in the picture is known as John.   John goes into partnership with his father.   He precedes him down the street and breaks the windows which his father afterwards mends.   Except for occasional encounters with the minions of the law, the partnership works famously.

Meanwhile the plot begins to thicken.   John's mother has become a rich stage celebrity and indulges her maternal instinct in an unpretentious way by playing Lady Bountiful to the children of the slums.   John and she have already met and have just naturally taken a shine to each other.   But with the sudden illness of John, the villain enters.   Charlie confesses to the doctor that he is John's father only by force of circumstances, with the result that the orphan asylum authorities are called.   With them Charlie has a battle royal, is defeated but recovers John at the very gates of the asylum.

But meanwhile John's mother has found out that he is her son.   He is again snatched away from Charlie, who wanders about in search of him until he falls asleep from exhaustion.   He dreams that he is in Heaven, where he finds John and all the rest of the inhabitants of the neighborhood.   On awakening he is led to the house where John and his mother have been happily united.

Such a picture cannot be retold in words.   It is a miniature epic of childhood in the comic manner in terms of the screen. There is infinite humor and swift pathos and subtle satire.   Con-

sider the beginning of the child's career. His mother deposits him
in a limousine but he immediately lands in an ash can; very un-
dignified, very incongruous, but is it not just like the chance we
take of being born with that silver spoon in our mouth? Luckily
we do not know enough to care at the time and, if we did, is it
so sure that we would all choose the silver spoon? John certainly
had more fun with Charlie Chaplin as his father than he could possibly have had with any duke.

         Or take the Chaplin vision of heaven. (To be sure the sub-
title labels it "Fairyland"!) A slum street suddenly festooned and
garlanded and all the people wearing white wings tacked on to their
otherwise unchanged clothing. They have not changed at all in any
other respect, except that they can fly about ludicrously on invisible
wires: a cross between a cabaret and a children's ball. The people fight and envy just as before and a policeman with wings has to
enforce brotherly love with his pistol! What an ingenious travesty
on our easy beatitudes!

         The episode of the fight with the orphan asylum officials,
exaggerated as it is, presents an excellent burlesque on institutional-
ism and illustrates the difference between individual and machine
care for children.

         Chaplin's main concern in The Kid is to give us a picture of
childhood and fatherhood and to show us how boy and man get along
in this world of ours. That kid and his father love each other and
it is the charm of their relation against egotism and unconcern of
the rest of the world which makes the picture so fascinating. That
is, after all, a simple matter for everybody to understand and it is
simply and beautifully handled. There is no doting, no slobbering
over the child, no attempt to achieve cuteness for its own sake. It
would have been a sweet and sentimental ending, for instance, to
have the mother marry the foster-father after she had providentially
discovered that his oddly surreptitious window mending had disguised
a stained window artist. We do not know what he did. Perhaps
he just went back to his job. Or perhaps the kid's mother fitted
him out with a regular pane shop. But whatever he did we may be
sure that John visited him frequently and that they had happy re-
unions.

         An astonishing picture, true to the common stuff of human
attributes. A picture that makes a very deep scratch in the possibilities of the screen. Millions will enjoy it, and many of those
who have stood aloof will have to admit, if only to themselves, the
supreme genius of the new Ariel who walks among mortals in the
most incongruous shoes that an immortal ever wore.
                              --Exceptional Photoplays, No. 3
                              (January-February 1921), pages
                              2, 6 and 7.

☐ THE KID BROTHER (Harold Lloyd/Paramount, 1927)

This newest of Harold Lloyd comedies takes its place among the popular comedian's best efforts. We place it well below The Freshman, just back of Grandma's Boy and Safety Last, and a thousand miles ahead of For Heaven's Sake.

The Kid Brother is a bucolic comedy. Actually it is a comedy Tol'able David. Harold plays Harold Hickory, youngest of the fighting Hickorys of Hickoryville. He is kicked about by the rest of the Hickorys until, like Tol'able, he proves himself. That all comes about after a pretty little girl of a traveling medicine show gets stranded in the hamlet. The strong man of the defunct troupe steals the village funds, the elder Hickory is suspected, but Harold recovers the coin and saves the family name.

The Kid Brother is full of snappy gags. Perhaps the best comes when Harold, hiding from the murderous strong man in a deserted boat hulk, puts his shoes on a little monkey belonging to the medicine show. The strong man chases the clattering boots all over the boat. There are scores of other good gags.

The bespectacled Lloyd gives a human, mellow comedy performance: He was never better than as the timid Hickory who saves the day. The Kid Brother marks the last appearance of Jobyna Ralston as Lloyd's leading woman. She does the medicine show girl with charm and appeal. Miss Ralston has been an excellent foil for Lloyd, and he isn't going to find it easy to get a successor.

Hand it to Harold! You'll want to see The Kid Brother. Lloyd never mixed a pleasanter blend of laughter and pathos.
                                              --Photoplay, Vol. 31, No. 4
                                              (March 1927), page 52.

☐ THE KING OF JAZZ (Universal, 1930)

A box-office picture can run for one week. If holding over, that must come from the extremely easy exploitation capable with this picture and the popularity of Paul Whiteman. As per the list of principals above, there are possibilities beyond the world-famous Whiteman and Whiteman and his band, but in the picture it's only Whiteman.

Taking the revue form of The King of Jazz as directed by J. Murray Anderson, on his first picture talker attempt, it could be said that the revue form is rather late, but that is stood off at this time by Paramount on Parade, also late, but over. So it remains up to Anderson, with Universal resting a production that cost $2,000,000 in his inexperienced hands.

If there is one big thing the Whiteman band is identified with, besides its leader, Paul, it is George Gershwin's "Rhapsody in Blue." The millions who have never heard the great Whiteman band play this biggest of all jazz melodies won't hear it here, either. Mr. Anderson has seen fit to scramble it up with "production." It's all busted to pieces, and, while it's all there, it's not the Whiteman number it would have been had it been played simply straight as a musical composition by the jazzing orchestra that does it so well and as it should have been.

Anderson does a lot of experimentation, as it looks, in the early section. He gets some effects out of it, but they count for nothing at the box-office. Mostly these effects are colors and backgrounds. Nothing here counts excepting Whiteman, his band and the finale, "The Melting Pot." This latter is an elaborately produced number, and produced in the same manner that Anderson or Ziegfeld would have put it on in a stage show. Many flocks of people appearing and disappearing. It's imposing, mainly because it comes at the finish, and the numbers before meant little. They were also staged by Anderson, mostly at long range, and valueless for that reason.

The Russell Markert girls can do anything, but what's the good of that if they look like a collection of shadows, with the close-ups seemingly always in wrong?

In comedy the revue is almost barren. A few blackouts, some from the last Anderson musical revue on Broadway, and the others just as light.

In songs the picture is more fortunate. It has two outstanders, both ballads. "Dawn," by Milton Ager and Jack Yellen, is already an assured hit through the radio, and "Monterey," by Mabel Wayne, sounds just as likely for a selling success. John Boles sings both, and well, with each extensively produced. They will help, but can't make the picture. The Ager-Yellen "Bench" number may come through. It's there.

In comedy William Kent gets the best chance, upon two occasions. Paul tries for a little comedy himself now and then, once by having a dancer double for him and exposing it. Most of whatever comedy there is occurs at the opening, when a cartooned Paul is chased by a lion in the African jungle. Some fun to this, and just cut off in time.

Charles Irwin makes a pleasant master of ceremonies, who does not obtrude, and runs off the revue performance nicely. Others flit in and out, scarcely noticed or recognized. Jeanette Loff sings a couple of songs while the Sisters G merely make one wonder why they were brought over from Berlin for the little they show here. Stanley Smith is the juvenile, and good enough. For example, maybe Grace Hayes was in the picture.

A "Bridal Veil" number is put on in a big way.   Bringing
the brides through the years to date, probably.   But if that isn't
Ziegfeld's first production scheme for a stage musical, it was
Anderson's.   This picture is all too much Anderson from the stage.
It quickly proves he did not realize the camera's scope.

Anderson is a class producer for the stage.   He never has
been credited with knowing much about comedy, and surely bears
out that rep in the Whiteman talker.

Paul Whiteman does admirably, whether talking, kidding or
leading.   His voice is Al for the screen, while the recording is
exceptional.   As Whiteman is well known as an expert on sound,
he reserving for himself the privilege of always being in the recording room when his band is making phonograph records, an unusual
demand with the disc makers, the recording here may go to the
Whiteman credit.

A 98-minute picture that can stand a loss of 10 or 15 minutes without worry.   There are neat camera and other tricks in it,
but, again, they don't count at the gate.   All in Technicolor, with
coloring smartly done.

Whiteman will hold up the picture, here and abroad, for the
Whiteman music is box office in any language.

But what this picture muffed is a pity.
                              --Sime Silverman in Variety, Vol.
                              99, No. 4 (May 7, 1930), page
                              21.

                    *   *   *

Here's that Paul Whiteman revue at last--and when fans fight
over which revue is best, this will have heavy backing!   Two factors greaten it--Whiteman's music, and the daring innovations
wrought for the screen by Stage Director John Murray Anderson.
In color, lighting, spectacle and photography he has opened new
fields.

Items: Gershwin's "Rhapsody in Blue" is tremendously
played and pictured.   How John Boles and male chorus sing that
"Song of the Dawn"!   Gorgeous beauty in the Wedding Veil sequence.
For sheer spectacle, the Melting Pot finale can't be beaten.   Jeanette Loff blondely lovely; John Boles lustily vocal; William Kent
freshly comic.   Whiteman's Band is great!--and those Rhythm
Boys... !

If you like revues--oh boy!
                              --Photoplay, Vol. 38, No. 1
                              (June 1930), page 56.

☐ THE KING OF KINGS (DeMille/P. D. C. , 1927)

Here is Cecil B. DeMille's finest motion picture effort. He
has taken the most difficult and exalted theme in the world's his-
tory--the story of Jesus Christ--and transcribed it intelligently and
ably to the screen.

DeMille has had a variegated career. He has wandered,
with an eye to the box office, up bypaths into ladies' boudoirs and
baths, he has been accused of garishness, bad taste and a hundred
and one other faults, he frequently has been false and artificial.
One of his first efforts, The Whispering Chorus, stood until this as
his best work.

The King of Kings, however, reveals a shrewd, discerning
and skillful technician, a director with a fine sense of drama, and,
indeed, a man with an understanding of the spiritual.

The King of Kings is the best telling of the Christ story the
screen has ever revealed. DeMille has achieved some tremendous
climaxes.

The winning of the Disciple Matthew, the raising of Lazarus
from the dead, the betrayal of Judas, the meeting of Christ and
Pilate, the tortuous way of the cross to Calvary and the Crucifixion
provide mighty film episodes as DeMille develops them. DeMille
has not hurried from tableau to tableau. He frequently pauses to
humanize and reveal his principals. One of the best things in The
King of Kings is his revealment of Pontius Pilate, the Roman governor of Judea. For the moment Pilate, puzzled, hounded by the
high priests, compassionate and seeking the path of least resistance,
lives and breathes.

You are going to be amazed at the complete sincerity of De-
Mille's direction. Nothing is studied. There is no aiming at theatrical appeal. DeMille has followed the New Testament literally
and with fidelity. He has taken no liberties. Frequently, in his
groupings, he has followed famous Biblical paintings.

It is difficult to analyze the performance of H. B. Warner
as Jesus. We can conceive of no more difficult rôle in the whole
field of history and literature. Mr. Warner meets the accepted
ideas of Christ and gives a very well sustained performance.

The surprise of the big picture is Victor Varconi, as Pontius
Pilate. Here is an intelligent and splendidly conceived bit of work.
Rudolph Schildkraut gives an admirable portrayal of Caiaphas, the
high priest of Israel. Among the disciples, all well played, Ernest
Torrence stands out vividly as Simon Peter. It is a fervent and
moving characterization. Jacqueline Logan is excellent as Mary
Magdalene and Dorothy Cummings has several moving moments as
Mary, the mother.

The King of Kings is a tremendous motion picture, one that, through its sincerity, is going to win thousands of new picture goers. DeMille deserves unstinted praise.   He ventured where few would dare to venture, he threw a vast fortune into the balance and he carried through without deviating.   Congratulations, Mr. DeMille. And a measure of praise, too, to the battery of cameramen, headed by Peverell Marley.

> --Frederick James Smith in
> Photoplay, Vol. 32, No. 1
> (June 1927), pages 54-55.

☐   THE KING ON MAIN STREET (Famous Players-Lasky/Paramount, 1925)

The story isn't a knockout.   It's the suave personality of Adolphe Menjou, who enacts the rôle of the King of Molvania, that puts it over.   It's a Menjou picture from the start to the finish. His subtle and captivating charm acts as a pivot on which the plot of the story rotates.   The picture is centered around a series of spicy and ultra-sophisticated situations which Monta Bell, the director, has logically developed with skill and freshness without shocking the censorious.

The story shows in a humorous and entertaining way the life of a bored king who longed to be loved as a man.   Bessie Love is the sweet little young girl with whom the King has a delightful romance.   Greta Nissen's beauty and gowns are a treat for the eyes. We're warning you--don't miss this.

> --Photoplay, Vol. 24, No. 2
> (January 1926), page 46.

☐   THE KISS (M-G-M, 1929)

Sweden's gift, Greta Garbo, makes silent pictures and you like them or else.   But you like them.   The Kiss is a stereotyped triangle yarn, but it is distinguished by another compelling performance by the mysterious Garbo.   The story involves the loves of three men for a woman.   The husband is shot and the wife goes on trial for her life.   Conrad Nagel is the "honorable" lover.

> --Photoplay, Vol. 37, No. 1
> (December 1929), page 55.

☐ A KISS FOR CINDERELLA (Famous Players-Lasky/Paramount,
    1926)

        It has no plot, this Kiss for Cinderella, except the beautiful
old plot of the Cinderella legend. It has no more sex than sunshine. It has no fashion parade. But it is exactly what its ad-
vertisements call it, "A Christmas Gift for All."

        Charm and laughter and youth it has, and while it marks no
great advance for Betty Bronson, it ranks Herbert Brenon among
the really important directors.

        Because she is starved and cold, she gets a blessed fever
that transports her to a fairy ball where she wears the glass slip-
pers and the beautiful gown and meets the Prince, who is really
her friend, the policeman. And then when she gets well again--
well, you go see for yourself. And take every one of the children,
even the baby. It's their lollipop.
                                    --Photoplay, Vol. 24, No. 3
                                    (February 1926), page 49.

☐ LA BOHEME (M-G-M, 1926)

        King Vidor's version of Henry Murger's short stories of the
Latin Quarter of Paris from which the Puccini opera was suggested,
is a picture of striking beauty, wonderfully directed by Vidor and
acted with much skill by John Gilbert. The theme is simple, as
delicate as the tension of a lyre, and tells the story of Mimi, a
seamstress, and Rodolphe, a struggling playwright, against a colorful and romantic background.

        A note of tender pathos pervades the entire piece and the
ultimate tragedy is too heartrending for words. Lillian Gish is
seen in another of her wistfully appealing but familiar characterizations. Renée Adoree, Karl Dane and George Hassell are included
in the cast.

        This production is a triumph for Metro-Goldwyn, for Vidor,
and for John Gilbert, and will prove a real joy.
                                    --Photoplay, Vol. 24, No. 6
                                    (May 1926), page 48.

                        *   *   *

        A pretty dismal entertainment, with Lillian Gish and John
Gilbert.
                                    --Robert E. Sherwood in Life, Vol.
                                    87, No. 2266 (April 8, 1926),
                                    page 32.

☐ LADY OF THE PAVEMENTS (Art Cinema Corporation/United
   Artists, 1929)

      Honors for Lupe Velez! This startling personality with the
emotional mechanism of a great actress IS the picture. In this
slight story, concerning the French Court, revenge and diplomacy,
D. W. Griffith misses many chances for that fine poignancy which
characterized his earlier work. Jetta Goudal is as strangely fascinating as ever, William Boyd is pale, but Lupe gives a magnificent performance.
                                    --Photoplay, Vol. 35, No. 3
                                     (February 1929), page 54.

                    *   *   *

      The excellently compiled and invaluable Film Daily Year Book
carries a full-page, uncaptioned portrait of D. W. Griffith, which
implies a greatness that is not reflected in his latest picture, The
Lady of the Pavements. It might have been the work of some director who would have to put his name under his photograph before
we knew who he was. I like D. W. personally. He is an amiable
and agreeable chap. But I wish he would realize what a terrific
handicap he places himself under by his complacent acceptance of a
greatness that has been accorded him by tradition rather than
earned by achievement. It is not humanly possible for him to make
a picture great enough to match his conception of his own greatness. And his assumption that he is so great that it is superfluous
to put his name under his photograph, makes it natural in every
picture he makes. If Lady of the Pavements had been directed by
an unknown no doubt I would have left the projection-room to hail
the advent of a new director who had done a fine piece of work, and
with a disposition to be lenient with the picture's weaknesses on account of the unpretentious attitude of the director. But it is the
work of the mighty Griffith! United Artists publicity bids me view
it reverently, on bended knee. It is by Griffith, therefore is above
criticism, and if I can not see that it is great, it is because I am
a poor worm. That is, such thoughts might enter into my consideration of the picture if I could think of anything but the picture
when I am viewing one; but it none the less is the handicap under
which D. W. works. And it is his own fault. He should take a
leaf out of the book of that exceedingly wise director, John Ford.
Have you noticed that Jack always follows a big picture with two
small and unimportant ones? He followed Four Sons with Hang-
man's House, which was supposed to be a small picture, but, unfortunately for Jack's system, its locale was in Ireland, which he
dearly loves, and he was tender with it, and sympathetic, and he
invoked the aid of banshees and fairies to help him tell his grim
story through a haze of Irish poetry, with the result that his little
picture was given a place on most lists of the ten best of the year.
By way of atonement Jack then gave us Riley the Cop, the most
ridiculous offering of the season and one of the funniest things I
ever saw on the screen. He followed that with some baggage-
smashing opus which features Victor McLaglen and a pile of trunks.

I haven't seen it. These little pictures having made us forget that
Jack gave us Iron Horse, Four Sons and some other screen master-
pieces, or having fastened in our minds the thought that poor old
Jack used to be good, he is at work now on a production that will
startle us once more into a realization that he is a great director.
The advantage of his system is that we are permitted to forget John
Ford between his big pictures. We never are allowed to forget
D. W. Griffith. He is ipso facto great. He is his own tough spot
on a program to follow. When we view a picture directed by an
unknown, its strong points impress us, standing out by virtue of the
fact that we did not expect to find them. When we view a picture
directed by Griffith, its weaknesses impress us, standing out for
the same reason, that we did not expect to find them. And a title
informs us that this one was "personally" directed by D. W. Griffith, which is an exhibition of egotism so great that it is funny.
How can a man direct a picture in any other way? I am amazed
at the lack of showmanship that this method of introducing a picture
reveals. It gives the audience the impression that something extraordinary is coming, and when merely a good picture follows all the
bombast, the audience feels that there is something lacking. Lady
of the Pavements has all the externals of a good picture, but it
lacks a soul. The story is a poor one. Difference in social rank
as a bar to marriage no longer is a good theme in this country,
and is becoming less so even in Europe. The performance of Lupe
Velez surprised me. She looked so angelic in her opening shot that
I did not recognize her until she went Lupe and began to beat up
one man and bite another. Too much footage is devoted to her
antics, but on the whole she does very well. That always excellent
actress, Jetta Goudal, makes a big contribution to the picture, as
do George Fawcett, Albert Conti and William Boyd.

> --Welford Beaton in The Film
> Spectator, Vol. 7, No. 7 (March
> 9, 1929), page 8.

☐ LADY WINDERMERE'S FAN (Warner Bros. , 1925)

The plot by Oscar Wilde was not so original. With Wilde's
epigrams it became literature. With Lubitsch's subtle translation
it is delightful.

Irene Rich is charming as Mrs. Erlynne, the naughty mother
of little Lady Windermere (May McAvoy). Ronald Colman is a
suave Lord Darlington.

Not for children.

> --Photoplay, Vol. 24, No. 3
> (February 1926), page 50.

☐ THE LAST COMMAND (Paramount, 1928)

The Last Command is filled with dramatic episodes which
von Sternberg handles with extraordinary appreciation of their values.   Evelyn Brent is a revolutionist to whom Jannings takes a
fancy.   She pretends to return his infatuation, and lures him to her
room, her purpose being to shoot him.   When she rises and points
the gun at him her resolution wavers, for Jannings' bravery awakens
her admiration.   He takes her in his arms.   It is an intensely
dramatic scene, but it is played as quietly and as devoid of heroics
as if coffee drinking were the only thing in which the two were interested.   There is much in von Sternberg's direction of this sequence which Hollywood might study with profit to itself.   In a scene
showing a woman about to shoot a man the situation is dramatic.
It is not necessary for the parties to it to act dramatically, for
such acting can not add to the drama there is in the intention to
murder.   Few directors seem to appreciate this.   Given situations
dramatic in themselves, they overdo them by making their actors
dramatic also.   The only effect that this treatment can have is to
distract the attention of the audience from the drama in the situation
to the drama in the acting, which I do not believe is good technic.
In his treatment of the sequence von Sternberg accomplishes the
double purpose of strengthening the scenes and saving Evelyn for
her big scene later, in which she lets herself go and to save Jannings from the mob, apparently becomes one of its most violent
members.   The mob sequence is handled admirably.   In it both
Jannings and Evelyn do their greatest acting, and it is great.   Von
Sternberg leads up to it impressively with scenes that are strong
both in drama and pictorial quality.   When Jannings defies the mob
that seeks his life he is truly magnificent.   Although he is the per-
sonification of tyrannical Russia, he never forfeits the sympathy of
the audience.   Evelyn saves his life by persuading the mob to take
him to St. Petersburg for his execution and she makes possible his
escape from the train that is conveying him to the capital.   After
he leaves the train a bridge collapses under it, and in a thrilling
scene we see it sink below the ice on a river.   Evelyn goes down
with it.   It is a refreshing departure to drown the heroine of a picture.   And The Last Command goes still further.   In the last sequence it kills Jannings himself--and the ending is a happy one in
spite of that fact, for we know that the lowly extra, who once was
so powerful, has come to the end of his suffering.   Bill Powell,
who in the early Russian sequences was shown as a revolutionist,
escapes to America and becomes a motion picture director in Hollywood.   He was subjected to harsh treatment by Jannings in Russia,
and the tables are turned when the two meet in Hollywood.   Jannings is working in a scene showing a night attack by Russian
troops, and he again dons a uniform to lead his troops.   He imag-
ines that it is real, and is so overcome by the intensity of his love
for Russia that he drops dead.   Over his body Powell, who is directing the picture, reverently places the Russian flag, and the
camera backs up until the body, the director and his assistant are
in the background, and three motion picture cameras are in the

foreground.   On this scene there is the final fadeout, a great ending to a great picture.   In spite of the fine performances it is a
director's picture, and when it is released von Sternberg will be
recognized as one of the very few directors who have made two
good pictures in succession, Underworld being the other one.   The
Spectator's prophecy has been fulfilled.

> --Welford Beaton in The Film
>   Spectator, Vol. 4, No. 12
>   (February 4, 1928), page 10.

☐   THE LAST LAUGH (Ufa, 1924)

    The Last Laugh--which is the footless and make-shift title
given the latest foreign film, first appropriately named The Least
of Men--is one of the most important pictures yet to be observed
on any screen.   Its influence on future picture making should be as
provocative as was that of The Cabinet of Dr. Caligari.   Unlike
The Cabinet of Dr. Caligari, its expressionism is that of the ra-
tional world, conveyed in terms of everyday objects.   It raises no
barriers of doubtful meaning.

    Essentially it is a picture of thought.   It is a comment on
the cruelty of an organized society to the individual grown too old
to serve that society.   This cruelty is not shown through precon-
ceptions of plot but through the impressions it creates in the mind
of its principal character.   It is a cinema visualization of a state
of mind as well as of a state of society.   It is less a narrative of
occurrences than a record of psychological experience.   It is told
perfectly in the medium of photography and the motion picture,
without artifice, without subtitles, without compromise.   (We are
not speaking now of the happy, humorous ending that was tagged on
to propitiate the gods of laughter and the fairy story, which ending,
too, by the way, is handled with the technical integrity of the main
story, which is stark and tragic in its implications.)

    The main body of the picture constitutes a perfect photoplay--
about the most perfect photoplay, if one also remembers and brack-
ets with it Shattered, that has ever been produced.   It is the photoplay of an old head porter who stands resplendent in his gold-
braided uniform at the entrance of a continental hotel, and grandilo-
quently superintends the handling of luggage of the arriving and departing guests.   It is not his body that is covered by the uniform so
much as his soul.   By that uniform he exists; it is the symbol of
his authority, of his spiritual well-being, in the tenement where he
lives.   Each evening he returns waddling in the huge, ornate coat
and is treated by the tenement dwellers with homage, as if he were
a general; he salutes them and is saluted.   Each morning he departs
clothed in its glory, walking pompous and superior, kindly but pat-
ronizing.   His mind is as poor as his pocket; it is the uniform that
enriches him, that makes him a figure in his imagination and in the

imagination of the people among whom he moves. Coming, one day, to take up his post before the door of the hotel, he finds a younger man in an identical uniform on duty. Stunned, he is called into the office and told that he is too old to work as the head porter any longer. The benevolent establishment gives him another job in recognition of his long service, but it takes his uniform. His new job is that of towel-boy in the men's lavatory. With the uniform gone, his pride is gone, his being is crushed, his world is destroyed. For a while, he manages to keep up the appearance of his former estate by stealing the uniform and wearing it home at night. But his deception is discovered when his old aunt, bringing him at the hotel a hot morsel, misses him at the front door, and is directed to the wash-room, where he cringes, humbled and despairing, before her horrified gaze. She carries the news back to the tenement. When he returns that night his shame is flung back at him by the gossip-loving, scandal-mongering neighborhood--by the same people who bowed before the symbol of his uniform. His doom, dumbly comprehended, unescapable, is thus brought upon him. He is alone with his torture. As he was upborne by the uniform on his back, so he is crushed by the towel of the menial that he holds in his hand for men to wipe their hands upon. Lear, outcast in the night and storm on the moor, is not more tragic. Indeed the cloak that he has been wearing is like the cloak of Lear and has been snatched from him by the ingratitude of the thing he has served.

Emil Jannings, who plays the part, is this man at every movement, in every little action, in every turning of his mind. He commands the part and fills it. His is a perfect realization of the character. The mind of the character is what his art of pantomime reveals, and the feelings of this old man lie open in Mr. Jannings' every look and gesture. Here, indeed, is an actor, and in his control the character bleeds in all its wounds.

To tell this simple and heart-rending story in motion pictures the pure use of the cinema camera is effected. The old Porter, celebrating his daughter's wedding, gets drunk; the condition of his mind and senses is reflected in the circling room, in the wavering building: the heads of the audience are made to swim, the gorge rises. A trumpet is tooted by a merry-making musician in the street beneath; the round mouth of the trumpet fills the screen, the photograph protrudes in brassy convolutions of issuing defocalized shadow: the braying sound is heard. On a screen of depth the sleeping tenements rise darkly in the empty street, dawn bursts and they stand stark, white, bloated, giving off waking, yawning noise in the tawdry daylight; bedding is shaken from the windows, forms in shawls appear in rapid movement on the iron balconies: the life of the tenement is fluttered sleazily forth to the audience. The old Porter retreats at night to the wash-room of the hotel, sits huddled motionless on the bench against the dark wall; the pavement light, cold in the grated skylight, falls above him: the photograph is numb, full of despair, of humiliation.

Far into the reaches of the possible art of motion pictures
this picture projects like a pointing finger; its shadow is on the future of the motion picture.

--Exceptional Photoplays, Vol. 5,
Nos. 3 and 4 (December-January 1925), page 1.

*   *   *

The American movie powers-that-be had so little faith in the
German-made The Last Laugh that, when they finally gave it a New
York hearing, they put in a vapid "popular" film to attract the public. The Last Laugh showed up the American photoplay as infantile
stuff. It was written by Carl Mayer, author of The Cabinet of Dr.
Caligari, and is a character study--related without subtitles and
wholly in pantomime--of an aged hotel porter disintegrating under
the heavy hand of age. The old fellow is superbly done by Emil
Jannings, who comes mighty near being the most eloquent cinema
actor of any land. Actually, The Last Laugh has more to recommend it than fine acting. It is a superb adventure into new phases
of film direction. We have never seen the camera made so pliable
to moods and moments. Frequently the camera takes the place of
the white haired porter and, through the eye of the lens, you see
as did the dimmed eyes of the broken old man. The Last Laugh is
a splendid production.

--Will Hays, Jr. in The New
Yorker*, Vol. 1, No. 1 (February 21, 1925), page 28.

☐ LAUGH, CLOWN, LAUGH (M-G-M, 1928)

This is the best work of Lon Chaney since The Unholy Three,
and it is a great relief to have him minus his usual sinister make-
up. His characterization of Tito Filk is perfect.

Laugh, Clown, Laugh is the old story of Pagliacci, of the
buffoon with the broken heart. Tito, the circus clown, struggling
against the pangs of unrequited love for his beautiful adopted
daughter, Simonetta, becomes afflicted with an erratic nervous dis-
order. Another man of wealth suffers from a contrasting malady.
The two meet in the office of a nerve specialist and become friends.
Then follows the rivalry of the two for the girl. Nils Asther, as
Luigi-Ravelli, the millionaire, is more than satisfactory. Loretta
Young, as Simonetta, reveals an unexpected display of dramatic
ability.

--Photoplay, Vol. 34, No. 1
(June 1928), page 52.

---

*This was the first film review ever published by The New Yorker.

☐ LAZYBONES (Fox, 1925)

      Buck Jones gives a splendid characterization that is quite
different from his usual wild and woolly Western he-man stuff. It
is rather doubtful if this will please his fans who like Buck when
he is shootin' up the town. A story of small town people which is
told in a direct and wholly unpretentious manner. The supporting
cast consists of Madge Bellamy, Jane Novak, ZaSu Pitts and Leslie
Fenton.

                                  --Photoplay, Vol. 24, No. 2
                                  (January 1926), page 49.

☐ THE LETTER (Paramount, 1929)

      It may possibly be no more than an accident that the first
really sensible and mature talking screen drama produced by our
new mechanistic medium was manufactured in the East. I mean,
of course, The Letter, and I hope you do not think I am being too
arrogant a New York patriot when I suggest that it is not at all unnatural that such an important pioneer effort should have been made
along the Atlantic seaboard. Rather than being disagreeably chauvin-
istic, I am endeavoring to be entirely friendly in my warnings to
Hollywood. *

      It seems very likely, though, that any possible admonition
now may be too late. Certainly, the success of The Letter makes
the East Coast immediately the serious rival of Hollywood in the
making of talking photoplays. I do not make any wild claim that
California as a producing center is definitely doomed. I do believe,
though, that the complacent monopoly on film manufacture so long
and tightly held in the West, is at least threatened and that complications face the efforts to maintain it. With stage and screen
now engaged in mortal combat for precedence in the new medium,
New York, which still manages to be the theatrical capital of the
world, may possibly manage to take advantage of the battle.

      Perhaps you will forgive me if, in presenting my case for
the potentialities of New York as a center of film production, I
quote rather liberally from a story of mine on the subject in The
Herald Tribune. I should hasten to explain that I do so, not out of
any particular admiration for the wording of the article, but merely
because it represents my ideas on the subject as well as could any
paraphrase I might devise.

      Anyway, I wrote that "since the current capital of the cinema
industry was first knocked from its complacency by the arrival of

---

*The Letter was filmed at the Paramount Astoria Studios on New
York's Long Island.

synchronized conversation, it has been trying desperately to buy up
all the actors, directors and writers of Broadway in its effort to
dominate a dramatic method dependent on the stage for its value.
When a Long Island studio, making its first full-length picture in
the new manner, succeeds in providing the most dramatically effective one yet devised, it must suggest that the stage people will not
have to travel as far as California to participate in the profits of
film-making.

"It is difficult to deny that Hollywood, with its more adapt-
able topographical and climatic sweep, its concentration on one industry and its general real estate features, was a comparatively
ideal place for the production of silent films that depended on movement, scenic values and other advantages of the outdoors for their
quality.   The arrival of talking pictures, however, with their call
for stage experience, theatrical craftsmanship and certain cultural
qualities, more indigenous to New York than to Hollywood, means,
I suspect, the increasing importance of the East and the ever growing difficulties of the West as a production center.   Dialogue films,
it is probable, will, for many years, have to go completely to the
stage for their method, and Manhattan, for all its weaknesses, is
hardly likely to give up its title as theatrical capital within the half
decade.   By taking up an alien cinema manner, Hollywood gives
evidence of having been suicidal to its own domination of a mighty
industry. "

No matter, though, if The Letter happens to be, as a sample
of future products of the East Coast studios, merely a deceptive
accident, it is certainly a first-rate photoplay.   As in all talking
pictures, it goes chiefly to the stage for its manner and inspiration,
as well as its story, but, unlike most of them, it makes use of
recognized cinematic qualities as well.   It has movement, pictorial
values, some effective camera work and all the other virtues that
were found in the pioneer silent films of a dying day.

Then, too, it has Jeanne Eagels.   As almost every one has
pointed out, it is being regarded as pretty much of a joke at the
expense of the Actors Equity that its banishment of Miss Eagels
from the stage for two seasons as a severe punishment for her sins
has merely succeeded in throwing her into ranks of the film players,
whence she emerges with the most brilliant performance the talking
pictures have yet provided.

Certainly her characterization of the faithless, homicidal
heroine of the Maugham drama is an enormously moving piece of
work.   The word, "brilliant," is so carelessly employed in criticism
that I hesitate to use it here again, but it is so obviously the right
term that it is impossible to avoid it.   Incidentally, it is not surprising to note that such a distinctive person as Miss Eagels offers
an entirely different portrayal from that of the incomparable Miss
Cornell, who created the role in the American stage version.   Miss
Eagels makes the man-killing lady harder, colder, less frankly sympathetic and less the lady than did her predecessor.   Yet the mere

fact that she refused to work for obvious sympathy in her part made it seem all the more effective, I thought.

One almost epoch-making thing about the picture is that, for probably the first time in cinema history, it changes an important point in an author's play and thereby improves on it enormously. You may possibly recall that a great weakness of the drama was that the climactic scene of the second act was merely an interlude, in which the heroine did not appear. The lady's lawyer went to a Chinese brothel to buy back the incriminating letter the Oriental mistress of the murdered man had in her possession. In the picture version, the Chinese woman demands that the wife come in person for the letter, so that she can humiliate her. Such a change ties up a once incidental episode to the central situation in a way Mr. Maugham really should have thought of.

One other change has been made that is less helpful. Both stage and screen versions ended with the heroine declaring, "With all my heart, I still love the man I killed." In the original, her tormented cry was the sign of her tragedy, the despairing outburst of one doomed to inexorable punishment. In the film, the line is addressed to the husband, rather than to the lawyer, and by that slight change, a different point is made. No longer is she indicating her punishment. Now it is her vengeance. Out of jealousy for the murdered man the husband is dooming his wife to remain for life on the scene of her crime, and it is to taunt him, not to scourge herself, that she tells of her love. I strongly prefer the Maugham version, but, anyway, The Letter is an exceptional picture.

--Richard Watts, Jr. in The Film
Mercury, Vol. 9, No. 18 (March
29, 1929), page 4.

☐ THE LIGHTS OF NEW YORK (Warner Bros. , 1928)

Announced as the first all-talkie, this melodrama of Manhattan night life aroused a lot of attention from the New York critics. The Warners originally intended this to be a short talkie subject, then they got enthusiastic and enlarged it to seven feature reels. It's full of murder and attempted crime.

The cast, headed by Helene Costello, Wheeler Oakman, Cullen Landis and Gladys Brockwell, struggles hard with the pioneer problems of sound filming. None of the players emerge with particular glory. Sound films will have to work out a better technique to advance--and, of course, they will. This film, however, is a landmark of the sound movie.

--Photoplay, Vol. 34, No. 4
(September 1928), page 57.

☐ LILAC TIME (First National, 1928)

     Another thrilling, romantic war drama, in which Colleen
Moore covers herself with glory.

     "Lilac Time" is a small farm near the French front, where
seven of the Royal Flying Corps are quartered. Its lilac garden
forms an exquisite setting for this love story. It is essentially a
beautiful love story, but the war background is as realistic as if it
were the central theme. It is, necessarily, reminiscent of other
air pictures, but it also has much that is new and breath-taking.

     Colleen Moore, as Jeannine, and Gary Cooper, as Captain
Philip Blythe, do beautiful work in the romantic rôles, and an excellent supporting cast assists in the spectacular activity, the result being one of Colleen's most compelling and elaborate pictures.
It's too good to miss.

--Photoplay, Vol. 34, No. 3
(August 1928), page 56.

*   *   *

     By long odds a greater picture than Wings is Lilac Time,
Colleen Moore's contribution to the air epics of the screen. It is
greater than the Paramount picture because it is equally thrilling
and, in addition, has what Wings lacks, a connected, coherent and
dramatic story from which it does not depart for as much as one
foot of film. Lilac Time might be taken as a model for pictures
that are planned as supers. From the opening scene until the last
it seems to concern itself only with telling its story. As it lets
nothing interfere with the telling, the story moves swiftly along its
logical course and holds our interest in it as a story. The same
story set in any other environment would hold our interest. That
is the test that any story should pass before it is screened. If it
does not have enough inherent strength to keep us interested when
it is told in a shanty, it lacks strength enough to warrant it being
told in a palace. Lilac Time has strength enough to warrant it being told in any setting. But it is told in France, and it is war time
when young fellows take their seats in planes and grin as they fly
towards death; when foes meet above clouds and have it out up there
until one combatant falls through a cloud, and the other wipes his
wounds and looks for another fight; when romance remains alive
though nations pass away. Lilac Time is a romance possessing all
the terrific trimmings that war could adorn it with. I saw it before
it had some of the trimmings that will be added prior to its release. It was strictly silent when I viewed it, but when it is released it will have talking sequences and sound effects that should
improve it immensely, for it is a picture that will lend itself admirably to the application of sound. But it is great, even as a silent picture. Colleen never before has appeared in anything with
such dramatic and pictorial sweep. And she never gave a better
performance. She is in the story logically by reason of being a

French girl at whose farm aviators are stationed. At no place
does the story strain itself to keep going. It is quite unlike the
story of Wings which commits suicide when it takes Clara Bow to
France. George Fitzmaurice directed Lilac Time. The last previous picture of his that I viewed--Rose of Monterey--was so beautiful that it was not true, and I had grown to look upon Fitz as a director who had no peer in spreading beauty on the screen, even if
he had to sacrifice drama to get it. I take it back. Fitzmaurice
has done a magnificent job with his direction of Lilac Time. At no
time does he sacrifice drama to beauty, but in several sequences
he mixes the two, giving us scenes of exquisite beauty and dramatic strength. In some shots showing a road crowded with people
who are evacuating a village, Fitzmaurice uses a row of eucalyptus
trees as a gorgeous frame for the action. The shots above the
clouds are not as impressively beautiful as those in Wings, but
George did not have as much latitude in framing them. A director
on the ground can not control very well the work of actors on the
other side of a cloud. I am surprised, though, that a director
with such a highly developed artistic sense as Fitzmaurice possesses, should give us in close-ups a love scene set among lilac
bushes. He had everything at hand to combine into a love scene of
surpassing beauty and tenderness, but in throws all of it away and
gives us the kind of shots that the public is tiring of. There is
another scene that is weakened greatly by close-up treatment. Gary
Cooper is leaving on a flight that means almost certain death, and
is saying farewell to Colleen, whom he loves. The leave-taking is
shown in an exceedingly stupid closeup. It should have been a
medium shot, with the line of planes showing dimly in the background, thereby retaining as part of the scene the grim thought
back of it. Gary Cooper gives a splendid performance in Lilac
Time. He is more human and likable than I have seen him in most
of his pictures. Eugenie Besserer is fine as Colleen's mother, and
several others in a long cast distinguish themselves. The picture
is one that I recommend without reservation to all exhibitor readers
of The Spectator.

--Welford Beaton in The Film
Spectator, Vol. 5, No. 9 (June
23, 1928), page 8.

☐ LILIOM (Fox, 1930)

Molnar's play ventures courageously upon the screen under
its own name instead of bidding for patronage with the kind of lurid
re-baptism Hollywood has accustomed us to. That is the first thing
in its favor, though the actors who play in it seem to disagree rather radically about how the name should be pronounced. Secondly,
it sticks with unusual fidelity to its original, in spirit and in lines
--even to some lines that to an American audience are so foreign
as to seem rather silly. There has been an elaboration in one sec-
tion--some rather giddy conversation between Liliom and the Heavenly

Magistrate added, presumably to keep things from getting morbid
and depressing--but it may be forgiven because it keeps Mr. Warner on the screen longer. Thirdly, it has been directed and mounted
with obviously the best of intentions to be dignified and beautiful.

However, it doesn't make a thoroughly satisfactory motion
picture. Its meaning, never easy to pin down definitely either on
the stage or between book covers, becomes even harder to get at
in the more scattered form that the cinema puts it in. A young
tough kills himself to escape arrest, leaving to mourn him a girl
whom he has often beaten, who is about to bear him a child. After
some years he is permitted to return to earth for a day, and the
only significant thing he does is to slap the daughter whose birth he
did not live to see. Then he is whisked away again, while mother
and daughter talk about beatings that do not hurt. Well may a hard-
boiled movie goer ask what it's all about.

Liliom and Julie--he with his contradictions, she with her
love--are characters that have delicate overtones in the intimacy of
a stage production; one gets fluttering intimations of their souls,
and a feeling of being close to some of the mysteries of love and
death, almost close enough to look into them. Putting the play on
the screen has something of the effect of presenting it in an outdoor
auditorium: its peculiar poetic mingling of literalness and mysticism
is all blown away, the meaning we were almost grasping--with our
feelings if not with our minds--gets lost in space, and the magic
is gone.

The only person who comes near to doing what the whole
play ought to do is Rose Hobart. She is believable, if not explain-
able, by sheer force of being always intensely there, loving. It is
a performance full of unusual beauty. Charles Farrell is picturesque
but juvenile--so juvenile that there is a distinct flavor of Penrod
about him. Liliom was after all a man, not a pre-adolescent up to
childish mischief, and his charm a definitely virile one in spite of
the bad-boyishness that lingered in him. Mr. Farrell would have
seemed very much better in a silent version of the picture.

The other people in the cast, as characters, are just background to help along the story and supply atmosphere: as actors
they fill the characters exceptionally well, with an old-world effect
that Mr. Borzage is expert at in his direction. Individually, Lee
Tracy, with economical but telling strokes, tosses off one of the
outstanding bits. Estelle Taylor might be called opulent, and suc-
culent if not seductive--she necessarily misses some of the miserly
and hungry qualities that are in Liliom's employer. H. B. Warner
is such a courteous and affable Heavenly Magistrate that it would be
almost a pleasure to be damned by him.

The pictorial effect of the picture is a bit affected and arty:
the modernistic elements seem more an attempt to get into an up-to-
date style than a sympathetic effort to supply a visual mood for the
play. The train that takes Liliom into the after-world is a clever

idea, but its fantasy has rather too much of the literal about it; it
looks like nothing in the world so much as a mechanical toy.

The music is especially effective, both in its composition
and in its use.

--James Shelley Hamilton in
Cinema, Vol. 1, No. 8 (December 1930), pages 37-38.

☐ LITTLE ANNIE ROONEY (Pickford/United Artists, 1925)

Several months ago Mary Pickford asked the readers of
Photoplay what sort of type they liked to see her play. And there
came an immediate and overwhelming number of votes for Mary in
kid parts. In a way, Little Annie Rooney is an answer to Photoplay's readers. And the only truthful thing we can say is that we
like their judgment.

For this is the Mary Pickford who will always be loved and
welcomed. This is Mary at her best and at her truest. She isn't
playing a character from any special book; she isn't really acting
a part. She is just the embodiment of anybody's little girl. The
story is set in the slums of New York with Mary as the leader of
a gang that looks like a junior League of Nations. Annie Rooney
is Irish and the daughter of a cop. In spite of the nearness of the
majesty of the law, she's a great little gangster until the tragedy
of lawlessness finally hits home. And the scene in which Annie
learns of the death of her father in a dance hall fight is one of the
greatest she has ever done. Here is Mary playing with so much
sincerity that she fairly wrings your heart.

Most of the picture, however, is just sheer joyousness.
Mary seems honestly happy to get back to pinafores. During most
of the scenes, she plays with children--the funniest bunch you ever
saw. The opening scenes which show Mary in the center of a
mean Irish fight are simply great. And the benefit show for Gari-
baldi, the Wop's horse, is another great episode. There is just
enough hint of a love story to give it a nice little lift at the end.
But you'll like Annie when she undergoes a blood transfusion to
save a dying man, all the time believing the operation means death
to her.

As for Mary's problem to find stories, she can make as
many more like this one as she finds time to film.

--A. S. in Photoplay, Vol. 28,
No. 5 (October 1925), page 50.

☐ LITTLE LORD FAUNTLEROY (Pickford/United Artists, 1921)

     Mary Pickford's best picture, and one of the most beautiful
things ever filmed. The children's classic story has become a
classic of the screen, and it is entirely fitting that "Our Mary"
should immortalize it. It is the sweetest, the most delightful of
all her performances; she plays Dearest, the mother, and Cedric
Errol, the Little Lord, in the greatest double exposure scenes ever
made. Cameraman Charles Rosher has done many wonderful things
in his long career as Little Mary's photographer, but this is his
most notable work. The film at first drags, but this is more than
made up for in the later scenes, which are dramatic and pathetic
and charming and funny. We take issue with the self-appointed
critics who write that Mary is not a good Little Lord; that she is
always Mary Pickford, hardly a little boy. To our mind, she is
perfect in the part. Her diminutive little velvet-clad figure, her
swaggering walk, her boyish mannerisms all evidence her great art.
Her Dearest is one of the screen's loveliest portraits. All the
pathos and the beauty of motherhood are masterfully painted. The
direction, by Alfred Green and Jack Pickford, is consistent, but
we suspect that Mary, more than anyone else, is responsible for
this picture. Claude Gillingwater gives the best performance of any
actor's this year, as the grouchy, gouty Earl of Dorincourt, whom
Cedric teaches to smile. His scenes with the star are touching,
and she generously made him her co-star in them. Take the chil-
dren--take the whole family!

                             --Photoplay, Vol. 21, No. 1
                             (December 1921), page 60.

☐ LITTLE OLD NEW YORK (Cosmopolitan/Goldwyn, 1923)

     One of the pleasant things the screen can do is to mirror the
re-creation of things and people gone by. This capacity gives a
definite charm to Little Old New York quite distinct from the story
itself.

     Set down in east lower Manhattan a hundred years ago, one
may just see the sights of the embryo metropolis, and let the tale
that is spun there wander along, bringing one here and there face to
face with personages long dust and sites long changed by skyscrapers
and elevated railroads. To the antiquarian there is considerable to
awaken the interest. There is Fulton's steamboat, and the old prize
ring of the fire-house, the office of John Jacob Astor, the eating-
house set up by the first Delmonico, and a residence or so of the
fashionable where the young bloods of that day quaffed their claret
untroubled by any prophesy of the coming a hundred years hence of
Mr. Volstead and his prohibition act. If one wishes to get back to
the story there is Marion Davies masquerading as an Irish lad in
knickers, a stranger in a strange land but surely on her way to put-

ting it over old Mr. Astor and winning a fortune and a cheer for
the Irish--which is almost as good as the mother-love stuff.   Miss
Davies makes a charming boy.

Unfortunately most of the characters are not personages but
are clearly observed to have been made up and painstakingly directed.   This is too bad when such an authentic background has
been provided by Joseph Urban for them to move against.   It is
chiefly this background, nearly always effectively photographed, that
makes Little Old New York an outstanding production.

--Exceptional Photoplays, Vol. 4,
Nos. 1 and 2 (October-November 1923), page 3.

*   *   *

A picture must be almost perfect to get by the New York
newspaper reviewers without adverse criticism of some sort.   They
are a hard-boiled, long-suffering aggregation, oftentimes taking
their work too seriously, approaching every picture with the firm
determination to live up to their title of critics regardless of its
entertainment value.

Little Old New York opened with unanimous approbation.
Marion Davies earned a place in the first line of stars for her
work in When Knighthood Was in Flower.   She firmly established
herself in Little Old New York.   It is a charming love story of
Old New York at the time when Vanderbilt was a ferry operator,
when Delmonico first opened his little restaurant, when Washington
Irving was a gay young blade, when John Jacob Astor was laying
the foundation of the great family fortune, when Robert Fulton invented the first steamboat.   As Patricia O'Day, a beautiful colleen
who is forced by her father to come to America impersonating her
dead brother as heir to an estate, she could not have been surpassed by any actress on any screen.   She should be decorated by
the Irish Free State for distinguished service.

Medals should also be sent to Sidney Olcott, who directed
the picture with a song in his heart, to Luther Reed, who adapted
Rita Johnson Young's stage play, to Joseph Urban, who framed it
in technical beauty, and every member of the cast should be cited
for splendid performances.   Harrison Ford plays young Delevan,
whom "Pat's" father seeks to deprive of the legacy by masquerading
his daughter as his dead son, with rare understanding.

Even the Authors' League must admit this is art.

--Photoplay, Vol. 24, No. 5
(October 1923), page 72.

☐ LONESOME (Universal, 1928)

        Barbara Kent and Glenn Tryon present a modernistic romance
of young love. It has a big city and beach resort background and an
earn-your-living flavor and would be more impressive if it were the
first picture relying on trick shots for novelty and dramatic mood.
Both Barbara and Glenn acquit themselves as masters in two of the
best human interest scenes yet filmed. You won't be sorry you saw
Lonesome.
                                        --Photoplay, Vol. 34, No. 2
                                        (July 1928), page 56.

                          *   *   *

        Fejos recently completed for Universal his second picture.
It is called Lonesome, and while it is not as bold in conception as
The Last Moment, it is a departure from the routine, and further
strengthens my conviction that Fejos is a director of great ability.
It would have been a better picture if it did not contain some totally
meaningless titles that now mar it. There is no story, wherein
lies its strength. A girl and a boy, unknown to one another, are
lonely in a great city. They come together and fall in love. That
is all. Every step taken until the paths of the two parties to the
romance converge is directed admirably. In a beach sequence, and
in one showing the concessions street of a resort, Fejos has too
much animation in his backgrounds, the only flaw I can find in the
picture. It was too long when I viewed it, but I assume that fault
has been corrected. What surprises me about the production is
that it was made. There is nothing in it that producers insist must
be in every picture to assure its success. In trying to discover
how it happened I learned that Carl Laemmle Jr. , battled everyone
on the lot on behalf of the script and finally won his father's con-
sent to its production. The result is a picture of which Universal
has reason to be proud. I think it will make money, but in any
event, it is a fine thing to have done. It would have been finer if
the studio had been brave enough to leave out all the titles.
                                        --Welford Beaton in The Film
                                        Spectator, Vol. 5, No. 9 (June
                                        23, 1928), page 7.

☐ LONG PANTS (Harry Langdon/First National, 1927)

        In the spring a young man's fancy turns to Long Pants--and
when Harry Langdon gets his first pair of long pants he's sitting on
top of the world. So much so that he casts aside the little country
gal and falls madly in love with the vamp, who is incidentally a
bandit. Harry soon realizes his mistake and returns home. Not
much of a story for six long reels, but Langdon is always funny and

so who cares a great deal about the story.
>   --Photoplay, Vol. 32, No. 1
>   (June 1927), page 56.

☐ THE LOST WORLD (First National, 1925)

This is a man's picture, for men love to go puttering through
wildernesses seeking big game and women like to wear pretty gowns
and powder their noses. A scientist asserts that he has found the
huge pre-historic mammals that were supposed to be extinct ten
million years ago and is promptly called a liar. Wallace Beery is
the scientist and anybody who calls Wallace a liar better prepare
for a battle. An expedition sets forth for "The Lost World." They
find it with its hundred-foot dinosaurs, brontosaureses, diplodocuses
and Bull Montana, playing the part of a huge ape. They leave Bull
in the wilderness but start back with a dinosaur. Arriving in London the dino breaks loose, knocks down buildings, breaks down London bridge and finally swims away into the ocean.
>   --Photoplay, Vol. 27, No. 5
>   (April 1925), page 38.

*   *   *

Some amazingly lifelike prehistoric reptiles and some lifeless humans mixed together in a moderately effective interpretation
of Conan Doyle's famous thriller.
>   --Robert E. Sherwood in Life,
>   Vol. 85, No. 2210 (March 12,
>   1925), page 32.

☐ LOVE (M-G-M, 1927)

Love is right. The original title of Anna Karenina would
have been wrong. It isn't Tolstoi, but it is John Gilbert and Greta
Garbo which, after Flesh and the Devil, is what the "fans" are crying for. Tolstoi's devastating analysis of the tragedy of illicit love
is almost completely made over into the recounting of a love affair
between a desirable woman and a desiring man, beautifully presented and magnetically acted.

You will have tremendous sympathy for Anna and Aleksei
Vronsky, two honorable persons who are the victims of an anti-so-
cial force. Even in the new set of circumstances invented for them
by Frances Marion, there is something of the original strength of
their characters. And Anna throws herself under the grinding
wheels of a train at the end, thereby risking an unhappy ending as
one little concession to Tolstoi, the censors and those who love the

novel.   But if you think that the finer side of the book--the romance
of Kitty and Kostia Levin--is even hinted at, you are nothing but a
silly.   The movie has separated the wheat of sex from the chaff of
preachment.

And so the film comes to us as a glamorous and picturesque
romance, untroubled by stern moralizing and flecked by comedy
generously presented to Tolstoi in the person of George Fawcett
as a Grand Duke.

Credit Gilbert with a double assist.   Not only does he give
a great performance, but he assisted Edmund Goulding in the direction.   Greta Garbo is beautiful and touching.   Brandon Hurst, as
Karenine, also gets in on the glory.

--Photoplay, Vol. 32, No. 6
(November 1927), page 52.

☐ THE LOVE PARADE (Paramount, 1929)

Sparkling as Burgundy, and almost as intoxicating, The Love
Parade is one of the outstanding pictures of the year.   It is Lubitsch's most brilliant effort since The Marriage Circle.   The little
director here conquers light opera!

After the dashing nobleman marries the Queen of Sylvania,
he gets durned tired of constantly obeying.   So he bludgeons the
queen into letting him be head man.

Maurice Chevalier, a great favorite after his first American
picture, despite a weak story, is grand as the prince.   His songs
are triumphs.   Jeanette MacDonald is an eye-feast as the queen,
and sings well.   Lupino Lane amuses.

The music is relatively unimportant, although "Dream Lover"
and "Nobody's Using It Now" may be popular.   Don't miss The Love
Parade.

--Photoplay, Vol. 37, No. 1
(December 1929), page 52.

*   *   *

Here is excellent, gay entertainment, and a very sizeable
step forward in the evolution of musical comedy on the screen, a
special treat for those who enjoy what they call sophistication.

The story has lots of novelty.   A Chevalier sort of gentle-
man--a man with an engaging smile and infinite La Vie Parisienne
virility--is representing his native Sylvania in some diplomatic capacity in Paris.   Because his amorous escapades have reached the
scandalous point he is sent back to his queen, Louise the First, for

discipline. Louise--young, lovely, unmarried--is the kind of queen
who wakes in the morning with a lusty song on her lips about her
dream lover--she renders it complete, rising in her nightie, with
chorus accompaniment from her ladies-in-waiting, and then steps
into her bath in full view of the camera, showing plenty but not too
much. She is manifestly ripe for just what is coming to her--
Maurice Chevalier. It is easily managed for this attractive young
man to rise quickly through an accommodating accolade to Prince
Consort. But the queen has taken him for only--well, husband purposes, leaving him no functions outside the royal chamber. His
manhood rebels, and in the cleverest last part of the picture he
accomplishes a polite taming of the shrew that puts the queen completely in her feminine place. Some hints from the life of a certain Queen of Great Britain and Ireland must have crept into the
later episodes.

It is all done very cleverly--cleverly is just the word. And
most entertainingly, except for occasional lapses into song, which are
awkwardly managed in the fashion of the old-time cue-for-music
kind of thing, with the songs notably commonplace both in music and
words. These ditties are probably there because M. Chevalier has
a reputation as a singing comedian and Jeanette MacDonald has a
voice that ought to be used. They really interrupt, rather unjusti-
fiably, an amusing flow of first-rate comedy.

The whole movement of it--barring stoppages for singing--is
very skilfully arranged. This must have been pre-arranged in the
script, but Lubitsch, with his famous "touch, " will get most of the
credit. No doubt he deserves it. It is impossible to think of any
other director who could have put this story on the screen with so
many happy results.

M. Chevalier has a personality that rides this fable with
superfine, elegant ease. "It, " with a French accent, he has aplenty.
If he objects to adoration he had better hurry back to France before
this picture has made the rounds. Lady fans will just love him,
and gentlemen ditto will enjoy learning from him.

Jeanette MacDonald has something more than an unusually
good voice--and what it is is not hidden under any bushel. As an
actress she is just a sweet American girl--it might be from Kansas
City--and being sat on all the thrones of Europe wouldn't make her
any different. Her lingerie will be widely admired and envied.

Lillian Roth is pretty and blatantly Broadway--maybe it is
not her fault, or indeed a fault at all--and Lupino Lane does the
same kind of cockney knock-about stuff he has been doing intermin-
ably for several dogs' ages. They both add the common to the
Lubitsch touch. The Afghan Ambassador supplies something quite
uncommon.

To be deadly solemn about a gay and lovely thing, The Love
Parade is cinematically important quite apart from the pleasure it

gives. It breaks away from many a trite way of doing such things, and proves what has not been so convincingly proved before, --that musical comedy can be done on the screen as no possible stage could do it.   The farewell to Paris number--sung by Chevalier, Chevalier's valet and Chevalier's dog--is one of those proofs. In such a notable piece of pioneering it is perhaps ungracious to harp on the banality of the songs and some of the secondary comedy-- they are really poor only in comparison with the abundant best of the picture, and they are not poor at all when compared with most of the photographed musical shows.

--James Shelley Hamilton in
Cinema, Vol. 1, No. 1 (Janu-
ary 1930), page 38.

☐ MADAME SANS GENE (Famous Players-Lasky/Paramount, 1925)

Here is a motion picture answer to the croakings of the cyn- ics.   In it Gloria Swanson sets herself securely in motion picture history as a great actress and the Paramount company earns un- stinted credit for the manner in which it has screened this fine stage classic of Sardou and Moreau.   Filmed against authentic back- grounds of the French revolution, perfectly costumed, wonderfully cast and acted, and edited with rare judgment and finish, the entire production is a credit to motion pictures and reflects unlimited credit on the organization that produced it.

Primarily Madame Sans Gene (Madame Devil-May-Care) is a comedy, but as it is produced on the screen it is one of the finest educational pictures ever made.   In it Madame Rejane made one of the great triumphs of her notable career, and the great rôle was a fitting wedding present from her company to Gloria.   The only mem- ber of her supporting company with whom we are familiar on the American screen is Charles De Roche, who plays her husband, Sergeant Lefebvre, who becomes a Marshal of France.   Emile Drain, probably the foremost portrayer of the rôle of Napoleon in the world today, is magnificent, and the producers were not afraid to contrast their star with some of the most beautiful women of the French stage.

Sans Gene was a laundress in the days when Napoleon was a struggling lieutenant of artillery.   The revolution made the wash- woman a duchess and her experiences in trying to conduct herself in the French court are terrifying and amusing.

This report would be incomplete without credit for the splen- did work of Forrest Halsey, who adapted the story, and Julian John- son, who edited the picture.

--James R. Quirk in Photoplay,
Vol. 28, No. 1 (June 1925),
page 48.

☐ THE MAGICIAN (Metro-Goldwyn, 1926)

Disappointing stuff from a once great director, this latest Rex Ingram production is entertainment only if the morbid and unhealthy are of interest to you. Adapted from a story by Somerset Maugham, it tells of Margaret Dauncey, who has been a nice gel except for a magician's evil eye. The cast, with the exception of Alice Terry, who gives a colorless performance, is as foreign as the backgrounds. Decidedly not for children.

--Photoplay, Vol. 31, No. 2
(January 1927), page 54.

☐ THE MAN WHO LAUGHS (Universal, 1928)

This picture may get by in Europe under the name of Art, but in this country it will have little interest. Dragged into a super-production by extremely slow action, it loses the dramatic value of a story which might have succeeded under the name of "something different." Historically it gives an insight into the lives of the yokels of the King James II period. Conrad Veidt does a splendid piece of acting.

--Photoplay, Vol. 33, No. 6
(May 1928), page 55.

☐ MANHANDLED (Famous Players-Lasky/Paramount, 1924)

Once again we can record a further stride ahead for Gloria Swanson. This story by Arthur Stringer isn't very much but the star lifts it into genuine interest and vitality. Tessie McGuire is a little shop girl, whose sweetheart is a garage mechanic with an invention for a new carburetor. Tessie catches her boss' roving eye, gets invited to a wild party, plays with fire for awhile, becomes an imitation Russian countess in a smart modiste shop and, tired of the men she continually encounters, returns to her old love, now a millionaire by way of his invention. Pretty inferior stuff as dramatic literature, but you will forget all that in Miss Swanson's absorbing work. She does a Charlie Chaplin imitation that will surprise you and has several really moving moments. Incidentally, the story is sexy-plus.

--Photoplay, Vol. 26, No. 4
(September 1924), page 43.

☐ MANSLAUGHTER (Paramount, 1922)

          Cecil DeMille's illness of last winter seems to have been as
good a thing for him as Lydia Thorne's penitentiary term was for
her.   Lydia Thorne emerged from the gray walls a human being.
Cecil DeMille came from long imprisonment in a sick room with a
new touch of sentiment and sincerity to add to his sense of brilliance
and timeliness and the result is Manslaughter.   This photoplay is
the best thing Mr. DeMille has done.   It is not perfect.   It has
theatric lapses; it collapses with the Pollyanna regeneration of the
heroine in prison and the out-of-character slip to the depths of the
district attorney.   Yet it is an admirable commentary on rich, rushing, headstrong Young America, done with a fullness which no stage
production could possibly approach and shown with a descriptive detail which no novelistic word painter could hope to equal.

          The biggest stories are easiest to summarize in a sentence
because they hammer home a single theme.   Manslaughter is a one
theme parable--the parable of the platinum-plated, utterly free, arrogant, young American girl, who has come to believe that the
world was created to be her playground and all mankind to be her
servants.   Such is Lydia Thorne, who is oblivious to suffering because she has never felt its pang.   Dan O'Bannon, young district
attorney, both loves and deplores her, and when in a moment of
reckless disregard she causes the death of an honest young officer
only trying to do his duty, it is O'Bannon who fights for her conviction on a charge of manslaughter and puts her away where she
must think, eventually repent, and begins to learn.

          Leatrice Joy as Lydia Thorne meets her great opportunity.
Thomas Meighan's work as O'Bannon is one of his finest performances worthy of this real actor.   He is a fixed star, not a comet.
                              --Photoplay, Vol. 22, No. 6
                                (November 1922), page 65.

☐ MARE NOSTRUM (Metro-Goldwyn, 1926)

          A most disappointing film from the man who directed The
Four Horsemen.   Most of the New York critics dodged the issue,
because of its foreign atmosphere and the reputation of Rex Ingram.
Doubtful of its entertainment value they attributed to it artistic merit
which it does not possess.   A repulsive quality to it sent this writer
to a soda fountain to get the bad taste out of his mouth.
                              --Photoplay, Vol. 24, No. 5
                                (April 1926), page 56.

                    *   *   *

          Rounding out a quartet of big special productions sponsored
by the Marcus Loew forces which are being presented simultaneously

on Broadway for long runs at advanced prices, and thereby estab-
lishing a record, Metro-Goldwyn is offering the Criterion Theatre
Mare Nostrum (Our Sea), a Rex Ingram production featuring Alice
Terry and Antonio Moreno adapted from the novel by the famous
Spanish writer Blasco Ibáñez, the author of The Four Horsemen of
the Apocalypse and other notable screen successes.

Deriving its title from the term dating from the Roman era,
affectionately applied by those living along its shores to the Mediterranean, Mare Nostrum which in English signifies "Our Sea," is a
story woven around this great body of water extending from Gibraltar
to the Suez Canal lying between Europe and Asia and Africa whose
shores through the centuries have been the ampitheatre for many of
the greatest happenings in the world's history.

Ibáñez has embodied the spirit of this sea and its hold upon
its people in the persons of the Ferragut family of Spain, the male
members of which for generations had been seafaring men and cry-
stallized it in the character of Ulysses Ferragut. At the opening
of the story we see Ulysses as a lad becoming imbued with the fascination of the Mediterranean. The year 1914 finds him the owner
of a fast freight steamer which he has endearingly christened Mare
Nostrum, which because of the huge losses he has sustained he is
about to give up.

The outbreak of the World War changes all this and brings
almost fabulous wealth for each cargo. A picture of the goddess
Amphitrite typifying this sea and known as the sweetheart of the
sailors, has always fascinated Ulysses who married without love a
shrewish woman of his family's choice and has one son, Estaban,
whom he idolizes. Amidst the ruins of Pompeii he sees a beautiful
girl and although he does not recognize until later that it is because
she personifies Amphitrite he is strangely attracted to her and falls
deeply in love with her. This woman, Freya, an Austrian spy, under orders accepts his attentions and Ulysses becomes so infatuated
that he neglects business, family, everything, and to show the depth
of his love even pilots a boat to a rendezvous where fuel and supplies are transferred to a German submarine. In the meantime his
son Estaban, who has come to Naples looking for him, starts back
home. A passenger steamer is torpedoed by the submarine and
Ulysses learns that his own son was among those who were killed.
Stung with remorse he thirsts for vengeance. Freya who has become sickened with her work and is no longer of use to her super-
iors is sent to France on a mission which means her capture. She
sends for Ulysses who comes to her but the memory of Estaban and
her responsibility causes him to cast her off. Wholeheartedly he
turns over his ship to the French. Freya is executed as a spy and
Ulysses' ship carrying troops is torpedoed. With his last shot he
sinks the submarine but is himself swallowed up by the sea. Sinking in its depths his spirit joins the spirit of the woman he loved
who typified "Mare Nostrum."

Filmed in the actual surroundings in Italy and Spain and on
the Mediterranean this production is a pictorial gem with quaint

scenes in the old European villages, palaces, impressive remains
of a past civilization at Pompeii and beautiful scenic shots, all
serving as a vital part as the background of the story and in bringing out the spirit of the theme.

Characteristic of Ibáñez' works in Mare Nostrum there is a
deep underlying note. Here it is really the sea itself and in only a
slightly lesser degree the horror of ruthless submarine warfare
which claimed as its prey women and children. This idea, Mr.
Ingram has effectively transferred to the screen, preserving the
power and impressiveness of the theme. His work shows imagination, artistry, finish, great care and infinite detail. Much footage
is used in establishing the atmosphere and the earlier reels up to
the point where Freya discloses her identity as a spy are largely
narrative. With the appearance of the German submarine the dramatic interest quickens and there is tremendous drama in the idea
of having the hero being unwittingly a factor in the death of his own
son. The same is true of the deaths of Freya and Ulysses, situations which will be totally unexpected by the average movie fan.

Mr. Ingram's treatment of the submarine angle is quite different from other current films dealing with the World War, and
not even the films made during the war have shown the Germans
in a more unfavorable light. This extends to the type of men portraying these roles, their every action even to the gloating of an
officer over sinking the passenger ship and the attempt of another
to escape from the submarine by striking down his own men.

Mare Nostrum, insofar as the human element is concerned,
is a tragedy despite the allegorical ending. There are, however,
effective lighter moments in the character of the old family cook,
a monstrously fat fellow, admirably and amusingly played by
Hughie Mack. The story is powerful and impressive. It holds
your attention and makes you think, for there is much that is allegorical, with considerable of its meaning and psychology not instantly evident on the surface.

Alice Terry, always beautiful, never looked more stunning
than as Freya, and superbly handles this role. Aided by Mr. Ingram's excellent direction she makes this character a continual
enigma. There is a strange fascination surrounding this woman,
you are never quite sure as to whether she is the goddess personified or merely her physical counterpart, her attitude at times suggests first one and then the other.

Antonio Moreno is fine as Ulysses. He handled the role with
distinction and presents a striking appearance that will bring flutters
to the feminine heart.

Mr. Ingram, presumably in faithfully following the Ibáñez
story, while he has made his leading characters interesting and human has not attempted to make them sugary or heroic. One does
not readily sympathize with a man who, infatuated by a siren, for-

sakes even an unloved wife and a son or a woman who uses this
love for ulterior purposes, although the later repentance of both
softens the effect.   This, however, does not prevent their story
from being interesting, even fascinating.

Mr. Ingram has undoubtedly produced a big picture.   Technically, artistically, from the standpoint of acting, direction, scenic
investiture and in the power of its theme and the sincerity with
which it has been transferred to the screen without compromising
with the conventional, it is superb.

In its psychology Mare Nostrum diverges from many of the
familiar screen formulas and it is on the attitude of the masses
toward these changes that its general audience appeal will largely
depend, for everything else is in its favor.   Undoubtedly it will
command a large following especially among those who grasp its
deeper significance.   It is the kind of picture that will be widely
discussed and this in itself, as every showman knows, is a box office angle of no inconsiderable value.

> --C. S. Sewell in The Moving
> Picture World, Vol. 78, No. 9
> (February 27, 1926), pages 785-
> 786.

☐   THE MARRIAGE CIRCLE (Warner Bros. , 1924)

It is becoming more generally recognized by producers that
a story can be told on the screen with pictures, plus intelligence,
and does not have to have a title every thirty or forty feet.   Also
it can be told clearly, concisely and straightforwardly, without
"flashbacks" or other nuisances.   Mr. Chaplin did it with A Woman
of Paris, and Ernst Lubitsch has done it again with The Marriage
Circle.   What stands out in this picture is its simplicity.   Here is
a story with a number of human characters in it.   The picture
starts, the characters themselves reveal the story, which runs
smoothly along to its logical ending.   There is no straining for effects, no effort to be spectacular.   It's all very simple, very human, and immensely entertaining.

The story deals with the complications which beset a young
wife who tries to steal the husband of her best friend.   The plot is
extremely thin and has no distinction whatever.   It has certain farcical angles which are most amusing, but it is the treatment which
makes the picture.

Mr. Lubitsch has been notably economical even in his use of
incident.   The scenes are laid in Vienna, but there is no attempt at
scenic effects.   It is just everyday life and surroundings.   The cast
is uniformly good.   There are two wives, admirably played by Marie
Prevost and Florence Vidor, and two husbands, played by Monte

Blue and that delightfully sophisticated actor, Adolphe Menjou.
Creighton Hale also contributes an excellent performance. It would
be hard to award first place to any one of these five. The women
probably will give it to Miss Prevost, but there is something positively enchanting in the work of Mr. Menjou. He's such a "wise egg."

                                        --Photoplay, Vol. 25, No. 5
                                          (April 1924), page 61.

☐ MERRY-GO-ROUND (Universal, 1923)

        When Erich von Stroheim had completed Foolish Wives, and
launched it on its spectacular career, it was announced that his
next production would be a Viennese drama entitled Merry-Go-Round.

        Von Stroheim had established himself as a real directorial
genius--wilful, inspired, daringly original and painfully erratic.
His Blind Husbands and The Devil's Pass-key were both weird, unusual, incoherent pictures which touched the heights of pictorial
artistry, and the depths of literary stupidity. Foolish Wives covered an even wider range. Von Stroheim spent a vast fortune on
it, building sets of incredible magnificence and employing large
mobs of extras in most of the scenes. He used up several hundred
thousand feet of film in photographing the picture, reducing it to
less than ten thousand feet in the finished product. It was wanton
waste, and put a terrible dent in the bank roll of Carl Laemmle,
the president of the Universal Company; but Foolish Wives was a
singularly interesting picture--and observers of the movie industry
were anxious to know what the picturesque von Stroheim would do
in Merry-Go-Round.

        When Merry-Go-Round was released, a year and a half after
Foolish Wives, it proved to be superior in every respect to the previous von Stroheim productions. It possessed the qualities of genius
which had marked these earlier pictures, and distinguished them,
and it lacked the incoherence, the extravagant exaggeration, the
total disregard for form, which had marred them. Like the others,
it was distinctly Continental in flavor: its scene was a Viennese
amusement park, and its characters humble show folk and lordly
members of the Austrian nobility. In this respect, it was typical
of von Stroheim's work.

        There was one emphatic catch, however. In the finished
print of Merry-Go-Round, as it appeared on the screen, was the
announcement that the picture had been directed by Rupert Julian.
Von Stroheim's name was missing.

        Von Stroheim had started Merry-Go-Round, quarreled with
his employer, Carl Laemmle, and then quitted Universal City in
what is technically known as "a huff." His relations with the officers of the organization had been none too happy since his financial

splurge on Foolish Wives, and the ill-feeling evidently came to a
head when it was found that he intended to follow a similarly costly
policy in Merry-Go-Round. So the work of completing this picture
was intrusted to the competent, as it later appeared, hands of
Rupert Julian.

Those who saw Merry-Go-Round, and appreciated its excellence, were anxious to know just where von Stroheim left off, and
Rupert Julian began. Their interested queries on this subject were
answered by Mr. Julian himself, in the following communication to
the New York Times:

"Mr. von Stroheim started the production on August
25, 1922. I was placed in charge on October 7, without
any opportunity whatever for preparation. I assumed
charge, therefore, and in order to progress with as little
chaos as possible, I retained the staff and most of the
original cast engaged by my predecessor. Naturally, in
the circumstances, I entered the situation facing varying
degrees of antagonism, as the staff and cast had been
selected personally by von Stroheim.

"The original script of von Stroheim's totaled over
1,500 scenes. When I was placed in charge von Stroheim
had shot 271 scenes, using 83,000 feet of film at a cost
of $220,000. If I had attempted to complete the production
as mapped out it would have been one of footage which
could not possibly have been used. And in addition to
this matter of excessive footage, the censorship question
would have been a serious one, if ever the original script
were followed. So when I assumed charge I discarded the
original script, and from day to day built the story and
characterizations of Merry-Go-Round as it now stands.

"Following several weeks' work on the production, I
called in Harvey Gates to collaborate with me on the story
I had in mind. And the love story of Merry-Go-Round as
it was presented is absolutely original. In the production,
as it stands, the entire footage, with the exception of approximately 600 feet, was directed by me. The introduction of Norman Kerry, Dorothy Wallace and Sidney Brace,
the groom, was not part of my work. One scene of Kerry
in a carriage and also that of the banquet sequence and
that of the elopement of the Countess with the groom were
not mine.

"All the scenes carrying the theme of the story were
directed by me, and also all the scenes in which crowds
were employed. The retreat of the Austrian army sequence was 'shot' in forty-five minutes through the use
of eight cameras.

"I finished the production on January 8. The cost
sheet stood at $220,000 when I took the picture over. I
spent $170,000 in making all the rest of the production as
it was shown on the screen. The reason for my giving
these figures is to correct the impression that I was re-

sponsible for spending an excessive amount of money in
the making of this film.   Seeing that I was forced to begin operations with a very expensive cast drawing high
salaries continuously, I have been highly commended for
holding the cost of production within the figures I have
mentioned.

"I had no part in any quarrel or controversy between
Universal and Mr. von Stroheim.   I have had no thought
of raising any question concerning the situation in which
I was placed, except that I have discovered that through
a misunderstanding some of the New York newspapers
have credited von Stroheim with making important sequences in this production, when these sequences actually
were originated and directed by myself.

"In the original script there were approximately 4,000
feet of titles alone.   Due to the fact that it is impossible
to present a production with commercial success with a
length of more than ten reels, at the most, in practically
all the theatres of the country, and with the exhibitors
clamoring for less footage, it easily can be understood
that it was imperative to change the story of Merry-Go-
Round, if for no other reason than the fact that 1,500
script scenes and 4,000 feet of titles could not under any
circumstances be produced finally under 20,000 feet.
And, moreover, it would mean the photographing of several hundred thousand feet of film in order to have the
material with which to cut the production.

"Of course, I do not mean to say or imply that Mr.
von Stroheim might not have made a successful picture,
and even a complete one, from his script.   I do say,
however, and undoubtedly Universal felt that way, that it
would have been a tremendously expensive production.
The point upon which I wish to lay especial emphasis is
the fact that the film now being shown is my work, with
the exception of a few hundred feet...."

From this it would appear that von Stroheim furnished the
atmosphere of Merry-Go-Round--the costumes, the settings and the
general mannerisms of the Viennese characters.   Mr. Julian furnished the story and the directorial details.

Although an enforced collaboration of this kind usually ends
in disaster, in the case of Merry-Go-Round it worked out beautifully.   The European flavor that von Stroheim imparted to the production was marvellously effective.   I am no authority on Viennese
amusement parks, but it seemed to me that the details were perfect in every way.   The tawdry tinsel of the place, the semblance
of hilarity, and the undercurrent of black tragedy were reproduced
vividly on the screen.   In contrast to this world of painted canvas
and cheap side shows was the gilded magnificence of the Austrian
court, centering in the person of Emperor Franz Josef, perfectly
impersonated by Anton Vaverka.

This atmospheric aspect was von Stroheim's contribution to the film. The rest of the credit--and there was plenty to spare-- belonged to Rupert Julian.

The heroine of Merry-Go-Round was a pitiful little girl who dusted the wooden horses, lions and giraffes on the whirling car- rousel. She was coveted by her villainous boss, a burly showman with a mean eye, and loved by a miserable hunchback who tended the menagerie ape.

Then there appeared on the scene a pompous officer of Franz Josef's court, a stiff, swaggering fellow with an inflexible sense of duty to his emperor and a regrettably malleable sense of honor. The little merry-go-round girl caught his fancy, and he made the customary advances.

Unfortunately, the haughty officer was compelled, by movie convention and the menace of the censors, to undergo a transition from base desire to pure, honest love. He decided that he wanted to marry the girl, and with that thought uppermost in his mind, went to the Emperor and confessed his troubles. But Franz Josef had other plans, and forced the officer into a loveless marriage with a blonde, portly countess. So the girl's romance was blighted.

Then came the war, to crush Austria and to level its top- heavy social system. The officer, wounded, battered and gray, re- turned to the park to find the girl whom he had loved and deserted in the good old days of 1914.

This story had its weaknesses, but it also had moments of great dramatic strength. Mr. Julian, as a director, atoned for his own deficiencies as a writer. He devised one episode, in partic- ular, which was as vitally terrifying as any passage in The Murders in the Rue Morgue. The villainous proprietor of the merry-go- round had beaten the ape and oppressed the hunchback, its keeper. One night the ape's cage was left open for a moment, and the gro- tesque beast saw its chance for revenge. It crept stealthily to the home of the evil showman, clambered up the wall with its great, powerful arms, and poised itself on the window sill. Here Mr. Julian achieved some remarkably effective pictures. He photo- graphed the ape from the room, so that the animal made a hor- rible, hairy silhouette in the window. Then the ape climbed in, crawled across to the villain's bed and did away with him in a de- liberate, efficient and utterly relentless manner. The actual mur- der was left to the audience's imagination; but the spectator could pierce the darkness of the room and conjure up the terrible scene for himself.

In acting, Merry-Go-Round fell a little short. The various players were not quite worthy of the quality established in the di- rection of the picture. Mary Philbin, however, gave an admirable performance as the harassed heroine, and Norman Kerry, whose acting is usually wooden, was satisfactorily stiff as the Austrian officer.

George Hackathorne made a definite character of the hunchback, and his colleague, the ape, was incredibly good.   I don't
know whether this strong rôle was played by Snooky, Joe Martin or
some less celebrated animal; it was certainly one of the outstanding
performances of the year.

Of the others in the cast, Dale Fuller, Cesare Gravina and
Dorothy Wallace were the best.

Merry-Go-Round represented a large expenditure of money,
but it was well spent.   If we must have huge, spectacular pictures,
this is the best way to have them.   The complaint against colossal
productions is not inspired by their size so much as their stupid
wastefulness.   Merry-Go-Round was intelligently produced, and for
this reason, it deserves the lavish praise that it has received.

--Robert E. Sherwood in The Best
Moving Pictures of 1922-1923
(Small, Maynard and Company,
1923), pages 85-92.

☐ THE MERRY WIDOW (Metro-Goldwyn, 1925)

Unless the spectacle of John Gilbert in twenty dashing uniforms has dazzled us into utter incompetency, this is one of those
fatal pictures that is going to cause untold havoc.   The adaptation
of Franz Lehar's great light opera is successful beyond the most
glowing hopes, and it has so much gay beauty, high romance and
brilliant spectacle that you can scarcely believe it is the work of
the same Erich von Stroheim who directed the sordid Greed.

Certainly he seemed to be right at home when he set forth
the most sophisticated love story ever presented on the screen.
There are moments in the picture that are either going to kill or
cure the censors.   But most of them are redeemed by a fine strain
of romance--the first time that von Stroheim has ever caught this
illusive quality.

But best of all there is John Gilbert in a role that ought to
make him the greatest of them all.   Gilbert is not only a Gift to
the Girls but he has qualities that redeem him for the men.   There
is, for instance, the scene in which he crowns the weakling crown
prince with a vase.   And he knows how to act, too; his Prince
Danilo is a human being.   However, let's rush on and say some
nice things about Mae Murray.   Hers, too, is a fine performance;
well shaded, deftly drawn and, above all, bewitching to the eye.
As a matter of fact Miss Murray is largely responsible for the picture in its production and had to fight her director every inch of
the way to its finish.   Another magnificent performance is given by
Roy D'Arcy.   As for the waltz scene, it is one of those lyric moments you'll never forget.

However, just one more word. Tell the children if they go
to The Merry Widow, Santa Claus won't bring them anything for
Christmas. But don't miss it yourself.
> --A. S. in Photoplay, Vol. 28, No.
> 5 (October 1925), page 51.

☐ METROPOLIS (Ufa/Paramount, 1927)

A story of the City of the Future, weirdly imagined, technically gorgeous, but almost ruined by terrible acting and awful
subtitles. The settings are unbelievably beautiful; the mugging of
the players is unbelievably bad.

It's a tale of future mechanistic development carried to such
an extreme that human beings are merely slaves to machines. The
film has daring, originality and some great spectacular melodrama.
What a pity that the German producers, themselves, are such slaves
to their own technical magic that they forget the human values of
their stories! What a pity that American editors distort what is
essentially a Jules Verne fantasy with preachy subtitles!

Nevertheless, Metropolis is a great spectacle, thanks to the
wizardry of its art directors and cameramen.
> --Photoplay, Vol. 31, No. 6
> (May 1927), page 52.

*   *   *

Only those who view with pessimism the fate of the human
race can derive satisfaction from Metropolis as a piece of fiction,
but those who are pessimistic regarding the development of the
screen must become optimists when they view it. It is an extraordinary motion picture, in some ways quite the most extraordinary
ever made. One must admire the minds that conceived it and
brought it into being. Eric Pommer, the supervisor, and Fritz
Lang, the director, are raised to a new dignity in screen art by
this production, the former for the magnitude of his conception, the
latter for the greatness of his screen interpretation of the conception. It was a brave thing to undertake for it was an adventure into
a realm of fiction that it is hazardous to exploit. I have my own
ideas regarding the trend of civilization and the state it will have
reached when our great-great-grandchildren are adults. You also
have your opinion. No doubt it differs from mine. Eric Pommer
has his, and it may differ from both yours and mine. He puts his
in a picture and asks you and me to accept it. I, for one, will do
no such thing. I refuse to believe that a century hence workingmen
will be slaves who live underground. If Pommer wished to produce
a story laid in a mythical country, and showed me bullfrogs driving
rabbits tandem, I would not quarrel with him, for it is his own
mythical country and I must accept all that his brain peoples it with;

but when he says "this is what your descendants will be doing one
or two hundred years hence," I refuse to follow him, for definite
knowledge on the matter being unobtainable, I do not see why I
should dismiss my own opinion and accept his. The whole trend
of civilization is in a direction opposite to that which Metropolis
takes, which makes the picture none the less entertaining, for at
least it stimulates discussion. I do not believe that we ever will
advance to a time when capital concerns itself with laborers as in-
dividuals whose bodily comforts and domestic welfare are of major
importance to it from a sociological standpoint; but I do not believe
for a moment that it will forget that it can realize upon its invest-
ment in labor only in the degree that the laborer is efficient. In
Metropolis we have laborers reduced to their lowest point of efficiency. The improvement in transportation makes reasonable the
prediction that in another century or so men can live hundreds of
miles from the scenes of their daily occupations. This will tend
to spread the population over great areas and give each man his
quota of sunshine and garden. Metropolis assumes that civilization
will burrow below the surface of the earth and that men will become
clammy things with colorless skins and white eyes. It assumes
also that men will work long hours, in spite of the fact that the
tendency towards shorter hours is marked. None of the things that
Metropolis says time will do to society seem reasonable to me.
Capital never will make slaves of workingmen because it is not
good business so to do. For all these reasons I could derive no
satisfaction from following the story of the picture. But as a picture I found it fascinating. Let us consider it purely as a picture
and not as a piece of literature.

       Metropolis was made to be released in twelve reels. Such
was the footage in which the whole story was told. All the intimate
phases of the story, the development of the love of the boy for the
girl, the views of the home life, and the social existence of the
characters, were sacrificed to production when five reels were
eliminated from the original film to bring it down to the standard
seven-reel feature length. I believe the American version would
have been a much better picture if the human element had not been
reduced so greatly. When Channing Pollock revised the film to
make it fit our conditions--a job that brought him twenty thousand
dollars and his name in gigantic letters on the screen--no doubt he
was persuaded by Paramount's salesmen that production value was
what the public craved, consequently he eliminated everything that
would have given the story any plausibility. Lang's direction reveals more aptitude for movement than for acting. All his mass
shots and those in which the machinery was featured were handled
in a manner that shows that Lang is a master in the treatment of
such subjects, but when he directed his actors he was not so much
at home. The father gives a convincing performance, in a quiet,
repressed way that made the portrayal a powerful one. The son
overacts all the way through, and gives a performance that entirely
lacks conviction. Apparently the director allowed his actors to give
their individual conceptions of the characters, without regard for
their relation one to another. Metropolis is rather an argument for

dual direction. If Lang's efforts with the material aspects of the
production had been supplemented with a Lubitsch's skill at making
the characters human we would have had a better picture, although
the story militates against it being a perfect one. When Ufa made
Metropolis it did not arbitrarily place its time one thousand years
hence. As I understand it, Eric Pommer's idea was to depict life
one or two centuries hence. Paramount's press agents, with their
usual flair for exaggeration, made it ten centuries, thereby preparing the public for something more weird than it received. Technically the picture is a revelation of what can be done with models
and a camera. The scenes of city life, airplanes passing among
buildings, taxicabs dashing along elevated streets, pedestrians moving along sidewalks, were done so realistically that they must as-
tonish anyone who is not familiar with the manner in which such
things are done. It will interest Hollywood to know that these
scenes were shot as we shoot our cartoon comedies: cardboard
cut-outs being advanced after each shot. It cost less to shoot the
scenes by this method than it would have to have used moving models, even though it took no less than nine months to complete them.
The most striking shots in the picture were those showing the illuminated rings passing up and down around the dummy to which the
face and form of the girl were being transferred. I have no idea
how it was done. Another effective shot was that showing several
columns of people converging on the tower of Babel. It gives the
impression that many thousands of people were used. If you looked
closely, however, you could detect evidences of it being a divided
shot, or whatever it is called--the same bunch of people being shot
half a dozen times. No matter what degree of entertainment you
derive from Metropolis you must give it credit for being a great
intellectual feat as well as an example of the extraordinary possibilities of the screen. It is to be hoped that some day Eric Pommer
will find himself so situated in Hollywood that he can attempt something else equally daring and ambitious.
                              --Welford Beaton in The Film
                                Spectator, Vol. 4, No. 1
                                (September 3, 1927), pages 4-5.

                    *   *   *

     Hollywood lives for money and sex. It borrows or buys its
art. It is the Germans who are the perpetual adventurers in the
cinema. They gave the camera its stripling mobility, its restless
imagination. They played with lights in the studio and achieved
innumerable subtleties in the use of black and white as a medium.
Even in their scientific miniatures they have worked with a virtuoso
camera. And it was the Germans who injected fantasy into the
camera.

     Metropolis, for all its thesis and its subtitular dialectic com-
pounded for American comprehension by the enlightened Channing
Pollock, is much more akin to the romantic vagaries of Siegfried
than to the realities of The Last Laugh. For Fritz Lang, who directed both Siegfried and Metropolis, is not a cinema radical. Like

Murnau in Faust he thinks in terms of sheer visual beauty, composition, and group rhythms rather than of dynamics. He is still
of the theater of Reinhardt in the fluency of his groups and the
rhythmic progression of his pageant. Although Karl Freund, the
cameraman for The Last Laugh and Variety, has worked here in
the same capacity, Metropolis lacks cinematic subtlety. It is only
in the shots of machinery in motion and in the surge of the revolutionists that it is dynamic. The camera is too often immobile, the
technique that of the stylized theater.

Yet here for the first time the chill mechanized world of the
future, which only barely revealed itself in R. U. R., has been
given reality. Here is the city, that tormented circus of buildings
which touch the sky, of tunnels that disrupt the places under the
earth. Through the air man has hurled his obstructions, his
bridges and traffic ways. Yet only the machines seem real; gigantic
purring gods grinding down life. Machines, machines, machines,
sliding through the earth, challenging the cosmos, pounding out human resistance as they set the awful tempo of life.

There is no loveliness here, except in the garden of the
rich, high above the levels of the city, where space and light are
not mortified for efficiency. Below the surface of the earth the
workers and their children crawl through a timed eternity, strapped
to the dynamos like so many numbered robots. There is no rest,
no beauty, no life below the gardens of the higher levels. Man is
inanimate. Life is metronomic. It is only the machines that are
alive. The machines and the careless children of "Brains."

As Lang has directed it, Metropolis is more stylized fantasy
than realism. Even in the torrential revolt of the workers as they
pour through the machine-rooms, alive, demoniacal, there is an air
of unreality. This is not revolution as the Russians stage it. It
has neither taste nor smell. Yet it is magnificent. Even the most
careless groupings are beautifully composed. Lang is too much the
artist to deny the imagination.

R. U. R. was a satire, but Metropolis is utterly devoid of
humor. Thea von Harbou, its author, wrote it originally as a novel
and then adapted it to the screen. Only her concept of Metropolis
itself is intellectual. The rest is sentimental symbolism. There
is no individualization within the type. Her persons are puppets.
There is the Capitalist, his Son, Mary the spiritual leader of the
workers, et al. The Son is the eternal mediator who, with the
help of the woman Mary, although only after a revolution intervenes,
brings "brains" and "brawn" together for the final fade-out.

Perhaps it is because of its original form that Metropolis
lacks concision. One of the most interesting episodes of the entire
film is that in which the inventor transmits the shape and likeness
of Mary to the woman of his creation by encircling bands of elec-
tricity, yet it is only partially developed. The robotess, or creature of human invention, breeds revolution and is stoned by the mob,

but the formula which gave her life is never mentioned again.   The
inventor is himself hurled from the cathedral roof by the blond and
shining John, the hero; but what of the formula?

It is Metropolis itself, the city of domed basements and
curving machinerooms, of massed buildings that conceal the sky,
of aeroplanes that ply their corner-to-corner traffic, of trains that
seem to shoot into unmeasured and untracked space, that makes
Fritz Lang's film so significant.

> --Evelyn Gerstein in The Nation,
> Vol. 124 (March 23, 1927),
> pages 323-324.

☐ THE MIRACLE OF THE WOLVES (Historic Films, 1925)

The Miracle of the Wolves is a noteworthy French picture
done in the classic tradition of French drama.   In this it differs
markedly from films of other Continental countries and from American films.   It is a stately, sincere and serious effort to portray
dramatically one of the important moments of French history.

The director, Raymond Bernard, has chosen the pageantry
form of motion picture art as the method of presenting the story,
so the acting in its delineation of character has a somewhat imper-
sonal touch.   This is not derogatory criticism for this impersonal-
ism achieves a heightened abstractness to which a more intimate
portrayal seldom rises.

The moment of history that the film records is the ascension
to the throne of all France of Louis XI.   Because of the protection
given to Louis when Dauphin, or heir to the throne, by Philip the
Good, Duke of Burgundy, both the Duke and his son, Charles the
Bold, are affronted when Louis becomes king and refuses to follow
them in building up the power of the nobles.   Louis XI is looked
upon as the maker of the modern homogeneous French nation because he stood with the people and for an all powerful central government against the growing power of the nobles who would separate
the State into many small and warring factions.

Interwoven in the diplomatic contest, open warfare and final
peace with Charles the Bold, is the love story of Jeanne Fouquet
and Robert Cottereau.   Perhaps the film is really about Jeanne after
all, for she is one of France's national heroines, the famous Jeanne
Hachette, Jeanne of the Axe, whose heroism so inspired and helped
the perilous cause of the king.

The film was produced with extensive cooperation of the
French Government and important national bodies such as the French
Academy.   It is authentic in historical detail and the old walled city
of Carcassonne was used as the setting of one of the important situations of the story.

The Miracle of the Wolves has the stately dignity of narration at its best, heightened and accented by moments of dramatic
action and dramatic intensity.   In the beginning of the film, for example, some time passes in an interesting but not dramatic sequence
of scenes--until the scene where just as Charles attacks Jeanne the
King enters.   It is true that after that episode there is more continuous action, yet it is the movement of narrative and not that of
the closely woven drama such as is found in some American films.

Besides the successfulness of this picture in carrying out
what may be called the classical mode of film technique one should
applaud the effect obtained throughout the film of the 15th Century
atmosphere.   Louis XI and Charles the Bold, besides being real
personages of the era, move amid the age of turmoil, daring,
strangeness and beauty, all enveloped in an authentic air.   The ancient quaintness of the festival which Charles arranged for the
King's entertainment, the Morality play with its accompanying crowds
of the common people, is a master touch.

So too is the remarkable air of the supernatural given to
some scenes in the sequence of the attack of the wolves on Jeanne,
where, after the balked and frightened pursuers see the wolves
making friends with Jeanne instead of rending her, they exclaim,
"It is a miracle. "   This effect, coinciding with the dramatic feeling
of the moment, is the result of true motion picture art.

The acting in the film, one will note, is of a part with the
best traditions of the French stage.   It is carefully studied, finished
and with a kind of retarded movement.   Do not look for the intimate
effect toward which American film acting tends.   The work of these
French actors has a serious and important relation to the broad effect the entire film is intended to produce.

Charles Dullin in the part of Louis XI is every inch what
one's imagination might picture this crafty but great monarch.   As
one of the titles states, Louis XI was a fox in his crafty skill, and
his little eyes and his slow thin smile see and comment on the happenings around him with successful guile and intuitive wisdom.
Yvonne Sergyl as Jeanne has the difficult task of giving us one
moment the most restrained and subdued acting and the next moment
the movement across the scene of a fury.   Vanni Marcoux as
Charles the Bold, and Romuald Joube as Robert Cottereau, give
their parts a tremendous air of fitting into the age.   Here too, we
should not ask to get into close, human touch with them.   They are in-
terpreting in a restrained art form the essence of the classic mode.

We believe that every lover of motion pictures should see
this picture because it represents a fine and successful example of
a historical story presented in an interesting manner and with a
dignity and singleness of effort in artistry that is worthy of emula-
tion no matter what technique is employed.

                                   --Exceptional Photoplays, Vol. 5,
                                     Nos. 5 and 6 (February-March
                                     1925), page 2.

☐ MISS LULU BETT (Famous Players-Lasky/Paramount, 1921)

Miss Lulu Bett in its screen version makes an attractive entertainment on its own merits.   Here is a story that has successfully appeared in novel, stage, and screen form.   Much could be
written about the metamorphoses which it has undergone, but it is
sufficient to say that most of them were inevitable in the process
of adaptation of matter to form, while the others are not important
enough to cause serious grief to the devotees of the book.

The success of the picture is due to a very large degree to
Lois Wilson's charming interpretation of Lulu Bett.   Miss Wilson
deftly subordinates her personality and looks to Lulu the drudge until the change in her fortunes takes place and then acts the lady
with a convincing touch of uncertainty, largely expressed through a
piece of millinery which just misses being very becoming to her.
It is a sincere piece of work.

Most of the rest of the members of the cast rather miss
their opportunities.   Theodore Roberts as Dwight Deacon again suffers from the chronic exaggeration which has overtaken him of late.
He is apparently under the impression that his manner of chewing
his cigar and his method of thrusting forward his chin like a cluck-
ing hen are what used to make people call him a fine character actor of the old school.   It is time for Mr. Roberts and his directors
to reform and give us some more original interpretations.   Milton
Sills is decorative if not convincing, and the part of Grandma Bett,
depending so largely on clever lines, is one which by its very nature cannot be very successfully rendered on the screen.   The part
of Monona, the obnoxious little girl of the novel, on the other hand,
is exceptionally well done.

                              --Exceptional Photoplays, Vol. 2,
                                No. 1 (January-February 1922),
                                page 11.

☐ MOANA (Famous Players-Lasky/Paramount, 1926)

Moana of the South Seas is obviously one of the very few entirely beautiful pictures (beautiful in the sense of the painter's
beauty, the lover-of-life's beauty) that the screen has given us.
For here the camera has been used consciously as an instrument
to reflect the beauty in this world.   The result is nothing that the
public need fear; the picture should make a tremendous appeal to
the public.

In this photoplay we follow the son of an important Polynesian
family as he leaves adolescence, becomes an adult member of the
tribe, courts and marries, Mr. Flaherty having presented this pro-
cession of events with all its practical and poetical meanings.   Slowly and simply the audience receives a sense of complete life.

Moana is something new, as Nanook of the North was something new. In Moana as in Nanook a different kind of plot is perceptible, one that is more profound than the dramatist's or the
scenarioist's, and of that description which the motion picture above
any other medium seems peculiarly adapted to render. In a story
way Nanook concerned itself with a struggle for existence that was
optimistic in spite of its hardship, its colors were bleak, its movement arduous. Moana's concern is with an acceptance of life graceful, akin to the lotus eaters' kind of bliss. Over the film is a
warmth, a golden ease and naturalness, the sense of life intoxicat-
ingly idyllic, of a power to enjoy life that is both child-like and
god-like. But no less than Nanook is it exciting philosophically and
in the images it conveys, on the one hand so steeped in decoration,
on the other so profound in their connotation of a companionship
with existence manifested by customs formed from the past by a
people's needs, environment and imagination working together.

Technically, Moana indicates perhaps the most perfect way
that the motion picture can go about doing this sort of thing.
Photographically, the practice is one of compelling camera values--
lights, shades, composition--to give the same effect that the painter's brush can give. The sky has the appearance of being blue,
the leaves of the trees green; the skin of the people seems brown
and of a texture exquisitely molded, their garments strike one as
patterns of rich color--the audience can feel and smell and see
these things. Cinegraphically, the method is one of rhythm, like
the prose that, using bright and exotic words, weaves them slowly
and chimingly into a picture that charms and moves the reader.
To perform all this with the camera, Mr. Flaherty has used no
color photography nor any tricks. To construct it dramatically,
he has chosen those activities and interests of his characters' lives
that pictorially represent them, linking these pictures together in
their natural sequence and inevitable dramatic implication. The
idea has been to recreate the beings of the primitive Polynesians
by letting us see them simply as they were, by cinegraphic means
the least artificial, the most sumptuous, and suggestively the most
indicative.

Thus, this picture shows thorough feeling for that rarely understood but vitally important essential in the use of photoplay medium, the need for constant pictorial interest. Mr. Flaherty's
camera-eye roves over the tropical verdure and the daily comings
and goings of these primitive folk and with inquisitiveness but always with good taste discloses them at their work and play, feasts
and festivals, sometimes following them into their homes and often
into the water where they are as much at ease as on land. And
yet behind all this apparently casual and natural work of the camera
is an alert and discriminating selection. Almost any one of the
thousands of separate pictures taken on the film, one feels, could
be clipped out and found to be interesting in itself; for, in spite of
the constant movement of characters and camera, the waving palms
and turbulent sea, each separate picture thrown on the screen is a
well balanced and beautiful composition--the view of the girl's hand,

sensitive, exquisitely alive, gracefully resting on the rich, decorative shell of the captured tortoise; the sequence of scenes showing the youth Moana being tattooed--the ordeal in the Polynesian rite of coming to manhood--in which are disclosed the anguished features of Moana, the faces of his mother, his father, his sweetheart, and that of the old artist of the tribe, as the camera eye moves from one to the other as though following a thought; the picturing of the betrothal dance of Moana and his sweetheart where the camera concentrates on the significant, symbolically moving figure--all of these scenes are of a description where nothing is jumbled, nothing uncertain, and the effect is completely aesthetic. The scene of Moana dancing, in particular, is at once one of the most beautiful and most interesting of the film. The grace, poise, rhythm, feeling of the dancer give us a peculiar insight into the mind and heart of his people, into their purity, and into their sense of the meaning of life. It is a pantomime of joy and pride and noble well-being.

As an indication of the extraordinary care taken in the preparation of the film, it should be stated that for two years Mr. Flaherty lived among the little Polynesian group, gaining their sympathy for what he was attempting to do as well as getting for himself a sympathetic insight into their lives. This period gave him leisure to put his thought and observation into his picture, and to experiment in order to find the best way of achieving it. Such extravagance of time is the way of the conscious creator with his material. Unless this time and thought are given to seriously projected achievement in motion pictures, motion pictures cannot rank with Moana--a film that is tremendously suggestive, tremendously helpful, to future motion picture makers who will analyze what Mr. Flaherty has done.

--Exceptional Photoplays, Vol. 6,
No. 2 (November-December
1925), page 1.

☐ MONTE CARLO (Paramount, 1930)

Somewhere long ago, when movies were young, the idea evidently got about that intelligent pictures might be interesting, but they could not be entertaining or amusing, and most assuredly they would not be popular. Ernst Lubitsch, being a foreigner, probably wasn't told about that when he landed, so he went right ahead making pictures for people who could understand things, and they turned out to be not only highly entertaining but pretty well liked by a whole lot of people. Then when sound and effects came in everyone went back to the old idea of eliminating intelligence and taste and discrimination and they catered once more to that lowest common denominator of audiences.

Lubitsch couldn't see that sound should have such a dismal effect on films, and he proceeded to make pictures under the same

formula as before, using sound to further his ends. As a result
Lubitsch remains one of the few motion picture directors, and The
Love Parade and Monte Carlo have been the best of their kind and
people are actually reported to like them. It must be pretty con-
fusing to those old cynics who say that the public has always got the
sort of film it deserves.

It's no small matter nowadays to turn out a screen musical
that people will enjoy; to get them to go at all is a minor triumph,
so poor have been most of the examples. The point of difference
between the Lubitsch musicals and almost all others, with the possible exception of the Ramon Novarro pictures, is that he recognized
that a comedy with music didn't have to be a "musical comedy," in
the stage sense, and that to transfer these tinselled operas from
stage to screen accomplished nothing but a decrease in their interest and a magnifying of their shortcomings. Taking a motion picture and utilizing both music and sound to the best advantage is a
much better policy, and Monte Carlo is as good proof of that as
anything else.

Monte Carlo has no chorus ladies tripping gaily in and out of
boudoirs, no Albertina Rasch girls appearing miraculously at the
little informal party of the Countess de Soandso, and very few instances when you feel, with a certain sinking at the stomach, that
the principals are about to give birth to a song. What sound there
is is used skilfully: Jeanette MacDonald is riding on a train, running away from a distasteful marriage to a rich nobleman, and as
the rhythm of the wheels beats itself into her mind, she falls into
the rhythm and sings a song which is an unusually brilliant example
of adapting music to a situation.

As she passes open fields where peasants are at work, they
stop and wave and a chorus of voices seems to join hers and sing
the song back at her.

Again, when Jack Buchanan, who has fallen in love with her,
keeps calling her on the telephone, she takes it off the hook, whereupon he sings to her, "Give me a moment, please," and she falls
asleep with the melody running through her head. For some time
after another song she keeps hearing the tune, and when little toy
figures on a clock come out to blow the hour, the notes they play
seem to be those of the song.

This continuity of sound and repetition of sound motifs is
probably Lubitsch's greatest contribution to the audible musicals.
Its effect is undoubtedly charming and natural, as well as psychologically clever. To this he has only to combine a knowledge of
how comedy should be directed and how love scenes should be managed and how satire can be painlessly inserted and a product like
Monte Carlo is the result.

Even the story, an unsubstantial one about a princess who
runs away from a rich marriage and falls in love with her hair-

dresser, is told with a different twist. Although the identities are
known all along to the audience, she does not learn that her charming attendant is a nobleman in disguise until he takes her to see a
performance of Monsieur Beaucaire, at which she perceives the
parallel in time for a happy finish. And finally, the performances
are a reflection of the direction, with Jack Buchanan gathering more
honors for himself as one of the most attractive and charming of
leading men, and Jeanette MacDonald having her moments now and
then and contributing a really lovely voice, and ZaSu Pitts being
properly lachrymal, and everybody else just right. And now they
can preserve the reels of The Love Parade and Monte Carlo and
burn all the rest, and nobody will even notice the loss.

--James Shelley Hamilton in
Cinema, Vol. 1, No. 8 (December 1930), pages 38 and 41.

☐ MONTE CRISTO (Fox, 1922)

        Score another triumph for William Fox, whose screen ver-
sion of The Count of Monte Cristo, the hero of Alexandre Dumas'
famous tale, has just had its premier at Tremont Temple, Boston,
and bids fair to continue to attract capacity audiences for many
weeks to come. The story is familiar to readers of literature.
To theatregoers it has been made equally familiar through the excellent histrionic work of James O'Neill in the stage version. As
a screen offering, it is a gigantic spectacle, rife with thrilling
events and episodes, and it brings the story of Edmond Dantes, the
Count of Monte Cristo, before the public in a most vivid and picturesque manner.

        One would look far to find another story in which there is
so much and varied material at hand for dramatic treatment, and
he would indeed be ultra-critical who can look upon it and not find
it far above the usual filming, and not declare it actually brilliant.

        Naturally in so stupendous a tale, with so many thrilling
passages and highly interesting situations, much of necessity has
to be left out in the filming. But so artistically has the story been
told in picturization, and so great attention has been paid to the
details, that the continuity remains unbroken and the rapidly succeeding events can be followed as closely and in as connected a
form by those who have not read the book, as by those who are
familiar with Dumas' classic.

        In its direction, Emmett J. Flynn had accomplished a notable
piece of artistic realism, while the cast selected for this great picturization reads like a "Who's Who in the Films." John Gilbert,
the hero of Shame, essays the role of Edmond Dantes, the Count,
in a most admirable manner. Not only is he the happy, ingenuous
sailor, but, as the Count of Monte Cristo he is the sophisticated,

courteous but implacable foe, not willing to rest from his labors until his three enemies' lives are ended. Estelle Taylor, whose rise in the films has been a rapid one, takes the part of Mercedes most delightfully. Robert McKim fits well into the part of the corrupt judge, De Villefort; William V. Mong, the Merlin of Connecticut Yankee fame, portrays the character of Caderousse, and Virginia Faire is the Princess Haydee. To George Seigmann is given the amusing role of Luigi Vampa, and Spottiswoode Aitken is cast as the mild and gentle Abbe, the prisoner of the fortress who enables Monte Cristo to recover the gold and jewels that raise him to the high position he later occupies.

Monte Cristo abounds in beautiful scenic effects and the photography shows the work of master craftsmen. In the delineation of the great scenes Mr. Flynn's direction is excellent. His artistry is manifest at all times. He never dallies over scene or situation and he excels particularly in the pictorial, the splendid feature settings. Infinite detail adds materially to these many and varied creations, too many and too varied to enumerate, but it almost appears at times as if the very spirit of Dumas is creeping into the film. Action, too, stirs him to excellence, and as a whole his telling of the tale is far in advance of anything he has done thus far.

At best, The Count of Monte Cristo is a highly involved tale and it is a wonder that Mr. Flynn has been able to straighten it out into the tense, dramatic narrative that is depicted. In a word, Monte Cristo has "arrived" and it may be characterized as a clearcut, well-done photoplay of most excellent parts. Mr. Fox easily may place it at the head, or very close to the head, of his long list of super-productions. It should prove to be a big money-maker for any exhibitor.

--C. M. Inman in The Moving Picture World, Vol. 55, No. 5 (April 1, 1922), page 548.

☐ MY BEST GIRL (Pickford/United Artists, 1927)

A romance that will take its place among the most beautiful that have been presented on the screen, a superbly acted production and one of the best directed of the year--My Best Girl, Mary Pickford's latest picture. For the first time we have Mary in a straight love story, and unless her untold millions of admirers throughout the world hail this picture as her greatest, I will be much surprised. Personally, I am of the opinion that Sparrows is the finest thing she has given us, but it is not the kind of picture her friends would expect from her. My Best Girl is a Pickford picture, and in it she gives a magnificent performance. In one sequence she rises to heights I never saw her attain before. Her pathetic attempt to disillusion the young man she loves, and who loves her, is among the

finest things that the screen has given us. It is done superbly, the
heart-breaking smile that shines through her tears being a poignant
bit of acting that only a great artist could make convincing. One
of the most exquisite moments in screen history is her final confession that her pretense can not conquer her love, a moment when
her shoulders droop, when the false smile vanishes and she throws
herself into her sweetheart's arms. It is a scene that will cause
a display of handkerchiefs in every audience that views it. Still
My Best Girl will provoke more laughter than anything that Mary
has done before. It is full of delicious comedy, subtle touches that
preview audiences caught at once. There is none of the senseless
"playing down to the audience." Sam Taylor's direction is based on
the assumption that the audience is intelligent, and as a consequence
this picture is going to gain him recognition as one of the most intelligent directors we have. He has filled it with little directorial
gems that make it one of the best directed pictures I ever saw.
The opening sequence showing the interior of a large five-and-ten-
cent store is particularly effective. First we have a close-up of a
cash register clicking out its nickel and dime receipts; then a dis-
solve to a counter, and finally the scenes enlarge until we have a
long shot of the entire store. Taylor has reversed adroitly the
hackneyed program of opening with a long shot and progressing
backward to a close-up. He builds instead of tearing down. The
store scenes, as well as the street scenes and others which have
many people in the background, are handled perfectly. He keeps
the screen full of action without distracting the attention of the
viewer from the principal characters. The direction is equally
flawless throughout. Taylor makes his comedy funny, his romance
beautiful and his pathos tender. Mary's performance shows that
she was happy in working with her director. And Taylor must have
been happy in working with such a star and such a cast. Charles
Rogers plays opposite Mary. His work is a revelation. This picture is going to make him. He romps through the part with an engaging joyousness that audiences will find contagious. There is not
a suggestion of staginess in one of his scenes. Like Taylor, he is
equally at home in comedy and in his serious moments. He is a
clean looking youth who makes his character one that all audiences
will love. The whole picture is cast admirably. There is not one
bit that is not played perfectly. Lucien Littlefield is a delightful
old letter carrier. His performance is one of the best of his notable career. Sunshine Hart and Carmelita Geraghty also provide
excellent characterizations.

--Welford Beaton in The Film
Spectator, Vol. 4, No. 4 (October 15, 1927), page 3.

* * *

With a story by Kathleen Norris, an adaptation by Hope Loring, and "America's Sweetheart" to play in it, the picture could not
fail to be interesting. Not the story, which is flimsy, nor all the
comedy running through it (and it is frequently slapstick), makes
you remember the picture. But you will carry away memories of
the beautiful love episode between Mary Pickford and "Buddy" Rogers.

You might not think of romance in connection with a ten-cent
store, but, when Mary was stock girl in Merritt's store, she discovered a wonderful beau, whom she tried to train in the business.
Thereby hangs the tale.   The love scenes between these two are
marvelous--beautiful, clean, and gripping.

The best picture Mary has made in several years.
                              --Photoplay, Vol. 33, No. 1
                              (December 1927), page 52.

☐ NANOOK OF THE NORTH (Revillon Frères/Pathe, 1922)

There have been many fine travel pictures, many gorgeous
"scenics," but there has been only one that deserves to be called
great.   That one is Nanook of the North.   It stands alone, literally
in a class by itself.   Indeed, no list of the best pictures, of this
year or of all the years in the brief history of the movies, could
be considered complete without it.

The potential value of the movies as an educational medium
is frequently stressed by men of prominence and triteness; and as
a result, the word "educational" in connection with a motion picture
has become almost synonymous with dullness, dryness and boredom.

The screen is no blackboard, and the prime test of every
film that is projected on its surface is that it shall be interesting
to the spectator.   It may be teeming with genuine instructive value,
it may contain what is generally called a "message," but if it fails
to hold the audience's attention, the value and the message will be
lost.

Robert J. Flaherty realized this when he produced Nanook of
the North.   He wanted to make a picture of Eskimo life (and, to the
average mind, there is no character that is colder or less enthralling than an Eskimo), and he wanted to record the tremendous vitality, the relentless force, of the Arctic.   He knew that there was
good material here, but he also knew that this material would be
worthless unless he presented it in an interesting way.   He appreciated the fact that mere photographs of Eskimos in their various
daily activities would be hopelessly dull if he treated his subject as
instruction instead of as drama.

The backbone of every motion picture is the continuity--and
by this I do not mean the plot.   Nanook of the North had no plot
whatsoever, and struggled along very well without it, but it did have
continuity.   The arrangement of scenes was sound and logical and
consistent.

Mr. Flaherty selected one character, Nanook himself, to
serve as the protagonist of his drama.   Nanook was the center of

all the action, and upon him was the camera focussed.   In this way
Mr. Flaherty achieved the personal touch.   Another producer, attempting to do the same thing, would have been content to photograph "A Native Spearing Fish" or "Another Native Building His
Igloo. "   Moreover, he would have kept himself in the foreground,
as is the way of all travelogue rollers.   Mr. Flaherty made Nanook
his hero--and a fine, stalwart hero he was.

Nanook of the North, however, was not all Nanook.   There
was a co-star in the title rôle, and that was the North.   The North
was the villain of the piece, the dread force against which Nanook
and his kind must continually battle.   So Mr. Flaherty showed us
Nanook, fighting sturdily to obtain food, and warmth and shelter,
and he showed us the North hitting back with its gales, its blizzards and its terrible, bitter cold.

Here was drama, rendered far more vital than any trumped-
up drama could ever be by the fact that it was all real.   Nanook
was no playboy, enacting a part which would be forgotten as soon
as the greasepaint had been rubbed off; he was himself an Eskimo,
struggling to survive.   The North was no mechanical affair of wind
machines and paper snow; it was the North, cruel and incredibly
strong.

The production of this remarkable picture was no light task.
Mr. Flaherty had to spend years with the Eskimos so that he could
learn to understand them.   Otherwise, he could not have made a
faithful reflection of their emotions, their philosophy and their endless privations.   He had to select from among them those who were
best qualified to tell the story of their race.   He had to do his
photography, his developing and his printing under terribly adverse
conditions.   He had no studio, no artificial lights and only the crud-
est of laboratories.

In the preface to this book, I say that the motion picture
represents the combined talents of hundreds, sometimes thousands,
of different people.   But Nanook of the North is the notable exception to that rule; it was essentially a one-man job.

Of the difficulties which confronted him in producing Nanook
of the North, Mr. Flaherty writes as follows:

"The film Nanook of the North is a by-product--if I
may use the term--of a long series of explorations in the
north which I carried on in behalf of Sir William Macken-
zie from 1910 to 1916.   Much of the exploration was done
with Eskimos.   I have been on long journeys for months
at a time with only two or three Eskimos as my companions.   This experience gave me an insight into their lives
and a deep regard for them.
"In 1913 I went north with a large outfit--an exploring
ship with lumber and material for a wintering base and
food for eight men for two years.   A motion picture outfit

was incorporated. I hoped that the results from it might
help defray some of the costs of what were now beginning
to be expensive explorations. I had no preliminary motion picture experience, other than some two weeks with
a motion picture camera demonstrator just before leaving.
We wintered in Baffin Land on this expedition, which was
of a year and four months' duration, and during those intervals while I was not seriously engaged in exploratory
work, a film was compiled of some of the Eskimos who
lived with us. Naturally the results were indifferent.
But as I was undertaking another expedition in another
part of the north I secured more negative and chemicals,
with the idea of building up this first film.

"On this expedition I wintered on the Belcher Islands,
which I had re-discovered and explored. Again, between
explorations as it were, I continued with the film work
and added to the first film very materially. After a lot
of hardship, which involved the loss of a launch and the
wrecking of our cruising boat, we secured a remarkable
film on a small island ninety miles out at sea, of walrus-
hunting. This picture particularly, and some interesting
stuff of native life, together with scenes showing the dis-
masting of the Laddie, our exploring ship, which owing to
our condition was broken up and used for fuel, formed the
nucleus of what I hoped would be a good picture. After
wintering a year on the islands, the Laddie's skipper, a
Moose Factory half-breed, and myself, finally got out to
civilization along with my notes, maps and the above-
mentioned film.

"I had just completed editing the film in Toronto when,
through gross carelessness of my own, the negative caught
fire, and I was minus all (some thirty thousand feet of
film). The editing print, however, was not burned, and
this was shown to some private groups several times--
just long enough, in fact, to enable me to realize that it
was no good. I knew then that the reason I had missed
out was that the whole thing was episodic. But I did see
that if I were to take a single character and make him
typify the Eskimos as I had known them so long and well,
the results would be well worth while. To make a long
story short, that is what happened. I went north again,
this time solely to make a film. I took with me not only
motion picture cameras, negative and developing outfit,
but apparatus for producing electric light so that I could
print and project my results as they were being made;
thus I could correct the faults and re-take wherever necessary, and more particularly still, my character and
his family who lived with me through the year could understand and appreciate what I was doing.

"Though Nanook and his crowd were at first highly
amused at the idea of the white man wanting to take pictures of themselves, the most common objects in all the
world, as soon as I got my projection apparatus going and

showed them some of the first results, they were completely won over. As luck would have it, the first picture that was made was the walrus hunt, which many of
the younger generation had never seen. I shall never
forget the night it was first projected, on a white cotton
sheet in my wintering hut. The audience--men, women,
babes and children, squatted on the floor--completely forgot that what was unfolding before them on the sheet was
a picture. They yelled, screamed and shouted their ad-
vice where the four stalwarts were shown in the walrus
tug of war. In the language of the trade, that first picture was a knockout. From that time on they were with
me to a man. Indeed, they vied with one another to be
cast in the angerooka's big aggie (picture). "

After Mr. Flaherty had completed the picture, and had
brought it to New York, he encountered a new set of problems: he
ran into the movie distributors. He learned that the Eskimos were
remarkably tractable as compared with these important gentlemen
who are empowered to decide what the public shall see and what it
shall not see. He had been backed on this Arctic expedition by
Revillon Frères, the furriers, but Revillon Frères could not sell
his picture for him.

He took Nanook of the North to five different distributing cor-
porations, all of which turned him down flat. They told him that
the public is not interested in Eskimos; the public wants to see people in dress suits. Finally, he effected a deal with Pathe, and
Nanook of the North was timorously submitted to the exhibitors.
One of them, Samuel Rothafel of the Capitol Theatre in New York,
decided to give it a try, although he was frankly dubious about its
possibilities as a box-office attraction. The week that Nanook of
the North played at the Capitol Theatre, it did $43,000 worth of
business.

It was instantly hailed by every critic in New York, and the
public (which wants to see people in dress suits) responded nobly.
Nanook of the North has since proved to be a substantial if not a
sensational box-office success.

One of the distributing companies, the Famous Players-Lasky,
which elected to throw Nanook of the North back into the cold from
whence it came, has made amends in an honorable and emphatic
way. Jesse L. Lasky has sent Mr. Flaherty to Samoa to make a
Polynesian Nanook. Moreover, he has made no restrictions as to
money, time or quality--so that we may expect, eventually, to see
the first real representation of the glamourous South Sea Isles on
the screen.

There was a tragic sequel to Nanook of the North which did
not appear in the film itself. Some time after Mr. Flaherty departed from the Arctic with his negatives and his prints, the gallant
Nanook died of starvation. The villainous North finally won in its

mortal combat, and Nanook became the first hero in movie history
who has gone down to ultimate defeat.   But his soul goes marching
on.   His shadowy form still flickers across the screen, to prove to
distributors and other short-sighted persons that Eskimos are human beings, after all.

> --Robert E. Sherwood in The Best
> Moving Pictures of 1922-1923
> (Small, Maynard and Company,
> 1923), pages 3-8.

*   *   *

   Upon coming away from a view of Nanook of the North, the
first reaction is that the picture is one of the most suitable hot
weather attractions within reach of exhibitors up to the present
time.   It is an epic of the snowlands so real and so interesting in
every detail that it carries the spectator right into the heart of the
snowstorms, ice and bitterest cold.   The mental effect will have a
physical result of cooling off the victims of the most torrid sort of
weather, and the manager who shows the picture will receive the
approbation of his clientele.

   Nanook of the North was produced on the East Coast of Hud-
son Bay for Revillon Frères by Robert J. Flaherty, a fellow of the
Royal Geographic Society and a noted explorer and engineer.   It is
a picture that defies classification.   It is not the adaptation of a
"story" in the accepted sense of the word, yet it has drama--the
drama of life where mere existence is a continual battle against the
forces of nature in their most cruel form.   It is not a scenic in the
accepted sense of that word even though its scenic splendors are
magnificent, because it is a real, true human document.   It cannot
be placed under the general head of an educational, but it brings the
South up to and through the door of the vast North and shows how it
lives.

   It is a stark, staring disclosure of the only life known to the
Eskimo, a race of people that endures the greatest hardships, knows
only the severest climate and has the least advantages of any other,
and yet is probably the happiest among all the races.   And you
laugh with them.   It is the dramatization of a slice of the life of
Nanook, the great hunter, and his continual struggle to feed his little
family.   It has vital interest for everyone.   Nanook of the North is
a screen classic.

   Nanook of the North is the first picture of its kind to reach
our screens.   It is distinctive and different, to say the least.   It is
a cross section of seasonal life of the Eskimo that, it should be
repeated, is surcharged with drama and stippled with humor, although there is no plot in the accepted sense.   If Nanook of the
North does not please your patronage you will have unusual difficulty
finding stuff that will.

> --Fritz Tidden in The Moving Pic-
> ture World, Vol. 56, No. 8
> (June 24, 1922), page 735.

☐ THE NAVIGATOR (Metro-Goldwyn, 1924)

        A Buster Keaton farce in six reels--and funny practically
every inch of the way.   Which is an accomplishment, because it
isn't easy to be laughable for six thousand feet of film.   Buster
plays the heroic Sap who finds himself with his sweetheart on an
ocean liner cut adrift by enemies of the owner.   The Sap becomes
the captain, crew and cook until the vessel strands upon a cannibal
isle.   Then Buster dons a deep sea diver's suit and keeps the can-
nibals more or less at a distance until a submarine comes to the
rescue.   Of course, like all farces, this doesn't stand analysis,
but the tale is studded with hilarious moments and a hundred and
one adroit gags.   Keaton was never funnier than in The Navigator
and he has a pretty foil in Kathryn McGuire.   It's a picture you'll
enjoy.
                                        --Photoplay, Vol. 27, No. 1
                                          (December 1924), page 50.

☐ NELL GWYN (British National/Paramount, 1926)

        This is the first English production to reach these shores that
will meet with the approval of American audiences.   Perhaps this is
due to the appearance of our Dorothy Gish in the cast.   Never have
Dorothy done such creditable work, and, as the little impish gamin
who becomes a favorite of the King, her performance ranks as one
of the finest of the month.   Just for the grown-ups.
                                        --Photoplay, Vol. 24, No. 5
                                          (April 1926), page 56.

☐ NOAH'S ARK (Warner Bros. , 1928)

        This picture has been heralded as a super-production, has
been ages in the making, and thousands of people appear in it.   The
story is fundamentally a modern one, with its theme derived from
the Bible.   It is historical, allegorical, symbolical, etc. , but the
Biblical sequence does not disappoint, as the sets and scenes are
so massive and so realistically impressive that we have decided to
be on the safe side when the world is destroyed again.   We are
still wondering how the flood scenes could have been made without
loss of life.

        The modern sequence is laid in France, at the time of the
war.   The story revolves around the romance of a beautiful German
girl and an irresistible American boy.   The two fall in love when
they are caught in a train wreck, just before war is declared.
These rôles are played by Dolores Costello and George O'Brien,
and rarely have they done such beautiful work.

The war episode is all one could ask, but the intimate scenes between O'Brien and Guinn Williams, his buddy, are exceptionally fine and appealing. It is to Michael Curtiz's credit that he has directed such a huge spectacle and at the same time so beautifully handled the love story.

The picture has a large and capable cast, and is tremendously interesting, for the most part; exceptionally thrilling and awe-inspiring in many parts, and will be discussed by every school child in the country, to say nothing of what will happen among teachers and religious enthusiasts. You will not be properly informed if you miss this.

--Photoplay, Vol. 34, No. 5
(October 1928), page 53.

☐ OLD IRONSIDES (Paramount, 1926)

James Cruze need not care who makes the laws of this country as long as he can make its historical films. Old Ironsides pictures this country's pioneering as a sea power, just as The Covered Wagon showed our winning of a land empire.

It's a glorious story of a glorious achievement. The hero is the frigate Constitution, the lone vessel that freed the sea of Tripolitan pirates. The heroine is the barque, Esther, rescued by the Constitution, from the pirates. There is a human love story, too, a poetic romance of a landlubberly boy and a girl who is the embodiment of the sea. And there is gorgeous comedy in the adventures of two sailors and a colored cook, played with salty gusto by Wallace Beery, George Bancroft and George Godfrey. Also on the honor roll are Charles Farrell, a newcomer, and Esther Ralston.

The greatness of the film lies in Cruze's sure grasp of the principle involved--"Millions for defense but not one cent for tribute"--and in his uncanny ability in recreating the very spirit of the times. He makes you see America as a young and vital nation, before she was concerned in dollar diplomacy and Sunday School legislation. It's a stirring ideal and the screen ought to be proud to hold it before the public.

A feature of the showing in New York is the Magnascope, a device that widens the screen to give more scope to the magnificent battle scenes. But Old Ironsides is in itself a magnascope, for films like this double the dimensions of the power and influence of the screen.

--Photoplay, Vol. 31, No. 3
(February 1927), page 52.

☐ THE OLD SWIMMIN' HOLE (Charles Ray/Associated First National, 1921)

There have been two samples of titleless pictures recently that have lent strength to the arguments of those opposed to them. One was The Kid, in which Charles Chaplin found it practically unnecessary to explain in print either the intentions of his characters or the lapses in his story. The other, Charles Ray's The Old Swimmin' Hole, goes even farther and has not so much as a single sub-title throughout its six reels of length. Of course it is not a story that demands titles. No one in it could possibly have anything worth titling to say, and there is no story at all in the plot sense. It is a day in the life of a small-town boy, a rather overgrown and clumsy small-town boy, necessarily, as Ray plays him, but a lovable, human, untheatrical type. It could go on and on for sixteen as easily as for six reels and, so long as it was kept as human and as true to the general acceptance of a small-town boy's life, as Ray and his director, Joseph DeGrasse, keep this much of it, it would be an interesting and enjoyable picture.
--Burns Mantle in Photoplay, Vol. 19, No. 9 (May 1921), page 51.

☐ OLIVER TWIST (Jackie Coogan/Associated First National, 1922)

The performance of little Jackie Coogan in the name part of this new film version of the Charles Dickens' novel is highly sensitive and well sustained. Otherwise, the version strikes us as being more careful than inspired.

The present Oliver Twist traces the waif from Mr. Bumble's workhouse roof to the sheltering library of Mr. Brownlow and--since Jackie couldn't grow up for one film--ends right there. The brutal Bill Sykes, the arch scoundrel Fagin, Monks, "The Artful Dodger," Nancy Sykes, and all the other folk of the London slums are there but they are pretty pale reflections of Dickens' imagination.

We fear Jackie's Oliver Twist will fall somewhere between the Dickens' lovers and his own fans, missing both of them. The first half will consider that Dickens has suffered and the other half will want more of Jackie.
--Photoplay, Vol. 23, No. 2 (January 1923), page 65.

*   *   *

In finish, in ability to tell a story effectively, Oliver Twist is a commendable, a successful picture; in fidelity, in ability to tell Dickens's story, it is measurably a failure. Even the fine work, the very fine work, of Jackie Coogan as Oliver does not fish

the chestnuts out of the fire--does not defeat the argument that the
photoplay must fall short, when it attempts to draw from them, of
its sources in literature.

Yet the fault in this particular picture cannot be laid entirely
at the door of the cinema medium. George Siegmann could have
been Bill Sykes, Lon Chaney could have shadowed forth Fagin,
Gladys Brockwell, less scrubbed of attire and feature, could have
shown us Nancy. In the treatment of these three arresting characters of Dickens, emphasis on the brutal, the cruel and crafty,
the degraded struggling momentarily up to light, would have given
something approximating the original. Why, then, was it not done?
The answer is censorship--fear of the censors.

Oliver Twist has the making of a great underworld picture--
a melodramatic photoplay of the sordid and the unredeemable--a
panorama of sinister shadows lurking in the filth of a London slum.
When the emphasis is placed on the machinery arranged by the
novelist to keep in motion his rather feeble character of Oliver,
all that is artificial in the story is brought to the surface and all
that is real is pushed out of sight. In going easy on "the rough
stuff" the producer has done a service to Jackie Coogan and to the
long beards with the shears, but he has done a mischief to the
work of Charles Dickens--to that dark and brutal canvas whereon
Nancy is shown murdered, and Fagin in prison pursued by the everlasting fiends, and Bill Sykes retracing his haunted footsteps to the
scene of his crime. Without these overmastering details, presented fearlessly, horribly, Oliver Twist is not Oliver Twist, and
it is not a picture such as Oliver Twist should be.

For what it remains--a well-made, well-photographed, well-
behaved, in its repressions capably acted, production, it is here
recommended.
                                    --Exceptional Photoplays, Vol. 3,
                                    No. 1 (November 1922), page 4.

☐ ON WITH THE SHOW (Warner Bros. , 1929)

One hundred per cent everything--singing, dancing, talking
and technicolor. The color photography makes it unique.

The situations have whiskers, but the transitions from back
stage drama to footlight hey-hey are well done. There is a large
chorus with lively dance routines, and tuneful music. The conversation consists of snappy comebacks, 1910 variety.

Performances from the large cast are almost uniformly good,
with Joe E. Brown standing out with sparkling comedy interpolations.
Sam Hardy scores as the harassed producer, and Betty Compson is

optically entertaining.   The Blues singing of Ethel Waters is a high-
light.   Alan Crosland's direction is competent.   All Talkie.
                        --Photoplay, Vol. 36, No. 3
                          (August 1929), page 54.

☐ ORCHIDS AND ERMINE (John McCormick Productions/First National, 1927)

        Here is an amusing hour for everybody.   A nice little come-
dy, featuring Colleen Moore and Jack Mulhall.   Another rags to
riches story of a telephone operator in a hotel who meets a mil-
lionaire--and of course they marry.   Colleen, the direction and the
titles take the Cinders out of this Cinderella yarn and make it just
one grand laugh after another.   Jocelyn Lee is quite interesting as
a gold-digger.   A pleasant way to spend an evening.
                        --Photoplay, Vol. 32, No. 1
                          (June 1927), page 56.

☐ ORPHANS OF THE STORM (Griffith/United Artists, 1921)

        When Dad who answers the questions asked in the advertise-
ments was a youngster he used to see the billboards wildly announc-
ing Kate Claxton in The Two Orphans, and if he was a lucky kid
his Dad took him to see the weepy old D'Ennery melodrama with
Miss Claxton playing both the orphans and piteously making the
blind Louise's plight the principal feature of the play.   And Mother
Frochard was most evil in her treatment of Louise and the brothers
fought a great knife-duel and the youngster was much impressed.
Kate Claxton played the piece until most people in the country probably thought she was the only one who possibly could play that sort
of emotional stuff, and then, years after, Grace George went out in
an all-star cast playing the two sisters for a time.

        But in the Griffith picture now offered the girls' parts are
not "doubled" but are charmingly acted by the sisters Lillian and
Dorothy Gish and in the picture the blind girl does not have most
of the emotional acting to do.   That falls to Lillian who is given
much work to do that is not at all remembered as coming from the
old play--and need it be said she does it well.   As the protector of
the innocent blind sister she is not only sisterly but motherly; as
the brave girl helping the injured Danton and thereby winning the
gratitude of the man who is to save her life at the end of the play,
she is delightfully womanly and sweet; and as the girl in love with
the noble Chevalier she is certainly all that a girl in love ought to
be.   A delightful piece of characterization it is that Miss Lillian
gives throughout the play.

Dorothy Gish's portrayal of the blind girl is delicate, interesting and most pathetic in the scenes of her distressful plight in
the squalor and poverty of old Paris, and in the scene in which the
sisters come so near to be re-united--only to be kept apart when
Henriette is arrested for harboring an aristocrat--her playing was
most effective. Mention, too, should certainly be made of the excellence of Joseph Schildkraut as the hero, Monte Blue as Danton,
and Sidney Herbert's extremely fine portrayal of Robespierre.

The picture as Mr. Griffith has made it rests more on Car-
lyle's French Revolution and Dickens' Tale of Two Cities for its
environment than it does on the old D'Ennery melodrama, although
the salient points of the story of The Two Orphans are all utilized.
But the power of the play is in the big pictures of those turbulent
times in France when the people seized the rights so long denied
them and went to terrible excesses of cruelty and injustice in en-
forcing those "rights." The scenes of the French Revolution--like
the assault on the Bastille, the horrible pageantry of the guillotine,
the wild harangues before the crowds that attended the evil courts
of "justice" that were established--these and many others certainly
had their appeal to a director of David W. Griffith's imagination.
And in his scenes of the crowded streets, of the battles, the bar-
ricades, the prisons, the place of the guillotine, the wild ride of
Danton and his followers to save the lovely heroine and her lover
from the falling knife--these are all made tremendously effective in
the art of the producer.

--Walter Brown in The Moving
Picture World, Vol. 53, No. 9
(December 31, 1921), page 1125.

□ OUR DANCING DAUGHTERS (M-G-M, 1928)

Gals with gold-digging aspirations can see this and learn.
The story depicts life in the younger set and deals with the struggle
of two gals for one lad. The presentation of youth is a lovely one,
what with a yacht club and cocktails. The main issue is: Will the
rich young hero succeed in rectifying the tragic mistake he made by
choosing the wrong girl? Light romance--and good. One thrill you
won't forget, nor the girl--Anita Page. Hers would be the outstanding performance if Joan Crawford and Dorothy Sebastian were not
also in the picture.

Nice restraint in the work of John Mack Brown, leading man.
Nils Asther's fervent kisses not too good, but his jealousy is real.
Eddie Nugent, a prop-boy turned actor, is well started.

--Photoplay, Vol. 34, No. 3
(August 1928), page 56.

☐ OUR MODERN MAIDENS (M-G-M, 1929)

As Joan Crawford's first starring vehicle, this vivid picture
of ultra-modern youth, as the movies see our younger folk, will
undoubtedly create quite a stir.   This is Josephine Lovett's sequel
to Our Dancing Daughters.   Then, too, it is the first time Joan and
Douglas Fairbanks, Jr., have played together.

Joan plays the rôle she does so well, that of a pampered
play-girl bored with the world her rich father gives her to play
with.   The climax of the picture is based on a thoroughly original
and unique situation.

Joan is exquisitely poised and gowned, and her acting highly
commendable.   Douglas Fairbanks, Jr., gives astoundingly accurate
impersonations of John Barrymore, Jack Gilbert, and his own dad,
Douglas, Sr.   Probably a tremendous box-office hit.   Part Talkie.
--Photoplay, Vol. 36, No. 2
(July 1929), page 54.

☐ PARAMOUNT ON PARADE (Paramount, 1930)

Paramount on Parade, if we are to take the title at its face
value, is the best the studio can do in the way of applied showmanship.   We have a right to assume that the production is a parade of
everything in the entertainment line that the organization possesses,
that it represents its full mentality, the full extent to which it can
employ its stars, its writers, its musicians, its dancing masters,
and its art directors in a united effort to create entertainment and
spectacle by which its creators can be judged.   View Paramount on
Parade with that thought in mind and you will be disappointed.   It is
merely a photographed vaudeville show consisting chiefly of indifferent acts, and totally devoid of that suggestion of continuity of thought
that successful screen entertainment must possess.   Under a title
that was not a confession that it is the best Paramount can do, the
picture probably would be regarded as fairly diverting entertainment.
As it is, it is more of a reflection on Paramount than a credit to
it.   When a studio goes into the revue business it challenges comparison with similar products of other studios.   Universal is presenting to the world its idea of what a revue should be.   There is
more thought, more art, more spectacle, more entertainment, better
music and singing in the Melting Pot number in the Paul Whiteman
revue than there is in the entire length of Paramount on Parade.
What the Paramount picture lacks chiefly is brains.   What cleverness it possesses is that of its individual artists who struggle manfully to make satisfactory entertainment out of unsatisfactory material.   Those behind the scenes are responsible for the poor showing.
Such artists of proven talent as Ruth Chatterton, Clara Bow, Nancy
Carroll, Helen Kane and Maurice Chevalier are wasted in numbers

that have little merit.   The outstanding artist is little Mitzi Green, whose imitation of one of the Two Black Crows is the best bit in the production.   Paramount overlooked a bet when it did not transfer to her capable little shoulders the duties it assigned to its masters of ceremony.   That at least would have been novel.   In a picture of this sort we have a right to expect novelties, some scintillating spots that stand out and bear testimony to the brilliant minds employed by the producers.   Paramount on Parade is singularly devoid of such brilliant features.   Its only musical numbers that have a chance to be included in the repertories of those who whistle popular refrains, already have been heard on the radio so frequently that the public will get the impression that they were borrowed for the production and that they did not originate in it. I think it is unwise of producers to make musical compositions public before the release of the pictures for which they were written.   There is nothing in this Paramount production that has not been done before in scores of others, and in many instances they were done better.   The picture can not escape being compared with the Universal revue, as the two will be showing simultaneously, and the Paramount offering is going to suffer woefully by such comparison.

--Welford Beaton in The Film
Spectator, Vol. 9, No. 11 (May
10, 1930), pages 9-10.

☐   THE PASSION OF JOAN OF ARC (Société Générale de Films/
M. J. Gourland, 1929)

Just as the rest of us seem determined to do away with the very institution of the silent cinema, the French, of all people, come along with one of the grandest of all motion pictures in the perishing tradition.   I won't go so far as to say that The Passion of Joan of Arc is the greatest photoplay I have ever seen, but, unquestionably, it is one of the four or five indisputable masterpieces of the dying medium; a superb indication of what could be done with old art form if efforts had really been made to develop it seriously. As a matter of fact, I am willing to go even further in my praise-- I think that The Passion of Joan of Arc is not only a magnificent film, but that it is one of the greatest and most significant achievements of twentieth century art, no matter what its form.

The work explains, with all conclusiveness, the attitude of the vanquished minority I belong to towards the talking pictures. Even in its subtitles, the French film is completely visual in its purpose and achievements.   Now, it is by no means my contention that the audible pictures cannot produce effective drama.   The Letter and Hearts in Dixie would prevent me from holding that belief. When, however, the success of an imitative medium threatens a purely pictorial form capable of Potemkin, The Passion of Joan of Arc, Greed, Variety and the Chaplin comedies, I somehow cannot

feel completely friendly to it.   When synchronized dialogue imperils
an art form capable of such works, I cannot help feeling, rather
bitterly, that its triumph means the destruction of one of the grand-
er manifestations of the modern spirit.   How, not only unnecessary,
but how completely a handicap speech would have been to any of the
old-time cinematic masterpieces!

Though the French picture belongs, as I have more than
suggested, in that epic company of Potemkin and The End of St.
Petersburg, it is entirely distinctive from them in manner.   To de-
scribe its methods I must fall back on one of the definitions of the
motion picture advanced, my recollection was, by that brilliant
young cinema philosopher, Mr. Seymour Stern.   One of Mr. Stern's
divisions of the screen form was, as I recall it, "sculpture in motion. "   That is the best description imaginable of the style and purpose of The Passion of Joan of Arc.

Essentially the picture is medieval French sculpture suddenly given movement.   In cinema phrases, it would have to be described as a series of close-ups.   The method is to offer, in the
form of subtitles, transcripts from the testimony in Joan's trial
and then photographed the reactions of mobile, beautifully carved,
figures to it.   A subtitle shows you a question the judges put to
their victim and the camera, thereupon, with a superb sense of design and lighting, captures the fleeting changes of expression by
which the inquisitors accompany it.   Then, Joan's reply is given
and, magnificently acted, you see the girl's reactions to the prose-
cution of her foes.

I have so often denounced subtitles as crude handicaps to the
medium of pantomime, as explaining, if not justifying the use of
dialogue, that I feel I owe them an apology after seeing The Passion
of Joan of Arc.   In it, they are an essential part of the work, providing a sort of chapter headings for the pantomimic drama that is
to follow them.   Were the questions and answers of the drama presented audibly, the entire mood of the picture would be viciously
ruined.   The complete effect of the film demands that everything be
visual and even the captions, which provide a necessary key to the
sculpture in motion of the drama, are not an intrusion but an inte-
gral part of the photoplay.

The most important single contribution to the excellence of
the picture, despite the brilliance of the Danish director, Carl
Dreyer, is the performance of Mlle. Falconetti as Joan.   Of course,
acting is so often the result of good direction that it is usually
dangerous to make such a distinction.   Yet there are things this
actress does that transcend outside management.   As Mlle. Falconetti portrays her, the Maid is a puzzled, sorely tried little peasant girl, devoid of grace or distinction of feature.   Under the persecution of her judges, however, she somehow stands transfigured,
until, without change of makeup, she assumes the unearthly spiritual
beauty of a great soul.   Never does she seem an actress simulating
sanctity; never does the mystic power with which she manages to

invest her characterization appear the work of artifice it, of course, must be. Somehow you feel that you are watching a great and noble woman. In the most difficult of histrionic feats, her triumph transcends all histrionics.

The picture probably is no great philosophical contribution to the lore of Joan of Arc. It treats only of the trial and execution of its heroine, and presents Joan, with utmost simplicity, as a helpless peasant girl, persecuted by cruel, but equally puzzled ogres, who grow more and more confused at finding themselves confronted by the miracle of sainthood. Unlike Shaw's masterpiece, Saint Joan, which showed the inquisitors as upright men, driven to persecution by the inexorable logic of their intolerance, the picture offers no such explanation and is satisfied to show the judges as leering, savage brutes. It does, however, offer them the excuse of the terrible bewilderment and even horror they felt in the face of that unaccountable sainthood.

I could find no such thing in the picture as any psycho-analyzing of Joan. For though the picture is modern in spirit to the extent that it employs such a recent dramatic form as the cinema, it is, in essence, a beautiful transcription of medieval art and the medieval devotional spirit. In it the fantastic sculptured figures of the fifteenth century are in motion before you; saturnine gargoyles come to life from some medieval cathedral and you see some idea of what the middle ages must have meant by sanctity. The result is something of rare beauty.

A Dane directed it, it is true, but the work is completely French in style, acting and locale. It comes, therefore, as a sort of tragic irony that one of the hitherto most backward nations in silent film manufacture arrives with something great, just as America, the home of the cinema, is gleefully giving up the medium.
                                    --Richard Watts, Jr. in The Film
                                      Mercury, Vol. 9, No. 20 (April
                                      12, 1929), page 6.

☐ THE PATRIOT (Paramount, 1928)

Only a great artist would attempt to play the rôle of Paul the First of Russia. There are too many odds against him. Yet Jannings, with his characteristic assurance, assumes the personality of the Mad Czar so completely that we forget the actor. His uncanny ability to get the intimate nuances of a character makes his portrayal both technically and psychologically accurate. In fact, Lubitsch's flawless direction gives all the characters the stamp of reality.

The story is like a brilliant piece of mosaic, with fearstruck Russia for a background. Silent, watchful ministers and the subtle

intrigues of the royal court pivot about the grotesque figure of the
mad ruler, whose life-long fear of sudden death has made a mega-
lomaniac of him.   The one man he trusts is Count Pahlen, superbly
acted by Lewis Stone.   It is the count's sad duty, because of his
unswerving love for Russia, to betray his friend by heading a con-
spiracy to throne the Crown Prince, beloved of the people.   In this
plot, Countess Osterman, who loves Pahlen, is his unwilling accomplice.   Failing to understand his high purpose, she, in turn,
betrays him to the emperor.   Florence Vidor is excellent, though
her characterization lacks vigor and fire.

Only such a master as Jannings would brave the competition
of so fine an actor as Lewis Stone, in giving him the title rôle and
the more sympathetic part.   Unlike Jannings' other American-made
pictures, this is more of an intellectual than an emotional triumph.
You will watch the picture with breathless suspense.

--Photoplay, Vol. 34, No. 1
(June 1928), page 53.

*   *   *

After watching Emil Jannings portray the mad Czar Paul in
The Patriot, it is impossible to deny that he is infinitely the greatest actor yet produced by the motion picture.   But that, it is true,
was already practically axiomatic.   What it is difficult to dispute
now is that he is the finest player current in any form of dramatic
art anywhere.

Of course his role in The Patriot is particularly well suited
to the peculiar talents of the man.   As the cowardly, homicidal,
brutal, lecherous, pitiful maniac who ruled Russia in 1801, he has
a part that calls for all the richness of detail, the heightening of
dramatic points and the stressing of emotional effects that the
mighty Teuton so revels in.   These qualities fit so completely into
the portrait that the actor could probably have acted all over the
place, with a modicum of thought as to the minor matters of restraint and credibility and still have been effective.

It is the chief glory of the Jannings performance that he
didn't take this easiest way to characterization.   He played his
sadistic imbecile with all the broadness of emphasis that was demanded by the role, and yet he added to this a subtlety, a restraint
and, above all an enormous human sympathy that many observers
have announced that he lacked.   It has been the claim of his de-
tractors that he marred his performances by mugging and the other
forms of over-acting, and that he was chiefly acclaimed by cinema
devotees because they confused histrionic violence with great acting.
Such a charge is pretty conclusively confuted by The Patriot.

In the early sections of the film, Ernst Lubitsch has impressed his individual qualities on it so strikingly that what is essentially a moving tragedy for the moment [turns] into sly and brilliant sex comedy.   And here the supposedly heavy Mr. Jannings is

at his best. I have no intention of suggesting a paradox when I say
that he is enormously light and deft when portraying the ponderous
amorousness of the mad czar. His scenes with his mistress--
charmingly played by the lovely Vera Veronina--and with the Countess Osterman (Florence Vidor) are delightfully done and when he
listens to Count Pahlen telling of his own sex adventures and gets
pretty excited in the course of the narration he is superb. I hate
to use that overworked word, but here is a place where it is thoroughly justified.

If by any chance you are interested in knowing my favorite
moment in both Jannings' work and the picture, I would confess that
it is the scene in which the czar, having been roguishly slapped on
the cheek several times by his mistress, suddenly awakes to the
importance of his position and socks the lady in the jaw with considerable violence. So far as I know this admiration arises from no
particular suppressed desire, but only from the pleasure of watching
an amusing and unexpected incident perfectly played. Then, too,
every time Jannings put the lady's dog out of his room, I found high
comedy prevailing.

Worthy of vigorous praise, too, are those scenes that merge
high comedy with tragedy, the Jannings subtlety. Under this classification comes the episodes showing the earlier relations between
the czar and Count Pah[len, who is his] confidant and his murderer.
Paul's admiration, affection and utter dependence upon the Count and
his momentary attempts to be petulent to him are beautifully handled.
He merely has to slam the door in Pahlen's face and then, the next
moment, open it shame-facedly to register his relationship with his
war minister with all its humor and all its pathos.

In the final, tragic episodes, showing the piteous helpless-
ness of the czar before the conspirators, Jannings performs one of
his greatest feats. The early scenes are chiefly devoted to portraying Paul as a cheap clown and a merciless murderer, as taking
from him any right to the slightest trace of human sympathy. Now
this was probably not so difficult for an experienced actor to accomplish, just as it should not have been so complicated to show
the betrayed emperor as the pathetic figure he is at the picture's
close. But to put both of these moods into one characterization
and never once to give the feeling that the resulting portrait is
confused or inconsistent or lacking in unity is, I proclaim, a genuine feat.

To sum it all up this sermon is, as you may possibly have
gathered, intended as a little street-dancing for one of the greatest
performances of our time. In Variety, in The Last Laugh, in Deception, in a dozen other pictures, Jannings has been magnificent.
But I suspect that, never before, has he grouped together all the
qualities of vigor, vividness, understanding, significant detail, richness of shading, gusto, humor, infinite resource and subtlety so
perfectly.

I admire, too, the courage Jannings showed in The Patriot.
To an excellent supporting actor, Lewis Stone, he conceded what
was at once the title role, the more sympathetic characterization
and the part having the really moving closing scene. Few actors
of either stage or screen would, I imagine, have the graciousness
or the courage to do such a thing, no matter how arrogant their
self-confidence. There were some at the New York premiere who
proclaimed that, as a result of his opportunities, Stone took the
picture away from its star. Such a view seems to me utterly absurd.

It is not that I am unappreciative of Mr. Stone's portrayal
of the man who was "a bad friend and an unworthy lover," a murderer, a betrayer of both his best friend and his sweetheart--and
an unselfish patriot who sacrificed even his honor for what he considered the interests of his country. Here is a magnificent, complex and glamorous role, and Mr. Stone plays it understandingly,
sympathetically and believably. It is a splendid performance and
should win for him the histrionic recognition he has long deserved.
But to class it with Jannings' tremendous portrayal is so wild as to
detract from its real value. Any attempt to put a sure and competent performance ahead of a great one can only result in such an
inaccuracy of judgment as to make one skeptical of the merits it
really possesses. And that would be unfortunate, for Stone is really so good that there is no reason why any one should have to over-
estimate him.

In closing a word should be said about Lubitsch's direction.
In combining his usual grand sex comedy with real tragedy and doing it with restraint, good taste, fine intelligence and sure dramatic effect, he gives us a really outstanding motion picture.
                              --Richard Watts, Jr. in The Film
                                Mercury, Vol. 8, No. 15 (Au-
                                gust 31, 1928), page 6.

☐ PECK'S BAD BOY (First National, 1921)

It is a rare acting talent and a lovable personality that
Jackie Coogan brings to the screen. But his directors will be hard
put to it to find stories to fit him. Probably never again will he
have the chance that Charlie Chaplin gave him in The Kid. He
misses it in Peck's Bad Boy, largely by reason of the contrast this
picture offers to the master comedy in which he made his debut.
But he is still a fine little actor, surprisingly unconscious of the
camera and capable of holding an audience's undivided attention so
long as he is in view. As the mischievous Henry he filches the
grocer's prunes and dried apples, fools father out of circus money
and finally fills the same unhappy parent's lumbago pad with ants,
causing more or less commotion when father carries the ants to
church with him. We fear for Jackie, after seeing him carried

around New York and kept constantly on exhibition for the benefit of
the publicity men of his organization. But we hope for the best.
It would be a great pity if his little head should be hopelessly
turned--turned so far, that is, that he suddenly would find himself
running backward in place of forward.

--Burns Mantle in Photoplay, Vol.
20, No. 2 (July 1921), page 59.

☐ PEG O' MY HEART (Metro, 1922)

Here is a photoplay almost anyone will like. The celluloid
Peg has all that the stage Peg had, even to the Irish brogue (thanks
to the excellent titling), and it has Laurette Taylor, the creator of
this beloved character. Moreover, Miss Taylor acts with a very
good sense of screen values--and photographs excellently.

Peg, of course, is just another variation of the eternal
Cinderella theme. Peg goes to the English manor of the Chiches-
ters rather an ugly duckling but she blossoms forth in a way that
wins over her snobbish relatives and captures the heart of the English lord who lives close by. The screen "Peg" goes back into the
girl's past to show her a restless wanderer with her beloved father
--an Irish gypsy in truth. And it extends on to show Peg being
received by the king. Possibly this addendum isn't necessary, but,
on the whole, Director King Vidor and his scenarist, Mary O'Hara,
have done a very satisfying job with the popular play, never deviating in any essential particular from J. Hartley Manners' original
footlight thesis.

Miss Taylor's screen work is unusual. Her performance is
very well sustained and there are but one or two perceptible let-
downs in spontaneity.

Peg o' My Heart rather encourages us in regard to Mr.
Vidor. It is workmanlike and sincere. Somehow, we can't understand why Vidor has been in eclipse recently. Surely no one had
a more human touch in his direction. But the ways of motion picture business are many and varied. Maybe this accounts for the
Vidor stagnation. Now let us hope that he will be able to return to
the direct and poignant dramas in which he revealed an amazing
promise.

--Photoplay, Vol. 23, No. 3
(February 1923), page 64.

☐ PETER PAN (Famous Players-Lasky/Paramount, 1924)

When Sir James Barrie wrote Peter Pan he unconsciously
created one of the finest scenarios for a motion picture that any

director could wish. Here are action, imagination, and the unreal
situations that only motion picture art can make authentic. Here
also is that charming disregard of time and geography which, mis-
used, makes so many motion pictures silly, but which, when properly related to the story, can become a delightful fourth dimension
that no other graphic art possesses.

The "land of make-believe" is obviously a field where motion
pictures can find new and worthy laurels. With the aid of double
exposure, concealed mechanical helps and all the tricks of the trade
--used with art--nothing that happens in the domain of fairies is
too difficult to be reproduced on the screen.

What could be more delightful than the picturing of Tinker
Bell as a brilliant ball of light, flitting swiftly through the air and
which, when alighting, is disclosed to the wondering audience as a
tiny creature in wind-blown draperies--all flame and unreality and
beauty? Or the defying of gravity by Wendy and Michael and John
when they essay to fly at the behest of Peter? They do fly and
marvelously at that, first round the room in riotous joy and at last
through the window, upward to the Never, Never Land.

Yet tricks do not make an art and Peter Pan, happily, has
more than clever mechanics to recommend it. The director, Mr.
Herbert Brenon, gives with rare charm the make-believe of childhood, seeing again, as Barrie saw, the grown-up land of parents
through the eyes and whimsical imagination of children. That the
stage play has been followed so closely and so successfully is due,
we believe, in large part to the fact that Barrie, as we mentioned
before, wrote an excellent scenario when he wrote the play. It is
often too much to ask of directors and scenario writers to give a
literal following of the stage version. Many situations effective before the footlights are ineffectual in a picture and either have to be
left out or translated into more dramatic incidents. This is legitimate motion picture art. Perhaps the day will come when all stage
plays--and books, too--when filmed will be prefaced by the announcement, "Adapted from" with the word adapted underscored.

The story of Peter Pan, so well known, does not need to be
retold here. It is a bare plot at best but like all children's stories
it is the telling that makes it. Nana, the big dog, whom Mr. Darling got to care for the children because no nurse maid could stand
his "fidgetting," looks after the children in just the way Barrie
must have imagined--and as any child would picture. It is this light,
fantastic, and beautiful make-believe foolishness that carries over the
tale.

A picture like Peter Pan makes it hard to place one's critical
finger on a scene and say, "Here is motion picture art"--something
done in a way peculiar to motion pictures and which cannot be done
in any other art medium and give the same thrill. All through the
film is an artistically satisfying air of reality, of childhood dream,
re-pictured for the enjoyment of our older youth. Perhaps in the

scenes in the Never, Never Land this beauty of fairy country rises
to its greatest height. Old Captain Hook, played so viciously and
delightfully by Ernest Torrence, and his crew of swaggering cut-
throats, help form many a scene where interest and art combine to
make a thrilling moment.

Betty Bronson, in her part of Peter Pan, one feels, has
worthily filled the elfin shoes of her two predecessors, Maude
Adams and Marilyn Miller. Miss Bronson gives a most whimsical
portrayal of this daring boy "who never grew up" and adds a curious air of impersonality, an aloofness from mundane boys and girls,
which throws into relief her quaint antics, elfin and fantastic, so
alien to everyday life of parents and other stodgy elders. Miss
Bronson has achieved a difficult thing in making charming and intelligent a role which in the stage play depended for part of its attraction on the spoken word. She has youth, which is an asset in
this part, but she also has a charming conception of the character
--roguish, daring and with that air of utter freedom that this play
boy of fairy land should have.

Considering Peter Pan as an exceptional motion picture, we
know that there have been other films, more dramatic, others with
more master touches of interpretation, in both direction and acting,
but this film, we believe, is one of the most delicate and whimsical presentations of character and situation so far put on the screen.
The picture has about it the veritable air of fairy fantasy and ranks
as a noteworthy pioneer in the penetration, by motion pictures, of
still another realm of thought expression.
--Exceptional Photoplays, Vol. 5,
Nos. 3 and 4 (December-Janu-
ary 1925), page 2.

*   *   *

Everybody in America should see this picture. It is more
than a tonic, because it not only revives memories of youth, but
makes you youthful. If you are young, you will live and triumph
with Peter Pan in all the glorious episodes that your imagination
ever dreamed. If you are old, you will find yourself young again.

There is so much good to this picture that one is left wondering how it was all done so flawlessly. Sir James Barrie wrote
the story, Herbert Brenon directed the picture, and Betty Bronson
lived Peter Pan. Mary Brian was the spiritual Wendy. Every
other member of the cast is also entitled to praise, from Ernest
Torrence down to the tiniest tot in the picture. The performance
of each was flawless.

Peter Pan proves that all the fairies are not dead. In our
childhood we believed in them, in fact, we knew there were fairies.
If, in after years, we came at times to doubt their existence, we
learned from Peter Pan that our doubts were wrong. Peter Pan
could not have been produced without fairies to guide it through the
beautiful scenes.

The more we think of Betty Bronson, the more we marvel
at her perfect performance. Not only the expression in her face
but the way she stood and walked, and the grace that she showed
every instant caused us to feel that she was truly an ethereal child
who never could grow up. And anybody who can do that is, in
reality, Peter Pan.

There is another phase of the picture that caused us to marvel, and that was the photography. The beautiful bits done by Virginia Brown Faire as Tinker Bell lent an enchantment that was
needed to make the picture perfect.

And that is what it was--a perfect picture of a perfect story,
with a perfect cast.
--Photoplay, Vol. 27, No. 4
(March 1925), page 44.

*   *   *

Peter Pan with its Pirates, Redskins, Never-Never-Land and
all the other accessories that make up the dreams and ambitions of
youth came to Broadway on Sunday at both the Rialto and Rivoli.
Peter Pan, the boy that would never grow up, who ran away from
the home the day he was born; Peter Pan, the Pirate killer; Peter
Pan, who makes you clap your hands if you believe in fairies,
proved one thing, if nothing else, that Betty Bronson is the find of
years as far as pictures are concerned.

To Herbert Brenon must go a full share of credit for having
turned out a picture that with its fantasy holds the attention. At
the early performances at the Rivoli Sunday the children shrilled
their delight over the adventures of the Band of Lost Children, and
the older kiddies were just as spellbound by the suspense the director managed to weave into the fantastical tale of the noted English playwright.

But above all it is Betty Bronson who achieves the big things
in the public eye as far as the picture is concerned. At times she
reminds one of Marguerite Clark of the earlier days of screen history. She has that same dash of youthful verve; then in another
moment will come the gentle hint that she is as Mary Pickford was,
and a combination of those two names means only millions at the
box office in time, provided, of course, she is properly guided.

Then as Wendy, Mary Brian proves to be another youthful
find for the screen. Sweet, demure and with a sort of self-effacing
manner she wins the hearts of those in front. Ernest Torrence as
the famous Captain Hook, the pirate leader, is another delight and
scores very neatly indeed.

The production is remarkable for its beauty, and in it was
an opportunity for Brenon to work in his mermaids again. While
shooting that scene his memories must have harked back to other

days when he was with Fox. The scenes in Never-Never-Land and the home of the Lost Children underground were exceedingly well handled, but the real thrill came with the pirate ship and the battle on its deck, with the little youngsters worsting the pirate band.

Peter Pan is a picture that will go down the years as a delightful fantasy and crop up again as time rolls along, and with each return be welcomed with a new joy by a new band of children, who will join the ranks of the never-grown-ups.

On the first de luxe show on Sunday the Rivoli started to "stand 'em up" as early as three o'clock, and that, after all, is the sure sign whether or not the picture will get the money.
                              --"Fred" in Variety, Vol. 77,
                                    No. 7 (December 31, 1924),
                                    page 26.

☐ THE PHANTOM OF THE OPERA (Universal, 1925)

        As absolute a contrast as could be found in humanity to Colleen Moore's "Sally" is Eric, the Phantom, played by our doublejointed friend, Lon Chaney.

        An ambitious spectacle adapted from Gaston Leroux' story, a weird and morbid tale, it is nevertheless an intensely entertaining picture. Lon Chaney seems to delight in such horrible rôles as the Hunchback of Notre Dame and the Phantom. Certainly, there is no one on the screen who can play such rôles so convincingly.

        There is not a ray of sunlight, a spark of tender passion, or a real vivid comedy relief in the whole production, and yet, the atmosphere of mystery, the tense coil of suspense, the morbid quality of the story, the lavishness of the whole production is such that we pronounce it excellent screen entertainment. In his production, Rupert Julian has carefully avoided extremeness in his depiction of horror, and for this he deserves great credit.

        It is a story of a great musician, cursed with a face so hideous that he is a monster. He haunts the labyrinthine cellars of the Grand Opera, and wreaks his monstrous vengeance on managers and performers who dispute his unseen domination. Cristine Daae (Mary Philbin) has the misfortune to inspire his love. She has never seen him, but he has made a great singer of her, and demands her love as his reward. This terrible menace keeps Cristine and the man she loves, Raoul De Chagny, played by Norman Kerry, apart. Foiled, the musician brings death and destruction, but in a series of exciting episodes Cristine is rescued. The monster plays his own requiem and dies. In spite of the horror of his rôle, Lon Chaney wins, at times, sympathy.
                              --Photoplay, Vol. 27, No. 6
                              (May 1925), page 45.

* * *

The work of reconstructing France has gone on in Universal
City at a prodigious rate. Two years ago, a considerable portion
of Paris was rebuilt for use in The Hunchback of Notre Dame, and
now the remaining districts of that celebrated city are added in
The Phantom of the Opera.

If Carl Laemmle had only expended his vast resources on
the devastated areas in France itself instead of in southern California, there would be no traces of the Great War left.

The Phantom of the Opera is not nearly so magnificent in
scale, nor so stirring in theme, as The Hunchback--but as represented on the screen it is a more consistently thrilling story. It
is spook melodrama at its wildest and weirdest, and it is beautifully
done.

The scene, as one might surmise, is the Paris Opera House,
and the principal character a shadow who doesn't turn out to be
Lon Chaney until the story is almost over. This strange phantom
is employed as a threat, and a darned potent threat he is, too; he
terrorizes the opera house from property room to gallery, and
maintains an exceedingly taut state of suspense. When he finally
emerges from the shadows, the initial strain breaks, and the story
develops into an orgy of wild, blood-curdling action.

Rupert Julian's direction of The Phantom of the Opera is excellent; he has emphasized his pictures rather than his drama, and
has thus achieved an optical illusion which could never have been
gained by any direct appeal to the intelligence.

The acting, though undistinguished, is appropriate to the
general tub-thumper quality of the story. In other words, it is of
the variety that is usually known as "ham."
                              --Robert E. Sherwood in Life,
                              Vol. 86, No. 2235 (September
                              3, 1925), page 24.

☐ THE PONY EXPRESS (Famous Players-Lasky/Paramount, 1925)

When James Cruze starts shaking the dust from American
history, then you have a picture that makes you sit up and take notice. For this director can resurrect our picturesque past with so
much vividness and imagination that one of his films is better than
a hundred orations on patriotism.

The Pony Express is not another Covered Wagon, it runs on
its own legs. Henry James Forman's story is so crowded with history, so dramatic in its outlines and so rich in incident that it is

more a pacemaker than a follower. It tells how California, by a
slim thread of cross-country messengers, was saved for the Union.
Most of the action is laid in Sacramento and at the station in Jules-
burg, Colo., at the time of Lincoln's election. It's a story of Indian fights, of gun duels and of deeds of daring. It is animated by
the figures of the tenderfoot Mark Twain and of the young Bill Cody.

The cast is composed almost entirely of players who are
well-known "picture stealers." The hits are about evenly divided
with Wallace Beery and Ernest Torrence tying for first place and
with George Bancroft as a close second. Then there is Ricardo
Cortez who, wonder of wonders, makes the hero a really interesting person instead of just the fellow who gets the girl. Betty
Compson has but few important moments, but at least the picture
fades on the finest close-up Miss Compson ever had taken.

Now as long as Mr. Cruze seems to have a gift for this
sort of thing, will he please tell us about Columbus and the Nina,
the Pinta and the Santa Maria? If necessary for a good movie, he
can have Columbus marry Queen Isabella.

--A. S. in Photoplay, Vol. 28,
No. 6 (November 1925), page 48.

☐ POTEMKIN (Sovkino, 1925)

The Film Arts Guild and the Russian organization, Sovkino,
have given a private showing of the Russian film, Armored Cruiser,
Prince Potemkin, to three hundred invited guests. The picture is
for sale in America. Max Reinhardt and Douglas Fairbanks unite
in saying that it is great art, the best motion picture either has
ever seen. Already it has had, as well, a tremendous commercial
success in Germany despite defeats in certain German cities by
political censorship. Will Hays, who seems never to forget that
the average mental age of the American public is fourteen years,
and is so very careful lest the movies help mature us, was not
present on Tuesday. There is no final word therefore as to whether
the picture is to become a legend among the cognoscenti, or be the
sensation of the movies this year.

In making the picture Director Eisenstein used members of the
Moscow Art Theater and hundreds of nonprofessional actors from the
Proletcult (Organization for Proletarian Culture). The story, based
on the official report in the Admiralty files of the Czar, and on the
recollections of eyewitnesses and participants, describes the revolt
of the sailors of the armored cruiser Potemkin of the Black Sea fleet
outside the harbor of Odessa during the 1905 Revolution, the demon-
strations of the common people at the tent-bier of the sailor who led
it, the attack on the mourners and revolutionists by the Cossacks,
and finally the escape of the cruiser Potemkin with the conniv-
ance of comrades on the other cruisers of the fleet to the Ru-

manian port of Constanza.   Here is epic material, full of pity, terror, and truth.

        Someone muttered in the audience, "This is only newsreel."
There could be no higher praise for the reality conveyed.   So it
was, indicating at last in which direction the art of the movies is
to lie, if the screen is to be something more than a vehicle for
exploiting the personalities of stars and a distractor of the public
gaze from public and private conflicts.   There was no star in the
picture, unless perhaps the cruiser itself, or the sailors, or the
masses of Odessa.   Certainly not the sailor who rose to give command and who died in the fighting.   The eyes of the audience beheld, sensed, understood all that happened on those significant three
days.   Captions were few and simple, muted down, whispered di-
rections to those who have forgotten history.   The continuity halts
nowhere for explanations.   The eye but followed as the ear might
hearken to a tune.   The sailors, at work, asleep in hammocks in
sultry and cramped quarters, waking, going to their decks and engines, to roll call, grumbling about the rotted meat.   The doctor,
looking at the meat through his glasses.   Nests of wriggling mag-
gots.   The doctor says the meat is good, to wash it off in salted
water.   The sailors know that in the prison camps of Japan their
comrades are better fed.   The commander of the cruiser will have
none of grumbling.   It smacks of mutiny.   He commands the firing
squad.... Sailcloth is thrown over the malcontents.   "Fire!"
"Fire!!" ... Fire!!!"... But comrade will not fire upon comrade,
and the revolt has come.   Words convey but feebly the tremendous
impression of being everywhere at once which the all-seeing camera
was able to give.

        This was more than newsreel.   The camera, like some holy
invisible, watched and recorded.   Of all this population that Director
Eisenstein commanded, not one lingered before the camera.   Life
was the thing--masses of men, sweating at the furnaces, at mess,
fighting; faces, arms, legs, engines, thermometers, the big guns
with nostrils scenting danger, the restless flow of the common people of Odessa across the narrow file of the breakwater to where
the dead sailor lay in common state; the faces of the mourners, the
student and revolutionist exhorters; the crowd in panic--things like
these have never been seen so well in life or theater before.   Nor
has machinery, monster and servant in the modern world, been so
emotionally comprehended, or the relations between those who physically manipulate it and those who own it been so dramatized.

        The audience was divided between those who were nervous
and puzzled by the social conflict which was the theme of the film,
and those who were deeply moved not only by the revolutionary
theme but by the revolution in movie technique bringing in its wake
a vision of the new developments in the one art the machine age
can call its own.   Whether the public sees this picture or not, it
will before long experience the influence of the new technique, the
use of masses, the feeling for motion and machinery, a new swift-
ness and naturalness.   Director Eisenstein, when he has finished

the picture he is now making in Moscow, a film concerned with
cattle-breeding and cream separators, I am told, will spend six
months in Hollywood.   He has been granted leave of absence by the
Soviet Government to direct one picture for United Artists.
                                      --Ernestine Evans in The Nation,
                                          Vol. 123 (September 15, 1926),
                                          page 252.

☐ THE PRISONER OF ZENDA (Metro, 1922)

        One of the first of the imaginary kingdom novels.   Done into
a picture by Rex Ingram, who has managed to capture the spirit
and the color of the book and transfer them, almost intact, to the
screen.   A vivid plot of impersonations and conspiracies; of treachery, love and adventurers--gentleman and otherwise.   Lewis S.
Stone takes the double part of Rudolph Rassendyll and King Rudolf
with a fine swagger.   He presents a figure heroic enough to set
any feminine heart a-flutter.   Robert Edeson is a genuine Colonel
Sapt and Malcolm McGregor is reminiscent of Valentino before he
was a star.   Stuart Holmes is one of the villains and Ramon Samanyagos, who does a fine bit of acting as Rupert of Hentzau,
seems a decided find and an entirely new type.   While the beauty
of the lady villainess, Barbara La Marr, makes the blonde loveliness of Alice Terry seem almost weak at times.

        So much for the cast, which merits almost any amount of
praise.   As do the exquisite settings and the truth of the atmosphere.   One cannot help wondering why, with everything so perfectly in tune, Rex Ingram dimmed the harmony of it all with unnecessary and ugly bits of slapstick.   There are butlers who trip over
rugs, men who throw over-ripe bananas, servants with flying sus-
penders.   Not many of them--but enough to enter a jazz note that
is not welcome.   This minor fault does not keep the picture from
being splendid.   Not another Four Horsemen, perhaps--but decidedly
worth while entertainment.   And Rex Ingram has had the courage to
venture an unhappy ending because the book read that way!
                                      --Photoplay, Vol. 22, No. 2
                                          (July 1922), page 52.

                          *   *   *

        Back in the eighteen-nineties Anthony Hope hit upon a liter-
ary formula that has been more imitated than any other style of
romance in the last fifty years.   A mythical kingdom with a beautiful lady of royalty, and a heroic English or American gentleman to
fall in love with her--it is still a reliable standby in the all-fiction
magazines.   But The Prisoner of Zenda, with its sequel, still remains the best, as it was the first, of its kind.

        It served the Famous Players for their first American pic-
ture back in the dawn of the feature-picture, with James K. Hackett

in the parts of Rudolph and the king. Now Rex Ingram, who has
ranged from Blasco-Ibáñez and Balzac to the bucolic comedy of
Turn to the Right in the last two years, has done it over again,
with all the advantages of the most modern equipment and technique.
He has made a good job of it.

      The story comes to the screen by way of a stage version
that was popular some quarter of a century ago, but it covers the
ground of the book pretty faithfully. One misses the tea-table episode, but that is more than made up for by an attempted assassina-
tion at the palace and a corking fight at the castle of Zenda.   Rudolph Rassendyll goes to Ruritania, gets entangled in a plot against
the king, outwits the king's enemies and wins the heart of the Princess Flavia, and goes away again, just as in the book.   It is done
with dash and glamor and a wealth of romantic atmosphere.   The
opening scenes of the extremely plausible European railway coaches
and the little station of Zenda with its Slavic-lettered signs have
all the effect of carrying the spectator bodily into a foreign country, so that he is ready to accept the crooked old streets of Stres-
lau, the cathedral, the hunting-lodge, and the castle, as the real
things even if they were not as picturesquely suggestive as they
actually are.

      The story moves with the real spirit and tingle of romance.
Brave and loyal men fight gay-heartedly, fair ladies tread the earth
with something of the enchantment of angels, and love and honor
are high, heroic things.   Modern psychologists may call it what
they will, but the thrill of the thing remains in it still.

      Several moments in the picture are particularly vivid in
emotional tenseness. The old servant mounting guard over the
locked cellar where the unconscious king has been hidden--the coro-
nation in the cathedral, where all the mass movements make such
an eloquent background for Black Michael's first defeat--the dwarf
climbing up the outside of the palace wall--and the last breath-
catching fight for the rescue of the king. In these scenes Mr. Ingram has a chance to show his skill in directing a kind of action
that his other recent pictures have not called for.

      Mr. Ingram has always had a keen eye for the right people
to play the right parts, but in this picture he was either a little
careless or he couldn't get the actor he wanted. H. B. Warner
would seem to have been the ideal actor for Rudolph. Short of him
perhaps Lewis Stone does as well as anybody; he is a practised
maker of correct gestures and facial expressions, but he lacks the
thing we call personality that would have lifted the part into the
sphere of exceptional romantic acting. Stuart Holmes trails such a
cloud of past villainies behind him that only by a miracle could he
achieve a thoroughly new and distinct characterization as a bad
man--and he just misses the miracle. Robert Edeson, marvellously
disguised in a Bismarckian makeup, creates by far the most vivid
character among the men, and close upon his heels are Ramon
Samanyagos [Ramon Novarro] and Edward Connelly. Alice Terry is

a lovely and charming princess--a little coldish, but Flavia always
did have something crystal-like about her, in the book and in the
play. Barbara La Marr makes a rich contrast to her as Antoinette
de Mauban.

There is one distinctly jarring element in the picture--the
slap-stick relief at the beginning, where no relief of any kind, even
if it were genuinely comic, is called for. Mr. Ingram, in spite of
well-known examples, does not need to go in for that sort of thing.

> --Exceptional Photoplays, Vol. 2,
> No. 2 (March-May 1922), pages
> 5 and 6.

☐ THE QUEEN OF SHEBA (Fox, 1921)

In contrast to Lubitsch's Deception, J. Gordon Edwards' production of The Queen of Sheba is sorry endeavor studded with beads
of perspiration. It tries and tries but it is never anything but a
conventional movie tale with the characters given historical names.
A little diluted history is added here and there, and the whole thing
is done with typical ineffective expense.

Basing their plea upon the theory that little is really known
of the legendary Solomon, the Fox forces jotted down one or two
facts and went to work. According to H. G. Wells, Solomon was a
much over-praised ruler. He was neither wise nor magnificent,
nor did he pause at murder or extravagance. For instance, he
unhesitatingly murdered his brother who, in The Queen of Sheba, is
the villain of the opus.

Mr. Fox and Mr. Edwards think better of Solomon, and he
is shown as a highly religious ruler who, however, lapses just a
bit when the Queen of Sheba appears in a neat traveling costume of
a pearl or two. You could hardly blame Solomon, since Sheba is
Betty Blythe.

Anyway, there is a child, and all sorts of tribulations happen
to the boy, thus padding out the spectacle. Fritz Leiber plays
Solomon in a religiously emotional way, but the real interest of the
production is Miss Blythe. Her beauty fairly takes one's breath
away. The rest of the court is very weak. You notice this when
Miss Blythe is off the screen.

The direction is uninspired. The crowds storm and cheer
with equal nonchalance and nothing seems real. Yet a fortune must
have been expended on chariot races, camels and all the usual
American incidentals of fil-em spectacle.

> --Frederick James Smith in Motion
> Picture Classic, Vol. 12, No. 5
> (July 1921), page 88.

☐ THE RED KIMONO (Mrs. Wallace Reid/Vital, 1925)

        Something terrible. It started out with a good story by
Adela Rogers St. Johns and was directed by Mrs. Wallace Reid.*
But somewhere the great qualities of those ladies' talents got completely lost. It's the one about the innocent, downtrodden girl, the
city slicker, the white slavery, the slicker falling for the other girl,
and offering her a wedding ring, the shot, the trial, repentance.
And then what do you suppose comes? Surprise, surprise, c'est
le war. No matter how much trouble it is, avoid this one.
                                   --Photoplay, Vol. 24, No. 4
                                     (March 1926), page 123.

☐ REDSKIN (Paramount, 1929)

        The story opens in a government Indian school. If, from
that, one can't tell how it is going to end your head is as empty as
the Grand Canyon. The hero, Richard Dix, is not accepted by the
Whites. His tribe renounces him, but he wins the girl. Not even
the magnificent color sequences, nor the fact that oil gushes from
volcanic rock for the first time in history saves Redskin from mediocrity.
                                   --Photoplay, Vol. 35, No. 3
                                     (February 1929), page 54.

☐ RIO RITA (RKO, 1929)

        A faithful screen transcription of the Ziegfeld musical come-
dy that is careful to follow the original stage production almost
scene by scene. It is helped by a couple of new numbers, the
astonishingly effective voice of Miss Bebe Daniels and the fact that
its original comedians, Bert Wheeler and Robert Woolsey, prove
to be more amusing in the film than on the stage. The liveliness
of a soubrette named Dorothy Lee is helpful, also.
                                   --Richard Watts, Jr. in The Film
                                     Mercury, Vol. 10, No. 11
                                     (November 1, 1929), page 6.

                        *   *   *

        This is another musical spectacle, gorgeously and unimag-
inatively photographed. It isn't worth while getting all het up over

*Mrs. Reid merely supervised the production, which was directed by
Walter Lang.

whether this kind of thing couldn't be done a lot better. It seems
to satisfy plenty of people as it is, just as cabaret shows do. Rio
Rita is a good deal like a superlative cabaret show. It has glitter
and fun and singing and dancing, lavishly strung together on a sort
of plot. Villainy and heart-break intrude now and then, to remind
us that there is a plot, but they are neither terrifying nor thrilling.
Spectacle is about all the thing is, and it is probably perfectly sufficient.

       The singing is notably pleasing. Bebe Daniels, it turns out,
has a light soprano voice of real freshness and sweetness, and
though she often sings with a pained expression she is far from
being painful to listen to. John Boles has an excellent tenor, which
reproduces excellently. As an actor he continually suggests an
amiable choir singer trying to cut up at a fancy dress party. But
light opera heroes are seldom better.

                                   --James Shelley Hamilton in
                                     Cinema, Vol. 1, No. 1 (January
                                     1930), page 42.

☐ THE RIVER (Fox, 1929)

       Quite the most bewildering feat that the sound device yet has
performed is its presentation of a musical prologue to The River,
which Frank Borzage directed for Fox. The story by Tristram
Tupper is fairly well known, having run serially in the Saturday
Evening Post. It is set in the rugged out-doors, where strong men
make axes bite into stalwart trees, which fall and are carried by
rushing streams to sawmills in the valleys below; the out-doors
that consists of scarred mountains that wear timber on their sloping
sides, of rocky gorges that shoot rivers from one level to another,
of draws up which summer winds carry the perfume of lower meadows and blizzards in winter shriek their maddened way. In this
setting Tupper puts his people, and there they work out their drama
of human emotions, a stark, elemental drama that depends for its
value as screen entertainment largely upon the fact that not one foot
of the film even suggests the existence beyond the camera limits of
another world where there are cities in which dress suits are worn,
and bands play and street cars run. When the picture reached the
New York office--it is in the New York offices, you know, that all
the motion picture brains are to be found--it must have been decided that the Borzage production would do better if it had a musical prologue that would put the mind of the audience in tune with it,
one that would suggest the primitive vigor of it. If we can believe
the string of credits that precede the prologue on the screen, half
the population of New York conspired to perpetrate the musical
opening. It is the most ridiculous string of credits I ever have
seen. But what follows is worse. A fat fellow comes to the foreground in the first shot and fixes his hands as if he were going to
dive into the orchestra pit; but he changes his mind and sings a

theme song.   To prepare us for the costumes of the woodsmen, he
wears a dress suit.   And the worst is yet to come.   A woman
joins him and helps him out at the end.   She wears an evening gown
and an expression that indicates that her singing pains her dreadfully.   I don't think anything more absurd, more out of keeping
with what it precedes, ever has been presented on any screen.   To
introduce such a picture as Frank Borzage has given us, it is positively criminal.   If the voices had been heard from off-stage, and
the screen devoted to a series of views in keeping with what we
later were to see, there would have been some sense to it; but as
it is now, it is an exemplification of the theme song craze at the
peak of its insanity.   But the picture is all right.   Borzage has
done a remarkable job.   I have indicated the setting.   In it the
director had only Mary Duncan and Charlie Farrell with whom to
tell his story.   For almost the entire length of the picture they are
the only characters we see.   A crow personifies a third member of
the triangle.   It is a psychological drama that gets little help in its
telling from the actions of its characters.   Farrell again demonstrates that he is an actor of rare ability.   He plays an unsophisticated boy who never has seen a city.   He gets right inside the
character and gives us a portrayal that is a work of art.   The
Eastern reviews of the picture that I have read did not treat Miss
Duncan with the consideration to which her intelligent work entitles
her.   She plays a young woman who has travelled the glittering
highways of life--put over effectively by the labels on her trunk--
and becomes the mistress of the manager of the lumber camp.   She
is regenerated by contact with Farrell.   I thought her performance
an outstanding one, even though I question the wisdom of casting
her in a part of the sort.   There should have been a suggestion in
the early sequences of more softness in the character.   As we see
her, there is too great a transition from her worldliness to her
regeneration.   But Mary Duncan is an actress of ability, with a
definite place on the screen.   You can't get away from that.   Harry
Oliver, an art director who is a rare genius, gave The River an
amazing production.   Out at Fox Hills he built mountains and forests, and ran a river through them, all so real that when you see
them you won't believe they constitute a man-made motion picture
set.   The synchronized score is not always in sympathy with the
scenes.   It builds to climaxes that aren't and leaves flat some that
are.   By chopping off the prologue and the melodramatic ending,
Fox can improve The River before it is released generally.
                              --Welford Beaton in The Film
                                Spectator, Vol. 7, No. 5
                                (February 9, 1929), pages 9-10.

☐   THE ROAD TO YESTERDAY (DeMille/P.D.C., 1925)

         Beautiful photography forms the background for a muddled
story.   It starts with Joseph Schildkraut defying God with a broken
arm.   He is married to Jetta Goudal, one of those wives in name

only. Involved in a train wreck, they go back to a dim past where
almost everything happens, entirely without visible reason. What it
all means you'll have to find out from Cecil DeMille, who created
it.
--Photoplay, Vol. 24, No. 2
(January 1926), page 48.

☐ ROBIN HOOD (Fairbanks/United Artists, 1922)

More than anything else, Robin Hood is a show. It seems
to be stretching the word photoplay to classify it under that name.
In fact it's the last thing in spectacles. We doubt if the silversheet
will go much further along this expensive road. Indeed, we sense
a movement along the way of intimate domestic type of play.

Doug Fairbanks must be given credit for making his version
of Robin Hood with a prodigal hand. He seized upon the half mythical character of the knight of Sherwood Forest--who went about
righting the wrongs of the commoners--and developed it into a
sweeping pageant of the stirring, romantic era of Richard the Lion
Hearted and the Crusades.

Outside of a tender--and almost lyric--love scene between
Fairbanks and Maid Marian in the first half, the whole acting honors
of this section go to Wallace Beery, who seems literally to have
stepped back eight centuries. He is Richard.

At no time does Doug seem Robin Hood. He is always a
twentieth century Fairbanks, although he puts such a sense of en-
joying himself into the proceedings that one almost forgets this fact.
Director Allan Dwan must be given great credit for his masterly
handling of the massive and seemingly insurmountable difficulties
of Robin Hood. The spectacle is his triumph.
--Photoplay, Vol. 23, No. 2
(January 1923), page 64.

*   *   *

I had my first glimpse of the wonders of Robin Hood while I
was in Hollywood in the spring of 1922.

At that time the inhabitants of Los Angeles' most celebrated
suburb were all conscious of the fact that great preparations were
on foot at the Pickford-Fairbanks studio on Santa Monica Boulevard.
Hundreds of carpenters, mechanics and painters were working on
the greatest scenic construction that Hollywood had ever seen--and
Hollywood, in its time, has watched many great cities, ancient and
modern, rise and fall.

The new Fairbanks set took the form of a mediaeval castle,
a Maxfield Parrish creation, with turrets and battlements that ap-

peared magically overnight. First the huge framework ascended; then it was covered with synthetic masonry; then the painters applied to it a semblance of age; then ivy crept up its walls. The central part of the structure was steel and on this was operated, by means of a donkey engine, the cumbersome drawbridge.

There was incessant activity, and the great "extra" population of Hollywood--that indefinite mass of pitiful souls who are employed by the day to work in mob scenes--started to revive the hope that had been flagging desperately during the lean winter. Business had dropped in the movie theatres of the world that year and production had waned in Hollywood. Several of the largest studios were completely shut down, and the rest were carrying on the work in a half-hearted way. Consequently, employment was scarce and most of the impoverished extras, rather than face starvation, were forced to renounce the hazardous pursuit of artistic glory and return to the nondescript jobs from which they had come.

The tremendous preparations on the Fairbanks lot betokened a return to prosperity, and plenty of work at $7.50 a day. So the extras rejoiced.

I went to see Douglas Fairbanks at his studio and there, in the room that served as his barber shop, he unfolded the story of Robin Hood. It was a most dramatic adventure; for Fairbanks, in his very soul, is a consummate actor. He breathes and exhales drama. Whether his audience numbers one or five thousand, he is always immersed in the performance of his rôle--and that rôle is a combination of all the gay, dashing, reckless heroes that have ever appeared in the pages of romance. Fairbanks in himself is a legendary figure, an inveterate mountebank, a cowboy with an Oxford training, a genuine artist and an incredibly likable chap.

He was wearing a pair of shabby flannel trousers, ancient tennis shoes and a "T" shirt, but as he related his narrative, he assumed all the majestic habiliments of the Middle Ages. As he talked, he waved vigorously a wooden sword, with which he felled imaginary enemies at every point of the story.

His recital was accompanied by the pounding and sawing of carpenters who were erecting the castle of Richard Coeur de Lion on a dry California field. Silhouetted against the sky beyond were La Brea oil wells, with engines chugging monotonously. It was a strange setting for this tale of pageantry, chivalry and romance.

Fairbanks told me of a knight in King Richard's Court--the Earl of Huntingdon, bold, stalwart, loyal and gentle. When Richard embarked on the First Crusade, Huntingdon left the side of his love, the Lady Marian, to follow his King on the long, perilous journey to Palestine. He was Richard's favorite, and second in command of the English forces.

Owing to the evil machinations of one Gisbourne, the tool of the treacherous Prince John, Huntingdon was brought into disfavor with King Richard, and was cast into a French dungeon to await the Crusaders' return from the Holy Land. With the aid of his faithful follower, Little John, Huntingdon escaped from the prison and returned to England. He found that the country was suffering under the tyrannical rule of Prince John, who had stepped to the throne in Richard's absence and was cruelly misusing the power that had been entrusted to him. Lady Marian, Huntingdon was told, had provoked the ill-will of John, and was dead.

So the Earl of Huntingdon vanished and in his stead appeared one Robin Hood, a wild, devil-may-care fellow who commanded an outlaw band of sturdy men in the forest of Sherwood. Robin Hood and his followers were dedicated to the task of protecting the poor from the depredations of Prince John's soldiers, and of depleting the coffers of those who were fattening on the proceeds of this dishonorable reign.

Robin Hood and his merry men gained in power and became a positive threat against the security of Prince John's throne. They captured the town of Nottingham and even invaded the royal castle itself. Finally Richard, disguised and unrecognized, returned from the Holy Land, and John's day was ended.

So Robin Hood resumed his identity as Huntingdon, Lady Marian reappeared from the nunnery in which she had been hidden, and all was well.

This was Fairbanks' own conception of Robin Hood, developed from his vast imagination, and he intended to follow it through to the bitter end--if he had to mortgage his Beverly Hills estate to do it.

He had read a great many books on the Plantagenet period, absorbing ideas from Sir Walter Scott, Howard Pyle, Alfred Noyes and all the others who have been inspired by the brave deeds of Richard Coeur de Lion. With these ideas swirling about in his extraordinarily active mind, he had built his story; it was a narrative that could not be set down in print and could not be limited to the confines of a play on the speaking stage. It was a moving picture story, which could be told only on the surface of the screen.

Fairbanks made a continuity for Robin Hood on one sheet of paper, which is reproduced in an accompanying illustration. It is an historic document, for it represents one of the earliest examples of a real photoplay. It is not an adaptation or "screen version" of a story that was designed for expression in some other medium. It is the outline of a narrative that must be absorbed through the lens of a movie camera before it can reach its audience. When we have more scenarios like this, and fewer second-hand products, we shall have more pictures of the quality of Robin Hood.

Fairbanks went into the production of Robin Hood with all the enthusiasm in his ardent system. He realized the truth in Will Hays's theory that it "isn't a one-man job," and he surrounded himself with a brilliant corps of collaborators: Allan Dwan, as director; Edward Knoblock, as literary consultant; Wilfred Buckland, as supervising director, and a cast that included Wallace Beery, Enid Bennett, Alan Hale, Sam De Grasse and Robert Dickey. He searched every available source for material on the customs, costumes and manners of the period, and saw to it that the details were as nearly perfect as it was possible to make them.

The result was a picture of magnificent impressiveness and exquisite beauty. To quote Laurette Taylor, Robin Hood was "a moving tapestry." From the moment when the picture opened, with the lowering of the drawbridge and the appearance of King Richard's court, there was no scene in the film that jarred on the aesthetic senses. It was all gorgeous to behold, and in the romantic flash of its drama it was intensely exciting.

Aside from Fairbanks himself, whose Robin Hood transcended anything he had ever done before, the outstanding performance of the picture was contributed by Wallace Beery as King Richard. Beery's impersonation of the lion-hearted one was not exactly in accord with the popular conception of this heroic monarch; he chose to play him as a coarse, jovial, crude product of the Middle Ages, rather than as a polished, graceful Arthurian prince. Although his interpretation disagreed with my own romantic picture of Richard, I must admit that Beery convinced me of the soundness of his ideas. For he managed to convey, in spite of his uncouth exterior, a remarkable sense of the chivalry, gentleness and nobility which have made Richard the heroic figure that he is.

Sam De Grasse was an adequately dark, sinister Prince John, and Alan Hale made Little John a bluff, hearty and thoroughly prepossessing fellow.

Of the motives that inspired him in the production of Robin Hood, Douglas Fairbanks writes as follows:

> "To produce a picture and then to stand apart from it and with a calm and judicial eye to appraise its value is a task way beyond me. I am afraid that the faculties of creation and criticism will always travel along widely separated, if parallel, lines; the creative mind will continue to do things at times better than it knows how, and the critical mind will continue to know how to do things better than it can do them. This means that hundreds of people can speak more intelligently of the merits and faults of Robin Hood than I can. For I only produced it, and my task ended there.
> "David Belasco once told me that it was a simple task for him to analyze a failure but impossible for him to analyze a success. I find myself in a similar dilemma.

Robin Hood is, of course, the most successful picture I
have made, but I am not sure that I can satisfactorily explain why.

"There is one misapprehension about Robin Hood that
still seems to linger. I have received many communica-
tions from intelligent people deploring the fact that the
picturized version of Robin Hood wandered so far from
the book. If these critics know what book they are talking about they have a distinct advantage over me. Robin
Hood was not taken from nor based upon any book. The
picture was almost pure imagination, projected against the
historical background of the Crusades. It was the fabri-
cation of a dozen dim legends in a form that lent itself
to the imagery of the screen.

"The idea of doing Robin Hood came to me in this fashion. For years I had received an almost continuous
stream of suggestions urging me to make a picture based
upon the legend of Robin Hood. But these left me quite
cold. The spectacle of a lot of flat-footed outlaws in
Lincoln Green, a few paunchy friars and a homeless min-
strel or two singing a roundelay in the shades of Sherwood
Forest did not strike me as anything to make a picture
about. I dismissed the idea as hopeless; considered doing
Monsieur Beaucaire, and even drew up a scenario of it;
resurrected The Virginian, which I have always wanted to
do; played with a sequel of The Mark of Zorro, and in
general fell prey to the period of restless indecision
which usually follows the completion of one picture.

"Then I came by chance upon some old manuscripts of
the period of Richard the Lion-Hearted and the Crusades.
The robust, heroic figure of Richard, crusading for the
Holy Sepulchre in Palestine while England was left to the
dark conspiracies of Prince John, stirred me at once.
The period contained every dramatic element: a strong
religious impulse, a kingdom undermined by treachery at
home while the flower of its knighthood sought adventure
in foreign lands, fair maidens won by valor in war or
tournament and left behind by their knights who followed
Richard to Palestine ... all the romance, the chivalry,
the color of the adventurous Middle Ages. To make it
complete, it suddenly occurred to me that this was also
the period of Robin Hood and that if, instead of sentencing
him to an indefinite term in Sherwood Forest, I could in-
volve him in the stirring history of the period, I would
have a real story. Since, according to some of the legends, he was identified with the Earl of Huntingdon,
Richard's most trusted friend, I was not taking too great
a liberty. I knew that in the coupling of the stalwart
figures of Richard and Robin Hood I had an irresistible
combination. The story that immediately suggested itself
was Richard's loss of faith in his friend and the later rehabilitation of Robin Hood as a national hero. I had
everything that I needed. The whole thing glowed and

beckoned to me like a rainbow.   I went to sleep with this
idea for many nights and awoke with it tingling in my
mind.
    "I mention this first burst of enthusiasm about doing
Robin Hood because with this kindling of the mind toward
an idea, the story itself seems to be born without labor
and to develop almost by its own momentum.   I enclose
a one-page scenario of Robin Hood which I prepared when
the idea first hit me.   It was a long journey from this
literary protoplasm to the final product, and without a
persistent enthusiasm which I have never felt about any
previous production and which was shared by all the members of my staff, it would have been hopeless.   It was a
motive force which sustained us through the long grind of
production with its constant disappointments and the distracting preoccupation with detail, and enabled us to meet
all discouragements with a vision of the completed whole
which never failed to stir us.
    "The great problem in making Robin Hood was to trans-
fer to the screen the mass of historical detail, the colorful pageantry, the scenic effects--all the pomp and herald-
ry of the period--without entirely swamping the story.
We tried to meet this by making the narrative as fluent
and dramatic as possible.   Some critics have felt that
the first part of Robin Hood was unnecessarily long.
They may be right, although I believe that without a thorough presentation of the hero in the character of the Earl
of Huntingdon, his exploits as Robin Hood would have been
much less effective.
    "Robin Hood marks the end of one cycle of picture
making for me.   It embodied nothing particularly new or
revolutionary.   In it I sought to do the best I could with
ideas and materials in current usage.   In the construction
of sets, in the photography, in the general method of
treatment, I tried to surpass what had been done before.
But there was no pleasant adventuring into the unknown,
no experimentation with the screen as a medium for a new
kind of expression.   This is precisely what I am attempting at present in The Thief of Bagdad.   It may not be an
improvement over Robin Hood, but it will at least be a
stimulating encounter with a new idea...."

Of The Thief of Bagdad I have heard much, but know nothing.
If it lives up to its advance notices, it will probably appear in the
next installment of this book--always provided, of course, that there
is another volume.

    In the meantime, however, I am satisfied to offer Robin Hood
as the best picture of the year.

                              --Robert E. Sherwood in The Best
                                Moving Pictures of 1922-1923
                                (Small, Maynard and Company,
                                1923), pages 37-44.

                                    *   *   *

     The point about Robin Hood in Chicago is $2. * That's the
top at Cohan's Grand, where the latest Douglas Fairbanks special
picture opened Sunday night. It opened to the best of this town's
400, and they will pay $2 or more for anything they want to see.
But this town also has Knighthood [When Knighthood Was in Flower]
at the Roosevelt, with a top of 80 cents. It is also a special.
Marion Davies' latest as well, and while this is in no sense a comparative review of the two films, one can't get away from the fact
of the prices, with Knighthood the first in here.

     Robin Hood, however, missed nothing in an exploitation way
coming to this city, inclusive of the "400," quite a feat in itself,
going with the rest of the publicity to the credit of Pete Smith and
his assistants. But Mr. Fairbanks' Hood will have to prove itself
in a picture house in this town, unless the dope reverses itself on
the $2 thing.

     As a picture, that comes in again. In Cohan's Grand it's
$2, and you can't overlook that when watching the picture in review.
It's a world-famous story made by a world-famous film star. Its
settings are stupendous and elaborate, and there are the adventures
of Robin Hood (Mr. Fairbanks), showing his home and lair, with
the Fairbanks daredevilry for his admirers, running along for 50
minutes. Before that, for 75 minutes the picture delves into a
showing of Richard the Lion Hearted, his court and affairs. The
people who pay are going to prefer the Robin Hood portion.

     Which leaves the balance sheet in this wise: Fairbanks and
Robin Hood for 50 minutes, together with perfect settings, costumes
and playing, as against the price.
                              --"Loop" in Variety, Vol. 68, No.
                                9 (October 20, 1922), page 40.

☐ ROMOLA (Inspiration/M-G-M, 1925)

     It is a beautiful and tiresome thing. Miss Gish never does
much more than drop a book in the whole sketch.
                              --Anonymous critic in The New
                                Yorker, Vol. 1, No. 10 (April
                                25, 1925), page 31.

───
*Robin Hood appears to have received its premiere in Chicago.

☐ ROSITA (Pickford/United Artists, 1923)

The combination of the names Mary Pickford, Ernst Lubitsch and Edward Knoblock sound like an alluring symphony from which one expects a great deal.

But the real attraction of the picture must remain Miss Pickford. Contrary to popular surmise she does not depart from her usual type in Rosita, --for she makes of the Spanish dancer, a charming, saucy, gay figure, --a blonde Spaniard, who is none other than our own Mary Pickford. But it must be recorded of Miss Pickford, that she sustains her part throughout to perfection, even in her tragic scenes she never forgets that Rosita is merely a street singer who does not acquire poise with her spangled robes, nor dignity with the palace the king has given her. She remains to the end only the impudent, pretty gamin who has attracted the king's wayward fancy, and in her most dramatic scenes never acts at variance with the possibilities of such a character.

As for direction, nowhere is the picture stamped with the Lubitsch touch as prominently as usual; still his hand is recognizable for the artistry that has made him world famous. The grouping is often noticeably unique; the mob scenes are deftly handled. The photography is good; some of the interiors and exteriors are exquisite.

Of the three persons first mentioned, Mr. Knoblock is the most disappointing. Rosita, his adaptation of Don Cesar de Bazan, leaves little of the original plot, in fact little plot at all. It is but a flimsy repetition of the old story of the king who falls in love with the beggar maid. The Rosita version included a clever queen who foils the king's plan to dispose of Rosita's lover, and thus the story ends "happily ever after" for Rosita, and as for the king, -- he returns to his royal consort, with speed, if not with grace. Of such frail material the tale is spun and Mr. Knoblock's only contribution of value consists in the titles (if they are his). They are excellent.

The actors' make-up deserves special mention. Miss Pickford suffered no crude blue eyelids, and the King's face was cleverly done up. Mr. Holbrook Blinn gave an almost perfect interpretation of the King, "so bold and gay, young maidens looked the other way." We may hazard a guess that such will not be the case with his public, who will probably find in Rosita good entertainment and much to enjoy pictorially.

--Exceptional Photoplays, Vol. 4, Nos. 1 and 2 (October-November 1923), page 5.

*   *   *

There has been a lot of worriment over the fact that Mary Pickford was going to grow up. Don't worry. Mary has grown up in Rosita, but she is just as charming, just as fascinating as ever and she does better acting than ever before in her career. There is probably no actress today who could portray the gay, graceful, coquettish, little street singer of Seville who "vamps" a king, as she does. The production is incomparably beautiful. The sets seem, many of them, almost fairy-like in their loveliness. The production shows why Ernst Lubitsch holds his place among the leading directors of the world. Except in one or two minor details, the direction is flawless and the story moves with a smoothness that is most satisfying. No, don't worry about Mary growing up.

--Photoplay, Vol. 24, No. 6
(November 1923), page 74.

☐ SAFETY LAST (Hal Roach/Pathe, 1923)

This new Harold Lloyd farce will become a classic of its kind, or we will miss our guess. For it is the bespectacled comedian's best effort to date. Lloyd has evolved his laughs from the skeletons of skyscrapers and the ledges of lofty buildings before-- but nothing has equalled Safety Last. Here he seemingly climbs a twelve-story department store all for the love of a girl--and to win enough money to make possible a wedding. A hundred times he hangs by an eyelash.

The shrieks of hysterical laughter that greeted Lloyd in the comedy in New York would convince even a hardened critic--but this reviewer left the showing in a state bordering on collapse, along with the rest. Who hasn't heightophobia? There are nervous thrills galore, as when a flock of affectionate pigeons descends upon the head of the fear-racked Harold. Then a mouse runs up his leg as he balances upon a ledge. After that an excited store customer drops a tennis netting upon the worried climber. But the climax comes when he misses his hold and seizes the huge hand of the store clock, as the face of the time-piece stretches into space.

But Safety Last isn't all a climbing stunt. There's a lot of good legitimate funmaking with Harold as a department store worker under the eye of a floor walking autocrat. There is one particular joyous moment when Harold, to impress the girl of his hopes, takes possession of the general manager's private office--and barely gets away with it.

This is easily one of the big comedies of the year. It is seven reels in length--but it speeds by with the rapidity of a corking two-reeler.

--Frederick James Smith in Photoplay, Vol. 24, No. 1 (June 1923),
page 65.

*   *   *

It is Harold Lloyd's policy to alternate between laughs and
thrills in his comedies so that the public may never quite know
what he is going to do next.   Safety Last was composed largely of
thrills--and terrible, spine-chilling thrills they were.   The major
part of the action took place upon the face of a high building with
Lloyd climbing up precariously from one narrow ledge to another.
On the way up, he met with every conceivable form of mishap and
when he finally reached the top, the audience was reduced to a
state of gibbering hysteria.

Although Safety Last was more mechanical than most of Harold Lloyd's pictures, it was certainly a superb mechanism.
                              --Robert E. Sherwood in The Best
                              Moving Pictures of 1922-1923
                              (Small, Maynard and Company,
                              1923), page 107.

☐ SALLY OF THE SAWDUST (Griffith/United Artists, 1925)

It's by all odds the gayest and most delightful picture ever
directed by D. W. Griffith.   And, in spite of the fact that it's a
trivial and flighty mixture of slapstick and romance, we venture to
predict that it will be one of his most popular.

For one thing, it brings W. C. Fields to the screen.   In a
season of great comedy, Fields ranks with the big ones.   He has a
wonderful personality; he's a fine pantomimist; he has a priceless
line of "gags."   He makes Professor Eustache McGargle, the circus faker, a memorable figure in screen annals.   He's a wow, a
knock-out, a riot.   That is to say, the boy's good.

The story of the film is a Cinderella tale of a little circus
girl who is really an heiress with a highly respectable and frozen-
faced Yankee grandpa.   With its circus atmosphere, it makes an
ideal structure for the unbeatable Griffith trimmings.   The climax
is truly remarkable because Griffith accomplishes the startling feat
of paralleling a pathetic melodramatic scene with a slapstick chase,
without losing the effect of either incident.

And it's a tribute to Carol Dempster that she can hold her
own against Fields.   In fact, in the climax it's just as though Lillian Gish were playing a heavy scene against the antics of Harold
Lloyd.   It sounds wild but it's so effectively done, that it is great.

Sally of the Sawdust isn't all clowning.   It is filled with
scenes that show Griffith's sensitive and beautiful instinct for the
truly poetic.   There is, for instance, a moment when the mother-
less Sally strews flowers on the grave of an unknown woman.   And

Miss Dempster plays it like an artist. While we are passing
around the praise, it is well to mention Alfred Lunt who is an unusual film personality.
                                    --A. S. in Photoplay, Vol. 28, No.
                                       3 (August 1925), page 50.

                         *   *   *

          Among the major tragedies of movie history has been the
decay of David Wark Griffith. This real pioneer in a new art, who
did first what Lubitsch, Ingram, Cruze and the rest have subsequently done better, has gradually descended from the heights to a
level of rank mediocrity.

          It is not pleasant to think that the man who made Intolerance
and Broken Blossoms could affix his name to anything so utterly bad
as Sally of the Sawdust.   And yet, considering Mr. Griffith's recent
career, it is not particularly surprising; since 1919, when he presented Broken Blossoms to an unappreciative audience, he has been
on the down-grade.

          Sally of the Sawdust is inexcusable.   It is absolutely incoher-
ent as to story; its attempts at pathos are illegitimate; its charac-
ters--with one exception--are artificial.   It is the work of a man
who has become so completely soaked with theatrical trumpery that
he wouldn't recognize reality if it stepped up and slapped his face.

          The one exception in Sally of the Sawdust is provided by W.
C. Fields, who manages to inject some of his own matchless comedy, and some of his own human warmth, into this otherwise blood-
less story.   Carol Dempster, who appears in the title rôle, is still
a very unconvincing counterfeit of Lillian Gish.

          There is a fine collection of ham sub-titles, all bearing Mr.
Griffith's trade-mark, in several of which he comes out boldly for
Mother Love.
                                    --Robert E. Sherwood in Life,
                                       Vol. 86, No. 2234 (August 27,
                                       1925), page 26.

☐ SALOME (Nazimova/Allied Producers and Distributors, 1922)

          To my mind, Salome is the most extraordinarily beautiful
picture that has ever been produced.   Nazimova chose to carry out
the Beardsley design in translating Wilde's play to the screen, and
succeeded admirably.   The effect of the picture was weird and wonderful.   Natacha Rambova was responsible for the correct interpretation of Beardsley's drawings.

Salome possessed many dramatic defects, but as a spectacle
for the eye, it was absolutely superlative.

> --Robert E. Sherwood in The Best
> Moving Pictures of 1922-1923
> (Small, Maynard and Company,
> 1923), page 103.

☐ THE SALVATION HUNTERS (Academy Photoplays/United Artists,
1925)

Few directors have ever set themselves the task that Mr.
Josef von Sternberg did when he decided to put his original scenario
The Salvation Hunters on the screen. The theme of this tale is the
effect of environment upon a young boy and girl and how their deep
imprisoned braver selves at last fight through the shell of cowardice
and benumbing existence that was their inheritance.

To comprehend the task of Mr. von Sternberg a slight outline
of the story is necessary.

A boy and a girl both still under twenty live on a river
scow, with rotting wharves and muddy river banks and their squalid
home making an unlovely background to dull drab living. And always the gigantic dredge that all day long plunges its open jaws into
the slimy water to emerge a moment later dripping and full of river
mud. To escape from this world that constantly shocks their sensitive selves they leave the scow and try their fortunes in the city's
slums. Here they meet a man who, posing as a friend, takes them
to a cheap room, promising work for the boy. But his real motive
discloses itself as he waits for that moment when discouragement
will force the girl into his power. The boy does get discouraged
and the girl almost fulfills the man's desire. At the last sordid
moment the cowardice of the boy is thrown off and he wins a triumphant victory over both himself and the man. Then out into the
country he and the girl go together, still tramps but now spiritually
free from their past.

The Salvation Hunters is partly a picturing of action within
the mind. Half the scenes have this purpose and should so be read.
Then, too, scenes such as the monotonous dredging in the first part
and the mud and filth of the water front give a picture of environment as seen and felt by the boy and the girl. Perhaps a passerby
would not have been impressed with all this sordidness. Yet to
present the world as viewed through the eyes of the characters--in
this case characters that saw a sordid world because their lives
were drab--is the aim of dramatic art.

The picture is not a perfect one by any means. It has many
faults, not the least of which is the titling, which is over-explana-
tory, often strained in thought and, where spoken titles are used,

too literary for the characters. But the faults of the picture are mainly shortcomings--a falling short of daring efforts at greater motion picture expression. However we will not discuss the faults, which are obvious, but desire rather to emphasize the efforts to reveal in an interesting fashion some realms of human life not often touched in motion pictures. Futile would it be to discuss whether or not the picture is art, except to say it has come near to the photographing of occurrences as they would actually happen and moods in people as they would actually be made manifest, and that throughout the creative impulse is to be perceived striving to express what is in its thought, although the thought itself may often be inadequate. And certainly the opening, with the different views of the swinging scoop, like a great, slow, tireless bird plunging for food, tying the scenes together in one design, is about as high in imagination as motion pictures have gotten.

How real is the battering on two souls of the constant fall and rise of the dredge, all day long, day after day. How dulling and killing this effect is on these two young minds, is disclosed to the audience by the slow moving, often motionless, poses of the girl and the boy on the scow. The slow tempo is far from the nervous action popularly supposed to represent motion picture art. And yet these quiet, monotonous scenes often reveal in an insistent manner the dull unhappiness of two persons imprisoned by circumstances.

There are other touches, too--such as when in the squalid room in the slums the two feel defeat creeping up the stair. They sit and look. That is all. But in the director's hands what does this almost motionless motion picture scene not tell us?

It is this creating in the minds of the audience something of the feelings of the characters that makes this picture noteworthy. Here is indicated the possibility of suggestion carried over to the audience by the quiet, almost static movement of the actors.

There is always a thrill for the audience in supplying through their own minds something that is not blatantly disclosed on the screen. Eventually, alert directors will capitalize this added interest in motion pictures and give us more films like this one. So Mr. von Sternberg may be commended for thus widening the technical art and narrative power of the motion picture.

George K. Arthur gives to the role of the boy none too certain understanding in his essay of a task that is made more difficult by the lack of any physical action, and asks our interest and our sympathy with a kind of motionless acting. The part of the girl, feelingly presented by Georgia Hale, shows a better artifice. Her first moody scene, her lack of vision, her half contemptuous acceptance of the boy's faith are brought out as perfectly as are later the gradual awakening and strengthening of her mental fibre. We feel reflected in Miss Hale's acting the girl's timid desire, her more persistent urge to believe, and the final joy in the conviction of the

Scaramouche 249

existence of a world of beauty. Rarely before has a screen actress
been called upon to play a part with less physical movement. Obliged to relinquish obvious gestures she has to rely solely on her
facial expression, which we realize springs from a complete inner
grasp of the processes of the girl's emancipation.

Mr. von Sternberg will doubtless venture again into the field
of motion picture art that he has in The Salvation Hunters so daringly entered. His admirers will then expect a motion picture that
will have all the excellence of this pioneering film and not so many
of its defects.

--Exceptional Photoplays, Vol. 5,
Nos. 3 and 4 (December-January
1925), pages 3 and 4.

* * *

A frightfully artistic picture, with some good acting, some
striking composition and almost no action.

--Robert E. Sherwood in Life,
Vol. 85, No. 2204 (January 29,
1925), page 32.

☐ SCARAMOUCHE (Metro, 1923)

This is one of the great pictures of the year. The French
Revolution is a big subject for any motion picture director to tackle.
Mr. Griffith did it successfully in Orphans of the Storm, and Rex
Ingram has done it again, fully as effectively, in Scaramouche. Mr.
Ingram has rather turned the Sabatini novel upside down. The author made the French Revolution incidental to the love story. In
the picture the love story is the incidental part. As a result of
this, the first half of the film, to those who have read the book,
seems a bit jerky. But when Mr. Ingram swings into the scenes
of the Revolution, the picture has a wonderful breadth and sweep.
The scenes of mobs of half-crazed men and Amazonian women racing through the streets of Paris, waving their rude weapons and
singing the "Marseillaise," are marvelously done. Nothing more
striking has been seen on the screen than Danton leading his terrible army to attack the Tuileries. The night scenes also, lighted
by bonfires, are almost terrifying. Mr. Ingram has used all his
great skill in making this picture and it is the best thing he has
done since The Four Horsemen. Ramon Novarro, who plays the
title rôle, has developed into an actor of power and charm. He is
ideal for the rôle. Praise of him in this production means even
more because he is playing opposite such a splendid actor as Lewis
Stone. Mr. Stone, as the villainous Marquis, gives a performance
that ranks with his finest. Alice Terry has little to do, but she
does that little well and is always beautiful. Special commendation
is due Mr. Ingram for his fidelity in casting. Danton, Robespierre,

Marat, the King and Queen, and Napoleon are all true to life. Settings and photography are remarkably good.

                              --Photoplay, Vol. 25, No. 1
                              (December 1923), page 72.

☐ THE SCARLET LETTER (M-G-M, 1926)

Hawthorne's classic and somber study of the New England conscience has been just as somberly translated to the screen.

Lillian Gish wears the red letter of sin with her stock virginal sweetness, failing to grasp the force of Hester Prynne's will power and intelligence.   She is a beaten child, not a courageous woman.

The camera work has been perfectly handled, but the Puritans have been seen with a slightly Swedish eye by Director Victor Seastrom.   They are dour rather than high-minded religious fanatics.   The performance of the piece is Lars Hanson's as Dimmesdale.   He suffers handsomely.

Take your handkerchiefs and the older children.   All self-appointed censors should be ordered to sit through it.

                              --Photoplay, Vol. 30, No. 5
                              (October 1926), page 53.

☐ THE SEA BEAST (Warner Bros. , 1926)

To the thousands who have been thrilled by Herman Melville's Moby Dick, the story of a white whale, this screen translation will be eminently satisfying.   Those who have not read the book have in store for them a motion picture that the Warners can conscientiously call a classic.

The outstanding feature of the film play is the exquisite love story of Ahab and Esther, beautifully played by John Barrymore and Dolores Costello.   The flowering of their romance, the sweet agony of their partings when Ahab goes to sea, the anguish caused by the misunderstanding that separates the lovers--are some of the most poignant moments ever pictured on the screen.

John Barrymore gives his usual finished performance.   His agony is almost too realistic in the scene wherein the sailors cauterize the bloody stump of the leg torn off by the sea beast.   It's too gruesome for sensitive souls.   And later, too, when he burns the tattooed name of "Esther" off his arm.

Dolores Costello's beauty is a delight to behold, and her acting is unbelievably good for a comparative newcomer.   The scene
in which she first sees the havoc wrought upon her lover by the
white whale reaches artistic heights that leave one trembling.   And
the scene is perfect pictorially.

Thrilling moments are provided in the sequences wherein
Ahab drives his ship through the waterspout in his mad chase for
vengeance on Moby Dick, the whale; and again where he fights to
the death his villainous brother.

George O'Hara as the scheming brother performs very well
and looks startlingly like John Barrymore in many scenes.

Director Millard Webb has put strength and beauty into the
telling of his tale.   A slight criticism might be offered, however,
that the story does not get started soon enough.
--Photoplay, Vol. 24, No. 4
(March 1926), page 55.

☐ SECRETS (Schenck/Associated First National, 1924)

Married life is made up of secrets--of moments that are
hidden away in the silent places of the heart.   The poignant secrets
of one marriage have been revealed in this picture--with Norma
Talmadge as the wife and Eugene O'Brien as the husband.   The
story is reflected back, across the years, from the pages of a
diary--held in the withered hand of a woman who is waiting to hear
of her husband's death.

The romance of youth, the elopement.   The struggle, as
pioneers in a new land.   The death of the first baby--during a battle for the lives of all of them!   Wealth, at last, and success--
bringing, however, the question of the "other woman."   Through all
of these tense situations we follow and if, at times, the tears are
close, we are not ashamed to admit it!

Miss Talmadge does as fine work, in this picture, as she
did in Smilin' Through.   In the hoopskirted costume of girlhood she
is a delight to the eye, but it is as the pioneer mother, and as the
woman of thirty-nine, that she really scores.   She rises--upon several occasions--to superb heights.   And, though Eugene O'Brien is
both good and convincing, he is left behind!

The photography, particularly in the first part of the picture,
is touched with real loveliness.   And the scenario, by Frances
Marion, is always searchingly human.   But it is the personality,
and the ability, of Norma Talmadge that makes this a thing worth
seeing.   This is a story that should mean much to all married

352 Selected Film Criticism

people. And to all people who expect to be married. It teaches a
lesson in devotion and tolerance.

--Photoplay, Vol. 25, No. 5
(April 1924), page 60.

☐ SENTIMENTAL TOMMY (Paramount-Artcraft, 1921)

The spirit with which a director approaches a picture is certain to shine through the screen, and John Robertson's love of
Sentimental Tommy has done a lot for this picture. Sometimes, it
seemed to me, it proved a bit of a handicap, in that in establishing
the characters of Tommy and Grizel, the Painted Lady and the good
Dr. McQueen, he forgets that the story, well known as to title
though it is, is still a generation old and only the Barrieites remember it well enough to get full value from it. It is a refreshingly wholesome picture, however, splendidly acted and beautifully
set, with a Long Island Thrums fairly steeped in Scotch atmosphere.
Here Tommy and Elspeth drift into the village and fly to the defense
of Grizel. Here the Painted Lady lives her pathetically short life
at the edge of town, where the respectables have shunted her, and
from here Tommy starts on his career as a literary man in London, later to return and shatter the heart of Grizel by his mystified
indifference to her shy, devoted love of him. And here, finally,
Tommy discovers a true affection for the unhappy girl, providing a
happy ending Barrie might not altogether approve, though we doubt
if he would seriously object to it. Through the story the clear art
of a fine little actress in May McAvoy flashes with a positive radi-
ance. Gareth Hughes as perfectly visualizes Tommy as any screen
actor could, and acts him much better than most of them would.
George Fawcett is the Dr. McQueen and Mabel Taliaferro the
Painted Lady.

--Burns Mantle in Photoplay,
Vol. 20, No. 2 (July 1921),
page 58.

* * *

The cinema touched another high-water mark last month in
John S. Robertson's tender visualization of Barrie's Sentimental
Tommy. Since Cecil B. DeMille literally hacked his way thru
The Admirable Crichton and vaingloriously termed the remains
Male and Female, we have shuddered at the thought of Barrie on
the silversheet.

But Mr. Robertson did intelligent and understanding work on
Sentimental Tommy, which is not only a film version of the whimsical Scot's Sentimental Tommy but of his Tommy and Grizel, as
well. The resultant photoplay runs eight reels and, towards the
end, grows tenuous. But, withal, it is charming and deft and subtle, in the main.

Mr. Robertson has succeeded in revealing that misty town
of Thrums, reflected so vaguely thru Sir James' rose glasses.
Best of all, he has caught that youthful dreamer and sentimentalist,
Tommy Sandys, who always conjured up such romantic fancies but
yet could never quite comprehend whether or not he was actually in
love. He is enmeshed in celluloid, from the vain little shake of his
head to his delightfully elusive day dreaming. Just now and then
you hear the grinding of the heavy photoplay machine behind Sentimental Tommy.

Sketched in, with a deal of the Barrie imagery, is little
Grizel, whose love for Tommy almost ends so tragically, her dear
daft mother, the Painted Lady, and that kindly but lazy old Doctor
McQueen, dozing in his dusty study. Let us pin our words of
praise where they belong. First, the scenario was adroitly managed by Josephine Levett. Then Mr. Robertson, who will be recalled for his colorful Dr. Jekyll and Mr. Hyde, deserves his lion's
share of the credit for his sympathetic direction. The photography
is a joy. And the acting--well, superb.

There have been two or three splendidly romantic and tender
characterizations in the history of the cinema. Henry Walthall's
Little Colonel was one of them. Richard Barthelmess' Yellow Man
was another. Gareth Hughes' Tommy Sandys comes mighty close
to this sacred gallery. And May McAvoy's Grizel will, alas, probably make her a star. She is Grizel. Mabel Taliaferro is the
Painted Lady as you and I have imagined her, and George Fawcett
is as lovable as old Dr. McQueen should be.

If you love the best in the realm of the screen, you will love
Sentimental Tommy.

--Frederick James Smith in Motion
Picture Classic, Vol. 12, No. 4
(June 1921), pages 54-55.

☐ 7th HEAVEN (Fox, 1927)*

It's the soul of Seventh Heaven that gets you, the soul put
into it by an understanding script, sympathetic direction and superb
acting. It doesn't matter much what else is in a story that has a
soul, nor where the soul comes from. This one comes out of a
Paris sewer and rises to sublime heights. It is a screen production
that glorifies the screen and atones for the sin of vulgarity that the
Fox organization committed when it made What Price Glory? When
the final returns are in from both these pictures it will be interest-

---

*The correct title of this film is 7th Heaven, but like most writers
since him, Welford Beaton persists in referring to it as Seventh
Heaven.

ing to compare the two grosses. As I believe there are more people in the world who prefer the clean things of life than there are those who like to wallow in its filth, I am confident that the Borzage picture will be much more profitable than the Walsh production. I am willing to go on record early and hope that in a couple of years Sol Wurtzel will produce the figures to prove me right or wrong. Seventh Heaven is a magnificently told story. There is not a foot in it that could be eliminated without harming it, nor is there a scene which could have stood more footage. It does not make pilgrimages into non-essentials and drag in irrelevancies that retard the story. In the first shot its spirit of optimism is born, its birthplace being an unlovely spot, the interior of one of the sewers of Paris. But even in such a place the spirit shines refulgently and continues to illuminate the story until the end. The only problem with which the picture deals is the relative social standing of two of its characters, a cleaner of sewers and a washer of streets, but to them it is a matter of as much importance as Mrs. Astorbilt's recognition of Mrs. Stuyvesant. Seventh Heaven proves what I often have contended, that it is the treatment which a story receives, not its ingredients, that gives it entertainment value. It does not possess extraordinary story value, but it is an extraordinary picture on account of the inspired manner in which it is presented. It should teach producers something. In a recent Spectator I told them that they could take some of the stories they are rejecting now, put real actors in them and give them good direction and they would have screen masterpieces. Seventh Heaven is a case in point. Nothing more drab than the setting for this story could be imagined. The interior of a sewer is the ultimate in unattractiveness. Nor is there a person in the story of the slightest importance to anyone. There is no white-haired grandmother to gain our sympathy, no child whose smiles warm our hearts, no beautiful settings to intrigue the eye--nothing but poorness that approaches poverty, drabness unrelieved by material things, but it is a beautiful picture because the souls of unimportant people are important, and because these souls are handled gently and tenderly by a great director. It could have been just another picture. The studios are turning out dozens each month which possess the possibilities that the Seventh Heaven script contained, but they have lacked the master touch of a Borzage to transmute the written scenes into golden screen entertainment. That all pictures made by Borzage do not rate as highly is attributable to the fact that greatness comes from all conditions being perfect, a good script, a capable cast and no studio interference. Given such conditions, the job is up to the director. Borzage did the job well.

Another thing that Seventh Heaven teaches us is that names are not of supreme importance to a motion picture. No one will be attracted to it by the fact that the name of Janet Gaynor heads the cast. I do not mean that names have no box office value. Hereafter, Janet's name will attract customers, but it will be because she came out of the unknown by playing a great part greatly. Seventh Heaven will be a tremendous money-maker solely because it is a good picture. The exhibitor who at first might be reluctant to buy it on account of its lack of box office names, will be impressed with the success it scores elsewhere and ultimately will provide his patrons with an opportunity to enjoy it. Stars' names are of no importance to him. His own name is what counts, and he wants pictures that will give his house a reputation. The star system is perhaps the most ridiculous extravagance our wildly extravagant business has indulged in. No good picture yet has failed to make a lot of money. I do not mean by "good" one that is a satisfactory example of screen art because it is perfect technically. I mean a picture that has universal appeal and that is done so well that none of the appeal fails to reach the public. If producers would forget names and devote their attention to making the best possible pictures they would make more money. Janet Gaynor will remain a box office attraction only as long as she appears in good pictures. She has everything that an actress must possess to be great. Her performance in Seventh Heaven is a wonderful one because her soul shines through it. Her first close-up grips the viewer although during its entire length she scarcely flutters an eyelash. Something from within her shines through her eyes and reaches a responsive place in the heart of the audience. One of the great moments of motion pictures is when she looks up and exclaims, "I, too, am a remarkable fellow!" She performs in that close-up a feat I do not remember having seen previously on the screen: she registers two conflicting thoughts simultaneously--her desire to see her sweetheart perform his duty to his country, and the great grief it causes her to contemplate his departure for the front. Simultaneously she smiles happily and weeps. It is not acting. It is the soul of an actress expressing emotions which it has absorbed. Janet's immersion in the part was complete, consequently her performance is even throughout. Her great appeal is something she brought with her to the screen. Six or seven months ago I saw her in an unimportant role, and there was some quality in her performance then that prompted me to write that the future held glowing prospects for her, but, even so, I scarcely was prepared for what I saw in Seventh Heaven. Of a piece with the artistry of her performance is the splendid work of the others in the cast. David Butler's street washer is a masterpiece of characterization, as are the taxi driver of Albert Gran and the "sewer rat" of George Stone. There is much feeling in all three performances. Gladys Brockwell was well cast and gives a very able performance. Through her viciousness and degradation there had to shine a suggestion of refinement to account for her rich relatives and to make plausible Janet's spiritual quality.

Charles Farrell's role in Seventh Heaven in some respects is an extraordinary one. Stripped to its essentials it is that of a conceited ass who boasts about being a remarkable fellow. The same business and the same lines in a different setting would make a character unsympathetic, a shallow person to be laughed at, not laughed with. But in this picture we love Farrell from the moment when we first see him, when he sings as he fishes for things that might obstruct the sewer. His initial acknowledgment that he is a remarkable fellow gains our hearty approval, and throughout the

256 Selected Film Criticism

picture we accept him cheerfully at his own valuation. There is a
pompous sweetness in his character that he depicts with consummate skill. For all his lowly station in life he is a great gentleman, and he is all the softer because he thinks he is hard. His
inborn sense of chivalry makes him go to the rescue of an ill-used
girl, but the influence of his environment makes him leave her lying
in the gutter while he goes contentedly about the business of eating
his dinner. We see the moment that his real nature asserts itself,
and for the rest of the picture we love him because we know him
better than he knows himself. It is a great characterization. I,
for one, was content to lose Farrell in most of the scenes in the
war sequence. The war was bigger than anyone in it, but the disposition of the producers of most of our war pictures was to create
the impression that it stopped to give the story characters an opportunity to do their stuff. History will thank Seventh Heaven for im-
mortalizing pictorially one of the most dramatic incidents in all
history--the dispatch in taxicabs of an army to defend Paris when
the torrent of advancing Germans seemed irresistible. I was in
France when it happened and thrilled with the French people at the
magnificence of it, a thrill I felt again when I saw this picture.
The photography all the way through Seventh Heaven is notable, but
reflected its highest art in the war sequence. Ernest Palmer and
J. A. Valentine, cameramen, have reasons to be satisfied with
their contributions to the picture. The production is not flawless.
Someone on the Fox lot with influence enough to impress his personality on a picture, deems one is not complete unless it shows
some sweet young girl undressing. There is such a scene in
Seventh Heaven, a wholly unnecessary one. It is more than merely
an exhibition of a tendency towards lubricity, more than merely a
sample product of a prurient mind. It is a poor thing from a story
angle. It would have been more consistent with Janet's whole characterization if she had sought seclusion while disrobing. But if they
had to undress her in public, why show her wearing underwear richly embroidered and of the finest texture? Such a girl would have
had on a cheap cotton garment. But perhaps the man on the Fox
lot who likes to see young girls undress has a nice taste in underwear. To some extent the close-up curse put its blight on this
picture. It assumed its most virulent form in that exquisite scene
showing the boy and girl performing their own marriage ceremony.
If ever there was on the screen a scene that should be devoid of
close-ups, it was this one. But it was treated otherwise. There
was another scene in which the two make love, the wedding dress
on the table between them. Its effectiveness was reduced greatly
by the manner in which it was cut into close-ups. But Seventh
Heaven is a wonderful picture. Katharine Hilliker and H. H. Cald-
well did the editing and titling. The titles are excellent. I know
of no finer set appearing in any picture. They are so nearly free
from errors in punctuation that it is all the more regrettable that
they were not perfect. Barney Glazer's adaptation was a truly
splendid piece of screen writing.

   Seventh Heaven repays study. Examine it closely and you
can discover technical errors in it, but you don't care. From its

opening sequence it is our friend, and we allow our friends to be
inconsistent or eccentric. The faults of the production are inun-
dated by its virtues. Even among picture people this view is held.
Those of the profession who view pictures technically and rate their
merits by the degree of their technical perfection forget all about
technic when viewing this one. Not since I have been in Hollywood
have I heard any other picture hailed by picture people as wholeheartedly as was Seventh Heaven. I have not heard one adverse
criticism. It appeals to the human side of picture people. Producers who have rejected every purely human story submitted to
them sing the virtues of this one. In the last Spectator I said that
producers would make a better job of pleasing the public if they
made more pictures to please themselves. When I wrote that, I
had not seen Seventh Heaven, consequently was unaware that the
truth of my contention was to be proved so promptly. The profession likes this picture and the public likes it also, demonstrating
that it would be good policy for producers to consult their personal
tastes more often. Ever since The Spectator was born I have contended in its pages that one of the needs of the screen was more
humanity in its pictures. Two greatly human pictures, Seventh
Heaven and Old Heidelberg, have followed one another in quick succession. Stella Dallas was intensely human, as were Beau Geste
and The Big Parade. Since there have been men, the most interesting study of mankind has been man, but the motion picture industry
is beginning only now to realize it. We will have many more such
pictures, but the majority of them will be very poor, for they are
the hardest kind of pictures to make. Any director can handle a
scene in which a man rushes into a room and tears his wife from
her lover's arms; very few can make convincing one showing a man
stroking the grey hairs of his mother. It takes no acting to produce
a thrill when a man enters a darkened room, a revolver in his
hand; but he has to put real art into the simple placing of a rose
before the photograph of a loved one who is dead. The more simple a story, the greater must be the direction. There is a lot of
difference between handling a murder and a mood. The success of
Seventh Heaven will lead to more pictures with heart appeal in them,
and most of them will be so poor that the public will tire of them.
Thus the industry will pass through another of its amusing phases.
Already producers are stating gravely that the public is demanding
human stories, and when the flock of poor ones fails to draw, just
as gravely will the producers ascribe the failure to the unstable
condition of the public mind. The truth is that the public mind
never wavers a hair's breadth from its desire for good entertainment. It always has wanted it, and I have advocated more of the
human interest pictures because they are the kind that have the
most universal appeal. There are some people who do not care
particularly for farces; others whose tastes do not run to tragedies,
but both of them like tenderness and sweetness and sentiment when
they are presented properly.

--Welford Beaton in The Film
                      Spectator, Vol. 3, No. 7 (May
                      28, 1927), pages 5-7.

*   *   *

One John Golden play plus one talented director plus two
brilliant young people equals one fine picture.   That is Seventh
Heaven.   It is permeated with the spirit of youth, of young love, of
whimsy.   A splendid picturization of the play that ran for two years
on Broadway.

Janet Gaynor and Charles Farrell are Diane and Chico, waifs
of the Paris slums, thrown together by merest chance to eventually
climb to the seventh heaven of ecstasy through the simple medium
of faith, hope and courage.   Chico is a sewer cleaner, a young
braggart, who saves Diane from her absinthe-crazed sister, only
to be forced to give the girl shelter.   Adoring him, her gratitude
turning to love, she mothers him until 1914 thunders into French
history and then the Fox company could not resist becoming epic.
There are battles and the usual shell-hole scene, but, when the
story again returns to Chico and Diane, you can forgive everything
in the beauty of their performances.

They are twin joys, those kids, their work entirely unmarred
by studied technic.   And this picture should plant them firmly near
the top of the picture world.   Chico's departure to the front is
superlatively done, but his return to the garret heaven, blinded, is
one of those unforgettable scenes.   Dave Butler is clever as Gobin
and so is Albert Gran as Papa Boul.   And don't forget to watch
Gladys Brockwell as the sister.

See this, by all means.   It's tender and tragic and wholly
appealing, splashed now and then with that grandly human comedy
for which Director Frank Borzage is known.

                              --Photoplay, Vol. 32, No. 2
                              (July 1927), page 54.

☐ SHADOWS (Preferred Pictures/Al Lichtman, 1922)

Shadows provides definite proof of the regrettable fact that
the best pictures aren't always to be seen in the best theatres.

It is an open secret that the great majority of first-run theatres in all parts of the country are controlled by four great pro-
ducing-distributing corporations--Famous Players, First National,
Fox and Metro, with an additional number that are devoted largely
to Universal, Goldwyn and Pathe.   These huge companies, which
are always at one another's throats, fight fiercely for control in
each city.   They desire to provide outlets for their own pictures,
and to block possible outlets for the productions of their competitors.

While these lords of finance grapple with each other, the
poor little independent companies stand helplessly by--knowing that,

regardless of who wins the big tussle, they are pretty sure to lose.
They find it almost impossible to get their pictures into important
first-run theatres; and must content themselves with those meagre
scraps that they are able to pick off the second string.

Shadows ran into this very difficulty.   It had been produced
by B. P. Schulberg, a picturesque young impresario who believes
in making money on box-office pictures--and spending it on what
Merton Gill calls "the finer and better things."   Shadows came under the latter head--and the exhibitors, therefore, viewed it with
alarm.   "It's too good to be profitable," was the consensus of
opinion.

Mr. Schulberg and his associate, Al Lichtman, tried to place
Shadows in one of the first-run theatres in New York (there are five
of them)--but it was met with nothing but rebuffs.   The proprietors
of these theatres had too many obligations to fill to the big companies that paid their salaries.

The National Board of Review, however, discovered Shadows
and lifted it from the obscurity in which it had been submerged.
As a result of their intelligent efforts, Shadows was brought to the
attention of those who are continually on the lookout for good pictures.

Shadows then started its career and, in spite of the handicap
that was saddled on it in New York, it proved to be financially successful.   Mr. Schulberg told me that he met with opposition from
exhibitors everywhere--and that he was compelled to make ridiculous
concessions before he could persuade them to book the picture.   In
every instance, however, the public's response was surprisingly
satisfactory.   A theatre owner in Seattle turned the picture down
completely; so Mr. Schulberg offered it to him on a percentage
basis--the exhibitor to pay for the use of the film in accordance
with its box-office receipts, just as a dramatist is paid a royalty.
This unusual suggestion was agreed to, Shadows was shown, and
Mr. Schulberg's share of the resultant receipts was far greater
than the rental usually charged for such a film.

Mr. Schulberg's exhibitor troubles started when he first decided to produce Shadows.   It was, in its original form, a story by
Wilbur Daniel Steele entitled "Ching, Ching, Chinaman."   It was
first published in the Pictorial Review and was subsequently selected
by Edward J. O'Brien for inclusion in his anthology of Best Short
Stories.   Mr. Schulberg realized its tremendous value as a motion
picture and, at the same time, appreciated the fact that it was too
original in its theme and its treatment to be grasped by the ex-
hibitors--who are lamentably wary of anything that has not been
done before.

His apprehensions were justified.

While "Ching, Ching, Chinaman" was in process of production, Mr. Schulberg received many protests from exhibitors.   "The

title suggests an Oriental story and the public doesn't want any
Chink stuff," they said.   So Mr. Schulberg changed the title to
Shadows.

Mr. Steele's story, however, was not changed.   In action
and in atmosphere, the spirit of the original was retained; what is
more, its realistic vigor was increased materially by the intelligence and the imagination with which it was developed as a moving
picture.

The scene of Mr. Steele's story was a small sea-coast town,
oppressed with the religious prejudices and hypocrisy which are
characteristic of all such limited localities.   A great storm came
up while the men of the village were out in their frail fishing
smacks--and while the sea absorbed many of these men into its
turbulent depths, it delivered up to the town a stranger--a China-
man--Yen Sin.

Naturally enough, Yen Sin opened a laundry, but he did more
than wash the citizens' clothes.   He laundered their very souls,
cleansing them of the hypocrisy with which they had been smeared.
When he found that the leading elder of the church was coveting the
young clergyman's bride, he exposed him--and forced repentance
down his throat.

In the end, the poor, benighted, heathen Chinee turned out
to be the truest Christian of them all.

Shadows was not only an unusually good story: it was a
forceful lesson in religious tolerance.   As such, it probably proved
offensive to many ardent churchmen who believe that intolerance is
a weapon entrusted to them, and to them alone, by God.

In the direction of Shadows, by Tom Forman, and in the acting, by Lon Chaney, Harrison Ford, Marguerite de La Motte and
John Sainpolis, there was a fine sincerity.   They all seemed to
realize that they were working on a picture that was destined to be
apart from the regular run of machine-made products.   They understood their obligations, and they fulfilled them.   Mr. Chaney's performance of the benevolent laundryman, Yen Sin, was the finest impersonation of an Oriental character by an Occidental player that I
have ever seen.

The adaptation of Mr. Steele's story by Eve Unsell and Hope
Loring was sound and logical throughout.   They told the story, as
it should be told, in a manner that was both forceful and direct.

I am glad that Shadows is included among the Best Pictures
in this book, for its production and its ultimate success have established two encouraging facts:

First, that the movie public is ready to receive and support
worthwhile effort--no matter how obscure may be its origin; and,

second, that there are motion picture producers to whom the desire
for "finer and better" things is something more than a trite, press
agent's phrase.

> I doff my hat to Mr. Schulberg. I hope he makes a great
> deal of money and a great many more pictures like Shadows.
>
> > --Robert E. Sherwood in The Best
> > Moving Pictures of 1922-1923
> > (Small, Maynard and Company,
> > 1923), pages 27-30.

☐ THE SHEIK (Famous Players-Lasky/Paramount, 1921)

E. M. Hull's Sahara Desert romance, The Sheik, a third or
fourth rate English novel which has recently been attracting much
attention in America, has at last reached the screen, via Paramount and Director George Melford. All the cheap banality of the
novel shines out of the screen version. And The Sheik is certainly
a pretty cheap brand of fiction, i. e. , a shocker designed to set
flappers blushing.

Herewith the story: A British girl sets out into the desert
as a lark and is taken prisoner by a fascinating sheik, who calls
himself Ahmed Ben Hassan, and who rules over certain tribesmen.
A prisoner in his lavishly furnished tent--which has all modern
conveniences from craftsman furniture to steam heat--she undergoes
a change and comes to love the man of the desert. It is not until
she has been captured by a neighboring sheik and rescued by Mr.
Ben Hassan that she comes to realize this. Then it is that she
finds that her hero is really the son of an Englishman and not an
Arab at all.

We expected much of Rudolph Valentino as the sheik but he
fails lamentably, at no time suggesting the self-centered, virile
tribal leader he was even in Miss Hull's puerile novel. Perhaps
the director is to blame. One never knows. Agnes Ayres does
little with the rôle of the English girl. The Sheik strikes us as being decidedly crude of direction.

> > --Frederick James Smith in Motion
> > Picture Classic, Vol. 13, No. 5
> > (January 1922), page 66.

                              *   *   *

The Sheik is fascinating as a study in local color, and the
love story of the English beauty and the desert chieftain will capture
the heart of youth. The coldly critical eye will discover that the
romance is quite ordinary, and the finish a compromise to convention that has served long and faithfully the writers of fiction.

Agnes Ayres is a beautiful woman and acts with feeling and finish.   And Rudolph Valentino is a romantic figure in his Arab robes, in spite of his trick of constantly showing the whites of his eyes.   But it is the shots of the gleaming sands and the charging horsemen that are the high lights of the picture.   George Melford has done wonders for the author of the novel, and the screen version is sure to prove one of the best money-makers on the Paramount program.   There are several exceedingly able impersonations to the credit of the supporting company, Adolphe Menjou as Raoul de Saint Hubert, Walter Long as Omair and Ruth Miller as a slave girl being on the list.

> --Edward Weitzel in The Moving
> Picture World, Vol. 53, No. 3
> (November 19, 1921), page 336.

☐ SHERLOCK HOLMES (Barrymore/Goldwyn, 1922)

You should see this if you are a devotee of John the Barrymore.   You should see it if you are a devotee of the Conan Doyle detective yarns.

It is one of the most artistic and unusual films ever made. Its settings and photography are amazingly fine.   Its cast is one of the few real all-star affairs.   Albert Parker, the director, has not been afraid to follow his imaginative impulses, with interesting results.

It's just a chapter from the life of that busy fellow, Sherlock Holmes.   There is a romance with Carol Dempster as the kissee. Dr. Watson is Roland Young.   Gustav Seyffertitz, a fine actor, is a splendid Dr. Moriarity.   Reginald Denny and Hedda Hopper are also present.

> --Photoplay, Vol. 22, No. 2
> (July 1922), page 52.

*   *   *

Sherlock Holmes was a rather free adaptation of the stories that Conan Doyle wrote before he started skating on the Styx.   Although John Barrymore chose to impersonate the great detective in a farcical manner, he realized the character perfectly.   Albert Parker reproduced the thrill of the original stories both in his action and his characterization.   The backgrounds, many of which were photographed in England, were exceptionally beautiful.

> --Robert E. Sherwood in The Best
> Moving Pictures of 1922-1923
> (Small, Maynard and Company,
> 1923), page 97.

Show Boat   263

◻ SHOW BOAT (Universal, 1929)

When you say that Universal's version of Edna Ferber's episodic and sentimental novel is a lavish production, you say nearly
everything possible about it.   The weakness of the film Show Boat
lies in the obvious direction of Harry Pollard.

Miss Ferber wrote a colorful novel that swept from a Mississippi river show boat to Chicago in the days of the World's Fair
and on to New York.   It had verve, spirit and fine atmospheric detail.   Some of this comes through to the screen.

Laura La Plante is the best of the cast as Magnolia but
Joseph Schildkraut overacts the rôle of Gaylord Ravenal.   So does
Emily Fitzroy in the rôle of Parthenia Ann Hawks, who rules her
show boat with an iron hand.
                              --Photoplay, Vol. 36, No. 1
                                (June 1929), page 55.

                    *   *   *

We know at the outset that Showboat is a good picture because Carl Laemmle appears on the screen and tells us that it is.
He is followed by Flo Ziegfeld, who makes assurance doubly sure.
It is tough on a picture to saddle it with the responsibility of living
up to such self-contained press agency.   But even with this handicap, Showboat makes good.   Although it is not true to either sound
or silent screen technic, it will rate as one of the finest pictures
of the year.   Harry Pollard directed it with rare intelligence.   The
story follows the career of Magnolia from the time when she is a
little girl until she returns with her white hair to live a life of retirement on the boat where we first made her acquaintance.   It is
her biography told in a series of episodes, difficult material to fashion into an engrossing motion picture, but Pollard has succeeded
admirably in making it entertaining.   It opens with some gorgeous
shots which plant in a striking manner what the showboat means to
the people in the Mississippi river towns.   Regarded from this
angle the picture might be considered an entertaining chapter in the
history of American drama.   While pictorially Showboat adheres
more closely to silent technic than to the new order of things, many
of its sequences contain dialogue.   The transitions from silent to
talking sequences, however, did not seem marked.   Perhaps this
was because Pollard did not rely too much on talking to tell his
story, using dialogue only as titles are used in the silent sequences.
Universal has given the picture a notable production, and can be
credited with a most praiseworthy contribution to screen art.   The
story is told in a leisurely manner, which may not prove popular
with those who have grown so accustomed to the rapid pace that
most of our pictures set.   The only place where I found it draggy
was towards the end.   Already it had gone on for nearly three
hours, but even while I thought it might be a little more brisk about
coming to a conclusion, I found myself interested in how the con-

clusion was being reached.   The closing scenes are so beautiful and
human that I am inclined to believe that audiences will be patient
with them.   In Showboat we have an exceedingly intelligent use of
the sound device.   Through many of the sequences there is an engaging obligato of Negro voices singing songs of the Mississippi.
Several selections from the musical version of the story were used
to good effect, both the words and the music of "Ol' Man River"
coming into the production at various times in a most welcome manner.   I am sorry to have to record the opinion that my friend
Laura La Plante is not well cast in the part of Magnolia.   Many
times in The Spectator it has been my pleasure to record my admiration for her fine work as a comedienne.   She is one of the
cleverest girls we have and is delightful in parts that suit her, but
among such parts can not be numbered that of Magnolia.   It calls
for dramatic acting and Laura is not at present a dramatic actress.
I believe she has talent enough to become one if she sets herself to
the task, but it was unwise to give her such a role before she was
prepared for it.   Laura plays Magnolia as a clinging-vine person
who did not show sufficient spirit to make consistent her rise to
theatrical fame after her husband left her.   The acting honors of
Showboat go to Joseph Schildkraut for his masterly characterization
of Gaylord Ravenal.   He gives a flawless performance which has a
great deal to do with giving the picture standing as an example of
screen art.   I hope that Schildkraut's work in this picture will lead
producers to keep him too busy in pictures for him to have time
for the stage.   We need more of his kind of art on the screen.
Emily Fitzroy gives a striking performance as Magnolia's mother.
In her opening sequences I thought her characterization a little
over-done, but as my admiration for her splendid acting grew, I
became reconciled to the part as she played it, and gladly give her
credit for contributing to the screen one of the finest characterizations that I have seen in a long time.   That always delightful comedian, Otis Harlan, is at his best in Showboat.   He has to his credit
a long list of fine performances, but nothing better than he gives in
this Universal picture.   The other members of the cast are adequate.   Showboat is a credit to Universal and a credit to screen art.

--Welford Beaton in The Film
Spectator, Vol. 7, No. 10
(April 20, 1929), page 6.

☐ SHOW OF SHOWS (Warner Bros. , 1929)

Mr. John Barrymore, who hasn't been altogether triumphant
in his screen adventures, manages to be quite the outstanding hit in,
of all things, the gaudy and spendthrift cinema revue which is mod-
estly called The Show of Shows.   Aided by his librettist, the late
Mr. William Shakespeare, and an anonymous scenic designer, he
boldly plunges into the midst of a chaos of stage and screen stars,
jazz music, chorus dancing, adagio performers and an attempt or
two at minor satire and comes forth with a classic interlude seem-

ingly as out of place as an Arab in the Bronx.   It may have been
artistic courage or merely shrewd showmanship, but certainly this
interjected soliloquy from the third part of King Henry VI supplies
not only the one striking and genuinely significant note, but also
the most popular episode in this latest and most lavish of the film
extravaganzas.

It is undeniable that Mr. Barrymore has been something of
a disappointment as a cinema star.   His earliest screen work, in
Dr. Jekyll and Mr. Hyde, Beau Brummel and even those slapstick
farces of his Famous Players days, revealed a talent for the new
medium as striking as his extraordinary gifts for stage playing,
but, after a magnificent start, he lapsed into the painful excess of
The Sea Beast, Don Juan, Tempest and Eternal Love.   Where it
had once been among his greatest virtues that he knew so accurately to what extent overemphasis in playing could be used, he soon
appeared to forget that a touch of restraint is important even in
overemphasis.   He indulged in frantic facial contortions and burlesque Lon Chaney make-ups and he was unhappy if he couldn't do
his Mr. Hyde vaudeville act in at least one scene a picture.   From
being the finest of the screen actors, he became not so very far
from the worst.

Now, in his soliloquy, he happily proves that he has really
lost none of his old-time magic, that the sins of certain previous
performances were merely an unfortunate lapse from grandeur.   It
is not that he shows the heights of restraint when he gives his brief
impersonation of the Duke of Gloucester or that he has given up that
propensity of his for doing Mr. Hyde all over again.   As a matter
of fact, he struts and frets his five minutes upon the screen amid
something of an orgy of facial contortions, offering few signs that
he recalls Hamlet's speech to the players which he used to recite
with such fine eloquence.   Yet he is so completely the master of
the art and the reticence of overacting, without which no player of
classical roles can really be distinctive, that his performance becomes not only the memorable event of the Warner revue, but likewise a pretty distinguished contribution to modern acting.

This is the report of one who still regards the Barrymore
Hamlet as the most thrilling performance of his theatre recollections.   It was not restrained and it was not classic in its calm,
and Mr. Hampden's blackboard lecture in the part was probably
more learned, but it was always thrilling, moving and excitingly
alive.   It revealed a feeling both for the poetry and the drama of
the role and it combined the two qualities into a synthesis of emotion and intellect that demanded your superlatives for any adequate
contemplation.   In his brief scene from Henry VI, where that en-
gagingly homicidal gentleman, who was to assassinate his way to the
throne as Richard III, first contemplates the philosophy of his mas-
sacres, he provides, in tabloid form, all the qualities that went into
his Hamlet.   That he makes faces a bit more violently than the
average player of straight realistic roles is reasonably unimportant
in comparison.

The Shakespearian interlude in The Show of Shows, has, in
addition to its demonstration that John Barrymore hasn't forgotten
that he was once our First Actor, another definite significance for
the motion picture. It proves with impressive force that the screen
is magnificently equipped to present a Shakespearian drama with
what is very likely more facility and dramatic forcefulness than the
stage can currently offer. The resulting cinema effort may not
quite live up to the original dynamic principles of the photoplay, but
with the opportunities provided for the mobility and the scenic effects suggested, if not demanded by the plays, there is no reason,
save possibly in the box office, why Shakespeare shouldn't yet prove
to be a scenario writer born a few centuries ahead of his time.

Whoever the unknown gentlemen are who provided the setting
and the lighting for the Barrymore episode, they deserve to stand
high among the more valuable citizens of Hollywood. I trust it
does not sound too sacrilegious to say so, but that background
against which Barrymore appeared and that ominous, symbolic suggestion of a mound of the dead upon which he stood seemed infinitely more impressive and dramatically atmospheric than any of those
emasculated Gordon Craig sets that were provided for that highly
praised stage production of Macbeth last season. The lighting, too,
was handled with a shrewd dramatic knowledge that the local theatre should try to emulate as quickly as possible.

The rest of The Show of Shows is elaborate, lively, fast-
moving and entertaining, but it can hardly be said that it lives up
to the possibilities it hints at. The trouble is not that the production contains more stars than it knows what to do with, or even
that there is not a real song hit to the picture. Most of us were
disappointed chiefly because it from time to time hits upon a grand
idea and then fails to take advantage of it. Such a charge certainly
cannot be brought against the chorus number in black and white that
Larry Ceballos has staged, and I suppose we should be grateful because, after deciding on presenting eight sister acts, the producers
have managed them with at least a minimum of offensiveness.
Some of the opportunities, though, are scandalously neglected.

There is, for example, an episode that endeavors to show
you what became of the six men who appeared with the Floradora
sextet. It is an engaging enough idea, but it is wasted in the
handling. That grand comic, Miss Beatrice Lillie, is given just
one appearance, but that one should have been not far from hilarious. Since the camera saw fit to cut her out of most of the scene,
however, it can hardly be said that she was used to advantage.
The "Bicycle Built for Two" number is pleasant, but it should have
been so much more effective. If the producers had spent more time
developing their better ideas and had left out the fantasy in which
an evil looking genii plays the terrible trick on Miss Myrna Loy of
setting down Mr. Nick Lucas before her as a gift, I think that others in the audience beside me would have been just as well pleased.
                                --Richard Watts, Jr. in The Film
                                   Mercury, Vol. 10, No. 13 (No-
                                   vember 29, 1929), page 6.

☐ SHOW PEOPLE (M-G-M, 1928)

This is the first time Marion Davies has ever shared honors
with anybody, while Bill Haines gave up stardom, temporarily, to
co-star with Marion in this picture.

Rarely have we had such a complete picture within a picture.
Marion and Bill depict most vividly the methods by which aspirants
get into pictures and what they get out of them.   Furthermore, you
have never before seen as many stars in any one picture.   Their
combined salaries would bankrupt the U.S. mint.   Among these
visiting guest stars are Charlie Chaplin, Douglas Fairbanks, Norma
Talmadge, John Gilbert, Claire Windsor, Polly Moran, Dorothy
Sebastian, Estelle Taylor, Aileen Pringle and Bill Hart.

The story is not new nor startling but Marion and Bill keep
you laughing.   Don't miss this.

--Photoplay, Vol. 34, No. 3
(August 1928), page 57.

*   *   *

The Hollywood epic is yet to be presented on the screen, but
Show People will serve as an entertaining interlude.   I hope it will
have the effect of impressing someone with power to make the necessary decision, that Marion Davies should appear in comedies
with a touch of human interest in them, and not in pictures in which
she is cast on the assumption that she is as great and as versatile
an artist as the Hearst papers insist that she is.   I don't think that
any other girl has been miscast as many times as she has, having
been given a succession of impossible characterizations that would
have checked the career of anyone who did not have the benefit of
such unwarranted exploitation.   Artistically it has been a sad hin-
drance to her progress, but finally she has caught up with it.   In
light comedy roles I don't know of anyone who can surpass her.
Certainly in Show People she is delightful.   The screen is lacking
in that variety of entertainment that recently she has demonstrated
her ability to provide so richly.   The picture also gives Billy
Haines a chance to show that he is a good actor.   His contribution
is a big one.   All in all, Show People is one of the most entertaining pictures that have come from the Metro lot in a long time.

--Welford Beaton in The Film
Spectator, Vol. 7, No. 2
(January 5, 1929), page 8.

☐ SIEGFRIED (Decla-Bioscop/Ufa, 1925)

A colossal and amazing achievement in film stagecraft and a
triumph for the German magicians who work their arts at the Ufa
Studio.

But it takes more than technique to make a great photoplay.
It takes heart and soul. In combining Richard Wagner's Siegfried
and Twilight of the Gods with the original legends, the adapters
have lost the vitality of the Niebelungen Lied. As a dramatist,
Wagner was repetitious and involved, but there is a robust, human and tender touch in his telling of the story that isn't in the
film. The rôle of Siegfried is marvellously played by Paul Richter.
Brunnhilde, portrayed by Hanna Ralph, is no Valkyr but a Queen of
Iceland. Siegfried will be presented as a special, with Wagner music. It is more than worth seeing.

--A. S. in Photoplay, Vol. 28, No.
3 (August 1925), page 50.

☐ SMOULDERING FIRES (Universal, 1925)

Tender realism and artful direction ladder this picture to the
topnotch heights of pleasing entertainment. Pauline Frederick, Laura
LaPlante and Malcolm McGregor deserve special mention for their
excellent work under Clarence Brown's guidance. Jane Vale, masterly business woman of forty, falls in love with a youth half her
age. When he becomes enamoured of her sister, she gives him up.

--Photoplay, Vol. 27, No. 3
(February 1925), page 57.

*   *   *

Pauline Frederick in the most intelligently constructed story
that has come out of Hollywood this year.

--Robert E. Sherwood in Life,
Vol. 85, No. 2222 (June 4,
1925), page 35.

☐ SO THIS IS PARIS (Warner Bros. , 1926)

Another variation of the domestic infidelity theme presented
by the sophisticated Ernst Lubitsch. The ultra touch of the German
director seems to wear pretty thin here and So This Is Paris turns
out to be the weakest of Lubitsch efforts to date. There are just
four characters to this comedy, a doctor and his wife, a classic
dancer and his better half. The feminine dancer is an old flame
of the physician while the doctor's wife flirts with the dancer. The
picture is jazzy, a bit rough in its humor. Assuredly not for the
kiddies. The cast is weaker than usual to Lubitsch. Lilyan Tashman is good as the dancer, Monte Blue amusing as the physician,
but Patsy Ruth Miller, as his wife, and Andre Beranger, as the
classic terpsichorean expert, seem weak.

--Photoplay, Vol. 30, No. 4
(September 1926), page 55.

☐   THE SON OF THE SHEIK (Feature Productions/United Artists,
1926)

Long will this picture remain in the memory of those fortunate enough to see it. The Son of the Sheik was Rudolph Valentino's
last effort before the silver screen. He was the old Rudy again
and his work, without question, ranked at the top of the best performances of the month.

Rudy's old desert, Rudy's old fire, his old love, Agnes
Ayres, his new love, Vilma Banky, his horses and his tents are
all here, and how! Romance fills the air every second Rudy's
visible.

The plot, if you insist, concerns the child of that marriage
between the Sheik and the Lady Diana, and what a child he grew up
to be! He rides like the wind, he fights like Doug Fairbanks on a
busy morning, and his lovemaking is more torrid than an August
afternoon in an account department.

In a troupe of French players, touring the desert, he beholds
his love. She is fair and has dove's eyes. At night, beneath the
desert stars, he woos her and she is very, very happy to be won.
But her father wants the young Sheik's money. Her father's confederate wants the girl. So drama comes in, when Rudy is captured, tortured and held for ransom.

Freed by his own men, he believes the girl has betrayed
him. He vows revenge and captures the girl, riding off to his tents
with her, frail and sobbing in his arms. The rest is what makes
this picture unforgettable.

Rudy plays both father and son, ideally. Vilma Banky is
perfectly lovely as the girl. And we expect every fan in the country to be saying, "It was Rudy's best. I can never forget him."
                                        --Photoplay, Vol. 30, No. 5
                                        (October 1926), page 53.

                    *   *   *

The vogue for celluloid sequels is spreading. We have seen
Douglas Fairbanks as Zorro and Don Q, the son of Zorro. Now
Rudolph Valentino is perceptible as the offspring of that celebrated
character, the Sheik, whose title has become a byword in every
American home. Before long, we may expect The Rebirth of a Nation, The Miracle Man's Nephew, The Fifth Horseman of the Apocalypse, and The Uncovered Wagon, in the last of which we shall see
the descendants of Will Banion traveling from Oregon to Florida in
a fleet of Fords.

The Son of the Sheik is a considerable improvement on its
distinguished predecessor. For one thing, it is a far better job

pictorially--and for another thing, it has the exquisite representative
of Central Europe, Vilma Banky, to augment the belligerent Rudy.
Miss Banky is a really adroit actress, although that fact is of complete unimportance to her legion of admirers (of whom the under-
signed is merely one).

Like Don Q, The Son of the Sheik resorts to a flashback to
its parent picture, with Agnes Ayres returning from Limbo to play
her former and still inconspicuous role.

> --Robert E. Sherwood in Life,
> Vol. 88, No. 2285 (August 19,
> 1926), page 24.

☐ THE SORROWS OF SATAN (Famous Players-Lasky/Paramount,
1926)

That D. W. Griffith is a great director and that pictures are
still in their infancy seem to be the two foremost traditions of the
industry. Like most traditions, there is little truth in either. It
is conceivable that a great director now and then might make a poor
picture, but no great director could make one so hopelessly bad as
Griffith made The Sorrows of Satan. Credited to some unknown director, it still would be hopeless, but the bright light of fame that
surrounds anything that the maker of The Birth of a Nation turns
out, brings this picture into prominence with its faults accentuated.
I never could see why Griffith was rated so highly as a director.
I attributed his prominence in pictures to the length of his connection with them, a period during which a good director would have
made a score or two of features that would bear testimony to his
skill. Only The Birth of a Nation and Broken Blossoms stand out
in my memory as productions that entitle Griffith to any degree of
fame. But I do not claim to be any great authority, and was willing
to accept the general estimate of his standing. I went to see Satan
strong in the belief that it could not be as bad as I was told it was,
and found it worse. It is a terrible picture. It drags its weary
way along for reel after reel that make a sum total of all the faults
that a director can commit. There was a good screen story in the
book, and perhaps its adapter wrote one, but the way it was told
on the screen robs it of any virtue the script may have contained.
One sequence that was designed to be striking is positively ludicrous. Adolphe Menjou and Ricardo Cortez alternately stride like
wooden soldiers out of the darkness into a high light, speak titles
and suffer eclipses. Each of their movements is forward, and the
light seemed to advance with them, giving me an opportunity to lay
a wager with my next-seat neighbor that they would reach the middle of the street before the sequence ended. I may be stupid, but
I could not understand the picture. The opening scenes contained
bands of white light that puzzled me and I grew more bewildered as
the thing progressed. Surely if Griffith has learned anything during
his long connection with the screen it is the science of lighting, but

this picture has the worst lighting I ever saw. Spots followed the
characters everywhere, lighting up their faces without regard for
the supposed source of the light illuminating the scene.   Carol
Dempster stands with her back to a window through which the sun,
the source of the room's light, is shining, but her face is lighted
brightly.   In another scene some flowers are in the high-light and
the faces of the characters in the scene in a half-light.   There
must have been a reason for such weird lighting, but what was it?
A bright light on a wall apparently came from a gas jet, for it
could come from nowhere else, but the gas wasn't burning.   A huge
cluster of electric globes casts no light to speak of in a hotel room,
while one oil lamp in another room illuminates it brilliantly.   Most
of the scenes were fogged without apparent reason.   No effort seems
to have been made in the editing to make medium shots match the
close-ups, a well established weakness of Griffith, who, as the inventor of close-ups, should know how to handle them.   I can see no
reason except very incompetent direction for the lack of merit in
The Sorrows of Satan.   There was nothing wrong with the material,
cast or production, but there was nothing right in the way they were
handled.

> --Welford Beaton in The Film
> Spectator, Vol. 3, No. 5 (April
> 30, 1927), page 9.

☐ SOULS FOR SALE (Goldwyn, 1923)

      This melodrama, written and directed by Rupert Hughes, is
a personally conducted trip behind the scenes of movieland--a Cook's
Tour of the empire of celluloidia.   As such, it will fascinate those
who have longed to visit a studio in operation--and, we suspect,
their name is legion.   It is for this reason that Souls For Sale
lands among our chosen six.   The story behind this journey through
filmland is false and trivial, tracing a young woman from extra to
stardom.   But, when Hughes places his camera behind the camera
and shows how make-believe becomes apparently real, then Souls
For Sale has high interest.   The action is loose, the story reeks
with heavy villainy, and the acting is never impressive--but the
background of studio life puts it over.

> --Frederick James Smith in
> Photoplay, Vol. 24, No. 1
> (June 1923), page 65.

☐ THE SPANISH DANCER (Famous Players-Lasky/Paramount, 1923)

      After being wasted in Bella Donna and The Cheat, Pola Negri
comes back to her own in this picture.   She is again La Negri of
Passion.   She has shed the veneer of sophistication and has reverted

to the primitive woman type. As the gypsy girl in this adaptation
of Don Caesar de Bazan, she gives a magnificent performance.
She portrays almost every emotion conceivable, and does each and
every one admirably. Herbert Brenon, the director, shares the
honors. Tony Moreno is a lovable scapegrace as the hero, playing
the rôle in a dashing, devil-may-care fashion. Wallace Beery adds
another to his long list of fine characterizations as the king of
Spain. With this production Paramount is keeping its promise of
bigger and better pictures.

--Photoplay, Vol. 25, No. 1
(December 1923), page 72.

☐ SPARROWS (Pickford/United Artists, 1926)

        Mary Pickford and a bunch of other kids who risk their pre-
cious necks to flee a slimy baby farm. That's Sparrows. There
are quicksands, alligators and, worse than any reptiles, Gustav Von
Seyffertitz, the keeper, as realistic a vile scoundrel as ever
breathed. It's not conducive to pretty dreams, but Mary is sweet
and wistful and kiddish and has some appealing scenes. Ten kids
are imprisoned in a swampy baby farm and when dimpled Mary
Louise Miller is kidnapped and deposited with them, Mary Pickford
pulls an Eliza-crossing-the-ice and takes her band by swamp and
tree to safety.

        In the cast next to Mary that cunning Miller baby wins the
gurgles. This may not be another Pollyanna but you will enjoy it.

--Photoplay, Vol. 30, No. 3
(August 1926), page 55.

☐ SPEEDY (Harold Lloyd/Paramount, 1928)

        All Harold Lloyd's pictures are successful primarily because
he is an excellent actor. Speedy is full of hilarious gags that in
themselves are funny, but the storms of laughter that they arouse
do not reach their peak until Harold, by some little stroke of actor's genius, gives them their final punch. In all his pictures
Harold has to compete for recognition with his gags, and the latter
always are so clever that they draw the applause and lead us to
overlook the fact that all of Harold Lloyd's success is due mainly
to the fact that he is one of the best actors on the screen. In
Speedy he gives what seemed to me to be the best performance of
his career. He gives us a boy that we like, not a frozen-face
Buster Keaton, nor a wisecracking pest like Bill Haines; but a
regular youth who can't hold a job, and doesn't care, and who is
ready to blow his last cent to give his sweetie a fine time. The
absolute cleanliness of the Lloyd pictures, of course, has contri-

buted greatly to their success.   When I have said that Speedy is
very funny and extraordinarily clever I have written my whole review of it.   Ted Wilde's direction is flawless.   Amusement and
hearty laughs are not all that I get out of Harold's pictures.   As I
watch them I wonder how under the sun the amazingly clever gags
are thought of.   I make obeisance to their creators!   I bow low to
the genius who conceived the idea of using the reflex action in a
total stranger's knee as a means of getting even with another
stranger who trod on one's toes.   The brilliance of such inspira-
tions dazzles me.   Speedy is full of them.   Harold makes one picture a year.   I think that's it, but, anyway, they come a long way
apart.   When we see one of them flit joyously across the screen it
gives us the impression that Harold and his gang made it one
morning when they were full of pep.   There is a spontaniety, a
sparkle to them that makes us feel that they were born of a moment's inspiration, and nothing to suggest that they were built slowly and that they progressed painstakingly from idea to idea.   And
despite the fact that he does not give us a great many pictures,
Harold has made a great many dollars.   I don't suppose even
Charlie Chaplin can match his fortune.   The financial aspect of the
Lloyd comedies interests me only as it supports my variously expressed opinion that there always is a market for mentality.   I have
said repeatedly that what most pictures lack is downright cleverness.   We turn them out now so rapidly that there is no time to
make them original.   If one of the big producers put Harold Lloyd
under contract to-day, Harold agreeing to the terms offered him,
we would get three, and perhaps four, Lloyd pictures a year.   They
would be like the Haines, Dix and other comedies and would make
some money, but not half as much as Harold makes now by his
one-picture-a-year policy.   As picture-making is a money-making
endeavor, I am surprised that other producers do not profit by their
contemplation of the Lloyd method.   Hasn't it occurred to someone
that if Buster Keaton were put on a one-a-year schedule, and that
the whole year were consumed in making the one as clever as possible, he soon would be making five dollars to every one that he is
making now?   His pictures would have time to be clever.   Cleanliness and cleverness constitute a screen combination that can't be
beaten.

> --Welford Beaton in The Film
> Spectator, Vol. 5, No. 6 (April
> 28, 1928), pages 10-11.

☐ THE SPOILERS (Paramount, 1930)

When movie kiddies gather around the gas logs for bedtime
stories pop tells about the famous fight between William Farnum
and Tom Santschi in the first version of The Spoilers.   That battle
made screen history, and Rex Beach's perennial novel has gone
ringing down the years.   In its third trip to the screen it becomes
a phonoplay and it's as thrillingly red-blooded as ever.   One of the

month's best through its excellent cast, and the sweeping, dramatic way in which the gold rush story is told. Gary Cooper is the most romantic of the Roy Glenisters who have fought for right in Nome. Kay Johnson again creates a distinct impression as the heroine, and Betty Compson is an appealing Cherry Malotte, the dance hall girl.

Action builds to the fight between Cooper and William (Stage) Boyd, and you've never seen a wilder brawl. The men tumble down the stairs, and finish in the street. No matinée stuff this. You should see Gary bite a hunk from Boyd's arm. It's all there, the loaded steamers for the Yukon, the coming of law into a lawless land, and the dynamite plot. Best of all, the story moves. Action is never sacrificed to dialogue. In a very fine cast outstanding support is given by Harry Green, James Kirkwood and "Slim" Summerville. Edwin Carewe's direction is excellent.

--Photoplay, Vol. 38, No. 6
(November 1930), page 53.

☐ STARK LOVE (Paramount, 1927)

A mighty fine picture, in some ways as noteworthy as Robert Flaherty's Nanook and Moana. Karl Brown, who had been Jimmie Cruze's cameraman, obtained Jesse Lasky's backing and took a studio staff into the Great Smoky Mountains of North Carolina. There he rounded up a mountaineer cast and shot a graphic and absorbing tale of the hills.

Stark Love, despite its garish boxoffice title, is a picture of genuine merit. It is astonishing how well the mountaineers act. Helen Mundy, a school girl hired in Knoxville, Tenn., is excellent as the heroine, while a hill boy, Forrest James, gives an amazingly good performance. An old timer, Silas Miracle, plays the boy's father in a way to outshine Wally Beery's best work. Don't miss this film.

--Photoplay, Vol. 31, No. 6
(May 1927), page 52.

☐ STEAMBOAT BILL, JR. (Buster Keaton/United Artists, 1928)

Generally when I view a motion picture I peer at it intently and find things in it to make catty remarks about. I laugh at funny things, but I do it sternly and judicially, and keep my eye peeled for faults the directors commit. When the picture ends I have notes in a little book, and I go home and sit in my backyard, hard by the hollyhocks and near the swing that is under the peach tree, and my two dogs and two cats gather around me while I write

profoundly, elaborating the notes in my little book. Donald* and I
went into a projection-room and viewed Steamboat Bill Jr. I never
made a blessed note, although I had my little book open under the
red desklight. I don't know how Chuck Reisner directed it, whether
he had senseless close-ups that should make me mad or huge kisses
that offend me. I don't know the name of the nice looking girl who
played opposite Buster Keaton. All I know is that Donald and I
laughed or giggled all the time the picture was running, and that it
kept me so amused that I forgot my little book. I am satisfied that
Reisner must have made a good job of the direction, for I am pretty
sure that I would have noticed any serious lapses. I know that
Buster and Ernest Torrence gave mighty fine performances and that
Tom McGuire was quite satisfactory. The important thing, however,
is that I laughed all the way through it and forgot that it was my
business to search for flaws in it. As the purpose of a comedy is
to make us forget business and have a good laugh, I must put
Steamboat Bill Jr. down as perhaps the best comedy of the year
thus far. Exhibitors should go after it.

--Welford Beaton in The Film
Spectator, Vol. 5, No. 9 (June
23, 1928), page 14.

☐ STELLA DALLAS (Goldwyn/United Artists, 1925)

    Photoplay recommends this picture, without the slightest res-
ervation, to every theatergoer, hoping that the public will demonstrate its appreciation of a great screen drama by rewarding its
producer with unmistakable approval. Say it with tickets--the song
of the box-office is sweeter music than the arias of the critics.

    Stella Dallas comes nearer being a perfect translation of a
novel to the screen than any picture in screen history. It is a
masterful piece of work, reflecting credit on its producer, Samuel
Goldwyn, its director, Henry King, its continuity writer, Frances
Marion, its author, Olive Higgins Prouty, and every member of the
cast and organization.

    Here, too, is one of the greatest performances ever given
to the screen--that of Belle Bennett in the title rôle. The rôle of
the dowdy, ill-bred wife of a rising young lawyer, developing from
a buxom girl of nineteen through to a tragic middle age and renunciation of her only child, is one of the most difficult that any actress has ever been called upon to do, and Mr. Goldwyn's selection
of her for the part was a stroke of genius, as was the work of the
director in guiding her through the characterization. As a matter
of fact, nearly every performance in the picture ranks as one of
the best of the month in a production that stands alone among its
competitors on these pages this month.

---

*Beaton's son, who also reviewed for The Film Spectator.

Lois Moran flashes onto the screen as a glorious addition to our younger stars; Ronald Colman, Alice Joyce, Jean Hersholt, Douglas Fairbanks, Jr., almost uncanny in his remarkable resemblance to his gifted father, all deserve praise far beyond the limited space of this report.

Go and see this picture or forever hold your peace about the art of the motion picture.

--Photoplay, Vol. 24, No. 1
(December 1925), page 46.

* * *

Stella Dallas deals with that most popular of all emotions, mother love--the same theme that animated such stalwart box-office successes as Over the Hill and Humoresque.

The mother of Stella Dallas, however, can not by any stretch of the imagination be confused with the gray-wigged, bespectacled, simpering, holier-than-thou old pest who represents the conventional mother on the screen. Stella Dallas is a coarse, gross woman, painfully devoid of the most ordinary social graces, gaudy but not neat--a ridiculous person and an inexpressibly pitiful one.

She had married a lonely young man, an aristocrat by birth, who had rapidly outgrown her and had left her to care for the daughter who resulted from their brief and none too appropriate union. But the father was unwise enough to bequeath to his daughter the sensitiveness and good taste which had been his own heritage, and when the girl grows up, it is evident that she too has soared above her mother's level of drab mediocrity.

The mother, of course, sees this--and the latter portions of the story are devoted to her laborious attempts at self-sacrifice.

In these two rôles--of mother and daughter--Belle Bennett and Lois Moran give performances of great beauty. Miss Bennett approximates perfection in her portrayal of crude vulgarity, and Miss Moran is incredibly lovely as a tender, loyal but vaguely distressed little girl. Another rich characterization is entrusted to the reliable Jean Hersholt, and Ronald Colman and Alice Joyce are acceptably good in neutral rôles. Frances Marion has done an excellent job on the scenario.

Henry King again demonstrates the directorial genius which dignified his work in Tol'able David and The White Sister (and which has been lost, strayed or stolen ever since). He has endowed this story, which might have been fearfully artificial, with a fine sincerity; furthermore, he has devised almost every scene with a considerable degree of technical skill. The high spot of the picture, to me, was an adolescent love scene between Lois Moran and Douglas Fairbanks, Jr., directed by Mr. King with fine delicacy and restraint.

There are just two bad elements in the picture. Miss Bennett's costumes are at times so grotesquely exaggerated as to destroy all the fine subtlety of her own performance. The weird regalia that she wears appear to have been gathered from the costume trunks of an old Zaza troupe. It is a harsh note in an otherwise harmonious production.

Then there is the trite ending, in which the mother stands out in the rain and watches her daughter tremble through the marriage ceremony. This same conclusion has been arrived at dozens of times before. It is stale.

--Robert E. Sherwood in Life,
Vol. 86, No. 2249 (December
10, 1925), page 24.

☐ THE STRONG MAN (Harry Langdon/First National, 1926)

Marching into stardom with Tramp, Tramp, Tramp, Harry Langdon's second laugh-provoker firmly establishes the wistful comedian in the front ranks of the screen's mirth-makers. Watch out, Charlie and Harold!

It's a grand and glorious laugh from the start to the finish. It begins with one laugh overlapping the other. Chuckles are swept into howls. Howls creep into tears--and by that time you're ready to be carried out. And we don't mean maybe!

The story runs along at a merry gait with Langdon keeping pace with his clever pantomime. Wait and see his interpretation of a cold. Gertrude Astor is outstanding as a big-blonde-mama vamp.

Don't be selfish--treat the whole family.

--Photoplay, Vol. 30, No. 6
(November 1926), page 52.

*   *   *

Harry Langdon has appeared in his second long comedy, The Strong Man. At almost any moment now our active discoverers of genius will view this man, have a rush of superlatives to the head, and bruit his name on the battlements. He has an ability to make himself cunning, pathetic, and overwhelmed by his surroundings that is devastating, and the news of his coming causes me to make merry moues of anticipation.

He renders one glorious sequence when he falls into the grip of a lady who wants to steal some money from the lining of his coat. He misinterprets her handlings and gives a rendition of outraged virtue that is worth going more than several blocks to see. And then again his attempts to fight off a cold are perfect.

The Strong Man is probably one of the poorest pictures that ever supported such excellent comicalities. In the middle it sags to the ground and after a very dreary stretch makes a few floundering efforts to rise, but even the pleasant antics of Mr. Langdon fail to revivify it. In an endeavor to gild the lily of Mr. Langdon's wistfulness the Hollywood merry-andrews have injected a blind girl into the story, and blindness is too terrible a thing to make a successful foil for comedy.

But you can be recommended to attend, for the two scenes touched upon and other stray moments will well offset the dull spots.
--Oliver Claxton in The New York-
er, Vol. 2, No. 31 (September
18, 1926), pages 50-51.

*   *   *

I don't know when I've seen anything more touchingly beautiful than Harry Langdon's performance in this. Probably never.
--Robert E. Sherwood in Life,
Vol. 88, No. 2293 (October 14,
1926), page 28.

☐ THE STUDENT PRINCE IN OLD HEIDELBERG (M-G-M, 1927)

Old Heidelberg will be a monument to the versatility of Ernst Lubitsch as a director. The Marriage Circle, Kiss Me Again, and So This Is Paris! demonstrated his ability to make frivolity fascinating, that he possesses a delicious sense of humor and knows how to pass it on for our enjoyment. Old Heidelberg reveals a Lubitsch who is deeply human, who can pull on our heartstrings with a force that is applied so subtly that we wonder where the power comes from. Also it is applied evenly, like a golden thread that traces a straight line through the fabric of the production. I have chuckled with the other Lubitsch, but with this new one I felt something at my throat that gave him a place in my heart that he never had reached before. A heart throb is a greater tribute to art than the contentment that a chuckle reflects. In those scenes that build up to the more compelling ones that they were aimed at, Lubitsch shows a mastery of detail and knowledge of screen essentials that have given him his place among the few great men of motion pictures. He resorts now and then to those shots that were features of foreign-made pictures, and he does it most effectively, particularly in one instance in which he interprets Ramon Novarro's glowing description of a trap ride which he intends to have with Norma Shearer. The legs of galloping horses are superimposed over the shot of Norma and Novarro, and then fade into the street in which we see the two seated in the trap, having a hilariously wild ride that conveys its joyousness to the audience. And that is the end of the joy in the picture. With dramatic suddenness comes pathos. The lovers

do not have the drive.   While Norma is preparing for it, her every
action indicating the happy song that her heart is singing, her
sweetheart is carried off to become a king.   The love story is born
in a field of daisies, over which a full-leafed tree stands sentinel.
It dies there when the boy is king and the girl still is bar-maid, at
a time when the daisies are dead, too, and the tree has lost its
leaves, its bare arms stretched above the grass whose green has
taken on a tinge of grey.   The love itself has lost none of its ardor, but its story is robbed of a happy ending by the dead greyness
of a king's importance and the sad drabness of a bar-maid's unimportance.   The screen has given us nothing more tender and sweet
and sad than this love story which Lubitsch tells so sympathetically.
In the last Spectator I suggested that when an aristocrat must fall
in love with a plebeian there should be at least one point of contact
between the two to make the love reasonable.   Generally the aristocrat is too highbrow to be convincing and the plebeian is too low-
brow to be believable.   In Old Heidelberg the love story is made
reasonable by the characterization of the crown prince as a regular
fellow and the girl as a pretty and refined lass.   The businesslike
manner in which she draws a stein of beer and accepts a tip for
serving it keeps us from forgetting that she is a bar-maid, thereby
establishing the fact and making it unnecessary to draw a broader
defining mark to illustrate the wide difference in the stations of the
two.   The line of demarcation between direction and great direction
is the absolute elimination of improbabilities.   Lubitsch is a great
director, and Old Heidelberg emphasizes his greatness as no other
of his pictures has.   It is a picture that asks you to take nothing
for granted, a clean-cut bit of art created by a master craftsman.

Among the greatest things that the screen has given us will
be numbered Jean Hersholt's performance in Old Heidelberg.   Months
ago in The Spectator I rated him as the greatest screen actor, and
his work in this picture alone would justify the rating.   It is a notable performance in spite of the fact that its greatest moments are
quiet ones.   He accompanies the crown prince, whose tutor he is,
to Heidelberg, where he went himself as a youth.   The new generation sings the same old songs.   Jean stands among them, a stein
in his hand, a smile of happiness on his face.   He sings with them,
sings again the songs that cemented friendships when he was young,
songs that inspired hopes of a brilliant future, of the great place
he would attain among men of affairs, that conjured up visions of
his triumphant return as a famous man.   And he was back now--a
tutor.   Still he sings, still sways time with his stein, but into his
eyes come tears to water his dead hopes, and as they tremble on
his eyelids they tell the story of a man who had been happy with his
unfulfilled ambitions until he brought them back to the place where
they were born.   So I, at least, read the close-up, with nothing to
guide me but a falling tear and a smile that trembled and became
sad.   It is the kind of acting that comes from an actor's consciousness and enters that of the viewer, a purely spiritual message that
leans but lightly on any physical manifestations.   It is of a piece
with Hersholt's whole performance.   He is a lovable, indolent and
untidy tutor, of little importance in the world, but after he is dead

a king who was his friend visits the room in which he had died and
strokes the pillow upon which his head had rested. This quiet little
scene is one of the most effective in the picture, and it is Hersholt's acting that makes it effective, for previous to it he so has
impressed his personality upon you that you feel his spirit in the
room with the king. As pictures are cut with regard for the star
and none for the public, I have no doubt that every effort was made
in the editing to keep Hersholt from stealing this one. Some day
producers will become sane and realize that the only thing that
matters is the best possible picture, and not the fate of any particular star. I may be wrong, but I imagine that this enlightened
reasoning did not govern the editing of Old Heidelberg. But I am
not disparaging Novarro's performance. He is delightful all the
way through and to put him in the part was an example of ideal
casting. Norma Shearer plays the bar-maid with sincerity and conviction, giving a much better performance than I have seen her do
in a long time. Edward Connelly, as the prime minister, handles
his role in a way that only a real actor could. It is a part that
does not permit one violent gesture. He walks through it quietly,
effacing himself as much as possible, but your eyes do not leave
him when he is on the screen, and you feel in this quiet man the
power that made him prime minister. The greatest surprise of the
production is the appearance of Bobbie Mack, an old stager who has
played atmosphere since D. W. Griffith was a boy. He gives a
splendid performance, distinguished by a long close-up that is one
of the artistic triumphs of the picture. It shows what capable direction will do. Philippe de Lacy plays the crown prince as a boy.
Once more the little chap shows what a fine actor he is. His first
meeting with Hersholt makes a delightful scene. The boy sizes up
the tutor who smiles down at him. At first he is suspicious of the
smile, but at last succumbs to it and starts the friendship that en-
nobles the whole picture. Gustav von Seyffertitz is every inch a
king as Novarro's uncle, and John S. Peters not only looks very
smart in his Heidelberg uniform, but gives an excellent performance
that indicates that he could take care of a larger part. Hans Kraly
wrote a notably excellent screen story, and the titles of Marion
Ainslee and Ruth Cummings are quite in keeping with the other
merits of the production.

--Welford Beaton in The Film
Spectator, Vol. 3, No. 7 (May
28, 1927), pages 7-8.

☐ SUNNYSIDE UP (Fox, 1929)

A screen musical comedy that is made into something superi-
or to the commonplace work its plot would suggest by the lovely
performance that Janet Gaynor, surprisingly adept at this alien business of song and dance, brings to it; by the pleasant, if unsensation-
al, work of Charles Farrell, the tunefulness of several De Sylva-
Brown-Henderson airs and an ingenious chorus number that gets

away with as much as they did in The Cock-Eyed World.

--Richard Watts, Jr. in The Film
Mercury, Vol. 10, No. 11 (November 1, 1929), page 6.

* * *

A trio of experts in writing musical stage shows wrote Sunny
Side Up especially for the screen. It is the most important attempt
yet made to create an original thing of this type for the sound picture medium. It is emphatically successful.

Musical comedies on the stage are pretty artificial--nobody
expects them to be anything else, even if the heroine does weep a
few tears when her course of true love runs temporarily askew.
Musical romance--The Desert Song or Show Boat kind of thing--gets
nearer to the difficult combination of music and a story where you
are really interested in what happens to the characters; but on the
stage a musical interruption, with its sudden focussing of spotlights
and a chorus opportunely dropping in, shifts the whole thing from
play to show--however pleasant it may be it is still artificial.

The screen can do it infinitely better--when it forgets the
stage and goes after the thing in its own way. That's what Sunny
Side Up does. Without the music it would still be a good romance.
Into this romance music is fitted just right--there is always a suitable reason for its being there, without jerking the plot out of shape
to inject an entertaining song or dance.

For anyone with a personal weakness for the Gaynor-Farrell
combination--like this here scribe--it is easy to like them in anything. It is easy to like them better in this than in their Seventh
Heaven and Lucky Stars. I really don't enjoy seeing Janet Gaynor
having too poor a time. Vicarious suffering is often quite pleasant,
experienced through watching the woes of some weeping heroine, but
it isn't vicarious enough when Janet Gaynor is being miserable. She
stirs up too strong a feeling that something must be done about it
right away--that you, personally, if the people on the screen don't
hurry up, must try to make things all happy for her again.

She is gay and radiant most of the time in Sunny Side Up,
and Charles Farrell is at last his own pleasant self, without melodramatic heroics. They both come through the "talking" test as
they might have been expected to do, with satisfying naturalness.
They sing, not operatically but like young people who sing because
they like to. And it all puts the right final touch to a picture play
that is in all its details admirably contrived and most admirably
directed.

--James Shelley Hamilton in
Cinema, Vol. 1, No. 1 (January
1930), page 38.

☐ SUNRISE (Fox, 1927)

      Sunrise in some respects marks the farthest spot the screen has reached in its progress as a developing art. F. W. Murnau, the director, and Charles Rosher, the chief cameraman, are the heroes. A great deal of the direction is inspired, and all of the photography is of a quality that gives the screen a new dignity as an art. It is a picture that is of tremendous value to Hollywood as a subject for study. Also it is interesting as the first production in this country of the man who sent us the epochal Last Laugh. Another point of interest is that it comes from the lot that gave us Seventh Heaven, another important picture directed by a man who was making pictures here before we began to notice the foreigners. From every standpoint Sunrise is important quite apart from its claim to consideration for the merits it possesses. Within his marked limitations Murnau is a director extraordinarily skilled in the use of the tools he works with. He deems the camera to be possessed of story-telling powers, and in making this picture he was fortunate in having at his command in Rosher a master of photography. He puts into his scenes a pictorial quality that matches their moods. I do not think the screen has shown us anything more sublimely beautiful than the shot of the sailboat leaving the shore after Janet Gaynor and George O'Brien have had their celebration in the city. The dissolving shots planting the spirit of vacation time possess the same rich quality in addition to being interesting as camera tricks. Murnau's direction demonstrates a point that I have urged constantly: that close-ups are a detriment to a picture unless inserted only when there are demands for them. Some of his most dramatic scenes are presented in deep-medium or long shots. This is logical treatment. The sets were erected with such scenes in mind; the lighting was arranged to preserve the moods of the scenes, the cameras placed and the characters grouped all for the purpose of building them up. As a consequence the scenes could be presented perfectly only to the extent that they presented all the features that were necessary to them. When a character's position in relation to another character is important to a scene some of its strength is lost when the other character is eliminated to allow the first to be shown in a close-up. Murnau gives us a few close-ups and each of them is necessary. In my opinion the most intelligent shot is that showing O'Brien terrifying Margaret Livingstone near the end of the picture. Because she had urged him to drown Janet, O'Brien, when he thinks Janet has been drowned, becomes infuriated and seeks the city woman with murder in his heart. When he encounters her the light is at his back and we can not see his face. Nor can we see Margaret's as she advances towards him with her back to the camera. But we see her lift her face to his, then turn and flee. There is a shot for our close-up hounds to study! I do not know of any other director who could have resisted showing us George's face distorted with rage and Margaret's registering terror. Murnau's treatment shows that such shots are unnecessary, as he uses the complete bodies of his characters to put over his drama. As soon as Margaret flees we

know that the expression on George's face must have terrified her,
and seeing the expression in a close-up would have told us no more
than we learned by not seeing it.   Another bit of direction that I
like is holding the camera on O'Brien for the entire time he is
rowing frantically to the shore after recovering from the insanity of
his idea of drowning his wife.   There is drama in every stroke he
makes, and Murnau sustains the drama by showing us all the
strokes.   All through the picture there are such examples of great
intelligence applied to direction.

　　　　But what is the net result of the masterly direction and the
superb photography?   Murnau has used his tools as skilfully as a
master sculptor uses his chisels, and gives us something as cold
as the marble that the sculptor uses.   There is not a heart-throb
in Sunrise.   What is a motion picture?   Is it an unfeeling thing of
camera angles, lighting, sets and photography, like Sunrise, or a
throbbing, living, human thing, like Seventh Heaven?   One of the
tools that Murnau used he passed to the hand of Frank Borzage:
Janet Gaynor.   In Sunrise her husband is about to drown her, and
as I view the scene I admire the direction and wonder how the
camera was anchored; in Seventh Heaven her husband is about to go
to war and as I view the scene I cry, and a lump hurts my throat,
and I can feel the spell of it again now as my pen pauses.   I did
not admire Borzage's direction, nor was I concerned with the camera.   I forgot that I was looking at a motion picture, something
that Murnau did not allow me to forget for a moment.   As an object to dissect in a screen clinic Sunrise is a masterpiece; as a
motion picture it is not great.   When Borzage directed Janet Gaynor
he explained the scenes to her, toying with her emotions until she
was pathetic little Diane, and then allowed her to act the scenes as
she wished, for having submerged her own personality completely
in that of the character, all of the manifestations of the character's
moods must of necessity be perfect acting.   I would gather from
Sunrise that Murnau used Janet to interpret his conception of her
scenes, and did not permit her to become in reality the character
she was depicting.   I imagine he treated George O'Brien in the
same way, but I have not the opportunity to make a comparison.
Murnau's direction reflects Germanic arrogance.   His players are
chessmen, and he moves them as such.   When O'Brien regains
Janet's confidence in him, he tucks her under his arm and the two
sidle along the sidewalk in a ludicrously unnatural way that would
have made pedestrians pause in amazement and stare at them.   Yet
no one notices them.   The ridiculous posture and gait are main-
tained until the two seat themselves in a cafe, again without creating the sensation that the entrance of two such grotesque creatures
could not help creating.   In the cafe sequence, though, we got our
only glimpse of the real Janet Gaynor, just a flash when she rises
after drinking wine.   Again in the barber shop we have an entirely
unnatural scene.   Arthur Houseman seats himself beside Janet and
begins to flirt with her in a manner so crude that it would have
provoked the instant protest of every barber in the place.   The
spectacle of a couple married for four years stopping traffic while
they embrace in the middle of the street is another one of the ex-

amples of straight movie stuff that rob the picture of all its wonderful opportunities to be poignantly human. Murnau is cold, too cold
ever to give us a truly great picture. He makes two of his characters advance along the sidewalk like a pair of crabs and tells us
that it is art. He puts an impossible wig on the character who
should get most of our sympathy, presents her throughout as both
physically and mentally unattractive and gives the impression of
ordering us to worry about her because he, the mastermind, so
commands. Extraordinary direction and beautiful photography are
no greater in a picture than the emotions they arouse. A man who
can make us cry is a greater director than one who only makes us
think. When we go to a theatre we do not wish to be lectured on
the art of picture-making; we wish to laugh and to cry, to become
distressed over the tribulations of poor Nell, and to develop an intense hatred for the villain. In Sunrise Murnau gives an extraordinary exhibition of motion picture mechanics, but he ignores the
only important thing: the soul of a motion picture.

     A combination of the Murnau mechanics and the Borzage hu-
manity would have made Sunrise the greatest picture of all time.
The German does not seem to understand people. If Sunrise had
been released before Seventh Heaven it would not have established
Janet Gaynor as an actress. Her characterization will not be popular throughout the world and will add nothing to her reputation. At
the same time I do not believe there is anyone in Hollywood who
could have done better in the part. Under Borzage's direction I
believe her performance would have ranked with the one she gives
in Seventh Heaven. There is everything in the role to awaken the
deepest sympathy for the neglected wife, but although I am absurdly
susceptible to the screen's emotional appeal, I was not moved in
the slightest way by one of Janet's scenes. I believe George
O'Brien's characterization was too much in monotone. We are
given no opportunity of becoming acquainted with him. Perhaps it
would have been easier to awaken our sympathy for his wife if we
had seen him as something other than a sulky, furtive weakling,
badly in need of a shave. If we are to judge their home life by
what we see of it in the opening sequence, it is possible that we
might view drowning as an easy way out for Janet. The opening
shot of the home would have shown a happy family group, O'Brien
and Janet at supper, that delicious baby in a high chair, and Bodil
Rosing--what a splendid actress she reveals herself to be in this
picture!--hovering about to lend an air of peace and contentment to
the scene. Then the luring whistle of the woman of the city and the
spilling of something in the baby's lap to take the women from the
scene, allowing O'Brien to make his escape and wreck the happiness
of the home which had been planted as a happy one. I would have
shown George treating the flirtation with Margaret Livingstone rather
lightly until his passion for her had been aroused, and then I would
have brought on the drowning suggestion with a suddenness that would
have staggered him. The transition from the happy home to the
diabolical plot to ruin it would have been dramatic. As Murnau
presents the sequence to us, we have a stupid clod in an unhappy
home, a youth so dull and such putty in Margaret's hands that it is

no triumph for her to bend him to her will. As we see him, her
passion for him is not convincing. I can not understand how such
an attractive girl could love such an unattractive man. And every
time he kissed her I was wondering what his beard was doing to
her face. Showing him so badly in need of a shave merely to lead
up to the barber shop sequence which has no place in the picture,
even though it is done very well, is a rather ridiculous straining
for an effect. Another unconvincing scene is the storm which overturns the boat. No storm on any lake ever acted like that one.
When a wind lashes a lake the waves come in orderly sequence.
In no way could a solitary wave like the one that swamps the boat
be produced. It was good direction, though, to show us the storm
first in the city. It makes us wonder what is happening on the
lake. The capsizing scene should have shown the lovers so happy
in an embrace that they neglected the sail, which catches the full
fury of the first blow and overturns the boat. That is the way it
would have happened, and we would have been spared the absurd
waves. When the men are searching the lake for Janet's body they
should not hold the lanterns below their faces. They could see
nothing with the lights shining in their eyes. But Sunrise is a most
worthy effort, despite its faults, and Fox is to be commended for
making it. It will not be a box office winner. One thing I like
about it is the opportunity it gives Margaret Livingstone to do something worthy of her ability. She is a splendid actress, but has not
been given many chances to prove it. Seventh Heaven was so rich
in humanity that it ran twenty-two weeks at the Carthay Circle.
Sunrise is so lacking in that quality that it will not run more than
eight weeks.

> --Welford Beaton in The Film
> Spectator, Vol. 4, No. 9
> (December 24, 1927), pages 4-5.

*   *   *

The sort of picture that fools high-brows into hollering "Art!"
Swell trick photography and fancy effects, but, boiled down, no
story interest and only stilted, mannered acting.

F. W. Murnau can show Hollywood camera effects, but he
could learn a lot about story-telling from local talent. The only
American touch is a fine comedy sequence in a barber shop. The
film has its moments. There is a love scene that smokes--liter-
ally. And there is a pathetic moment when the "hero" tries to
drown his wife.

Janet Gaynor does good work but looks all wrong in a blonde
wig which wouldn't fool anybody. George O'Brien acts like the
Golem's little boy. Worth seeing for its technical excellence.

> --Photoplay, Vol. 33, No. 1
> (December 1927), page 52.

☐ SURRENDER (Universal, 1927)

     Universal and Director Edward Sloman deserve congratula-
tions on their courage in filming this solemnly beautiful portrayal
of Jewish life. The story, of a Rabbi's daughter who sacrifices
herself to save her people, due to its almost reverent treatment,
emerges as a tensely realistic portrait of radical conflict. Ivan
Mosjoukine is an interesting prince. Mary Philbin and Nigel de
Brulier give performances you must not miss.

--Photoplay, Vol. 32, No. 3
(August 1927), page 55.

☐ TEMPEST (United Artists, 1928)

     Camilla Horn, making her initial bow in an American film,
is the most interesting item about this picture.

     For Miss Horn, the German actress who played Marguerite
in Faust in Europe, displays, in addition to her amazing beauty, a
histrionic ability which promises to offer keen competition to both
Greta Garbo and Vilma Banky. A decided blonde with perfect classical features and slanting brown eyes which are fathomless in their
subtle shadings of emotions, she all but steals the picture.

     The interpretations of the entire cast are consistently splen-
did. Although John Barrymore does excellent work which should
do much to further his motion picture ambitions, it is in no way
the star's picture. Louis Wolheim, George Fawcett and Ulrich
Haupt are equally capable in their supporting positions.

     The story is an interesting picture of the overthrow of the
Russian monarchy by the Red Revolution. The production was
started by the Russian director Tourjansky, aided by Lewis Milestone, and finally was directed by Sam Taylor. Although there is
some slow action, taken as a whole it is a credit to the man who
finally megaphoned it.

     John Barrymore is a peasant, Camilla Horn is a princess.
At their first meeting she whips him--yet for some hidden feminine
reason fails to report him to her father for a seeming effrontery.
The conflict of class hatred and inward yearning for this man of
lowly birth gives her the opportunity to display an unusual amount
of emotion. The revolution reverses their positions. By all means,
see the picture.

--Photoplay, Vol. 34, No. 1
(June 1928), page 52.

☐ THE TEMPTRESS (M-G-M, 1926)

While this Vicente Blasco-Ibáñez story is crammed full of melodramatic action--much of it preposterous--Greta Garbo makes the proceedings not only believable but compelling. Miss Garbo scored in The Torrent, also a messy Ibáñez tale, but it takes The Temptress to prove definitely her abilities.

The background switches from Paris to the Argentine. Elena, the wife of a weak South American, has the unhappy faculty of making all men her slaves. They all fail: bankers, bandits and heroic bridge builders. Suicide, ruin and disaster follow in her wake. And so she ends, a derelict of the Paris streets. Such a rôle strains at the probabilities, but Miss Garbo makes Elena highly effective. She is beautiful, she flashes and scintillates with a singular appeal.

From the moment Robledo, fresh from the Argentine, meets Elena at a mask ball in Paris, passions simmer and smoulder. Tragedy stalks after Elena--but she follows Robledo to the Argentine. Robledo repulses her, despite his love, but tragedy still follows. The great dam is swept away by the tropical torrents and the villain's TNT.

There is a whip duel, between Robledo and the scoundrelly bandit, Manos Duros, which is something new in film fights. Director Fred Niblo hits a directorial high spot in Robledo's return to the Argentine, galloping across the pampas. Antonio Moreno is effective as Robledo, but Roy D'Arcy does entirely too much mugging as the sneering bandit. As Elena's wealthy patron, Marc Mac-Dermott provides a neat bit. However, The Temptress is all Greta Garbo. Nothing else matters.

--Photoplay, Vol. 31, No. 1
(December 1926), page 52.

☐ THE TEN COMMANDMENTS (Famous Players-Lasky/Paramount, 1923)

The best photoplay ever made. The greatest theatrical spectacle in history. The greatest sermon on the tablets which form the basis of all law ever preached.

Strong words, indeed, but written two weeks after seeing it, after serious consideration of Griffith's Intolerance, and Birth of a Nation. It will last as long as the film on which it is recorded. It wipes the slate clean of charges of any immoral influence against the screen.

A tremendous picture in theme and execution, The Ten Commandments will run for years in the motion picture theaters of the
world, flashing its message continuously.

Not only the screen, but religion and civilization owes a debt
of gratitude to Cecil B. DeMille for this achievement.   Daring in
its conception because of its very massiveness it is the voice of inspiration and the work of genius.

To state that a thing is indescribable is a confession of inability in descriptive power.   We will let it go at that.

The picture opens with a prologue in color photography,
visualizing the persecution of the Israelites during their bondage by
the Egyptians, the flight under the leadership of Moses, the miracle
of the Red Sea, and the destruction of the idolatrous Pharaoh and
his army.   The screen has never approached this in beauty or
power, yet within a few minutes this too is surpassed in the episode
on the mountain top where the voice of God comes thundering and
flashing through the darkening skies, bearing the commandments to
Moses, the prophet of Jehovah.

When the prologue ends it seems that any modern story would
seem futile and unworthy.   Yet the modern story holds its own, and
is almost equally powerful.
                                   --Photoplay, Vol. 25, No. 3
                                   (February 1924), page 62.

☐   THAT ROYLE GIRL (Famous Players-Lasky/Paramount, 1925)

D. W. Griffith can't, apparently, make a poor picture.
Even when he steps out of character for a moment to depict swift
melodrama with jazz and younger generation, he does it pleasingly.

Carol Dempster gives a performance that skyrockets her into
any ten best list of players named from now on.

That Royle Girl presents a fresh idea on the screen--that is,
that a girl can mean different things to different men.   Daisy Royle
doesn't love the jazz orchestra leader, and she certainly is not a
bad girl; but she makes the very feminine error of leading a man
on and then trying to close the door in his face.   What follows is
highly dramatic and interesting, with the keen suspense that characterizes all Griffith's pictures.
                                   --Photoplay, Vol. 24, No. 4
                                   (March 1926), page 55.

                        *   *   *

Inaugurating a series of productions which he is making for
Paramount, D. W. Griffith's latest picture That Royle Girl is a

gripping underworld melodrama with fine characterization and human appeal, exceptionally tense drama and suspense, which works up to a tremendously thrilling action and emotional climax in a remarkable reproduction of a cyclone.

"That Royle Girl" is Daisy Royle, a product of the slums, daughter of a lazy drunken morally weak confidence man and a sickly mother who eases her suffering with drugs. A frail, delicate type but forced to look out for herself she grows up into a mixture of hoydenish tomboyishness and wistfulness, innocent of the world's evils and finding inspiration and solace in confiding her sorrows to the statue of her ideal, Lincoln. After many hard knocks she becomes a mannequin and gets in with a fast jazzy set, falling in love with Ketler an orchestra leader who has separated from his wife. Mrs. Ketler is murdered, Ketler is convicted on circumstantial evidence and Daisy is involved. Clarke, the district attorney, who looks down on girls of Daisy's type is strangely attracted to her, and although she does not love Ketler she determines to save him as she knows he was with her at the time of the murder. Learning from a rival gangster that Baretta, a gang leader, is the murderer, with the aid of a newspaper friend she attracts Baretta and plays upon the jealousy of his sweetheart until in a quarrel the truth comes out. Daisy and her friend are captured by the gangsters and imprisoned in a cellar. A storm which develops into a cyclone wrecks the building and Clarke finds her. Convinced that he has misjudged her and unable longer to fight down his love, he takes her in his arms, while Ketler, who has proved a cad, goes back to his old haunts.

Once the story gets well under way, the interest is held in a vice-like grip. At the beginning the story seems somewhat sketchy and the connection between some of the situations is at times vague. It develops, however, that these scenes are but backgrounds for the action that is to follow and that each has its niche in the story. The murder occurs early in the development and from this point on the dramatic interest and suspense continues to mount higher and higher. Through scene after scene from the time Daisy first goes to Baretta, the murderer, the dramatic tension increases and after she goes to the roadhouse the dramatic effect becomes so gripping that it keeps you right on the edge of your seat. In the handling of these scenes especially, Mr. Griffith again shows that he is a master director, for we have never seen a better example of securing the utmost of dramatic power out of a situation, not only in the way he keeps the tension continually mounting but especially in the way he holds it at an intense pitch through scene after scene without a touch of anti-climax or a moment's let-down. Even without the wonderful cyclone scene which blows houses about and buffets the heroine around, the picture would have a whale of a climax, so strong is the play upon the emotions.

In the title role, Carol Dempster has a part that is ideally suited to her and she gives a remarkable performance, holding your interest and sympathy every second she is on the screen, which is

290 Selected Film Criticism

during almost the entire picture. The other characters are of relatively minor importance. W. C. Fields is excellent and contributes his unique type of humor, but has very limited opportunities.
James Kirkwood gives a fine portrayal of the rather stiff role of
the district attorney and Harrison Ford is able as Ketler. Especial praise is due Paul Everton and Florence Auer for their exceedingly convincing portrayals of the gang leader and his girl.

The gripping climax to That Royle Girl should go over big
with any kind of audience and That Royle Girl looks like a splendid
box-office attraction, sure to immensely please the majority, for
despite its unusual length it holds the interest right up to the final
flash.

--C. S. Sewell in The Moving
Picture World, Vol. 78, No. 4
(January 23, 1926), page 342.

☐ THEY HAD TO SEE PARIS (Fox, 1929)

Mr. Will Rogers in a comparatively up-to-date version of
the old Man from Home theme. If you can stand the sight of Mr.
Rogers, the friend of kings and the toast of foreign capitals, pretending to be one of those hick patriots from inland America, who
despise the thought of effete foreign nobility, believe that one of
Uncle Sam's boys can lick any five foreigners and are furiously
snobbish towards any one unfortunate enough not to be born under
the Stars and Stripes, you may be able to bear this comedy, though
you are likely to find it a bit dawdling, anyway.

--Richard Watts, Jr. in The Film
Mercury, Vol. 10, No. 11 (November 1, 1929), page 6.

☐ THE THIEF OF BAGDAD (Fairbanks/United Artists, 1924)

Here is magic. Here is beauty. Here is the answer to the
cynics who give the motion picture no place in the family of the
arts. Here is all the color and fantasy of the greatest work of
imaginative literature, Arabian Nights, done so beautifully, so perfectly, that it is an everlasting credit to its producer and an everlasting joy to those who see it. Into the words of this great classic, Douglas Fairbanks has blown the breath of life. He has
achieved the much discussed possibilities of the camera. It is a
work of rare genius, and the entire industry, as well as the public,
owes him a debt of gratitude. If you miss this picture it is your
loss.

The production itself is almost flawless. It would be small
business, indeed, to use a microscope. Mr. Fairbanks spent al-

most a year in preparation. At his studio he assembled artists
from all parts of the world, as is told in the Rotogravure section
of this magazine. He spent over a million dollars. It is futile to
say that it is worth every cent of its cost because the great imaginative quality and beauty of the picture is something that cannot be
measured in dollars and cents.

Through the delightful fantastic tale of the Orient runs the
theme, "Happiness must be earned," and it is a remarkable tribute
to the story that it is so entrancing that you find yourself taking all
the marvelous effects for granted.

Go see this picture at the earliest opportunity. Your ticket
will be a magic carpet which will carry you with the hero of the
Oriental tale to palaces in the clouds, to the abode of the winged
horse, and to the citadel of the moon on wondrous adventures, and
you will learn that "If you love a princess, you must make yourself
a prince."

> --Photoplay, Vol. 25, No. 6
> (May 1924), page 54.

* * *

Douglas Fairbanks as the hero of an Arabian fairy tale that
is rich in beauty and spectacular effect. It is ideal holiday entertainment.

> --Robert E. Sherwood in Life,
> Vol. 84, No. 2196 (December
> 4, 1924), page 50.

☐ THREE FACES EAST (Cinema Corporation/P.D.C., 1926)

Yes, it's about the war--but don't let that or anything else
keep you away from this picture. It is not the conventional war
play. There are no trenches or barbed wire or dead soldiers.
The plot deals exclusively with the inside workings of the German
and English Secret Service.

It is a thrilling, fast-moving and entirely logical mystery
story, with Jetta Goudal giving a superb performance of a fascinating woman of intrigue. Not until the final scene do you find out for
certain who she is.

Rupert Julian directed the picture and has done a splendid
piece of work. He also appears in a scene as William Hohenzol-
lern. Clive Brook, Henry Walthall and Robert Ames are the other
actors who prove that a good story, well directed and capably acted,
needs no star.

> --Photoplay, Vol. 24, No. 4
> (March 1926), page 54.

☐ THE THREE MUSKETEERS (Fairbanks/United Artists, 1921)

A great picture: one that the whole world will enjoy, today
and tomorrow. Romance, adventure, humor--great direction, great
scenario, great acting--it is one of the finest photoplays ever produced, a real classic. You might know that a combination of Dumas
and Doug, Knoblock and Niblo would be effective, but they exceed
your expectations. To be sure, Knoblock has taken a few little
liberties with the story of Dumas père, such as making Constance
the niece rather than the wife of Bonacieux, so that Doug may
make love to her; and changing the affair of the buckle almost entirely. Some of the street scenes are obviously f. o. b. Hollywood; and Doug is an American D'Artagnan despite his French
mustache. But, considering the censors, considering everything--
it's great. The continuity is as smooth as any ever written, and
Fred Niblo has done justice to it, making the scenes dramatic and,
above all, beautiful. There is one shot of Thomas Holding, a
business-like Duke of Buckingham, outlined against a great window,
that is as effective as anything the Germans have done. Fairbanks
has never done better work; his performance is an everlasting credit
to him and to the screen. Nigel de Brulier's Cardinal Richelieu
is a marvelous piece of work. Mary MacLaren is a youthful,
chaste, and exquisite Anne of Austria: a censored queen. Leon
Barry, George Siegmann, and Eugene Paulette in the title roles
are immense. Adolphe Menjou as the King and Marguerite de la
Motte as Constance are good. Don't miss this!
                                        --Photoplay, Vol. 20, No. 6
                                        (November 1921), page 60.

☐ THE THREE MUST-GET-THERES (Max Linder/Allied Producers
    and Distributors, 1922)

Do you want to enjoy a highly amusing burlesque? Then follow Max Linder, the French comedian, in a mocking travesty of
The Three Musketeers. The picture is adorned with a rather cumbersome title, The Three Must-Get-Theres, but there's nothing
cumbersome or clumsy in the delightful absurdities even if deft
satire is missing. Don't think that the Linder piece encroaches on
the Fairbanks domains. Doug's picture is sheer romance; Max's
sheer tomfoolery. The gifted Frenchman's version may be called a
burlesque of any picture dealing with heroic hokum.

Max is too clever to remain in retirement. He comes forward here accomplishing his humorous moments with little apparent
effort. Will you laugh when as Dart-in-Again he is entirely surrounded by a small army of swordsmen, who are about to run him
thru with their rapiers, and makes his escape by the simple trick
of ducking, the guards toppling over from their own steeds? We
defy you to keep silent. This is only one of the extremely funny

episodes in a picture which preserves its comedy atmosphere in a creditable manner.

The gay Max is supported by Frank Cooke as Louis XIII, a bright study incidentally, and Bull Montana, who makes Rich-Lou a figure of beauty.

--Laurence Reid in Motion Picture Classic, Vol. 15, No. 3 (November 1922), page 102.

☐ THE THREE PASSIONS (St. George's Productions, 1929)

Either Rex Ingram has gone almost entirely to seed or else it is next to impossible for an American to make a good picture abroad. The formerly gifted Ingram has directed this subject with what has become known--on these shores at least--as a heavy English hand. The strange part of it is that Englishmen seem to lose this "heavy hand" when directing in America.

A few years ago Ingram might have made something out of this picture despite the fact that there is nothing very remarkable about the story. The plot, however, does allow of effective cinema treatment and, apparently Ingram has tried to achieve this. He has used the spectacular background of a huge British ship building yard and factory, and to his credit it should be stated that he has succeeded in securing some unusual camera angles.

He has failed, however, to inject into the picture the old mood and feeling, the strength and irony that formerly marked his screen creations. The cast appears to have been a handicap rather than an aid or asset--at least to American eyes. The players, who, with the exception of Alice Terry, are European, seem rather repressed and uninspired.

The Three Passions is a story which particularly calls for exceptionally potent playing on the part of the three principals if it hopes for success, and as this was lacking the picture at best becomes a mediocre offering.

The role of the father, in the hands of an Emil Jannings, would have been a tremendous and sympathetic character. Shayle Gardner has done fair with the role but is apparently inexperienced in camera work.

Alice Terry has bobbed her hair and makes an attractive appearance in blonde hair au naturel. Her part is not outstanding, however, and will create little enthusiasm among theatregoers. Ivan Petrovitch has a great role but makes little of it.

The Three Passions has plenty of production value, as far as massive sets and mob scenes are concerned. The emotional and

human elements in the story do not impress, however and the film
will be somewhat of a dud as far as American audiences are to be
considered.   Ingram's name may help at the gate but exhibitors are
advised against handing out promises on this one.
                              --Tamar Lane in The Film Mer-
                                cury, Vol. 9, No. 9 (January
                                25, 1929) page 14.

☐ THREE WEEKS (Goldwyn, 1924)

     The celluloid edition of a book that shocked us, a generation
ago, makes an entertaining picture.   True, in this frank age, the
story has lost much of its daring.   But it is well told, and well directed and interesting.   Some of the settings are exquisite, and the
lighting effects are good.   And the whole cast is excellent.   It is
Aileen Pringle, as the unhappy Queen, however, who stands out
cameo-like from the rest of the picture.   She sets a new style in
enchantresses--she never loses the wistful charm that will win the
sympathy of any audience.   The story of a queen who, bitterly disappointed in her marriage, allows herself one fling at romance and
joy.   Not quite a month--but every day crowded!   And then, again,
a life of repression that ends in the greatest sacrifice.   Not for the
children, of course!
                              --Photoplay, Vol. 25, No. 5
                                (April 1924), page 61.

☐ THUNDERBOLT (Paramount, 1929)

     A vigorous, well acted and handsomely produced crook melo-
drama of familiar design that somehow seems to sum up in itself
all the virtues and defects that have gone to make the American
motion picture both a world force and a sad trial to the sensitive
minded.   Brilliant and commonplace, powerful and feeble, ingenious
and lacking in invention, never particularly tasteful but always filled
with an enormous gusto, it becomes a sort of archetype of the Hollywood cinema.   If you feel you would be distressed by a lot of rowdy
comedy in the death house, it will hardly please you.
                              --Richard Watts, Jr. in The Film
                                Mercury, Vol. 10, No. 3 (July
                                12, 1929), page 4.

☐ TOL'ABLE DAVID (Inspiration/Associated First National, 1921)

     Easily the most romantic figure on the screen today among
the male stars, Richard Barthelmess scores a great personal hit in

his first starring vehicle. The story is laid in the mountain country of one of the southern states and the characters have been
chosen largely from the primitive folk which inhabit the region.
There is an engrossing human interest running all through the story
and ninety-five per cent of the material used has been selected with
excellent discrimination. The other five per cent consists of some
low brow comedy entirely unsuited to the mood of the story and the
personality of the star, and a few spots where the gruesome and
unpleasant have been overstressed.

There are many moments of spiritual beauty in the picture
and the production is in keeping with every demand. As David, the
earnest and finely molded young boy whose great ambition is to
drive the United States Mail Coach, Richard Barthelmess fulfills
every promise made by him in the past in characters that called
for fine qualities of heart and mind. It is difficult to find one flaw
in his impersonation.

The supporting cast contributes a long list of able characterizations. Gladys Hulette, Forest Robinson and Marion Abbott are
among the high lights.

> --Edward Weitzel in The Moving
> Picture World, Vol. 53, No. 5
> (December 5, 1921), page 589.

☐ THE TOLL OF THE SEA (Technicolor/Metro, 1922)

Toll of the Sea was another variation of the old Madame
Butterfly theme, photographed in color. It was the first colored
picture to achieve natural tints with any degree of accuracy. The
picture was extraordinarily beautiful throughout, and its dramatic
interest was heightened by the superb acting of a little Chinese
girl, Anna May Wong.

> --Robert E. Sherwood in The
> Best Moving Pictures of 1922-
> 1923 (Small, Maynard and Com-
> pany, 1923), page 101.

☐ THE TORRENT (M-G-M, 1926)

Monte Bell stands well in the foreground of those directors
who can take a simple story and so fill it with true touches that the
characters emerge real human beings and the resulting film becomes a small masterpiece.

Such work he has created in Torrent and for fans who are
slightly grown-up this picture will be a vivid delight. Greta Garbo,

the new Swedish importation, is very lovely.
> --Photoplay, Vol. 24, No. 6
> (May 1926), page 50.

* * *

The Torrent is another adaptation from the flowing pen of
Vicente Blasco Ibáñez, and is chiefly important in that it represents
an advanced effort by the rising Monte Bell, and introduces to
American audiences an extremely interesting Swedish actress named
Greta Garbo.

It is fairly violent in its emotions, but the potential hamness
is averted by Mr. Bell's delicate touches and Miss Garbo's heroic
restraint.
> --Robert E. Sherwood in Life,
> Vol. 87, No. 2264 (March 25,
> 1926), page 26.

☐ TRAMP, TRAMP, TRAMP (Harry Langdon/First National, 1926)

This picture takes Harry Langdon's doleful face and pathetic
figure out of the two-reel class and into the Chaplin and Lloyd
screen dimensions. Not that he equals their standing yet, but he is
a worthy addition to a group of comedy makers of which we have
entirely too few. Langdon has graduated and this picture is his
diploma. Tramp, Tramp, Tramp will introduce him to a wider
public, and the public which followed his two-reel career will be
doubled or trebled. The boy's good.

Harry plays a kid hobo, who enters himself in a transcon-
tinental hiking contest. He's just got to win the race to win the
gal, who is his inspiration, and Harry believes that all's fair in
love and war, and he's in both. He isn't exactly on the level in the
race, but you should worry about his sporting morals.
> --Photoplay, Vol. 24, No. 6
> (May 1926), page 49.

☐ TRIFLING WOMEN (Metro, 1922)

Rex Ingram, who wrote and directed Trifling Women, furnished further proof of his great ability as a director. I can't say
much for him as an author, for Trifling Women possessed an unnecessarily trifling theme. The picture's merit, however, was not
dependent upon its plot. It was filled with strong drama which was
derived from the pictorial qualities and not from its situations.

In these pictorial qualities, <u>Trifling Women</u> was the best production that Rex Ingram had made.   In constructing and composing his scenes he used a vast amount of imagination, so that the effect was always supremely striking to the eye.   Ingram also displayed his usual good judgment in the selection of his cast: Barbara La Marr, Ramon Novarro and Lewis Stone all fitted perfectly into the general weirdness of the scene.

> --Robert E. Sherwood in <u>The Best</u>
> <u>Moving Pictures of 1922-1923</u>
> (Small, Maynard and Company,
> 1923), pages 97-98.

☐   TUMBLEWEEDS (William S. Hart/United Artists, 1925)

For the first time in nearly two years a new William S. Hart production is being offered to exhibitors.   It is <u>Tumbleweeds</u>, which is being distributed by United Artists Corporation and produced under the direction of King Baggot.

The story which has been produced on a big scale deals with the driving out of the cattlemen and their herds from the Cherokee strip lying between Oklahoma and Kansas and the opening of this territory about thirty years ago to homesteaders.   Hart appears as Don Carver, a cattleman, who resents this act until he meets Molly, one of the incoming horde, seeking a home.   He determines to stake his old ranch at Box K for her.   Through the villainy of her half-brother he is arrested for entering the strip too soon when he goes to round up stray cattle.   Breaking out of the stockade he is able because of his fleet horse to outdistance the others but finds the villain ahead of him.   His action is misunderstood and the girl throws him down; however, it all comes out all right in the end.

The presence of William S. Hart in this picture is naturally the chief point of interest and his legion of admirers will find that he has been provided with a typical "Hart" role in the character of Don Carver and handles it in the manner which made him famous as a "western" star.   He is seen as a strong silent man, ever-ready to champion the weak and oppressed, whether human or animal; a cowboy intensely partial to his cattle, a man quick on the draw and deadly accurate with his gat, a virile he-man but a bashful lover. In short, he is the same William S. Hart that millions liked in a role cut and tailored to exhibit the characteristics that made him the idol of millions.

The title is the name of a desert plant that is blown about by the winds and which the cowboys have applied to themselves to indicate their roving nature.   Little of the story deals with cattle as the story opens with the ranchers being ordered off the land they have rented from the Indians.   A strong sympathy is built up for them and they are shown as naturally opposed to the incoming home-

steaders.   There are a number of effective shots of vast herds of
cattle as the cowmen are shown moving their stock off the strip.

Concentration of the story on the land rush gives good opportunities for stirring action and the scheming of the villains and
their defeat by the hero furnishes good punch melodrama, while the
romantic angle is pleasing.   There is an effective and typical Hart
touch where he uncomplainingly accepts the heroine's rebuke and
prepares to leave the country, believing he has lost her.

The picture starts off at a leisurely pace, but continues to
gain momentum and from the beginning of the land rush to the final
flash there is no dearth of rapid and effective action, which is
punctuated with good comedy relief supplied by Lucien Littlefield as
the star's eccentric pal.

King Baggot has smoothly and finely directed this production.
He has built up wonderful suspense in the scenes just preceding the
firing of the gun to start the rush, which will get the spectators'
nerves on edge, and has put over the stampede with a big punch.
This is handled on a gigantic scale with hundreds of men and women
of all classes and ages on horseback and in all kinds of conveyances
from high bicycles to prairie schooners dashing madly for the coveted property.   This is an honest-to-goodness punch, and Oh, boy,
the way Hart breaks from the stockade, mounts his horse and out-
distances everyone will provide thrill after thrill for all who like
fine riding.   Why, there are scenes where his horse's feet seem to
be leaping through the air, barely touching the ground.   These
scenes should "get" anyone who likes action.

Barbara Bedford is charming as the girl in the quaint dress
of that period and Littlefield contributes an effective characterization.   J. Gordon Russell and R. Richard Neill are all that could be
desired as the villains and the others are satisfactory.

In Tumbleweeds William S. Hart not only has a stronger
story with decidedly more punch and action than his more recent
productions, but a thoroughly congenial and typical role.   The star
will draw them in and the picture should please Hart fans and the
public in general and prove a good box-office attraction.
                                             --C. S. Sewell in The Moving Pic-
                                                ture World, Vol. 78, No. 1
                                                (January 2, 1926), page 60.

☐ TURN TO THE RIGHT (Metro, 1922)

About the last stage success to sell for a record figure before the present depression was the Winchell Smith-John Hazzard
footlight effort, Turn to the Right, which comes to us via Metro.

Turn to the Right, with all due apologies to the stage taste
of New York theatergoers, is just plain hokum.   In it you find the
honest youth who loves his mother but is unjustly sent to prison; his
self-sacrificing white-haired mother who keeps the light burning in
the window; the very coy sweetheart, the hard-hearted skinflint deacon with the mortgage; the wicked city slicker; the benevolent millionaire; two crooks ripe for reformation and friends of the hero,
and the comedy rube grocery clerk.   Every thing happens on schedule, for the honest youth gets the coy sweetheart and becomes the
jam king--or something--in the last seconds.

Just why Metro had Rex Ingram do Turn to the Right is beyond us.   Bucolic melodrama surely isn't his forté.   Apparently he
made up his mind to follow in Griffith's footsteps in making Way
Down East, i.e., he decided to do all the awful stage comedy as
awfully as possible.   Unfortunately he did not succeed in imitating
the vital element of Way Down East--the much miscalled human
punch.   Of course, Turn to the Right actually had no real vigor.
Yet the film version proves something we have steadily observed
in Ingram's direction.   He cannot build drama, being too concerned
in getting a series of fetching pictures.   He does not know where
and what to emphasize.   This is glaringly apparent in Turn to the
Right.

Actually, Ingram's failure with Turn to the Right is even
more palpable than we have indicated.   He completely failed to
transfer the story to cinema language.   There are long stretches
of action almost lifted bodily from the stage version.

Another item is to be checked against Ingram, who has been
rated as an able selector of players, probably because he fortunately hit upon Rudolph Valentino for his The Four Horsemen.   Ingram
picked Jack Mulhall and Alice Terry for the country lovers--and
we can find no two players more ill-fitted for these roles.
--Frederick James Smith in Mo-
tion Picture Classic, Vol. 14,
No. 2 (April 1922), page 87.

☐ UNDERWORLD (Paramount, 1927)

A strong story, plus powerful direction, plus three marvelous
performances combine to make Underworld one of the greatest pictures of the year.

It is raw, red drama, vivid as the front page of a newspaper, compelling as the bark of a machine-gun.

Bull Weed, murderer, gang leader, law defier and sentimentalist, loves his moll, Feathers, a beautiful queen of the underworld, and Rolls Royce, a bum who, on a whim, he stakes to a

thousand dollars. Sobered up, Rolls Royce becomes Bull's devoted
friend and the brains behind his campaigns. Bull thieves and kills
gloriously until he sees a rival gang leader attempting to kiss
Feathers. He promptly pumps him full of lead and is sentenced to
be hanged.

The suspense from this moment is nerve tightening as the
shriek of a fire engine. Feathers and Rolls Royce, knowing they
love each other, pledge their loyalty to Bull, but their attempts to
save him from the noose arouse Bull's worst suspicions. He breaks
away from jail to hunt them. Under police fire himself, he threatens their lives, only to surrender to the law, happy, as he beholds
for himself the strength of their fidelity to him and their love for
one another.

Credits are due in all departments from the story by Ben
Hecht, to the titles of George Marion, Jr. Joseph von Sternberg's
direction cannot be praised too highly. The photography is flawless. Characterizations of rare distinction are given by George
Bancroft, Evelyn Brent and Clive Brook. Leave the younger children at home but give yourself a treat.

                              --Photoplay, Vol. 32, No. 4
                              (September 1927), page 52.

☐ THE UNHOLY THREE (M-G-M, 1925)

If you really enjoy good crook melodrama, be sure to see
this. It is one of the finest pictures ever made, due to the able
and clever direction of Tod Browning. From the very beginning
the story grips you. The opening scene is a freak show. All the
freaks are shown--the human skeleton, the fat lady, the sword
swallower and many others. Also the midget, the strong man and
the ventriloquist--these three forming the main characters of the
picture. On account of being engaged in a brawl in the freak show,
the three get together to formulate their plans and become united
under the title of "The Unholy Three." The ventriloquist is the
master mind and naturally you wonder just what trick this queer
combination will pull off.

To divulge the remainder of the story would be unfair--it
would be just the same thing as taking the cream out of the cream
puff.

The cast is exceptional. Lon Chaney gives a perfect performance as the ventriloquist. Perhaps you will appreciate him because of his abandoning his makeup except during the moments of
his disguise. He wouldn't be a good crook if he didn't have a disguise, would he? Then comes Mae Busch, whose acting is proof
that she can handle emotional roles with feeling.

As for the midget, Harry Earles, he is a strange delight. He is quite a source of amusement, for instance, all dressed like a baby and smoking a big cigar.   Victor McLaglen is the strong man who doesn't do very much but show his muscles.

And poor Matt Moore is cast as the innocent victim of the gag.   However, we don't recommend it for the children.
--Photoplay, Vol. 28, No. 2
(July 1925), page 51.

*   *   *

There ought to be more melodramas like The Unholy Three. This is something that the movies can do superlatively well--and something that they do surprisingly seldom.   Melodrama, on the screen, is identified almost entirely with fast physical action: cowboys or sheiks or cavalrymen riding madly across country, men hanging by their teeth from the ledges of skyscrapers, railroad wrecks, duels, heroines floating on cakes of ice toward waterfalls, and every known form of automobile chase.

There are none of these wild thrills in The Unholy Three. Like The Cabinet of Dr. Caligari, this story maintains an atmosphere of mystery, of suppressed terror, without once resorting to the usual pyrotechnic display.   The foul play, of which there is plenty, is cerebral rather than muscular.

The result is a singularly fine picture.

The unholy three of the title are impersonated by Lon Chaney, Victor McLaglen and Harry Earles, and Mae Busch is their feminine accomplice.   They are all excellent--especially Mr. Chaney, who proves again that he can be just as sinister and terrifying without an unusual amount of make-up as he is when distorted into the weird shape of Quasimodo.

Tod Browning directed The Unholy Three with considerably more regard for the individual scenes than for the story as a whole.   Thus, the continuity is not always smooth.   But the various episodes are so admirably contrived, and the photography at all times is so perfect, that the occasional breaks are forgivable.
--Robert E. Sherwood in Life,
Vol. 86, No. 2234 (August 27,
1925), page 26.

☐ THE UNHOLY THREE (M-G-M, 1930)

The finest thing about this picture is that it discloses Lon Chaney's natural voice just exactly as it should be--deep, vibrant, and perfectly poised.

Chaney followers have eagerly awaited his first talking picture. Besides this, the silent version of The Unholy Three was
one of Chaney's best, so this production was warmly anticipated.

In the rôle of the sinister ventriloquist, Chaney uses five
voices, those of the barker, the ventriloquist, the dummy, the
feminine voice of the old woman, and the imitation of the parrot.
He actually does this, but the deeply satisfying thing through it all
is his own voice.

A splendid cast supports, but Lila Lee's work as the crook,
Rosie, is excellent. You'll get thrills a-plenty!
--Photoplay, Vol. 38, No. 3
(August 1930), page 55.

☐ THE UNKNOWN (M-G-M, 1927)

Tod Browning had just one idea when as author and director
he was working out The Unknown: a fake armless wonder who became a real one by having his arms amputated because he believes
the girl he loves will like him better that way; and while he is being pared the girl falls in love with someone else. One idea in a
story I'll admit is more than the average, but even in a picture that
is fortunate enough to possess one, there should be a few collateral
ideas to help make it entertaining. In The Unknown we are aware
all the time that there is but one idea and we can detect evidences
of the painstaking labor to build up to it. The idea itself is ridiculous, if we are to take the picture seriously, which I presume is
what Browning would like us to do. In any event, a production
with a star of the importance of Lon Chaney is important enough
to occupy a critic's attention. In writing a screen story you can
not base the biggest situation in it on anything in itself beyond
credence. Joan Crawford does nothing to show Chaney that she
loves him, yet he deliberately has his arms amputated because he
thinks she is going to marry him. It is unbelievable that a man
would do such a fool thing, therefore the whole story is unconvincing and uninteresting. Browning no doubt wanted to present
Chaney as a victim of the irony of fate, but overlooked an obvious
opportunity to do it effectively. He should have shown Joan madly
in love with the man she thought was armless. This would have
got away from the over-strain in registering Joan's purely manufactured distaste of men's hands, and it would have given a semblance of reason to Chaney's action in whittling himself down to the
dimensions that Joan loved. Fate could have stepped into the picture while Chaney was at the hospital and transferred Joan's affections from Chaney to Kerry, Chaney's unexplained absence being the
impelling motive. There would have been some irony in such a
situation, and it would have made it an infinitely better story. I
don't think Tod Browning ever will give us a great picture as he is
too firmly addicted to all the moss-grown methods of constructing

one. His habit of spoiling most of his sequences by showing them
entirely in close-ups plays havoc with The Unknown. He does not
seem to consider it of any importance to plant the relation of the
characters in a scene to one another. In one sequence in this picture Chaney and Joan speak titles into the air and there is nothing
to show that they are in the same county. At the end of the sequence Joan exits and joins Lon, which finally clears up the mystery of to whom each was speaking. The good director is he who
can put over a scene while keeping his main characters in it.
Browning never has revealed an ability to do this. In a measure
he has a fine pictorial eye and succeeds in intriguing our visual
sense without making any appeal to our brains. It is too bad that
the fine actor of Mr. Wu is wasted in such a grotesque offering as
The Unknown. Joan Crawford is very satisfactory in this picture
and to me her characterization is the only meritorious feature of
the production. Elaborate care is taken to acquaint the audience
with the fact that she has a fine figure, to which I certainly offer
no objection. I feel grateful to Browning for demonstrating to me
that she has beautiful legs. I also was glad to note, when my mind
was not occupied with its reaction to her legs and the rest of her
physical self, that she is coming on as an actress. Norman Kerry
and John George pleased me when they were not in scenes with
Joan. When they were I did not notice them.

> --Welford Beaton in The Film
> Spectator, Vol. 3, No. 13
> (August 20, 1927), page 7.

☐ THE VANISHING AMERICAN (Famous Players-Lasky/Paramount,
1925)

It might have been one of the outstanding pictures of the
screen. Impressive, gloriously beautiful in its natural settings, a
fine and worthy theme, with an original score worth the price of
admission itself. Yet, robbed of greatness by mawkishly sentimental and overwritten titles and mediocre direction of its intimate
scenes.

Our regret is that its direction did not fulfill its tremendous
possibilities, and our outstanding disappointment is that some parts
of it, especially the badly overdrawn characterization of a movie-
villain by that heretofore fine actor, Noah Beery, will permit the
film cynic to lean over and whisper, "Why do they do it?"

The film opens with some very fine and spectacular episodes
of the cliff-dwellers and their conquerors. The actual story begins
in the third reel with the opening of the modern story. Once the
plot is under way, it is an interesting narrative of a noble Indian
who goes to France to fight the white man's battle and returns home
to be projected into an episode in which government agents have
stolen his people's property to the last blade of grass and abused

their women. Pretending to be based on historical facts, this sequence is really unpardonable and improbable beyond words.

This picture isn't great enough artistically to weather the
blow of a tragic ending that will probably send the Dix fans home
in tears.

However, Richard's work is fine and sincere. He can check
up the picture as an artistic success for himself. To that extent
it's a feather in his cap.

You won't waste your money or your evening with this picture and you need not be afraid to take the little folks along--also
an extra handkerchief.

--Photoplay, Vol. 24, No. 1
(December 1925), page 47.

☐ VARIETY (Ufa/Paramount, 1926)

A critic's picture, if ever there was one. This absorbing
story of vaudeville life has more popular qualities than any German
production imported to America since Passion. It is a direct and
primitive study in passion, lifted to the remarkable by a fine performance of a middle-aged acrobat by Emil Jannings. This Jannings characterization deserves to rank beside his work in Passion,
Deception, and The Last Laugh.

Fascinated by a young dancer, the acrobat deserts his wife
and his baby. The man is not only passion-swept, but the girl
means a return to his trapeze work and to the applause of the theater. With the young woman as his partner, the man achieves
success. Just when he is a Wintergarten headliner, he discovers
that the woman is unfaithful. Another acrobat in his act, younger
and better looking, has stolen her away.

Then comes the big scene. He can drop the man to his
death by simply missing a catch in midair! Here is a terrific
moment, superbly built up by masterly direction and camera work.
We aren't going to tell you the denouement. You will have to see
Variety for yourself.

Because it is a strong study in unvarnished sex, Variety will
probably meet opposition here and there throughout America.
Another version has been shown in Los Angeles. In this the wife
and baby, together with the desertion, of course, have been eliminated. The recreant acrobat is married to the girl--in a subtitle.
Thus the intrusion of the other athlete becomes an invasion of sweet
home life.

The Virginian   305

    The direction of E. A. Dupont and the camera work of Karl
Freund make Variety technically a superb thing.
                          --Photoplay, Vol. 30, No. 4
                            (September 1926), page 55.

                        *   *   *

    The newest German picture, Variety, is showing at the Rial-
to, and it is very nearly all that a movie should be.   It is a simple story told without wandering and it is grown up.   It concerns
itself with triangles among sideshow and vaudeville folk.   There
isn't any originality to the plot, but there is in the straightforward
and mature handling of it.   The acting, with fleeting exceptions, is
perfect, Emil Jannings standing out as usual.
                          --Oliver Claxton in The New York-
                            er, Vol. 2, No. 20 (July 3,
                            1926), page 34.

☐ THE VIRGINIAN (Paramount, 1929)

    Owen Wister's novel is due for a revival after this picture
is released.   It is to be regretted that Dustin Farnum (who made a
very creditable silent version of this story in 1923) did not live to
see the present talking version.

    All the atmosphere of the range is here, with Gary Cooper,
The Virginian, in his first full-dialogue picture, delivering that famous line: "When you call me that, smile!"

    For the first time, a thousand bellowing cattle, with dozens
of yelling cowboys, are filmed with sound, in a thrilling roundup.

    Walter Huston, as Trampas, equals his work in Gentlemen
of the Press, and Dick Arlen has another rôle very like that in
Wings, and again he gets from it tremendous sympathetic response.
All Talkie.
                          --Photoplay, Vol. 36, No. 5
                            (October 1929), page 53.

☐ THE WAY OF ALL FLESH (Paramount, 1927)

    The opening sequences in The Way of All Flesh are done
splendidly.   They are acted admirably and serve to plant in an entertaining and mildly amusing manner just what the story calls for:
that Emil Jannings has a happy home life, that he loves his wife
and children and is a kind and indulgent husband and father; that he
has a position of trust and is a man of exemplary integrity; that he

is fond of clean amusement--in short, that he is a decent, contented
American citizen.   From these happy scenes there is a gradual
transition to a dull note, a note which the picture strikes and holds
with monotonous tenacity.   The greater part of the production is an
individual sorrow done in monotone.   It would have been a more entertaining picture if there had been a suggestion of a bright streak,
no matter how narrow, running through the drabness.   I do not
mean that there should have been comedy relief.   God forbid!   In
several scenes a note of relief could have been struck without departing from the spirit of the story.   For instance, Jannings, as
an old and broken man, is shown peddling hot chestnuts on cold,
winter streets.   There are hundreds of pedestrians among whom he
moves, but he never makes a sale.   The mere fact that a man with
such a past had to sell chestnuts on the streets contributed all the
pathos that was necessary to the scene.   To have shown him making a few sales would have relieved the drabness without lessening
in any way the scene's inherent appeal.   I am of the opinion that
Jannings's physical reaction to his sorrows is overdone.   I had the
feeling as I watched the picture that I could have felt sorrier for
him if he had stood up more bravely under the blow that fate had
dealt him.   His rounded shoulders and his shuffling gait almost got
on my nerves.   In the final sequence outside his home the expression on his face is that of a man whose mind seems to have lost
its power to function.   It makes the sequence less compelling.   I
am not going to waste much sympathy on a man who is himself in-
capable of being as sorry as I am for his misfortunes.   If his mind
has failed and he has forgotten his troubles there is no reason why
I should worry about him.   The whole closing sequence would have
been much more appealing if Jannings had been shown in possession
of both his mental and physical strength, impaired only to the extent that passing years and his great sorrow could not help affecting
him.   The picture swings too far in the other direction; it goes the
limit in showing him as a mental and physical wreck.   But it is a
fine picture.   Jannings's performance is superb.   What a master of
expression he is!   Purely as a vehicle for displaying the talents of
its star The Way of All Flesh is beyond criticism.   Victor Fleming's direction places him among the few really capable directors.
In my opinion the bank sequence is one of the best acted and best
directed parts of a picture that I ever have seen.   Jannings's subtlety and his nuances, his extraordinary ability to talk with his eyes,
and the ever-present impression of a sense of humor, make him
magnificent in this sequence; and Fleming has handled it with consummate skill.   Belle Bennett and that fascinating Phyllis Haver are
excellent.   Some day Phyllis's name is going to consume an enormous quantity of electrical energy.   The Way of All Flesh, however,
is practically all Jannings.   I hope he remains in this country a
long time and that he never makes a worse one.   If Paramount can
maintain such a pace we have in store for us some rare cinematic
treats.

--Welford Beaton in The Film
Spectator, Vol. 3, No. 12 (August 4, 1927), page 11.

☐ THE WEDDING MARCH (Paramount, 1928)

There is one scene in The Wedding March that shows the
perverse Mr. von Stroheim at his best and most characteristic. A
decadent Viennese nobleman and a vulgar millionaire tradesman are
grovelling on the floor of what may be evasively described as a
bagnio, and, as they crawl about in their stupid orgy, they drunken-
ly sign the marriage contract that will unite their children in what
will be quaintly called holy matrimony.

The episode has a bite to it that is fine drama, and a certain leering irony that is von Stroheim. It is, in its essence,
crude, heavy-handed and a bit unhealthy, but it also possesses that
incisive, original, powerful, thoroughly individual dramatic quality
that makes many of us think that the incorrigible Teuton is one of
those rare spirits of the cinema that approach greatness.

It seems to me, I regret to say, that there are unfortunately
few episodes in the long-awaited Wedding March that possess the
qualities which have made the von Stroheim idolators so loyal a
band of battling hero-worshippers.   The picture is too lethargic in
its pace, its story too unimpressive, its detail too full of minutiae,
its symbolism and its contrasts too obviously managed for us to
rate it as one of the first of the Stroheim works.   Its uninteresting
photography and its use of an absurd looking property bird to sym-
bolize the happiness of its lovers tend to make us a bit skeptical
over any possible charges that the cuts in the film have injured its
impressiveness.

Yet I don't think that any of us have reason, amid all our
disappointment, to begin questioning the greatness of our favorite
director.   With all its flaws, The Wedding March is still one of the
distinctive productions of the cinema, a film that is obviously the
work of a remarkable talent.

My intention in this sermon, though, is not to defend von
Stroheim as one of the important men of the motion picture, but
merely to dispute a charge brought against him by the more un-
friendly reviewers of The Wedding March.   It was the claim of these
ladies and gentlemen that the new film showed definitely that it was
absurd to call the director a realist; that, on the other hand, the
work proved conclusively he was the screen's most advanced romanticist, whose highly uniformed efforts were the final word in the
picturesque sentimentalities that are supposed to appeal especially
to the rather nebulous section of the cinema public known as servant girls.

In replying to all this, I hope you will not think I am trying
to sidestep when I say that none of the Stroheim devotees have ever
said he was merely a conventional realist.   Of course, that term
"realist" is perhaps the most widely inaccurate word in all our literary jargon.   Realism is supposed to indicate a portrayal of the

duller and more abject aspects of life and when you say that it
should be used to indicate the manner, rather than the setting of a
narrative, you are hardly likely to make much of an impression.
This, I should apologetically add, is no doubt highly bromidic to
those of you who read literary criticisms.

Of course, according to this conventional idea of realism,
Greed, which I still think is the most impressive film I have ever
seen, is the only von Stroheim picture in that mood. All the rest
of his works have been romantic and colorful in setting and highly
picturesque in events, and their characters have belonged in the
higher social circles, rather than in the less debonair class that is
supposed to furnish the material for naturalism. Yet each one of
them, and I particularly include The Wedding March, has possessed,
for all its surface romanticism, an unsentimentalized attitude
towards its people and their lives that are in the better sense of
the term, "realistic. "

Take, for example, the character the director himself plays.
Von Stroheim's love for trick uniforms and his amusing weakness
for indulging every aspect of his exhibitionist complex, should not
conceal that he has taken what would ordinarily have been a mere
romantic hero, a dashing Graustark dandy, and de-bunked it as
completely as could any self-conscious social satirist. The love
of the decadent prince Stroheim plays for the ingenue may likewise
be outwardly romantic in its aspects, but the film is almost savage-
ly honest in showing how much less than high tragedy the final
separation of the pair really was. Then, too, there was the character of the nominal villain, the boorish, dirty butcher who wanted
the ingenue and finally got her. Though shown as thoroughly bestial
in his pictorial qualities, this gentleman was at least given the
credit of going to jail for an honest, rather heroic, protest against
the casual brutality of the effete aristocracy that ruled him. Certainly, also, the scene I described originally is realistic in every
possible sense of the term.

In a word or two, I think that von Stroheim has, in his current effort, so thoroughly extracted the sentimentalities from the
romantic cinema school of the lovely Waltz Dream and even of his
own brilliant Merry Widow that, for all his affectations, you can
hardly avoid regarding him as both a conventional realist in his
methods and a biting dramatic satirist in his results. The curious
description of Erich von Stroheim as a manufacturer of servant
girl romances, whatever that means, strikes me as being pretty
absurd.

Quite incidentally, it should be added here that among the
director's feats in The Wedding March was his success in making
Fay Wray, whose other efforts at acting have been slightly abortive,
give a really moving performance as the deserted ingenue. It was
less surprising to watch that grand and sadly neglected actress, Za-
Su Pitts, giving a genuinely heart-breaking performance as the lame
heiress who knew that the prince, who was marrying her, really

loathed her.

--Richard Watts, Jr. in The Film
Mercury, Vol. 8, No. 22 (October 26, 1928), page 6.

☐ WHAT PRICE GLORY (Fox, 1926)

A lot of laurels are to be distributed on this film. First,
William Fox and Winifred Sheehan deserve wreaths for filming
What Price Glory when everyone said that it couldn't be done satisfactorily. Raoul Walsh, the director, must get a large share of
the credit for his sincere handling of the picture. A lot of credit
goes to the cast. At least one member of it, Victor McLaglen,
emerges from What Price Glory to stardom.

What Price Glory follows the original stage play of Maxwell
Anderson and Laurence Stallings with surprising fidelity. Just after
the Broadway hit of this play, Metro commissioned Stallings to write
an original war story. The Big Parade was the final result. However, What Price Glory reaches the screen after its offspring.

As a spoken play, What Price Glory attracted instant attention because of its caustic and bitter shafts aimed at the futility of
war. The drama, too, was studded with profanity. A spade was
called a spade in every other line. The film version follows the
spoken play in presenting the life-time enmity of two marines.
Most of the clashes have been over girls. In France the old flame
bursts out again over a peasant girl, Charmaine.

The profanity of the hardboiled marines' conversation remains entirely in pantomime, however. Director Walsh has developed his story with a great deal of power. The scene in the
dressing station after the battle is highly compelling. Aside from
McLaglen, praise goes to Edmund Lowe, Leslie Fenton, Dolores
Del Rio and Barry Norton.

--Photoplay, Vol. 31, No. 3
(February 1927), page 53.

☐ WHEN KNIGHTHOOD WAS IN FLOWER (Cosmopolitan, 1922)

Here is an American made romantic production gloriously
decorative. For this we must give our thanks to Joseph Urban,
scenic creator extraordinary. Director Robert Vignola deserves
his share of praise for keeping a fine grip on a difficult story.
Cosmopolitan spared no expense in filming the tale.

Back in the days of swashbuckling fiction, Charles Major
turned out this "best seller" of the gay reign of Henry VIII. Mr.

Major made the saucy, fiery tempered hoyden, Mary Tudor, his
heroine, revolving his romance around her turbulent love for Charles
Brandon and her ill starred royal marriage to Louis XII of France.

Marion Davies is the petulant Mary Tudor, the rôle once
done behind the footlights by the glorious Julia Marlowe. Miss
Davies puts more variety into the rôle than in anything she has
heretofore contributed to the silversheet. Forrest Standing is the
heroic Charles Brandon. Lynn Harding's Henry VIII has many moments of excellence but personally we prefer Emil Jannings as the
much married king. William Norris seems to overdo the senile
Louis XII but his moments just before his death are superbly
limned. There are a number of able players present but none of
them offers a more clean cut bit than George Nash in a few brief
moments as a roystering adventurer.

True, the photoplay lacks in character humanizing and in the
Germanic touch of historic reality. There are moments when it
seems to us Director Vignola could have attained greater suspense.
But, then too, there are moments to be long remembered. There
is the Urban arrangement of lights and setting when Mary Tudor
kneels in prayer. Here is superb cinema painting. And, then
again, there is a piquant glimpse of Mary Tudor in bed.
                              --Photoplay, Vol. 22, No. 6
                              (November 1922), page 64.

☐ WHERE THE PAVEMENT ENDS (Metro, 1923)

Where the pavement ends--there romance begins.

At least so said John Russell in his series of stories bearing
this general title. Rex Ingram has been singularly successful in his
visualization of this tale, The Passion Vine. Somehow it seems to
us to be his best picture. For one thing, he never loses his story
in the quest of beautiful photography. And he never resorts to awful
comedy. Here is just the tale of a missionary's daughter and a
young native. But there is yet more to it, the slow breaking down
of white civilization before the corrosion of the South Seas. Ingram
has caught this with superb skill. His screen catches--and radiates
--the sensual lure of the South Pacific. And Where the Pavement
Ends does one other thing--it establishes Ramon Novarro as an idol.
                              --Photoplay, Vol. 23, No. 6
                              (May 1923), page 64.

                    *   *   *

There have been many South Sea motion pictures, but this is
easily and by a long way the best of them. It has a better story
back of it, and more artistic skill in its direction. It is not the
best picture Rex Ingram has made, but it has the pictorial beauty

that is inseparable from anything he does, which in itself is enough
to lift it above the ordinary, and in intention it keeps faith with the
original story to an extent that almost amounts to bravery.

That it doesn't put John Russell's story on the screen so
faithfully in actual performance as in intent is due to weaknesses
in continuity structure, and to at least one serious mistake in casting. Mr. Ingram apparently is not a good dramatist--if he were
he would have built Where the Pavement Ends so that there would
have been psychological inevitability in the missionary girl's falling
in love with the Island chief; so that the broken lantern on the
church porch, replaced later by the crafty captain, would have
played the dramatic part for which it was intended; above all, so
that the perilous descent of the falls would have seemed absolutely
the only way to get to the shore instead of a rather far-fetched attempt at a movie thrill. As it is, these things seem to have been
put in the picture only because they were in the story, not because
they grew unescapably out of the characters and the situations into
which the characters got themselves. There are also faults in
clarity--the spectator has to correct his impression again and again
about how long the love affair has been going on, and that is pretty
bad technique unless--as is obviously not the case here--it is done
with a purpose.

Mr. Ingram was working at a disadvantage in having Alice
Terry as the missionary's daughter. Miss Terry, for all her
charm, does not at all suggest the starved woman who is making
her last desperate play for love and romance, and without such a
woman the story loses the chief thing that makes it different from
other movies.

Ramon Novarro is an ideal selection for the hero--the young
South Sea Island chieftain, Matouri, to whom the missionary's
daughter turns for love and protection, in her loneliness. By his
mere looks Novarro can suggest the sunniness and nobility of the
child of nature, and he is quite equal to what acting demands are
made upon him. Harry T. Morey is an admirable example of a
villain who is not allowed to be too villainous--a happy combination
of excellent acting and excellent direction.

Of the beauty of the picture too much couldn't be said, nor
is there any need to say much. That is something any Ingram picture is sure to have. But the very best motion pictures need something more, and it is a disappointment to find that such a good story
as Russell's The Passion Vine was not, as it could have been,
turned into a superlatively good screen drama.
--Exceptional Photoplays, Vol. 3,
No. 6 (April 1923), page 1.

☐ THE WHITE ROSE (Griffith/United Artists, 1923)

David Wark Griffith's The White Rose was at once the most interesting and the most disappointing photodrama of the early Summer. We have come to expect so much of the dean of the silver sheet--and The White Rose realizes so little.

Actually, The White Rose is a variation of Way Down East with Louisiana trimmings. It is the old, old story of the innocent girl who loves not wisely but too well. Griffith has tricked it out in beautiful photography and two tenderly moving moments but, stacked against these lyric qualities, are reels of hokum black face comedy, atrocious valentine sub-titles and a thousand and one inconsequentials. The theme itself becomes terribly cluttered up with these inessentials and continually wanders into blind alleys.

Whatever else one may say of The White Rose, it at least brings back Mae Marsh to the screen--and restores her to us with a smash. Miss Marsh plays the girl of the Griffith story, a wistful little waitress with a pitiful longing for life. Her performance throughout is a joy, replete with the subtleties of adroitly placed lights and shades. Twice she strikes a splendid height, as the flapper surrendering to love under the Dixie moon and, again, as the broken mother, face to face with death.

There are several newcomers in The White Rose. Ivor Novello is the young minister who almost brings death to the girl. From a photographic viewpoint he is superb. Dramatically he is superficially skilful, but his performance left us cold. Another newcomer, Neil Hamilton, reveals some possibilities. The fourth principal, Carol Dempster, does not rise to the opportunities of her rôle. She is the weakest link in the picture.

The White Rose leaves us rather puzzled as to the problem of Griffith. Somehow, he seems to us to be a great man living within a circle of isolation, surrounded by minor advisors. Genius out of touch with the world, as it were.

                          --Frederick James Smith in
                          Photoplay, Vol. 24, No. 3
                          (August 1923), page 63.

☐ WHITE SHADOWS IN THE SOUTH SEAS (M-G-M, 1928)

If this opera had not gone to sleep under a cocoanut tree, it would have been the greatest South Sea drama ever filmed. This is the film that was started by Robert Flaherty. And the cameraman has caught rare beauty with his lens. Pearl diving and its perils are shown in wonderful under-sea shots and, although drama dies with the sinking of a plague ship in a thrilling typhoon, interest

is sustained by a gorgeous travelogue.
                          --Photoplay, Vol. 34, No. 3
                          (August 1928), page 58.

                    *   *   *

      Nothing finer than White Shadows in the South Seas ever has
come to the screen.   It is a Metro picture, directed by W. S. Van
Dyke and featuring Monte Blue.   Frederick O'Brien's charming book
of the same name was the inspiration for the screen story.   All the
charm of the book is put on the screen.   It is a soothing picture
that makes one lazy, and instills a desire to dwell on a South Sea
island and pick a living off a tree.   We see stately palms waving
their branches, languidly yielding to a lazy breeze; crescent beaches
turning back rolls of foam which the sea sends to them; quiet pools
which reflect the riot of foliage that droops over their rims; brown
gods of grace who glide through crystal-clear water in search of
pearl oysters.   We go into the homes of the natives and see how
they live, how they eat and work and play--all things that we visualized when we read O'Brien, but which now come to us to alter our
imaginings to square with facts.   It is a photographic idyll of surpassing beauty, a poem which nature wrote and which the camera
caught.   And with it all we have a story, gripping, dramatic, that
saddens us, for it shows how white men--the White Shadows--grasp-
ing, debasing, went down there, destroyed the poetry in the name
of commerce, and for a life gay, sweet, and innocent, traded a
"civilization" that was sodden, immoral and corrupt.   It was a
splendid thing for Metro to do--the making of this picture--and
splendidly has it done it.   In it cinematic art touches one of its
greatest heights.   It was a big thing to do to send a company all
the way to the South Seas, a venture in screen commercialism to
make a great example of screen art, and so magnificently has the
venture succeeded in its artistic quest that it will prove to be a
commercial triumph.   White Shadows in the South Seas will be one
of the outstanding financial successes of film history, and as such
should encourage Mr. Mayer to send forth more expeditions of the
sort, and other producers to consider the advisability of emulating
him.   The picture will be a success, not because of its scenic
beauty, not as a lesson in geography, not by virtue of its sociological value, but because it is a regular motion picture that makes us
interested in people who move through it.   It was wise of Metro to
stress the story.   Reduced to its essentials, it is nothing but story,
the embellishments being things it picks up as it goes along.   The
viewer who is not intrigued by its pictorial splendor will follow with
interest its romance and its drama.   The viewer who can see nothing interesting in the life of the natives, will see much to interest
him in the acting of Monte Blue.   Monte gives a superb performance, one that is sincere and powerful.   It is a characterization of
many different phases, and he is brilliant in all of them.   I have
seen nothing finer on the screen in a long time.   This picture will
bring to the front a young woman who is destined to become a great
favorite.   She is Raquel Torres, a Mexican I believe, whom Hunt
Stromberg discovered somewhere and gave her her opportunity.   She

is splendid. She has a spiritual quality that makes her screen personality charming. It is the same quality that Janet Gaynor has in
such abundance, and Loretta Young, and a few others, the quality
that suggests sweetness and goodness, and instills in the viewer
confidence in a girl's integrity and intelligence. Robert Anderson
very capably plays the part of heavy, and there are many satisfactory performances given by natives. Van Dyke's direction is masterly. The story, splendidly written, brings out graphically the
misfortune that befell the South Sea Islanders when they were "civil-
ized" by traders. I wish it had gone farther and shown the evil
done by meddling missionaries, the unconscious accomplices of
greed and alcohol in destroying a life a thousand times purer than
the one that set forth to purify it.

> --Welford Beaton in The Film
> Spectator, Vol. 5, No. 9 (June
> 23, 1928), pages 7-8.

☐ THE WHITE SISTER (Inspiration/Metro, 1923)

     Lillian Gish scores another personal triumph in her much
heralded production of the popular Marion Crawford novel. As a
young girl, orphaned, turned out of her home by the cruel older
sister, and finally bereft of her lover, she goes through every shade
of emotion. When, after becoming a nun, the lover miraculously
returns to her, the situation reaches an intensity, a passion, that
calls for superb acting. The climax of the renunciation, and of the
following volcanic eruption that gives the lover a chance to die as a
hero, is well handled. Henry King's direction is good. Though
Miss Gish may not reach the peaks of expression that she did under
Griffith's supervision, her work is more evenly balanced and human. She is a woman, rather than a temperamentally high-strung
girl.

> --Photoplay, Vol. 24, No. 6
> (November 1923), page 74.

☐ WHOOPEE! (Goldwyn, 1930)

     For all the gorgeous scenes, unusually well done in Techni-
color, the beautiful girls and the unmistakable hall-mark of Samuel
Goldwyn and Florenz Ziegfeld, this picture would be a pretty tiresome affair if Eddie Cantor were not so funny. It is by far the
best attempt to make a screen musical comedy after the stage-
formula, and the result is not enthralling. The conclusion seems
to be that it just can't be done, even by master hands.

     It has the remnants of a comedy plot, and a grand plentitude
of comic episodes, and it is swell entertainment except when the

glorification business interrupts proceedings.   Somehow there seem
to be too many lovely girls--their maneuvers through long dance
routines, their endless parades across the stage in Ziegfeldish cowboy adaptations or elaborately head-dressed with feathers, are not
a feast to the eye any more than a kaleidoscope is.   Individual
beauty gets lost in the procession--and Technicolor, applied to faces
in motion, is very trying to the optics.

    But Eddie Cantor makes it all worth while, and Ethel Shutta
helps him notably.   The secondary gentlemen are pretty bad, hero
and villain alike, and the Indian business is particularly trying.
Conventional types, fairly endurable in stage musical shows, are
nothing short of deadly before the movie camera.
                                --James Shelley Hamilton in Cine-
                                    ma, Vol. 1, No. 8 (December
                                    1930), page 41.

☐ THE WIND (M-G-M, 1927)

    Out where men are men and weather is weather.   Where life
is a constant battle against wind and sand.   That's the background
for Lillian Gish's newest emotionalism.

    Miss Gish plays a little orphan Virginia girl who is taken
into a cousin's home.   To escape the distrust and hatred of the
cousin's wife, she enters into a loveless marriage with a rough
young rancher.   Does she come to love her diamond in the rough?
Of course, but not until she kills a scoundrelly cattle buyer who at-
temps to attack her.

    As the lonely, distraught girl, Miss Gish gives a fine emo-
tional performance, reaching genuine histrionic heights.   Lars Hanson, as the rancher husband, displays an excellent sense of repression and wins your sympathy.   It is Montagu Love who supplies the
convincing menace.
                                --Photoplay, Vol. 32, No. 6
                                    (November 1927), page 52.

☐ WINGS (Paramount, 1927)

    A great war spectacle of the air.   Thrilling airplane fights
and manoeuvers in and above the clouds.   Unfortunately the story
is weakly built and, with the exception of several touching scenes,
misses conviction.

    Two youngsters, both loving the same girl, quarrel over her
just before battle.   One lad is brought down within German lines

and is lost in the marshes. He steals an enemy plane and makes
his escape toward the Allied front. His pal goes on a lone hunt for
him, sights the German plane and blazes away at it. The other
boy is shot to pieces and, dying, is recognized by his friend.

The two lads are splendidly played by Buddy Rogers and
Richard Arlen. Clara Bow, as the girl, is too sophisticated for the
part. By all means see Wings.

--Photoplay, Vol. 32, No. 4
(September 1927), page 52.

☐ THE WINNING OF BARBARA WORTH (Goldwyn/United Artists,
    1926)

Here is a natural drama so powerful that it completely over-
shadows every living thing. The desert, cruel, beautiful, unrelenting, eternally struggling against the terrific forces of inventive
genius and nature. It is the story of the reclamation of the Imperial Valley, of the harnessing of the Colorado River into a gigantic irrigation project. Even a Duse would be submerged in this
conflict of the elements. Sam Goldwyn, with the assistance of
Henry King, the director, and Frances Marion, the scenarist, set
out to film that great love story of the West, Harold Bell Wright's
The Winning of Barbara Worth, but the simple love tale is swept
away by the vastness of the theme. There is still love in it, a
strong undercurrent of the poignant feeling incidental to the drama.
Vilma Banky is first seen as the pioneer mother, who loses her
life in a sand storm. Her performance is fine and true. Later,
Vilma is the daughter of that brave mother. She is exquisitely
beautiful, a perfect tribute to perfect photography.

The rôle of Willard Holmes offers Colman very little chance
for emotional work, although he characterizes the Eastern engineer
with typical virility. Gary Cooper, a newcomer, as Abe Lee, is
worth watching, and the Western characters played by Paul McAl-
lister, Charles Lane, Clyde Cook and E. J. Ratcliffe are perfect
to the alkali. But the tremendous theme--the desert, the sand
storms, the cloudbursts, the raging flood that sweeps the town of
Kingston--I doubt whether Sam Goldwyn realized its magnitude until
it unreeled before the eyes of a brilliant Hollywood first night audience at its world premiere at the Forum Theater.

--Photoplay, Vol. 31, No. 1
(December 1926), page 53.

☐ A WOMAN OF AFFAIRS (M-G-M, 1928)

One might be reconciled to silent pictures remaining a little
longer if all of them were as good as A Woman of Affairs, which

Clarence Brown has made for Metro, the clause in his contract that
provides that no one is to interfere with him while he is making a
picture, being responsible for the fact that it is good even though
it is a Metro production.   Although they call the woman of affairs
Diana Merrick she is none other than our old friend Iris March to
whom Mike Arlen introduced us.   You remember her, the captivating woman wearing the green hat.   What an exceedingly silly industry is this one of making pictures.   The Green Hat is a story either
fit or unfit for screen presentation.   If fit, then it should be presented under its own name; if unfit, it should not be presented at
all.   Will Hays, that sanctimonious monk in tarnished cassock, did
not pass upon the moral merit of the story.   He received his orders from Louis B. Mayer, and then consented to the filming of
the story provided the public was defrauded into thinking that it was
some other story.   It's an old custom that Hays brought with him
from politics.   You'll remember that he accepted tainted money as
campaign contributions and tried to defraud the public into the belief that it was derived from other sources.   Well, anyway, Clarence Brown made The Green Hat into a picture that rates highly as
an example of screen art and which will hold the close attention of
any intelligent person who views it.   In making this statement I am
assuming that the public will see it as I saw it and that Metro is
not going to tie pans and other things on it to make a noise.   The
picture is engrossing for the same reason that the book is engrossing, not for its story value, but for its delightful treatment.   Brown
had a superb cast--Greta Garbo, Jack Gilbert, Dorothy Sebastian,
Lewis Stone, Douglas Fairbanks Jr. , Hobart Bosworth and John
Mack Brown.   While it is a joint Gilbert-Garbo production, Jack
sat back and allowed Greta to earn all the bows.   Whether she will
prove to be your conception of Iris March depends upon what that
conception is, but she is my Iris March down to the flicker of her
eye-lashes.   In my opinion she never gave a more intelligent or a
more entertaining performance on the screen.   All the performances
are what we might expect from such a brilliant cast.   Young Doug
Fairbanks without question is destined to be a great actor.   At the
present moment the thing that he is in the greatest need of is a
haircut.   Clarence Brown's direction displays the same mastery
that made Flesh and the Devil an outstanding picture, although Woman of Affairs will not attract the attention the other did, as Arlen's
contribution in the way of a story is not as great as Sudermann's.
But there still is a touch of timidity in Brown's direction and not
until he gets over it will he show us what a really capable director
he can be.   In one sequence he swings his camera from a group to
a door through which a character exits, then swings it back to the
group of which the departing player was a member before he left.
It is a smooth manner of avoiding a cut, but Brown uses the idea
only once in that sequence and not once again in the picture.   His
grouping in medium and long shots always is intelligent and effective, but he is too timid to go a little farther and tell his story
with such shots.   He falls back on close-ups after he has demonstrated that he could do without them.   He is one of the most painstaking directors in pictures, one of the most thorough workmen, and
when he gets a little more confidence in himself he is going to give

us some extraordinary pictures. The titles in <u>Woman of Affairs</u>
are punctuated with that display of gross ignorance that has become
the Metro trade-mark. It is why the lion in the main title roars.

--Welford Beaton in <u>The Film</u>
<u>Spectator</u>, Vol. 6, No. 10
(November 24, 1928), pages 7-8.

□ A WOMAN OF PARIS (Chaplin/United Artists, 1923)

This picture is significant because, in its production, Charles
Chaplin proves that he is one of the greatest of all directors. But
it is not great, and it is for the sophisticated rather than for a
strictly family audience. Any fifteen-year-old child who appreciates
it should be taken home and spanked. But we do recommend it
most highly to readers of Photoplay who are interested in the technique of motion pictures, for in it Mr. Chaplin has given other directors a post-graduate course in the use of simplicity for the
achievement of effectiveness. Chaplin wrote the story, and you
are inclined to be angry with him for not permitting a good writer
to furnish him with a subject that would have been worthy of his
skill in direction. The critics have raved about this new revelation
of Chaplin's genius, but the truth of the matter is that he has demonstrated his peerless qualities in that respect in dramatic episodes
in many of his comedies. In brief, it is the story of a young
French girl from a small town who becomes the mistress of a
wealthy Parisian, but who learns too late that "Rags are royal rai-
ment when worn for virtue's sake." As a result of her work Edna
Purviance will probably be sought after by other producers, and
Adolphe Menjou, always a good actor, will be given the opportunities he has long deserved. Fortunately Mr. Chaplin is not to for-
sake the comedies which the world needs. He indicated that in his
little talk the night the picture opened in New York, when he said
he hoped the public would not take his effort too seriously. But
how we would like to see him essay a serious rôle like "The Music
Master"--once anyhow. We feel confident he would surpass any actor on the stage or screen in such a performance.

--Photoplay, Vol. 25, No. 1
(December 1923), page 73.

*   *   *

For many years it has been apparent in the comedies of
Charlie Chaplin that Charles Spencer Chaplin takes himself seriously. Now for the first time, in a photoplay written and directed by
him, but in which he does not appear, the general public has been
asked to take him seriously. The result is one of the few, in the
strictly artistic sense, fine motion pictures which have been produced since that potential art developed into an industry.

In A Woman of Paris Mr. Chaplin as a writer and director
has not done anything radical or anything esoteric; he has merely

used his intelligence to the highest degree, an act which has ceased
to be expected of motion picture people for many years.   He has
written and directed a story in which all the characters act upon
motives which the spectator immediately recognizes as natural and
sincere, and therefore A Woman of Paris breathes an atmosphere
of reality, and thereby holds the attention of any perceptive audience in thrall.

As a director Mr. Chaplin has attained to a great achievement, because he has succeeded in contributing his own fascinating
personality and subtle intelligence to his actors in their given situation.   The performance of Edna Purviance as the woman of Paris
is a thing of much charm, altogether aside from her physical loveliness.   The outstanding feature of the picture is the charm and
natural goodness she makes convincing in spite of her relations to
Pierre Revel, as played by Adolphe Menjou with great distinction.
This relation of Marie and Pierre Revel is undeniably in conflict
with the thesis that a union outside of marriage is invariably unhappy, is always entirely a thing of the flesh and involves indecency
of mind.   Marie and Pierre, while estranged in the end, are never
violently sorrowful and they are certainly not excessively fleshly.
Also, their feelings, if these are an indication of their state of mind,
are ones of genuine affection and respect for each other.   It would
be wiser to say about this attachment that it is a plea for charity
and understanding of such people by one who is charitable and un-
derstands them, than that it is a subtle stroke at the wholesome-
ness and desirability of marriage and lawful love.   For the emotional disaster that overtakes Marie is due to her desire for lawful
love and marriage, and in Pierre there is always an implied sympathy for the want in Marie's heart, as well as an urge to satisfy
it.   That this should be part of the drama of so fine a technical
achievement will doubtless be regrettable to many, and a point for
attack on the picture as a whole.   On the other hand, there will be
many who will perceive a treatment both clean and honest, a purpose both artistic and truthful.   Not a spot in this polished picture
is tarnished by anything cheap and vulgar, not one moment is spent
in pandering to low tastes or the craving for the sensational.

A Woman of Paris has the one quality which almost every
other motion picture that has been made to date lacks--restraint.
The acting is moving without ever being fierce; the story is simple
and realistic without ever being inane; the settings are pleasing and
adequate without ever being colossally stupid.   The result is a picture of dignity and intelligence, and the effect is startling because
it is so unusual.

The achievement of Mr. Chaplin indicates what should be
obvious, that 10,000 in the cast do not necessarily make a moving
drama, and directors of pictures made on that principle would do
well to see this picture often and take it to heart if it is the artistic motion picture that they are striving for.   The action is very
simple, and to tell the story would be unprofitable, because the
story is not at all unusual, which is the very thing that makes it

humanly interesting.   But to attain the simplicity and even flow
which his picture has must have cost Mr. Chaplin much effort.
He, as the director, undoubtedly deserves much of the credit for
the natural relations of his characters to each other as brought out
by Edna Purviance, Adolphe Menjou and Carl Miller.   It is easy to
see that these actors are doing exactly what they are told, and doing it as they would in their homes, if they happened to live in such
homes as Mr. Chaplin, the writer, has devised for them.

Incidentally, A Woman of Paris has some bits of comedy that
are typical of what has made Charlie Chaplin justly famous, but the
comedy is never forced in for relief but takes place as the natural
thing in the situation.   There is also an underlying vein of satire
which is a healthy sign in any study of the interrelations of human
beings in modern life.

> --Exceptional Photoplays, Vol. 4,
> Nos. 1 and 2 (October-Novem-
> ber 1923), page 3.

*   *   *

Charlie Chaplin, assuming temporarily the director's garb,
proves to the satisfaction of everyone that he is the first genius of
the silent drama.

> --Robert E. Sherwood in Life,
> Vol. 83, No. 2151 (January 24,
> 1924), page 31.

☐ A WOMAN OF THE WORLD (Famous Players-Lasky/Paramount,
1925)

Awake!   Negri fans, from your long siesta.   The fascinating, continental Pola is with us once again.   A dangerous, cynical,
tempestuous Italian countess she is, wearing a tattoo--insignia of
an amorous adventure.

Director Malcolm St. Clair deserves credit for the restraint
shown in the small-town scenes and types that must have tempted
exaggeration.   Not for the children.

> --Photoplay, Vol. 24, No. 3
> (February 1926), page 50.

☐ ZAZA (Famous Players-Lasky/Paramount, 1923)

Gloria Swanson in this picture definitely takes her place
among the leading actresses of the screen.   She leaves no doubt as
to her talent.   Many liberties have been taken with the story, but

the picture, while not so dramatic and absorbing as the play, is still extremely interesting. Zaza, as played by Miss Swanson, is more like Kiki, a gamin of the French stage--childish, petulant, given to fits of temper, kicking, biting, scratching, but always lovable and fascinating. The star is at her best in her quieter moments. The production is lavishly mounted and the supporting cast, headed by H. B. Warner, is exceptional. Mary Thurman and Lucille La Verne deserve special mention, as does Allan Dwan for his careful and intelligent direction. A picture very well worth seeing.

--Photoplay, Vol. 25, No. 1
(December 1923), page 72.